I0819637

PETER McLEAVEY

PETER McLEAVEY

The life and times of a New Zealand art dealer

Jill Trevelyan

First published in New Zealand in 2013 by Te Papa Press,
PO Box 467, Wellington, New Zealand

TE PAPA® is the trademark of the Museum of New Zealand Te Papa Tongarewa
Te Papa Press is an imprint of the Museum of New Zealand Te Papa Tongarewa

A catalogue record for this book is available from the National Library of New Zealand

ISBN 978-0-9876688-4-4

Design by areadesign.co.nz
Printed by Everbest Printing Co, China

Front cover: Peter photographed by John B Turner, 1969 (detail)

Back cover: Peter with John Reynolds' *Looking west, late afternoon, low water*, July–August 2007

Back flap: Jill Trevelyan at home, photographed by Michael Hall, 2013

Facing title page: Peter with Richard Killeen's *Interpretation*, photographed by Richard Killeen, 1979

Facing contents: *For Peter*, John Reynolds, 1989

Page 410: Upcoming exhibitions (gallery notice), 2009

Page 494–95: Peter and performer Sheba Williams with Bill Hammond's *Cave painting 4*, 2008, photographed by Amelia Handscomb for Alexandra Owen's Spring/Summer 2008–09 fashion collection

CONTENTS

FOR PETER 14-4-89
TWO
HUNDRED AND
FORTY-FOURTH
EXHIBITION
AT 147 CUBA STREET

INTRODUCTION

In 1967, the young Peter McLeavey tried to interest investors in a new and unusual venture – a dealer gallery in Wellington. He was candid about his prospects. A gallery could only be described as a '*highly speculative* investment'; it required backers who were willing to take risks. 'I can assure you that I would work long and hard to make it a success,' he wrote. 'I believe that I have the ability and judgement to create both financially and artistically the best art gallery in the country. One day I will do it.'[1]

This is the story of how he did it: how a cautious, rather reticent insurance clerk became a pioneering art dealer in New Zealand. It traces the careers of his artists and his relationships with them, from Colin McCahon and Gordon Walters to Peter Robinson and Yvonne Todd more than forty years later. It sketches the development of a professional art world, and it describes a period when New Zealanders discovered the art of their own country.

This project began in the Peter McLeavey Gallery archive – a great untapped source of New Zealand art history. It is a room packed with correspondence, exhibition files and diaries, and as I worked there I often had a sense of listening in on conversations between Peter and his artists. There was Colin McCahon, painting a lament for James K Baxter; Richard Killeen, describing his first groundbreaking cut-out works; Robin White, starting afresh in Kiribati after a fire destroyed her home and studio. And through all of these narratives is the voice of Peter himself – encouraging, reassuring and philosophical about the ups and downs of the artistic vocation. 'Art is a lifetime,' he observes.[2]

While the archive provided momentum, this book is also the result of many conversations with Peter and his circle – his family, artists and

Peter at his first gallery at 270 The Terrace, with paintings by Toss Woollaston and Milan Mrkusich, photographed by Marti Friedlander, 1967

collectors. Peter, now seventy-six, has been unfailingly helpful, juggling interviews with his ongoing commitment to the gallery. Although he is no longer its public face – his daughter Olivia has fronted the gallery since 2011 – he continues to be closely involved behind the scenes, overseeing the business from his home in Thorndon.

As I write, in March 2013, exhibition number 534 is showing at the Peter McLeavey Gallery: new work by Andrew Barber, who was born in 1978 – ten years after Peter opened at 147 Cuba Street. In those days, Peter looked to New York, where the model of the commercial gallery for contemporary art was well established. A specialist dealer organised temporary exhibitions, and marketed an artist's work in return for a commission on sales. But was that model really viable in New Zealand, where the art market was still in its infancy?

For the first three years, Peter's gallery ran at a loss, subsidised by his part-time job in a factory. All the time he was nurturing an audience and a market, however, and gradually the trickle of visitors grew steadier. Eventually, some of his artists were able to earn a living from exhibiting their work – an unthinkable achievement for an earlier generation. And even if earning a living was out of the question, Peter encouraged his artists to think of themselves as professionals. As Laurence Aberhart has noted, 'There wouldn't be a Laurence Aberhart, photographer, if there hadn't been a Peter McLeavey, art dealer.'[3]

Peter's gallery was founded on a romantic and almost religious belief in the transformative power of art: its ability to offer sustenance on a personal level, and enliven and inspire the wider culture. It is a belief that has buoyed him over his long career. As a young man, uncertain of his future, he discovered a sense of identity as a New Zealander through the paintings of Colin McCahon, Toss Woollaston and others. These artists offered a model of commitment and endeavour that spoke to his own unfulfilled longing: 'They had a view of themselves and this island state and its place in the world and what we could do here.'[4] Their example helped to form Peter's conception of art, which is grounded in the importance of place. 'You have to have a core and a strong sense of "yourself" to do much as an artist,' he wrote in 1979. 'To be able to sit and feel your past and the culture that has shaped you.'[5]

For Peter the gallery provided a vocation, and also a place of his own – connected to the world beyond, yet also slightly removed. 'I like to think of the stairs as a moat,' he remarked. 'The gallery keeps the world at bay. It protects me, sustains me. We feed off each other.'[6] Within his two small rooms, he retained complete control, and his

147 Cuba Street, 2012; the gallery is on the middle floor

attitude towards the gallery was protective, tinged with superstition and governed by an elaborate sense of ritual.

As a businessman, Peter was careful and punctilious, and took pride in paying his bills on time: each Eccles cake and coffee was noted in his expenses, and every handwritten receipt was promptly dispatched. But when it came to making decisions about art, he was driven by emotion and instinct. '[I] must follow my intuition, always,' he wrote in 1981. 'Not do anything because of what people say to me but, rather, follow my feelings. They always turn up trumps.'[7] It was crucial to him that he 'believe' in the art he showed in his gallery: 'I just can't sell it if I don't feel that special "something".'[8]

Many art dealers have commented on the role that intuition plays in their profession. As the American veteran André Emmerich has suggested, 'The whole game lies in being able to identify and experience trends in advance, by the seat of your pants, by feeling and enthusiasm.' Emmerich likened himself to a surfer: 'You can't make a wave. If there aren't any waves out there, you're dead. But the good surfboard rider can sense which of the waves coming in will be the good ones, the ones that will last. Successful art dealers have a feeling for hitting the right wave.'[9]

The challenge for the art dealer is to transmit that sense of possibility and excitement, and Peter was a natural salesman, a storyteller and allegorist who engaged and mentored his clients. 'I'm selling my dream of New Zealand,' he once explained. 'I have my reading of New Zealand culture and I frame everything I sell within that.'[10] Yet even today, when art is more than ever a commodity, he resists the idea of buying for investment. 'Ninety-five per cent of art depreciates,' he says. 'Buying art for investment is a bit like playing Russian roulette.'[11]

Peter opened his business at a time when the role of the dealer gallery was poorly understood in New Zealand, and he had to train artists and art officials in a new professional system. He was also fighting powerful conservative forces in Wellington, and his early sense of embattlement never left him. '[A]s an art dealer,' he wrote in 2006, 'I often feel like a boxer. You lace up, bright-eyed and bushy-tailed; jump into the ring; and start punching. Sometimes one can get a bit too confident, let the guard down and get floored. But, like Ezzard Charles, big Mike Tyson or the great Ali, you pull yourself together and climb to your feet and carry on. I've done 40 years… And while I'm no longer fresh as a daisy the hunger still burns. I'm still on my pins; still boxing on.'[12]

On a practical level, the need to change exhibitions every few weeks requires a high level of energy and commitment; moreover, as artist John Reynolds suggested, 'the dealer has to try, under one roof, to deal with all these narcissistic, egocentric, self-obsessed, often hugely talented individuals'.[13] Peter once described himself as a 'travelling psychoanalyst'; to this could be added the many roles of the committed dealer as mentor, counsellor, salesman and financial adviser.[14]

In my interviews for this book, many people spoke of Peter's calm, softly spoken manner, and remarked on his almost old-world sense of courtesy. That is the Peter McLeavey most people encounter, but it's just one facet of his complex persona. By nature he is turbulent, driven, obstinate, definitely 'a bit cranky'[15]; he insists on doing things his way. 'Art is something very special in my world,' he wrote in 1978, 'and I do not compromise when it comes to the handling or selling of it.'[16] Peter could be ruthless if he felt anyone had crossed him or failed to respect his professional standards, and those who witnessed his anger never forgot it. His friend and assistant Derek Cowie commented on the steeliness that lay beneath his disarming manner: 'Peter was the wolf in sheep's clothing... cunningly projecting an awkward, shy and difficult persona. The wolf was alive and well and watching everything.'[17]

For more than four decades, Peter welcomed all comers to his place at 147 Cuba Street: students, artists, bureaucrats and bums. As the exhibitions came and went, the gallery itself never really changed: the shabby entrance, a patchwork of graffiti and tattered posters; the creaky stairs leading to the first-floor landing; the untidy corridor cluttered with packing crates. Crossing the threshold, a visitor might notice the elegant proportions of the two modest rooms, domestic in scale, their white walls pitted and marked by decades of exhibitions. They might glance out the semi-circular window to the often raucous life on Cuba Street below. And there in his corner would be Peter himself, slight, neatly dressed, tapping away on his old typewriter or addressing invitations in his fountain pen to the next opening.

Each visitor to the Peter McLeavey Gallery was treated as special, and offered a narrative that linked the work on display to the world beyond. Peter shared his own enthusiasm; his vision of art as essential, bewitching, mysterious and endlessly enriching. Depending on his whim, he might retrieve a treasure from his storeroom: a drawing by McCahon, a construction by Brendon Wilkinson, or a photograph by Joel-Peter Witkin from his personal collection. A parcel, just arrived, might prompt an offer: 'Just a minute, I've got something to show you.'

'All good galleries are essentially autobiographical,' Peter once noted, and his remains the most personal and idiosyncratic this country has seen.[18]

This is his story.

ONE

He fed us, as children, on his dreams.

When Peter McLeavey's father died in 1992, at the age of eighty-five, Peter spoke at the Requiem Mass in Lower Hutt. He recalled his father's many years as a railwayman, constantly transferring from one small town to another, never settling long enough to put down roots. He described his father's forceful personality: his strong will and sharp mind, his taste for argument and love of a good story. Peter reflected on Les's dogged survival in his old age, during which he repeatedly defied his doctor's predictions. 'And now,' he concluded, 'he's made his last transfer.'[1]

Les McLeavey cast a long shadow over his eldest son, and his death was in many ways the lifting of a burden. Peter was fifty-six at the time, with a well-established business as an art dealer in Wellington. He had long ago proven himself in his unconventional career. He was to all appearances a credit to his family – a worthy son. And yet, for Peter, it was not quite so straightforward. Even as a successful middle-aged man, he could never be certain of his father's love and approval. As Les's health declined, Peter took to visiting him several times a week at Woburn Home in Lower Hutt, sitting with him for hours, and waiting. 'I wanted something from him. A word from him. Something he couldn't give.'[2]

Leslie Francis McLeavey was, as Peter once remarked, 'born with a silver spoon in his mouth'.[3] He grew up with a sense of privilege and entitlement, the youngest son of James McLeavey, 'a big, bearish man always dressed in a three-piece suit', who was described on his death in 1945 as one of Levin's 'most widely known and respected residents'.[4]

Peter's 'Grandfather James' had grown up in Makara, near Wellington, the son of Joseph McLeavey, an Irishman who was posted to New Zealand

Les McLeavey, c.1935

with the British Army and served in colonial garrisons during the late 1840s.[5] Young James McLeavey was ambitious and enterprising, and made his way north, managing a sheep station in Hawke's Bay in the 1880s. After marrying another Irish Catholic, Mary Murphy, in 1890, he moved to Ohau in the Horowhenua, where he leased land on the Papaitonga estate from the ornithologist Walter Buller, and farmed it for a quarter of a century. In 1897 his property was described as providing 'excellent pasturage for 1600 sheep and fifty head of cattle, the homestead being a comfortable eight-roomed house'.[6] James was active in community service, and McLeavey Road in Ohau is named after him.

James and his wife had six sons and a daughter, and instilled in them a strong sense of family pride and public service. Les was born in 1907 and grew up with the expectation that he would follow his father into farming, but the McLeaveys, like so many New Zealand families, were powerfully affected by the crises of the following years. The three eldest sons served overseas in – and survived – the First World War, but it had an adverse effect on their lives back home. By the time Les reached maturity, it was clear that there was nothing left for him: his brothers had run through the family capital. Les blamed alcohol and poor commercial decisions for his family's losses, but the McLeavey fortunes were also affected by the economic recession of 1921–22 that prefigured the Great Depression. Peter, who was born in 1936, grew up with the stories of what might have been, and the legend of his father's 'lost patrimony' was a leitmotif of his childhood.

In fact, Les's prospects were also affected by his health. As a young man he contracted tuberculosis and spent several years at Pukeora sanatorium at Waipukurau; by the time he was fit enough to work, the Depression was causing widespread unemployment. Desperate to find a job, he eventually secured his first post with New Zealand Railways, shovelling coal on the TSS *Earnslaw* at Lake Wakatipu in Queenstown. 'It was then,' Peter surmised, 'that his pride took that great knock'.[7] Les steadily worked his way up the ranks to become an inspector, but in the years when his children were growing up he was a restless and frustrated man. He was forever hoping to leave the Railways 'and the cruel shifts that almost broke him. He was always going to move on; up, away and go to another town to better himself and so realise those ambitions that he had. Ambitions that had been thwarted and almost burnt out of him by the Slump… He fed us, as children, on his dreams.'

A tall, handsome man with craggy features, Les McLeavey was charismatic, outspoken and argumentative. To his three children he was a powerful and unpredictable personality, outgoing and exuberant

Peter's father Les McLeavey (second from left) with his family, c.1919

on the one hand, morose and withdrawn on the other. He loved music, especially the songs of the popular American star, Jimmy Durante, and often invited his railway friends in for a party. 'Father played the mouth organ and the ukulele,' Peter recalled. 'And there was always someone, often a Maori chap, with a guitar. The flagons would come out – beer for the men, gin for the ladies.'[8] Like many of his workmates, Les found solace in alcohol. 'A lot of time he spent in the Masonic, or the Denbigh, or the Carlton. And he would smell of beer when he got off the bike and went inside to eat a dried up meal in a silent kitchen.'[9]

Peter's mother Betty – Elizabeth Theresa McLeavey, née Tiernan[10] – was born in a village near Boyle in County Roscommon, Ireland, in 1905. She came to New Zealand as a young girl, arriving in Wellington with her family in 1912. The Tiernans were fiercely republican in spirit and two of Betty's uncles had been imprisoned by the English, their houses burnt to the ground. 'Mother didn't like the British,' Peter noted. 'She identified strongly with the IRA.'[11]

Betty McLeavey, c.1935

Attractive, vivacious and always well dressed, Betty trained as a milliner in Wellington, and managed several staff at Whitehead and Pears drapery store in Cuba Street.[12] She met Les at church when he was stationed at Lower Hutt, but it was not until 1935 – after a six-year engagement – that they could afford to marry and establish their own home. A year later, they moved to Ohakune, and Betty set up her sewing machine in the sitting room, making garments for the wives of the local gentry. Musically, she had a taste for opera, which she listened to on the radio; she was also an avid film-goer and often took her children to the pictures on Saturday afternoons. 'For her background, she was quite knowledgeable about art and music,' her eldest son observed.[13]

Like her husband, Betty was a strong personality, confident and opinionated. She and Les often had rows – 'not physically violent, but it was a pretty raw world we lived in'. There was no middle ground for Les and Betty – it was black or white, right or wrong – and Peter and his siblings grew up in an environment of constant argument and debate. 'Lines were drawn; the stockade was erected; and we picked them off as they came over the ridge, just like in a Western. It was a place of great passion. Of Love and Hate. It was an exhilarating home for ideas were always discussed and we children found ourselves catapulted into the murky waters of religion, politics, international affairs, everything. Argument, argument, argument.'[14]

Peter Joseph McLeavey was born on 21 September 1936 at Raetihi Community Maternity Hospital, about 16 kilometres from Ohakune. Two years later, his parents moved south to Levin, where his siblings Michael and Marie were born in 1938 and 1940. Later they would move again – to Napier, Feilding, Waitara, New Plymouth and Lower Hutt – always living in the railway settlements on the outer fringe of town.

By mid-century, New Zealand Railways employed some 25,000 staff, most of them housed in the wooden cottages that were close enough to the tracks to rattle when a train went past. The hub was the kitchen, the largest room, with a coal range and a drying rack suspended above: as the poet Pat White, a former railway child, recalled, there was 'the smell of damp clothing, wet wool . . . and a line of raincoats on hooks in the back porch, hanging above a selection of gumboots'.[15]

Among the railway families there was a strong sense of camaraderie, but the community, like any small settlement, 'could get a touch claustrophobic. The men worked together all week, while the women clustered in houses crowded with kids'. There was a lot of 'looking over the fence' in such places. For Peter, the community was an entire world, a tribe of its own, just like that other great influence in his childhood – the Catholic Church. 'There were two distinct worlds when I was growing up – the world of the railway settlements, which was a kind of ghetto, and the world of the Church, which was another ghetto. I don't think I had any friends that weren't railway children or Catholic children, or both.'[16]

Transience, too, was part of life for the railway workers. 'We got used to being the new kids in town. We'd make friends, and then we'd leave. We always seemed to be moving on.' Fifty years later, Peter bought a 1955 photograph by Robert Frank, entitled *View from hotel window, Butte, Montana* – an image taken in a run-down guest house, showing a view, seen through flimsy net curtains, of a bleak industrial landscape.[17] 'That [was] my life ... looking out of the first-floor window of the boarding house at the town where we were going to make our future.'[18] Each move brought mixed emotions of excitement and anxiety: 'I think it gave me a sense of detachment. I always felt I was on the outside.'[19]

Like the other children of the settlements, the young McLeaveys played in the railway precinct. 'That was our back yard. We would go off with our coal sacks and collect the coal that had fallen off the tender. We always knew what time it was by the train that was passing.' Peter and Michael, so close in age, often played together. 'We got on pretty well,' Michael recalled, 'but Peter always liked to do things his way. I remember the Meccano set our aunty gave us. Peter would have the book of instructions and he'd say, "Oh no, you've done this wrong," and he'd be pushing me around, and then I'd lose my temper, and we'd be punching each other ... There was a bit of that.'[20] 'I probably was a bit bossy,' Peter admitted. 'I threw the cat at him once and it landed on his back. I hit him over the head with a hockey stick one day.'[21]

Temperamentally, the brothers were quite different: Michael placid and sunny-natured, Peter highly strung and introspective. Marie, who took after her elder brother, felt that her parents picked on the two of them. 'We were on tenterhooks the whole time. The strap would come out. We couldn't do anything right.'[22] Peter agreed: 'We did feel a lot of anxiety. I always felt Mother was about to explode. And I was afraid of my father in a way.'[23]

Michael was less affected. 'Father would shout at me,' he recalled. 'He'd say, "I'll give you a lift under the lug! Do you want a lift under the lug?" Oh yes, I was afraid of him, but it never really bothered me too much. They were tough, our parents, but I got on with them.' He felt that Peter and Marie bore the brunt of his parents' ire. 'Mother had high expectations of Marie, and she got a hard time. My father had ideas for Peter. He was clever at school, and he was supposed to get a big job. But they didn't really bother about me that much. I was probably lucky.'

Marie described Peter as her father's opposite. 'Father was big and powerful. Peter was little and quiet. You never knew what he was thinking – he kept it all to himself. He had moods, and I'd look at his face to see what mood he was in. Sometimes you knew not to talk to him. Peter was always different.' She remembered him as a largely absent figure: 'He stayed in his room, he was always reading. He was afraid to come out. It was the only place he could get away.' All his life, Peter would be drawn to small enclosed spaces – 'the curtains drawn, the windows closed, no draughts'.[24]

TOP: Peter (right) with Michael and Betty McLeavey, 1939

BOTTOM: Peter (left), Marie and Michael, 1940–41

Marie, Peter (centre) and Michael, c.1947

The atmosphere in the McLeavey home did not go unnoticed by visitors. Peter's Aunty Doreen, his mother's sister, came to stay regularly and took a special interest in the children. Marie recalled, 'I heard later that she would go home and say, "Something's wrong in that house. Those children are afraid of their parents." But no one said anything. No one did anything.'

As adults, Peter and his siblings often discussed their parents, trying to analyse what it was that had so affected their childhood. Why was their mother so controlling, so explosive? Why was their father so moody and unpredictable – perhaps he suffered from a manic-depressive condition? Or perhaps, after all, Les and Betty were not unusual in the context of their generation and its attitudes towards parenting. This was the view that Peter took in a letter to Colin McCahon many years later. '[M]y Mother and Father were good people but so marked by the Slump that they had enough problems to cope with. That, marked or coupled with Irish Catholicism made love pretty hard.'[25]

Peter later described his childhood as visually impoverished, but he was more fortunate than some of his contemporaries. He remembered sitting with his grandmother in Levin while she turned the pages of a book of Old Master paintings. The colours were overwhelmingly rich and sensuous, the images rhythmic, decorative and alluring. Later, he learnt that the paintings were by Raphael. 'At that point something clicked in my intelligence. But where in New Zealand could you see a Raphael?'[26]

There was little chance to see original art in the 'cow towns' of Peter's childhood, let alone a Raphael: 'There wasn't any Prado in this neck of the woods.'[27] At home, the only pictures were religious prints: the Sacred Heart in the kitchen; a large crucifixion in his parents' bedroom; and an image of the Catholic Church, a strong sturdy tree with the Pope at the top and the withered offshoots of Anglicanism, Presbyterianism and other denominations lying abandoned on the ground.

At St Patrick's School in Napier, art and religion were inextricably entwined. 'We didn't really have practical art. But we had catechism every morning, and the art was brought in to explain biblical stories or aspects of theology. Later I realised the pictures were by artists like Fra Angelico ... The religion was communicated to us by the art.'[28] The experience left Peter with a reverence for the beauty of paintings, and their magical ability to speak across time and place: 'Art was presented as a document, a plan and a map of another world.'[29]

At seven, Peter was confirmed into the Catholic Church and a third name, John, was given to him. 'It was a complete cultural immersion,' he recalled. 'Prayers every night before bed, the family rosary, Mass every Sunday, Benediction perhaps on Sunday afternoon.'[30] There was a strict hierarchy in this world: 'God was sitting in heaven, then there was Christ, and the Saints, and our parents. But between our parents and the saints were these strange creatures – the nuns. A great big thick belt around their middles. Great big rosary beads. All very devout ... Very articulate. I remember one or two of them talking about art, in Europe. They were floating between the world and heaven. One's relationship with them was very complex.'

Peter's Catholic upbringing instilled in him a strong sense of ethics, especially the importance of honesty and loyalty, and a keen awareness of the power of ritual. 'It was a very sensual world, the world of the Church,' he reflected. 'Think of Mass: there's the priest, who wears exquisite embroidered vestments. All his movements are carefully choreographed with the singing, the chanting, the beauty and gravity of the language. There's the incense, the sense of touch as you take the host – all the senses are working.'[31]

At primary school, Peter was a diligent student, equally at home in the classroom and on the sports field. 'I remember one time, I think it was Sister Julian, she tried to teach us how to play rugby. She showed us how to pack a scrum, a great big country girl with great big boots on and hands like great big hams. It was a strange world I grew up in.'[32] It was also a highly idealistic and exacting world, in which merit was measured by duty and self-sacrifice. Peter heard many tales of missionary service, and one story in particular made an indelible impression – that of a Jesuit priest, toiling in the wilds of South America, dedicating his entire life to a small, fledgling Christian community. 'My young heart raced when I looked out at the world from our place. We were to go out into the World, to save it. To show it what was what. All that Passion. We were baptised and a commitment burned in our tender hearts. To what? We only felt. We didn't really know.'[33]

Peter also grew up against a backdrop of war and the looming threat of Japanese invasion. In 1943, when a convoy of American servicemen was briefly camped at Napier, he and his family joined the crowds at Marine Parade to see them shipped off to their destination in the Pacific. As he stood watching, a soldier bent down and presented him with a stick of chewing gum. 'I was so happy,' he recalled. 'It was like a gift from another planet, or Parnassus.'[34] Just weeks later, however, he made a chilling discovery: 'Father came home from work and, as we sat around the table (with the picture of the Sacred Heart looking down on us all) Dad said that all those American marines had died. They went to Tarawa, he said, and ran up the beach on that atoll into the guns of the Japanese.' Peter never forgot the shock of that moment – nor the vision of the kindly American soldier, in the immaculate uniform, dying on a sandy beach in Tarawa.

In 1945, the McLeavey family moved to Feilding, 20 kilometres from Palmerston North, where Peter initially attended St Bridget's Convent School. He became an altar boy, cycling to church in the crisp early morning to arrive ten minutes before Mass at seven o'clock. '[W]e lit the candles and put out the gong, the water and wine cruets, and the towel. We practiced our Latin. Then we would know the right words for the responses. It always had to be the right words. In the correct sequence. If not, well, who knows? For the Archangel Michael might appear from behind the altar and with his rod clout us into the next world.'[35]

Peter's love of language was nurtured by his religious upbringing, as well as the poems and songs of Irish republicanism, but his childhood reading was mainly confined to comics: 'I loved *Film fun*, *The Champion*, *Mandrake*, *The Phantom*, *Dick Tracy*, and *Topix* – the Catholic comics.'[36] For Christmas in 1948, his parents gave him the biggest book he had ever seen – *The great encyclopedia of universal knowledge*, with more than one thousand pages crammed with facts and figures.[37] Michael soon noticed a change in his brother: 'He must have read the thing from cover to cover, and he'd be at you all the time, "Ask me about this, ask me about that, and I'll look it up." And he seemed to know lots of stuff. And Mother bought another book, *100 great lives*, and he read all that too.'

Reading fed Peter's imagination and encouraged him to daydream about life beyond the limits of the railway settlement. In his seventies, he recalled an incident from these years: 'On the other side of the railway line in Feilding there was a park, with a lovely Anglican church. I remember standing by the railway one day, watching some people over there: they were walking round the church, they had a car, they had two young blonde girls with them. And one of them was the most beautiful girl I had ever seen. And I thought, I want one of those. That girl and her family represented everything that I was completely separated from. The car, the clothes, the establishment – the sense of entitlement.'[38]

Near the end of his family's stay in Feilding, Peter began to attend the Marist Brothers' High School in Palmerston North – a shock after the comparatively benign rule of the nuns. 'The brothers were very hard – they would discipline the boys with the strap, and there was an element of fear. It was like a police state. I was glad when we moved.'[39]

When Les was transferred to Waitara in Taranaki in 1949, Peter enrolled at the local high school. 'It was my first public school, no nuns or brothers, and it was quite liberal. It was a great time for me. Life seemed to open up.'[40] One teacher in particular made a strong impression. 'It was the first period in the afternoon and we had a teacher called Mrs Palmer... She came into the classroom and said, "Today we're going to talk about Mesopotamia and the Italian Renaissance – two very old civilisations," and as she talked the horizon line shifted...

My imagination took hold.'[41] Captivated by the idea of European high culture, the twelve-year-old saved his pocket money and caught the train to Wellington for a major event on the arts calendar – a performance by the Italian Grand Opera Company, the first to tour the country since 1932. He went with his Aunty Rosie, one of his mother's sisters who lived in the capital: 'We used to listen to opera at home on the radio, but this was a completely new experience. I loved it.'[42]

Peter looked back on his years at Waitara as a settled and sociable time. He was reading more than ever, enjoying stories of travels to exotic places such as Richard Halliburton's *The flying carpet* and *New worlds to conquer*.[43] He also discovered a new passion in fishing. 'It became an obsession,' Michael observed. 'He'd be down the wharf all the time with his mates. We'd go to Mass on Sunday as a family, and as soon as it was over Peter was off, racing home to get his bike. We'd be walking home and he would fly past us in the opposite direction, down the wharf. He was always fishing.'

At home, Peter was quiet and self-contained: 'I was very much under the thumb of my parents, well behaved, passive, a bit intimidated.'[44] Like his siblings, he had taken 'The Pledge' on his confirmation, promising to abstain from alcohol until he was twenty-one. 'My parents were strict about drink and the Truth [the sensationalist weekly paper]… Both were forbidden fruit.'[45] Sex was another taboo, and Peter was left to piece together the facts of life from the rumour and speculation that abounded at school. He grew up with what he later described as 'the Catholic schoolboy's sense of sexual dread – sex as an overwhelming pleasure and overwhelming danger'.[46]

When Peter was fifteen, the family moved down the line to New Plymouth – 'it was the big smoke after Waitara,' Marie recalled. But for Peter, the early months in the new town brought fear and anxiety: 'I had a tough time at New Plymouth Boys' High School. I was a little wee chap and I was bullied and knocked around a bit.'[47] Unable to confide in his parents or his teachers, he retreated into himself, becoming emotionally and physically withdrawn. 'The experience stayed with me for years. I was afraid of any human contact, and I felt I couldn't trust anyone.' Until then, Peter had done well academically, especially in English and history, but in New Plymouth his grades suffered and he left school without taking the School Certificate examinations. With this decision his prospects dwindled: any chance of going to university was out of the question.

Peter (far left) form 5, New Plymouth Boys' High School, 1952

At this point, Peter's Uncle Arthur intervened. Les McLeavey looked up to his brother, a bank manager in Auckland – 'To my father he was the success.'[48] Arthur had always taken an interest in Peter, and now he arranged for him to start as a clerk at the Bank of New Zealand in New Plymouth. Les was delighted. 'My father had always wanted Peter to work in a bank, in a big job,' Marie recalled.

Peter joined the bank in January 1953 and flourished in his new role. 'I knew I was smart, but I didn't know what at. I discovered I was good with figures.'[49] Many years later, he acknowledged the value of this early training: 'I learnt those mundane (but essential) things like balancing the books and being neat, punctual, accurate'.[50] He came to see the money he handled as a commodity: 'It was completely demystified, stripped of all emotion – it could have been a sack of beans. That was an important lesson.'[51] Socially, too, he enjoyed his new milieu. He was articulate and personable, and found it easy to relate to a wide range of people – customers, fellow workers and supervisors. 'Joining the bank was like being part of a family. A world of very kind, good people, a complete cultural experience, like the church – people entered it for life.'[52]

Living at home with his parents, Peter bought books and music with his wages, and grew more adventurous in his reading: 'Dostoyevsky and the Russians, philosophy, in particular Aristotle and the Desert Fathers. I was interested in history; the missionaries, the Dominicans, Jesuits and Benedictines.'[53] Stories of the Catholic saints fired his imagination and he had no difficulty relating to ancient texts, such as the *Confessions* of the early church father, Saint Augustine. 'When he lived and wrote in 300 AD, he was living in Hippo in North Africa, at the outpost of the empire. I have always visualised that place as about the size of Foxton or Dargaville. And in relationship to Rome, the same as ours to Europe. So a lot of my knowledge came from a sort of hunger, a yearning... I knew that I lived in New Zealand, but my real home, my spiritual home felt to me to be overseas.'

To Peter, as to most Pākehā New Zealanders of the period, art was an activity associated with 'overseas', and mainly with England and Europe. He had no consciousness of local artists at all: 'My head was full of Raphael, and the painters of the past.' In fact, New Zealand art had little public profile beyond the regional art society exhibitions, where portraits of local dignitaries and decorous landscapes crowded the walls.[54] '[O]ur art shows are thick with banalities,' complained the poet and critic ARD Fairburn in 1947.[55] Meanwhile the public galleries, often run by art society volunteers, seemed trapped in the previous century: as Fairburn put it, some of the pictures 'ought to be in bottles of methylated spirits'.[56] Young artists like Eric Lee-Johnson deplored the preoccupation with academic British art: 'We have spent more than enough on museum pieces by dead English painters'.[57]

Although he was not yet aware of it, Peter had grown up in an era of considerable debate about the future of New Zealand art. In the pages of the *Year book of the arts* and Charles Brasch's literary quarterly, *Landfall*, critics discussed the need for a distinctive, independent national culture. 'Strictly speaking, New Zealand doesn't exist yet,' the poet Allen Curnow remarked in 1945. 'It remains to be created – should I say invented – by writers, musicians, artists, architects, publishers'.[58] The composer Douglas Lilburn summed up one of the key challenges – the exodus of 'younger people of talent' to England: 'They are unable to find ways of using their creative talent here, and they feel a lack of vital and progressive ideas to which they can ally their enthusiasms.'[59] Frances Hodgkins and Katherine Mansfield were among those of an earlier generation who had become expatriates, earning critical acclaim in England.

Lower Hutt Municipal Library
GRAMOPHONE RECORD LIBRARY
Name P. J. McLEAVEY
Address 247 Riverside Dr.
Lower Hutt.

Grand Catholic Dance
EPUNI COMMUNITY HALL
FRIDAY, FEBRUARY 7th, 1958
8.30 p.m. - 1 a.m.
☆
BRAZIER'S ORCHESTRA. EXCELLENT SUPPER.
Single Ticket: 5/-

Memorabilia from Peter's collection, 1958–59

By the late 1940s, however, there were signs of change. In the visual arts, young painters such as Toss Woollaston, Rita Angus and Colin McCahon had each developed their own distinctive style without the benefit of overseas travel.[60] Although they aligned themselves with modern art, and looked to contemporary international developments for impetus, they identified as New Zealand painters and shared a sense of leading the way for the next generation. To them, the art societies were a reactionary force. Their dissatisfaction came to a head in 1949, when the Canterbury Society of Arts rejected Frances Hodgkins' *Pleasure garden* – hardly one of her more challenging works – as an acquisition for the Robert McDougall Art Gallery.[61]

It was not until 1954 that Peter had his first inkling of the clash between the old guard and the new generation of painters. That year, reading the *Taranaki Herald* one evening by the coal range, he learned of a 'brouhaha that was then raging down the line at Stratford'.[62] The Stratford Art and Craft Society had refused to display a touring exhibition by Toss Woollaston, Colin McCahon and Harry Miller on the grounds that the paintings were crude and incompetent.[63] As Peter recalled many years later, 'Words like "experimental", "neo-barbarism", "hoax", "masquerading", "neurosis", "pigmentary depravity" peppered the pages as the argument built. The sanity of the artists was questioned and found wanting.' He was struck by a comment from a local doctor, who declared there was only one place for the display of such 'murky recesses of the subconscious' – and that was in 'the sympathetic privacy of the psychiatrist's consulting rooms'.

Peter's curiosity was piqued. Who were these artists who had prompted such hostility? What was it about their work that inspired such debate? He carefully clipped the article and filed it away for safekeeping. Soon afterwards, he purchased his first painting – 'a Van Gogh-ish night scene by Gary Reeves, a fellow bank clerk in New Plymouth. It cost about three guineas.'[64]

In January 1955, Peter's father was transferred for the final time. The new family home was a modest state house in Riverside Drive in the Lower Hutt suburb of Waiwhetu. Peter joined his parents a few weeks later, moving to the Wellington branch of the Bank of New Zealand, where his superiors recognised his abilities and mentored him as he took on new responsibilities. Later, one of them would tell Peter's mother that he could have 'gone a long way' in his career at the bank.[65]

After New Plymouth, the capital had much to offer musically, and Peter enjoyed the concerts of the National Orchestra and the Wellington Chamber Music Society;[66] he also developed a taste for jazz, buying LPs by Charlie Parker, Ben Webster, Lester Young, Art Tatum and others. At the Lower Hutt library he discovered the new Skira art books, with essays on famous painters and full-page colour reproductions: 'I fed on those. They were an important part of my education in art.'[67] By now he had friends with similar interests, among them Wilson Buchanan, a young commercial artist with an impressive collection of jazz and classical records, and there was an element of self-invention in his new persona. 'Peter went a bit hippy,' his brother Michael commented. 'He had long hair, and he used to wear a duffle coat with wooden toggles and a pair of brothel creepers ... My father didn't like that at all.'

In 1957, Peter turned twenty-one. Intelligent, enquiring, and aware of the limits of his schooling, his energies were very much directed inwards, 'channelling my emotional and sexual life into self-education'.[68] Although he was attracted to women, and dated occasionally, he was physically reserved and wary of emotional engagement. At the bank, his growing ambition to travel overseas set him apart from his colleagues. 'Most of the chaps I was working with had the same aim: to find a girl, buy a section, build a house and get married. That wasn't what I wanted ... I knew I had to go away. Perhaps I was escaping from something.'[69] Peter was determined to 'confront the past' from which he had come: 'The past which had been shaped by Catholicism, by certain utopian ideals, and by a fascination with the tribalism of Ireland.'[70]

Aware that his parents would put up strong resistance to his plans, he took his time in breaking the news. 'Oh, there were storms,' Marie recalled. 'My father thought Peter was mad, giving up a good job in the bank to go off travelling. Stark raving mad. Peter had to defy him.'

But for Peter, it was the beginning of his independence. 'I felt a great sense of release and peace after telling them, and began planning my trip.'[71]

TWO

The real purpose of my leaving New Zealand has been accomplished.

In the autumn of 1959, Peter quit the bank to pursue his dream of travelling the world. In his letter of resignation he claimed that the decision had not been easy. 'Nevertheless I consider that while I am still young and in reasonable health I should take the opportunity... For I believe that in going I will not only satisfy a desire that I have had since my earliest memories, but I will also improve my knowledge of the world and man.'[1]

As the date of his sailing approached, Peter bought a diary to record his new experiences. 'Today is the day!!!' he declared on 23 April. He had been taking driving lessons in the previous weeks – 'My hill work was frightful'[2] – and on the very morning of his sailing he failed his test. He never attempted to learn to drive again.

Peter's departure was unprecedented in the McLeavey family, and some twenty friends and relatives gathered at the wharf in Wellington to see the *Monowai* sail for Sydney. After years of anticipation he was finally on his own, yet his initial feelings were tinged with anxiety. 'As the Boat drew away from the wharf I felt rather sorry,' he noted. 'But I guess if I want to see these countries etc I have to make these sacrifices.'[3]

On arriving in Sydney on 27 April, Peter found lodgings through the Catholic Welfare Board. Within a week he had a job as a sales clerk at John Sands Ltd, a large firm of printers and stationers. 'We buy original Paintings and Photographs and we turn them into calendars,' he informed his parents.[4] Peter planned to save money to help finance the next leg of his journey to London, and he was unconcerned about the limitations of his new job: after all, he would soon be on his way. He noticed that his supervisor seemed to be quite contented, but that was hardly surprising: 'he is married and I suppose when you are married you lose all ambition to succeed etc.'[5]

Peter in Sydney, 1959

Peter in Colombo, 1960

Meanwhile, Sydney had its attractions. 'My word this Aussie beer is much stronger than the Kiwi equivalent,' he confided in his diary.[6] He was intrigued by television, only recently introduced in Australia, and often stopped to watch it in shop windows on his exploratory walks around the city. The shops were 'fabulous', he wrote home. '[I]t is very interesting just to sit and watch the people going in and out. There are always some very attractive and well dressed girls and women walking around.'[7] Within a week, Peter was sporting the latest in men's fashion – a tweed worsted suit with tapered cuffs. 'If I wore it down Lambton Quay in Wellington, people may say I was a Teddy Boy,' he admitted.

Peter was quick to check out the local cultural scene, reporting on Nikolai Malko conducting the Sydney Symphony Orchestra and a 'rather controversial' exhibition of Robert Dickerson's stylised, sombre portraits at the Blaxland Galleries.[8] 'The artist was a very sensitive thinker with an intense love of humanity,' he observed, but he found the pictures rather monotonous. Listing the many concerts, plays, films and exhibitions he had attended, as well as all the overtime he was working, he scarcely needed to reassure his family, 'I am not sitting around home twiddling my thumbs.'[9] Any spare time was devoted to reading, advancing his programme of self-education: Maxim Gorky, Chekhov, Huysmans, Thomas Merton, and biographies of William Blake and Saint Teresa of Ávila.

The church remained a focus in Peter's life, and by July he was dating a girl he had met at a youth dance. In August, he joined the Legion of Mary, a lay Catholic organisation; two months later, he was appointed secretary. With others in the group, including his girlfriend Jan, he made weekly 'street visitations' to spread the Catholic word. In his diary he commented on Jan's 'purity of soul' and great love of music. 'She is the most refined girl I have ever taken out ... The trouble with me, I think principally, is that I talk too much when I am with a girl. I *must* try and shut up once in a while because I think it gives people the idea that I am conceited etc when it is only my "emotional drive" and desire trying to make me more attractive in the eyes of HER.'[10]

By the new year, Peter was planning his departure, and wrote to his parents, reflecting on his stay in Sydney:

> I will be rather sad going from its pleasant climate, for I have had a truly wonderful time here. Concerts, Plays, Ballet and, of course, a very nice girl who I have referred to before. As a sort of a grand finale I took her out last Saturday night. First of all we went to a very cosy restaurant up the Cross (Champagne! – the works) and then ... we saw a performance of 'The Sleeping Princess' by the Borovansky Ballet. It was a memorable evening and we both enjoyed it. You may think this is wild extravagance but as I said before she is a particularly nice girl and I don't mind saying that she is a bit of a temptation for me to stay in Australia.[11]

Always careful about what he divulged, Peter refrained from mentioning another 'extravagance' in his final days in Sydney. Fascinated by the Aboriginal art he had seen in exhibitions, he purchased a pair of bark paintings, which only just fitted into his suitcase. They would travel the world with him, and eventually take their place alongside works by Colin McCahon and Gordon Walters in his home in Wellington.

From Sydney, Peter caught the train to Brisbane to visit the Queensland Art Gallery and see its new attraction – *La belle Hollandaise*, the first painting by Picasso to enter an Australasian museum.[12] Described as 'a picture of a young Dutchwoman wearing only a bonnet', it had caused a flurry of protest on arrival, and Peter had read about the controversy in

Pablo Picasso, *La belle Hollandaise*, 1905
Gouache, oil and chalk on cardboard
Queensland Art Gallery, purchased 1959 with funds donated by Major Harold de Vahl Rubin

the Sydney papers.[13] He now pronounced it 'very good'.[14] On 9 February, he set sail on the SS *Fairsky* bound for Southampton; stopping in Singapore a week later, he bought a copy of the Gospels as well as something more adventurous – Nabokov's *Lolita*, recently banned in New Zealand as 'indecent'. Peter commented in his diary, '[A]lthough the subject was a little repulsive, it was a beautifully written book. When I asked Fr Cass his opinion he gave what I thought was a very intolerant one.'[15]

After three weeks at sea, the ship arrived at Cairo, where Peter saw the treasures of King Tutankhamun at the Egyptian Museum and had the obligatory camel ride on a trip to the Pyramids. He was impressed with the grand boulevards and architecture of Cairo – 'a pretty go-ahead place'[16] – but his overnight stay in Naples three days later, his first taste of Europe, was a revelation. The *Fairsky* docked in the late afternoon, and Peter set off to explore the city by foot: two hours later, quite by accident, he found himself outside the famous opera house, Teatro di San Carlo, described by the French writer Stendhal as 'the most beautiful theatre in the world'. 'Before you could say Jack Robinson,' Peter wrote home, 'I was mingling with the very fashionable crowd in the foyer making my way to my seat' for a performance of Offenbach's *Tales of Hoffman*.[17] The dazzling theatre – a five-tier horseshoe of boxes, upholstered in red and decorated in gold leaf, with a frescoed ceiling by Guardini and sumptuous painted curtains – took his breath away. He could never have imagined such splendour.

It was an enchanted evening for the young man from Lower Hutt, but more astonishment was to come. Next morning he was up early to visit the Museo di Capodimonte, waiting outside the old palace for it to open. 'For the second time in about 12 hours I was dumbfounded for once inside I knew I was in for a treat. You see, inside the palace, it is decorated just as it was 200 years ago. You just walk in from the cold Italian morning, and crash, there you are in the 17th century with beautifully carved statues and a marble floor.' Peter saw paintings by Titian, Raphael, El Greco, Botticelli and others – 'I spent all the morning there and I only just got back to the boat in time' – but it was Giovanni Bellini's great *Transfiguration of Christ* that overwhelmed him. Peter was familiar with the painting from illustrations in books, but in Naples, confronting the original, he was astounded by its power and immediacy. 'In those days, you could stand right close to the paintings – there were no security guards; just the sound of someone coughing in the next room – and you could see the man who painted the thing. You could see the brush strokes, the bits of hair from the paintbrush.'[18] It was a crucial moment. Art had been a lofty, mysterious pursuit, associated with remote men of genius: now, for the first time, 'I realised art was made by someone, by a human being.'

Arriving in London in March, Peter stayed at the YMCA in Bloomsbury while he looked for accommodation. Within a week he had a short-term job with an insurance company in the central city: 'I am on the 5th

Giovanni Bellini, *Transfiguration of Christ*, c.1478–79
Oil on panel
Museo di Capodimonte, Naples

floor and when I look out of my window I see St Paul's Cathedral.'[19] His wages were £9 per week, half that of his previous job: 'What a let down after Aussie.'[20] In the evenings he planned a trip to Europe, and sent home an itinerary that took in the legendary places he had long imagined: 'I can see Father's face when he reads it!!!'[21] Despite his bravado, Peter was feeling rather intimidated by London and the challenges ahead. He counselled himself in his diary, 'I must have confidence in myself and go forward, forward.'

In May, he crossed the channel to Paris, staying at a grimy hostel run by the Communist Party near the Gare du Nord. On his first day he visited the Basilica of the Sacré Cœur on the hill of Montmartre – 'from there I got a great view of Paris';[22] next was the Musée d'Arte

Moderne, where he admired the work of Picasso, Matisse, Klee and Rouault. Like any young art aficionado on a first trip to Europe, he was determined to see as much as possible, and he ended the day at a museum of Romanesque art, emerging 'almost a wreck' hours later.

Back home, Peter had read the French poets in translation – Baudelaire, Verlaine and Rimbaud – and now, at the Bibliothèque nationale de France, he was able to see their letters and manuscripts. At the Louvre he studied the masterpieces he knew from books, including the *Mona Lisa* and the *Venus de Milo* – a wonderful, yet exhausting experience: '[I]t is a physical endurance test going around the Louvre,' he admitted. The Musée de Cluny offered a more intimate encounter with the past. Housed in an ancient abbey, it contains exquisite medieval statues and altarpieces, but it was the humble implements of daily monastic life that he found most affecting. Indeed, it was not just high culture that captivated Peter. Writing to his parents, he commented on the poise and elegance of young Parisian women; he also reported, rather provocatively, that wine was cheaper than milk.

Leaving Paris, he visited Versailles – 'magnifique!' – and Chartres to see the great medieval cathedral. From there he caught a ride to Biarritz, but the lack of cars made hitchhiking impossible once he crossed the Spanish border. The trains, however, were unforgettable: '[E]veryone takes their lunch and usually a bottle of wine and you are expected to share ... I was an object of great curiosity to my fellow travellers and they put me on a great fuss. During that trip I ate all sorts of odd things: smoked herring, black pudding, egg omelette ...'[23]

Peter's next destination was Ávila, the famous walled town northwest of Madrid. 'Avila is one of the great centres of Spanish pilgrimage,' he informed his parents, 'for it was here that 2 of Spain's most notable saints lived, Saint Teresa of Avila, and St John of the Cross.' As a child he had read about these saints and longed to walk in their footsteps; now he was able to visit the convent where Saint Teresa had lived, and see the grove of trees where Saint John had his hermitage. In Madrid, he spent two days at the Prado – 'perhaps the finest [museum] in the World' – where the paintings by Goya made a long-lasting impression. On a day trip to Toledo, he was dazzled by the cathedral, one of the finest Gothic buildings in Europe, but appalled by the souvenir industry: 'the commercialisation of this town made it stink'.[24]

By late May, Peter was back in France, visiting Avignon, the papal seat during the fourteenth century, en route to Italy. In Rome he spent a day in the Vatican Museum: 'I saw the study of Pope Julius II where the walls are covered with two great frescoes of Raphael ... It's funny how you change your views on painters for I used to think Raphael was too slick, almost commercial, but after seeing his work in the Vatican, which has the finest collection of his painting in the world, I have changed my mind completely. He was a genius.'[25] The young man from the antipodes was testing his opinions and becoming more confident in his taste.

Peter was enthralled by the Sistine Chapel with its famous ceiling painted by Michelangelo, but the Vatican Library offered more unexpected wonders: 'Letters from Henry VIII to Anne Boleyn and the Pope were on show amongst many other famous and precious things'. He was intrigued by the street life around the Vatican precinct: 'Chinese priests, Franciscan friars, nuns... and then poor peasants from the south who have come up to Rome to see St Peters – dressed usually in black with the heavy black stocking that the Spanish women wear.'

From a café in the Termini railway station, a striking modern building lined with shops, bars and restaurants, Peter wrote home to his parents. 'All over Europe they have these Bars or "bistros" which are small shops that sell all sorts of liquor and you can go in and sit down at one of the small round tables, buy a drink, and stay as long as you like. There is no six o'clock closing here... All through Europe wine, sherry etc is very cheap and I haven't seen one drunk in all of my travels to date. Anyway! I suppose by this time you must think I've been drunk sitting in bars frittering away all my money. I assure you I haven't.'

Nearing the end of his trip, Peter caught a train to Florence, where he made straight for the convent of San Marco to see 'the finest collection of Fra Angelicos in existence'.[26] At the Uffizi Gallery, he was captivated by Botticelli, especially his *Birth of Venus*, and sent his sister a postcard. 'What a great piece of art it is,' he commented, 'and for me it made the trip worth it just to see it.'

Back in London after a twenty-eight-hour train trip, he wrote to his parents:

> The real purpose of my leaving New Zealand has been accomplished and there is nothing more I wish to see in Europe. I have, for the last 7 weeks had a fairly extensive trip and I can say that I'm now completely satisfied. I have seen many things which I will store in my mind and which I will savour for many years. When I look back it almost seems like a dream, you know. But time passes, and we change and although it is very interesting to see and go to these places one can not go on like this forever and I will have to think now about returning to New Zealand or at least facing the future anyway.

Souvenirs from Peter's travels in Europe, 1960

Visitors at a private view of the Picasso exhibition,
Tate Gallery, 1960

For now, though, he was free to enjoy London. 'Facing the future' – his father's phrase – could wait.

In late June, Peter took a new job, working for the travel bureau of a large department store, Chiesmans of Lewisham. A few weeks later, he successfully applied for a promotion. 'I had to use a little cheek at first for I knew very little about the travel game but as time goes by I am picking it all up and making a pretty good go of it.'[27]

By now he was starting to miss the news from home, and he began to visit New Zealand House in The Haymarket to browse the *Auckland Weekly*, the *Freelance* and the *Listener*. He also discovered *Landfall*, which had helped to promote a sense of cultural identity since its inception in 1947. Here, Peter found art reviews and reproductions of contemporary New Zealand painting – work that surprised him in its vigour and modernity. One day, walking through Bloomsbury, a new book caught his eye in a shop window – *The New Zealanders*, a collection of short stories by the young Auckland writer Maurice Shadbolt. 'It stopped me in my tracks. *I* was a New Zealander. I went in and bought it, and I read it.'[28]

But Peter's dawning sense of New Zealand as a place with its own distinctive culture was still evolving. London had so much to offer – including, in the summer of 1960, the largest ever retrospective of Picasso's paintings at the Tate Gallery. For decades the Spaniard, now nearly eighty, had been influential among the more radical British artists but lampooned in the press; finally, it seemed, the rest of the country was catching on. Some half a million people saw the exhibition, journalists wrote of 'Picassomania' and the *Tatler* coined a new term: it was a 'block-buster'. Peter made several visits, as did other young New Zealanders temporarily based in London, the artists Pat Hanly, Billy Apple and Bill Culbert. Writing to his parents, he explained that all the works were hung in chronological order – 'so you can go along and just see how he has changed and developed as an artist. All this is extremely interesting for it gives you a far greater understanding of his work.'[29]

In October, Peter apologised for neglecting to write: 'I have been on the razzle dazzle a bit lately,' he admitted.[30] In the space of a few weeks he had been to see the Miles Davis Quintet, the Leningrad Philharmonic Orchestra, Chekhov's *The seagull* at the Old Vic, and exhibitions of the work of Paul Klee and William Blake – and much more. The next night he was off to the Blackheath Chamber Music Society to hear a concert of early music. 'With all this talk about theatres, concerts etc I guess you are thinking that I'm spending all my money on entertainments, and you would be 100% correct. You see I've decided that as I'm here in London I may as well go and see and hear as much as I can afford as I will never get the opportunity again. The result is of course that I am not saving a bean'.[31] He hardly had time to attend Mass, but he saw no reason to concern his parents on that score.

Peter also had news of a more personal nature: his love life was 'blooming'. In July he had met Rosemary – 'a very attractive girl with beautiful skin and the most expressive eyes I have ever looked into' – and on their first date they had visited the National Gallery.[32] He was enchanted by Rosemary's looks and sense of style, but noted in his diary that she was only sixteen-and-a-half: 'Too young and flirty I think!!'[33] He also enjoyed the family life that Rosemary provided, especially her mother's cooking: 'I keenly look forward to when I go round there as the meals are crazy (Great).'[34] But there seemed little prospect for their relationship, and he cautioned his parents not to get any 'rash ideas' about marriage.[35] '[W]e are both getting pretty keen on each other but as I'm definitely heading back to New Zealand next year I think I will have to try and slow the pace down a little.'

Instead of living in a boarding house, Peter was now flatting with a group of young men in Blackheath. 'I feel it is the best move I have made,' he told his brother, 'for they are all of my own age and they are a lively lot so there is always something going. Where I was previously I was more or less by myself, in a small room, and I was beginning (during the later stages) to get a little lonely, and depressed.'[36] With his new friends he visited Le Macabre, a beatnik coffee bar in Soho with murals of skeletons, bakelite skulls for ashtrays and Chopin's *Funeral march* on the jukebox. 'This was very dark and gloomy inside and instead of seats you sit on old tombstones and drink your coffee on coffins. It is all rather fun.'[37]

The early 1960s was a period of radical developments in the arts, and Peter gravitated towards the new and controversial. He told his parents about Karel Reisz's *Saturday night and Sunday morning*, one of the first British New Wave films – 'very harsh, very realistic, with a pretty hard-hitting story about a young chap in a North of England industrial town. I doubt very much if the uncut film would ever pass the New Zealand censor as there is a fair bit of bad language in it.' He mentioned the plays he had seen, including Harold Pinter's *The caretaker* and JP Donleavy's *A fairy tale of New York*. 'There is a big controversy in England at the moment over the theatre ... and these 2 plays represent the extreme movement of new play writing.'[38]

As the time for his return to New Zealand edged closer, Peter's whirl of art, music, theatre and film became ever more intensive. 'As you have probably gathered from my letters I like London very much,' he wrote to his parents, 'and it must be a great place to live in if you were on a salary of £20,000 a year.'

In April 1961, Peter left work and made a final trip to Paris, mainly to revisit the Louvre, but he also managed to see the jazz great Bud Powell at the Blue Note Café. His trip coincided with a crisis in the final stages of the Algerian war of independence, when a group of French generals, hoping to maintain the status quo, attempted to overthrow President de Gaulle. 'I have never seen so many armed police and tanks that were rattling around the centre of Paris,' he reported.[39] Returning to the UK, he hitchhiked through Wales to catch a boat to Dublin, but his stay in Ireland was cut short by a bout of pleurisy. Instead of exploring the land of his forebears, he spent several days in hospital.

Back in London, on the eve of his departure, Peter took Rosemary to a concert at the Royal Festival Hall. 'It was all rather sad when the concert finished and I looked around the hall for the last time. Later we walked over the Waterloo Bridge and along the Victoria Embankment and had a cup of coffee. She came down to Southampton to see me off.'[40]

Although he was ambivalent about leaving London, Peter felt he was ready to return home. He admitted to his parents that he was likely to find New Zealand 'a little slow' for a while: 'But with a bit of patience I hope I do not get too jumpy ... I do not think I will at the moment anyway for I feel quite contented and I am honestly looking forward to coming home.'[41]

Peter believed that his future lay in New Zealand – but what would that future hold? Where would he find an outlet for his artistic interests? By the time he embarked on the SS *Southern Cross* in late May, he had begun a novel – about a young man, a New Zealander, who was returning home after a long stay in London. There had been a relationship with a charming girl, but it was abruptly cut off by his departure.

Somewhere between Cape town and Auckland, Peter tossed his novel overboard.[42]

AGNUS
DEI
DONNA
NOBIS
PACEM

THREE

The paintings triggered off something inside and I saw my land for the first time.

Early on the morning of 5 July 1961, the *Southern Cross* sailed into Wellington and docked at Glasgow Wharf. A small welcoming party, including his parents and his friend Wilson Buchanan, braved the chill to meet Peter, but after the anticipation of arrival the reality was rather a let-down. 'My parents drove me home to the Hutt Valley and I kept noticing all the weeds growing by the side of the road. It was unkempt, like a frontier. So I went home and had a cup of tea.'[1] Marie McLeavey was delighted to see her brother again. 'He was the same Peter, so sensitive and serious. I remember him sitting on the couch in his horn-rimmed spectacles. He'd only just said hello to me, really, and he fixed me with a look and said, "Marie – what makes you tick?" Well! I had no idea what he was talking about!'[2]

After more than two years away, Peter had developed a keen curiosity about his own country's history and culture. '[R]eally it was not until I got to Europe, that I discovered I was a New Zealander,' he recalled. 'It was to be back here that spiritually I would live and flourish.'[3] He returned, too, with romantic ideas about his homeland: 'I had this feeling, very strongly, about New Zealand being almost a waif, something that was unloved, unappreciated.'[4] Idealistic and eager to commit himself, he wanted to nurture his own culture and assist its growth, but as yet he had no idea how to go about it. 'I needed a challenge … I needed a cause. I was waiting, waiting for something to come and claim me.'[5]

Besides, at the little state house in Riverside Drive, there were more pressing considerations. As far as his parents were concerned, Peter's years of travel and adventure had come to an end, and it was time for

Colin McCahon, *Agnus Dei, Donna Nobis Pacem*, 1966
Oil on canvas on board
Victoria University of Wellington Art Collection, purchased 1968

him to settle down and think about the future. The first priority was to find a job. As the reality of his circumstances set in, Peter's spirits plummeted. Restless, anxious, and uncertain of his future, he entered one of the most difficult periods of his life. 'I really went through the hoops,' he recalled. 'It took me a couple of years to settle back. And I had some pretty depressing times.'[6]

In August, Peter went back to a job as a clerk at the Bank of New Zealand, but 'I couldn't stand it... I had to go back the next day and tell them I was leaving.'[7] His father was appalled. 'You're mad!' he fumed. 'Giving up a good job!'[8] As the tension mounted, Peter retreated to his room, reading essays on art and literature by Herbert Read and Graham Greene.[9] By now he had decorated the walls with theatre posters from London, including one that spoke to his current predicament – Eugène Ionesco's satire on conformity and alienation, *Rhinocéros*.

Friends provided some consolation, and Peter enjoyed catching up with Wilson Buchanan, who was now planning his own overseas trip. Buchanan introduced him to a new acquaintance who would become a lifelong friend, a young Englishman named Ivan Bootham who had grown up in an artistic family and loved music and literature. Bootham was then working as a ticketwriter at Evans's fabric store, and making his first tentative steps towards becoming a writer and composer; he shared Peter's dry sense of humour and understood his longing to return to London.[10] 'Peter was quite unsettled,' he recalled. 'He would go into the travel agent one week and book his passage back, then go in the following week and cancel it. This went on for quite a time.'[11]

Bootham's parents had recently emigrated from England and settled in Whanganui, and he took Peter to visit them one weekend. Peter immediately felt at home with the Bootham family: Joe, who worked for a cousin's bakery; his wife Amy, an accomplished pianist; and their two daughters. It turned out that they had sailed on the SS *Southern Cross* with Peter; Joe, an artist, had even made a drawing of him in his shipboard sketchbook.

Early in 1962, Peter decided to get away from Wellington for a while. He planned to visit his old home town, New Plymouth, and enquire about job prospects, but when the bus pulled into Whanganui on a clear sunny day, the town looked so appealing that he decided to stay. Perhaps he was swayed by the thought of the hospitable Boothams. Within a few days he had a room in a boarding house and a job in the menswear department at the D.I.C. store – his introduction to the psychology of salesmanship. 'The head of menswear told me something that was useful to me later on,' he recalled. 'He said, "When the

Peter with the Bootham family, Sydney Place, Whanganui, 1962

farmers come to town, get them some socks or anything, it doesn't matter, but get them into the changing room. You've got to get them in the changing room."'[12]

In Whanganui, Peter regained a sense of independence for the first time since returning to New Zealand, and he also enjoyed himself socially, spending much of his spare time at the Bootham cottage at Sydney Place. Genial Joe Bootham was the first serious painter Peter had met, and he was deeply impressed by the older man's dedication and integrity. Watching Bootham at work, planning his paintings and reflecting on his progress, he understood that art was as much an intellectual pursuit as a technical discipline.[13] Ivan, who was a frequent weekend visitor, took a playful photograph that suggests the spirit of role-playing and comedy that prevailed at Sydney Place. Peter, posing in a jaunty cap between the elder Boothams, looks quite at home with his adopted family.

By the spring of 1962, Peter was back living with his parents in Lower Hutt. After a brief period as a clerk at the National Airways Corporation, he found a new job with good prospects, working as an insurance clerk in the shares section at the Australasian Temperance and General Mutual Life Assurance Society. One of the largest and most successful insurance companies in the southern hemisphere, 'T & G', as it was known, was housed in a handsome eight-storey building on the corner of Grey Street and Lambton Quay.

Peter found his new work more interesting and congenial, but he was still struggling to adjust to life in Wellington. His Catholicism had begun to wane while he was abroad, and he had largely stopped going to Mass. 'The Catholicism had been such an absolute, total thing,' he recalled. 'It never completely went away, but it lost its power for me in those years, and it left an emptiness. I was searching for something.'[14] He was also divided between two cultures, trying to get a foothold in New Zealand and recover a sense of belonging, but missing the vitality of life in London. New Zealand seemed very much on the edge of the civilised world, far from new developments in contemporary culture.[15]

Now that Wilson Buchanan had left for London, Ivan Bootham became Peter's closest friend in Wellington, and the two attended concerts and plays, and saw the latest avant-garde films by Cassavetes, Fellini and Bergman at the Paramount Theatre in Courtenay Place. One night, Peter took his friend to an upstairs coffee bar to watch *Top of the pops*, a new BBC programme that featured the latest sensation – The Beatles. Ivan was a regular visitor at Riverside Drive, spending hours in Peter's room talking about books and music. Peter lent him his copy of *Lolita* in its plain wrapper – 'Be careful who you mention it to' – and Ivan later wrote a poem about their friendship:

> those were the days in '62 –
> What was banned must be OK, right?
> And being young our duty was to keep up with the play.
> But the play I warmed to at Waiwhetu was of a 12 inch LP
> Sonny Rollins Way Out West…
> Tenor sax in its element riding bass and drums
> The jaunty good humour not a put-on:
> Who'd have thought 'I'm An Old Cowhand' was born to jazz?
> We jumped the horizon at the end of our noses
> (those nights of sorrowful countenance)
> Brought to life by the promise in the midst of ordinary things,
> Even if home for us was always away from home.[16]

During his holidays, Peter travelled the country by bus and train, taking with him books of New Zealand poetry and history to read. He visited the Bay of Islands, staying at a boarding house in Russell and exploring the tranquil grounds where the Treaty of Waitangi was signed in 1840. 'I remember looking across the water at Russell, at the land and at the skies, and feeling a sense of place for me here. And during this time I started to look at the art of my own country.'[17]

A turning point came in July 1963, when he saw a retrospective exhibition by Toss Woollaston and Colin McCahon at the Centre Gallery in Wellington. This was a landmark show for the two artists, who had been working since the 1930s and were regarded, at least by a small band of supporters, as the country's leading painters.[18] The retrospective did much to bring their work to a new audience and, for the young Peter McLeavey, '[I]t was an epiphany…I was knocked over.'[19]

Bold, rugged and unmistakably 'modern', the work of McCahon and Woollaston was as good as any contemporary art he had seen in Europe. That in itself was exciting. But McCahon's work affected Peter on a deeper level, reminding him of the thirteenth-century Italian paintings he had so admired on his travels: 'The colour and the brush-work were strong, expressive; the form, primitive and assured.'[20] McCahon's art seemed to link the old world and the new, and it affected Peter emotionally, as he explained to the artist years later. 'The paintings triggered off something inside and I saw my land for the first time. It was a crucial time for me as I was thinking of returning to England. But somehow I felt differently about being a New Zealander. This was our land. Your land and my land. New Zealand. And I wanted to give it something. My drive and ambition and love.'[21]

McCahon and his contemporaries answered a need among the intelligentsia of Peter's generation: they demonstrated the possibility of a vigorous New Zealand art, and their work helped to nurture a growing sense of national identity. As the poet Charles Brasch noted in 1958, 'The best contemporary painting (and literature, and music) is in fact *creating* New Zealand as a world of the imagination.'[22] For Brasch this was an exciting development: '[I]n these first stirrings of the native imagination an undiscovered world seems to be waking and opening before our eyes. In that world we may look for an expression of our spiritual identity as a people.'

Brasch was writing in a catalogue published by the Auckland City Art Gallery, which was leading the way in raising the profile of New Zealand art. Its dynamic young English director, Peter Tomory, had a mission for the gallery: to 'pump a continuous transfusion of the vital blood of art into the community, enrich its spirit and imagination and provide it with an active set of totems for its own adaptation of the European civilisation'.[23] With Hamish Keith, Colin McCahon and other staff, Tomory organised exhibitions like the McCahon–Woollaston retrospective, as well as a series of annual touring shows that surveyed the work of artists across the country.[24] Such exhibitions did much to develop a sense of confidence in the quality of New Zealand art – and a new optimism among young artists. 'Auckland Art Gallery was welcoming all comers,' painter Don Binney recalled, 'and it exerted that magical pull, drawing all the antsy intelligent eager people from all over New Zealand.'[25]

But other galleries lagged behind Auckland. As Tomory noted in 1964:

> [New Zealand] painting of this century is not properly shown in any gallery but Auckland's. It is as though somebody interested in New Zealand poetry were to find that certain New Zealand libraries did not stock it at all … We have ten Woollastons, for example, and the National Art Gallery has none at all. The McDougall Gallery in Christchurch has one; Dunedin has none. Yet Woollaston is now 55 and has been an established painter for 10 or 15 years …
>
> The public galleries could be doing much more to break down the old New Zealand snobbery that anything good must be done overseas.[26]

In Wellington, the National Art Gallery, under its long-serving director Stewart Maclennan, was hampered by poor funding and a conservative council dominated by members of the New Zealand Academy of Fine Arts – Wellington's grandly named art society. In 1958, the gallery had rejected the major exhibition *British abstract painters*, organised by the British Council, on the grounds that it represented 'a particularly extreme section of ultra-modernism in art' and 'was not considered to merit display'.[27] It also made a habit of turning down the touring exhibitions initiated in Auckland, much to the disgust of local painters such as Gordon Walters. Criticism became widespread during the 1960s. The editor of the *Evening Post* complained, 'An art gallery should be more than just a place in which to kill time on a wet Sunday. It should be a meeting place for the community – a place of colour, congeniality and controversy.'[28]

The shortcomings of the gallery were a concern for the Queen Elizabeth II Arts Council (the precursor of today's Creative New Zealand), established in 1963 to channel government support for the arts, but it would be another decade before it became directly involved.[29] Throughout the 1960s, the arts council's efficacy was limited by meagre funding and lack of direction, especially for the visual arts – a sore point among the art fraternity.[30]

Looking back on the early history of European art in this country in 1969, Hamish Keith made a sombre observation: 'Isolation and neglect were the conditions of an artistic life in New Zealand.'[31]

Traditionally, artists had limited opportunities to exhibit and sell their work, let alone earn a living. Many showed with local art societies, and some set up small selling displays in bookstores, libraries, and coffee shops like the French Maid Coffee House in Wellington, run by Dick Singleton. Described as 'the mecca of the writers and artists, singers, and the overseas community', the café had its first exhibition in 1940, showing the work of Theo Schoon, Sam Cairncross, Gordon Walters, Colin McCahon and others before it closed in 1951.[32]

Artists also clubbed together to form exhibiting associations, and in Christchurch, The Group was one of the most effective, providing an annual forum for McCahon, Woollaston, Rita Angus, Doris Lusk, Leo Bensemann and others. Another outlet was afforded by framers and artist suppliers such as John Leech in Auckland and McGregor Wright in Wellington, who showed original art as well as reproductions.[33] In the capital, the Centre Gallery, run by the Architectural Centre, was the leading place to see contemporary art, serving as a selling venue as well as a de facto public gallery. But throughout the country the situation was the same: sales were modest, prices low and there was little market for contemporary art, let alone modern art. Don Binney, who first exhibited in 1961, recalled, 'As often as not, a painting would be bought by another teacher, artist or writer in a gesture of collegial support.'[34]

By the mid-1960s, that situation was beginning to change. In some quarters, at least, there was a sense that New Zealanders, living in a period of prosperity and increasing national self-awareness, were ready to take a greater interest in the art of their own country. As the editor of the *Evening Post* commented in 1965:

> 'A car for every family' was once the cry of those who sought to give effect to the arrival of the affluent society. Now they are changing their tune. 'Two cars for every family!' is evidently more in keeping with the times...
>
> Where is somebody who, with enthusiasm equal to that of the champions of the motor car, will raise the cry: 'A painting in every home!' Or better still: 'Two paintings in every room in every home!'?[35]

In Wellington, Russell Hancock, the chairman of the Centre Gallery, was saying something very similar: 'We want to see paintings in boardrooms, paintings and sculptures in public buildings, in business offices and in shop windows.'[36] Opening the gallery's Christmas exhibition in 1965, he spoke of the popular image of New Zealanders as beer drinkers, rugby players, 'world-class fighters' and breeders of fine racehorses: 'I don't see why they shouldn't add to all these things by gaining a reputation for being cultured and knowledgeable in the visual arts. We've got the money, the time and the basic education for it.'[37] As Hancock recognised, the younger generation was potentially a keen audience for New Zealand art: having come through a progressive system of art education at school, implemented by Clarence Beeby and Gordon Tovey, they had at least some basic awareness of the subject.[38]

One of the limitations for artists was the lack of dealer galleries – a relatively recent phenomenon in the international art world, emerging in Paris and London in the late nineteenth century, and gaining momentum in New York fifty years later.[39] The modern dealer played the role of talent-spotter, showcasing the work of selected artists in short-term exhibitions in a permanent gallery. Moving between two distinct social and economic worlds – that of the artist's studio on the one hand, and the private collector on the other – they marketed the work, supported their artists and in return took a commission on sales. Art dealers had a key role to play in a professional art world, but there seemed to be little potential for them in New Zealand.

A precursor was Edwin Murray Fuller, who opened a gallery in Wellington in 1920, which represented Archibald Nicoll, Nugent Welch, John Weeks, Dorothy Kate Richmond and others. The business soon expanded to include British art, and it became Murray Fuller's chief focus: he and his wife Mary brought six exhibitions of British art to New Zealand from 1928 to 1940.[40] At a time when Pākehā New Zealanders identified with British culture, the art of the 'mother country' had far greater cachet than any local offering.

The first dealer gallery devoted to modern New Zealand art was opened in 1949 by a young woman with a passion for her subject. Stylish, energetic and ambitious, Helen Hitchings created a spacious gallery with a lively installation of paintings, ceramics, textiles and furniture in a warehouse in Wellington's Bond Street. She closed two years later to take an exhibition of contemporary New Zealand art to London, but her gallery provided a model for those who followed, most notably Peter Webb's Argus House Gallery in Auckland (1957–58)[41] and André Brooke's Gallery 91 in Christchurch (1959).

The Gallery of Helen Hitchings, showing the McCahon–Woollaston exhibition, August 1949

It was The Gallery (later renamed the Ikon Gallery) that led the way for a new generation of dealer galleries in New Zealand. Opened in Auckland in March 1960, it was the initiative of two young architecture students, Don Wood and Frank Lowe, who continued their studies while running the exhibition programme. Located in a basement in Rationalist House at 64 Symonds Street, The Gallery had a clean modern look, with plastered brick walls, coir matting and elegant lighting. It was a popular hangout for students and artists, and had close links to the nearby Auckland City Art Gallery; indeed, the idea of opening a gallery had been suggested by Tomory and his staff. McCahon, in particular, was very encouraging: having visited New York in 1958, he understood the role a dealer gallery could play in Auckland. It was he who provided a list of artists, and the first exhibition was opened by Tomory.

Peter with his first Colin McCahon painting, *Was this the promised land*, 1962, at his flat in Mortimer Terrace, Wellington, photographed by Robert Kennedy, c.1964

Wood and Lowe arranged exhibitions by McCahon, Jean Horsley, Keith Patterson and Alwyn Lasenby in their first year, and later held a number of important McCahon shows, including the 'Gate' paintings in 1961 and the 'Landscape theme and variations' series in 1963.[42] When Lowe left the business, Wood continued on his own, building up a small group of clients, most of whom were art-world insiders – artists, architects, curators, critics and academics. In his third year, he wrote to the expatriate artist John Blackburn, 'Things are still very difficult here for both painter and art dealer but are gradually improving… I have recently been going through a period of mild bitterness about the lack of patronage for arts supplied by the New Zealand public. They all pay lip service to the artist and his work but never reach into their pockets.'[43]

The Gallery – lively and youthful – was Peter McLeavey's introduction to the world of the art dealer in New Zealand. By 1963, he was becoming a collector, saving his wages to make the occasional purchase and visiting Auckland as often as possible. Buying a painting was a way of identifying himself as a New Zealander and committing to the culture. 'Just as an icon painting not only represents the Virgin, but *is* the Virgin, so a local painting was not just *of* New Zealand – it was a living, breathing chunk of New Zealand.'[44] It was a conviction that would fuel his future career.

In May 1964, Peter acquired his first McCahon, a luminous abstract painting entitled *Was this the promised land*, from Don Wood.[45] He met McCahon at the gallery when he was making his purchase, and accompanied him to the Kiwi Tavern for a beer; back home, he had his photograph taken outside his flat, proudly showing off his new acquisition.[46] In the following year, Peter bought a second McCahon, a three-part work entitled *Koru, 1, 2, 3* from the Barry Lett Galleries; later he acquired *Agnus Dei, Donna Nobis Pacem* (see page 38).[47] He also purchased works by Toss Woollaston, Don Peebles, Pat Hanly[48] and the young Wellington artist Jeff Macklin. In a few years he had acquired a small but outstanding collection of New Zealand art – one that favoured the most bracingly austere in contemporary practice.

Peter's interest in collecting was unusual among his circle in Wellington, and even his closest friends were sometimes startled by his acquisitions. 'People didn't buy paintings in the early 1960s,' Ivan Bootham recalled. 'And certainly not those kinds of paintings. I remember being quite taken aback by *Koru, 1, 2, 3*. I had seen McCahon's *On building bridges* at the Auckland City Art Gallery, which I could relate to, but the numbers paintings took a little more time.'[49]

Even for other artists, McCahon's work was challenging. As Ian Scott, who was still a student, observed, 'McCahon had his supporters

Colin McCahon, *Koru, 1, 2, 3*, 1965
PVA on hardboard
Museum of New Zealand Te Papa Tongarewa, purchased 2011

at art school, but many people didn't have a clue what he was doing.'[50] Scott recalled his first encounter with McCahon's thirteen-part *Numerals* at the Auckland Society of Arts in the mid-1960s.[51] 'We went in there, Rick [Killeen] and me, and we just looked at each other and said, "What the hell is that meant to be?" We knew we had to get to grips with it, we knew McCahon was important, but at that stage it was very difficult to take in.'

In tandem with buying paintings, Peter was collecting articles by the writers he admired: Peter Tomory, Hamish Keith and others. In 1964, Keith surveyed the recent changes in the art world in Victoria University's student paper, *Salient*. New Zealand artists were less isolated with the advent of air travel, he noted; they were also more confident, more professional and much more numerous. '[I]n the bleak years of the forties [we could] really only boast of two major painters, McCahon and Toss Woollaston. In the following 10 years the two have become five, from 1960 to 1962, the five 10, and in 1964 we have at least 20 painters and sculptors worth taking very seriously indeed.'[52]

Keith acknowledged the importance of dealers in the fledgling local art world: 'In Auckland the activity of at least two serious professional dealers has put more money in the artist's pocket in four years than the combined New Zealand purchases of the public galleries has in 20. While it is still practically impossible for the serious contemporary artist

Toss Woollaston, *Taramakau*, 1963
Oil on board
Brian Steele collection

to live by his painting or sculpture alone, he can at least look forward to increasing returns for his labours.'[53] Like Tomory, Keith lamented the fact that so many of the country's art institutions were dominated by old men – 'almost without exception they are out of touch'. Peter read such articles with great interest. A revolution of sorts was under way in the visual arts – one led by his generation. But how he could help the cause?

Initially, he began to seek out the artists who interested him, hoping to learn more about them and their work. Visiting Nelson in May 1964, he caught the bus to Greymouth to call on Toss Woollaston, who painted in his spare time and earned a living as a door-to-door salesman for Rawleigh's household products. Years later, he retained a vivid memory of that occasion. 'Greymouth was a ramshackle, raw, rawboned sort of place and it was a wet dreary day when I arrived at about 6PM. I put up at the Brian Boru and rang the artist. He welcomed me – "Like to come round this evening?" I went to the old house and was shown into the front room where the walls were covered in paintings and the Rawleigh products were stacked on the floor – back rub, liniment and vapour balm. That was Toss's studio.'[54]

After Woollaston had shown his pictures, Peter asked if he could be left alone with them for a while. 'There was one painting in particular, an oil on board of the Taramakau River, that attracted me [see previous page]. I went back to the Brian Boru, had a few beers – they were doing a roaring trade at midnight, half the town seemed to be there – and thought about the sixty guineas [nearly a month's salary] the artist had advised me was the price of the picture.'[55] Next morning he went back and bought it.

Woollaston was surprised and delighted to sell a painting to a complete stranger, and wrote to thank Peter: 'I wish you long enjoyment of it. A purchase encourages me & stimulates me to paint more. We all enjoyed your visit greatly.'[56] For his part, Peter had never met anyone like Woollaston and his wife Edith. 'I knew I'd come in contact with two remarkable people. Their home was an old-fashioned colonial house, but there was a wonderful warmth – it was a very warm, informal, nurturing place. They had brown bread. I'd come in contact with another civilisation.'

Peter found a new world opening up in these years. 'I was meeting men and women who were on the same wavelength as me ... McCahon and Michael Illingworth and Toss Woollaston and Gordon Walters and many others ... I found them a source of inspiration ... They had a view of themselves and this island state and its place in the world and what we could do here.'[57]

For Peter, the artists would become a second family, a close network of shared interest and purpose and emotional support: he would come to think of Toss and Edith Woollaston as his 'other parents'; McCahon and Illingworth as his 'brothers'. Art would become a passion, helping to fill the gap left by his waning Catholicism. 'The art became an absolute ... it had its apostles, it had its sacred texts, it had its heroes, it had its villains, it had its martyrs. That became an imaginary world for me.'

In 1963, Peter left the family home in Riverside Drive and took a flat in Mortimer Terrace, Aro Valley, in Wellington; later, he moved to Tinakori Road in Thorndon. He developed a habit of walking the streets late at night, fascinated by the elegant colonial houses in the neighbourhood. 'I'd see the glow of a lamp, a beautifully lit room, bookshelves, pictures on the wall. That's what I wanted, that whole life. It was completely different to what I'd grown up with.'[58] Meantime, Peter's favourite

Toss and Edith Woollaston, c.1966

haunts were the less salubrious St George Hotel and the Duke of Edinburgh, where he met his friends and enjoyed a pint or two. He also spent a lot of time reading: 'I'd often stay inside with my books all weekend, and save up all the dishes until Sunday evening.'

Since early childhood, Peter had been troubled by bouts of asthma, but the condition seemed to worsen after his return to New Zealand. Even more troubling, he was prone to anxiety and debilitating bouts of depression, which lasted for weeks. His doctor believed that his problems were related, and prescribed valium to calm his nerves, but Peter was reluctant to take the medication: 'Something told me that wasn't the answer.' Eventually, the doctor made another suggestion: perhaps psychoanalysis might help to address the unconscious roots of his

Mario Fleischl, 1948–49

anxieties? He recommended Mario Fleischl, a Polish Jew who had trained in Vienna and emigrated with his wife in 1936 to escape anti-Semitism and fascism in Europe.[59]

By the time Peter met him in 1963, Fleischl was in his fifties and had been practising as a psychoanalyst in Wellington for twenty years. A tall man with a strong European accent, and usually dressed in a three-piece Harris tweed suit, he worked in a small room in the Druid's Chambers in Woodward Street, conveniently close to Peter's office in Lambton Quay. Peter was immediately struck by Fleischl's subtle intelligence and wide-ranging learning, but it was only gradually that he became aware of his links to the local art world. The psychoanalyst's friends included painters, potters and musicians, and he and his physician wife Hilda had been among McCahon's earliest patrons in Dunedin in the 1940s, commissioning his major work, *Otago Peninsula*.[60] The Fleischls were part of a wider group of educated, dynamic European refugees – artists, architects and academics – who had brought a new verve to New Zealand cultural life in the post-war years.[61]

For the young Peter McLeavey, Mario Fleischl was a mentor and a father figure: kindly, supportive and understanding. His appointments took place three days a week, usually at lunchtime, Fleischl seated behind a large wooden desk while he lay on a chaise longue. Peter would talk freely about his childhood experiences, his dreams and anxieties, while Fleischl took notes and prompted further discussion. The relationship echoed to some extent that of the confessional, such a familiar part of Peter's upbringing, but in Fleischl's office the penitent, seeking a healing encounter with God, became the patient seeking self-knowledge and understanding.

Many years later, Peter described his experience of psychoanalysis. 'Mario and I are on the edge of a bay. There's an island out there at sea; we drag a boat out and we row to the island. As we walk up the island my foot stubs into the sand and it's a piece of marble, I realise it's a piece of a face. I find more fragments. A foot, and hand. I realise I've discovered an archeological site. I start to put the pieces together. And gradually I realise it's me.'[62]

This process of self-discovery was 'marvellous, wonderful, frightening and awesome',[63] helping Peter to understand his strengths and weaknesses, and move forward with confidence. He would come to see the psychoanalyst's couch as a bridge between the old Peter, the cautious insurance clerk, and the new Peter, willing to have faith in his own instincts and abilities.

FOUR

I can now devote my energies to the 'cultural revolution'.

As Peter recalled it, until January 1966 he was 'just someone who occasionally went to Auckland to buy a painting for my collection'.[1] He was settled in his job, earning a good income and enjoying his freedom as a young bachelor. Within a few months, his life had changed completely.

The change was prompted by a routine matter: Peter needed to find a new home because his flatmate was moving to Australia. One of the first flats he visited in the new year was at 270 The Terrace, conveniently close to the central business district. It was on the ground floor of an old Victorian villa, and had a large high-ceilinged room with a bay window overlooking the street, and a smaller room at the back. Peter was immediately struck by the light and sense of space. 'As soon as I saw that front room I knew ... there was something about it. In a fraction of a second I thought to myself what a beautiful thing to show paintings, contact some of these artists, get their works and show them, see what happens. Just give it a bit of a burl, you know?'[2]

Like a convert's account of a religious experience, Peter's story dramatises the moment of discovery – the sudden revelation, and the conviction of the way ahead. He regarded his 'birth' as an art dealer as an abrupt change of direction – an impulsive decision – and to some extent it was. But Peter had been fascinated by contemporary art for some time, and there were other developments that had led towards this moment.

In October 1965, for example, he had attended a discussion on the future of Wellington's cash-strapped Centre Gallery, which was largely run by volunteers.[3] Guest panellist Hamish Keith, in typically provocative form, stunned the audience with his advice: 'Close your doors and pack

Peter photographed by John B Turner, 1969

up.'[4] Keith argued that the gap in the market would soon be filled by a dealer gallery, which would be much more effective in promoting contemporary art: 'A private gallery would make a tremendous cultural change in Wellington.'[5] When Keith asked his listeners, 'Why is there no one here promoting New Zealand painting?' Peter thought to himself, 'Why not me?'[6]

Ivan Bootham learned of his friend's intentions late in 1965. 'Peter rang me up and asked me to meet him at Suzy's, the coffee bar. He told me he wanted to set up as an art dealer in some way. He didn't know how he would do it. I think he was to some extent inspired by Barry Lett in Auckland; in fact, as I recall he was even wondering if he should go to Auckland himself.'[7]

Peter had met Barry Lett in 1964, soon after Lett took over the Uptown Gallery in Queen Street and began to show the work of his fellow art students.[8] In May 1965, Lett went into partnership with Rodney Kirk Smith and Frank Lowe, who had previously been involved with the pioneering Ikon Gallery. The Barry Lett Galleries opened in Victoria Street as the Ikon closed its doors, taking over many of its artists, and it soon became the leading venue for contemporary art in Auckland. In 1967, Peter commented on Lett's achievement: 'On one hand it has given painters financial security by providing them with the outlet to exhibit – and sell – their work. Secondly, and just as important, is the fact that the Barry Lett Gallery has allowed Aucklanders the opportunity to see exhibitions of some of the best contemporary painting in New Zealand.'[9] Peter could have been describing his own ambitions. The Barry Lett Galleries provided a model; the question was, could Wellington support such a venture?

Peter was keen to test the waters, but first he discussed his plans with Mario Fleischl. 'Mario gave me much good advice,' he recalled. 'His stimulus gave me the courage to start my gallery.'[10] At this stage, Peter had nothing to lose: he could continue to work as an insurance clerk and run his gallery by appointment, with viewings on evenings and weekends. As Ivan Bootham observed, 'He was on a bit of a mission. In a sense, Peter saw the artists as the voices in the wilderness, and he wanted to have that voice heard. He was idealistic; he saw himself hand-in-hand as it were with the artists, helping them. He obviously wanted to make a living, but it was more of a shared cause.'

If Peter had little experience of art dealers other than Barry Lett and Don Wood at the Ikon Gallery in Auckland, and few models on which to base his new enterprise, in Wellington there was at least a precedent for selling work from a domestic setting. Madame Durga Lall, a well-known local personality and eccentric, held occasional exhibitions in her home in lower Pirie Street. Peter was a regular caller, and took Bootham along on one occasion: 'I remember black and white Franz Kline-like action paintings.'[11]

Eager for insights into his new profession, Peter read SN Behrman's racy, anecdotal memoir of Joseph Duveen, the first international celebrity dealer.[12] Duveen's career was based on a simple observation: Europe had a great deal of art and America had a great deal of money. He was shrewd, flamboyant and audacious, and cultivated a mystique around the art he purveyed: 'You're not ready for that yet,' he famously told an aspiring collector. Duveen pioneered a cult of the art dealer as a personality, and his example was not lost on Peter.

By February 1966, Peter had moved in at The Terrace and found a flatmate to help pay the rent. He had already discussed his plans with Toss Woollaston, who was keen to be involved, but he needed to sound out other artists as well. Taking two weeks' leave, he hitchhiked first to New Plymouth to visit Michael Smither, and then to Auckland, where he met Don Binney and Milan Mrkusich, and spoke to McCahon on the telephone. He also contacted Barry Lett, who agreed to send him some paintings on the condition that he share the commission on sales.[13] Back home, he ordered a large custom-built 'viewing wall', but progress was frustratingly slow. '[A]lthough the joiner has had the plan for three weeks, it is as yet uncompleted, and no amount of bullying, or shouting seems to have the slightest effect in hurrying this gentleman…'[14]

By now, Peter had informed his parents about his new project. 'I think they felt I'd gone stark raving mad. It was incomprehensible to them.'[15] Nevertheless, his mother put her skills to work, making new curtains for the front room, and a linen cover with matching cushions that transformed his single bed into a stylish divan. As long as he kept it tidy, Peter could transform his bedroom into a gallery in minutes.

On 21 May, he put his first advertisement in the *Dominion* – in the 'Amusements' column:

> COLIN McCAHON
> M.T. WOOLLASTON
> DON BINNEY
> A selection of Paintings including a major Binney oil, 'Alien Bird over suburban house', 1965.
> Telephone Peter McLeavey, 47561, for appointment to view.

Flyer for Peter's first gallery at 270 The Terrace, 1966

Looking for inexpensive forms of publicity, Peter installed a painting 'with a bit of a spiel' in Harry Seresin's popular coffee bar, upstairs at Parsons Bookshop on Lambton Quay.[16] He also rented a display unit in the Dominion Life Arcade, between Willis and Victoria streets, which was just big enough for a medium-sized picture. Soon, a Woollaston or a McCahon took its place among advertisements for local wares – bridal gowns, a haberdashery store and a clockmaker. Peter commissioned local artist William Jenks to design a flyer for his new gallery, and chose as his logo an angel in profile – 'a guardian, a protective device'.[17]

17th May 1966 №. 1

RECEIVED from I. T. Bootham

the sum of Ninety four Pounds

ten Shillings — Pence

being full payment of painting No 65/374. M. T. Woollaston

£ 94 : 10 : —

P McLeavey

Receipt for Peter's first sale, Toss Woollaston's *Mount Alexander*, 1966

At first business was slow at The Terrace: 'We'd average one person a fortnight.'[18] Peter was in the process of reinventing himself, and was not yet the dapper businessman of later years, as Ivan Bootham observed: 'He had a rather worn jumper with holes at the elbows of which he was quite proud. It might have been some kind of statement. Probably was! But even Michael Smither, who was no fashion plate – definitely not – even Michael remarked that maybe appearing in front of clients in that jumper was not quite the way to impress or generate sales.'

It was Bootham and his fiancée Audrey Welburn who purchased the first painting from Peter in May – a large Woollaston oil for £94, approximately one-tenth of Bootham's salary.[19] In the following years, he recalled, 'Peter would quite often ring me up to have an anniversary drink of receipt no. 1.' This first sale was a sign of things to come: a number of his friends became clients, and many clients became friends.[20] And initially, at least, Peter's desire to support his artists outweighed his business instincts. He offered to forgo any commission on sales to assist Woollaston, who had recently given up his day job to paint full time. 'Well, I was then working,' he commented. 'I had my job, I was being well paid for what I was doing there, and I wanted to help Toss.'[21]

Peter met Gordon Walters, who would become a lifelong friend and mentor – and a key member of his stable – when he came to view Woollaston's paintings. Walters, who had recently begun his now-celebrated 'Koru' series, was about to become a full-time artist with the financial support of his wife, the author and anthropologist Margaret Orbell. He was enthusiastic about Peter's plans for his gallery, lending him catalogues from the Museum of Modern Art in New York and introducing him to the influential American art magazine, *Artforum*.

Support also came from Gil Docking, the new director of the Auckland City Art Gallery, who invited three regional curators to select works for the annual survey of New Zealand painting: Peter McLeavey in Wellington, John Coley in Christchurch and Charlton Edgar in Dunedin.[22] Given the gallery's leading role in the art scene, this was a valuable endorsement of Peter's judgement. In his introductory text in the catalogue, Peter described the Wellington contingent as 'a hardy band of individualists' and noted the trend towards gifted young artists leaving the capital: 'Without the stimulation of a large buying public or dealer galleries that are continually exhibiting good local and national painting, Wellington painters are thriving in difficult soil.'[23]

Peter's early clients included several academics from Victoria University, just a short walk up the hill from The Terrace. In 1947, the historian John Beaglehole had established a committee to buy pictures for the staff common room, and in the following years he was aided by two lecturers from the music department: Fred Page, who was married to the painter Evelyn Page, and Douglas Lilburn, a close friend of Rita Angus.[24] All three were keen advocates for contemporary New Zealand art, and they helped to encourage an interest in collecting among their students and colleagues.[25] By 1966, John Beaglehole's son Tim was the key figure on the university's art-purchasing committee, and he soon made Peter's acquaintance. Tim Beaglehole was struck by Peter's manner: 'He was quite unusual with his big eyes, his glasses, and his very deliberate and considered form of address.'[26] He was also rather bemused by Peter's set-up. 'It was basically a bedsit. How there was room for him to live there as well as have so many paintings was puzzling … It left me with the impression that he was a slightly odd fellow. Living with all those paintings.'

David Gascoigne, then a young lawyer, knew Peter as an insurance clerk. He recalled his first meeting with him in his new role as 'a purveyor of fine arts':

> My father-in-law at that stage had a strong interest in the visual arts, and one Saturday I agreed to take him to see Peter about some paintings. So I drove him to the Terrace … and I said I'll pop out of the car and just make sure it is the right place. Well, it wasn't Peter's place – it was a bordello, to put it politely. There were

Peter with Toss Woollaston paintings,
photographed by Marti Friedlander, 1967

semi-clad people there, it was a wreck of a building, and I was treated as though I was a potential client. I wasn't, and I had to flee. I did ask them where Peter McLeavey was and someone said, 'He might be in that building over there, darling.'

So I went to the next door building and indeed it was Peter's place. It was effectively a bedsit... it was smallish and the main piece of furniture was a bed. He had a whole lot of paintings lined up against the wall, four or five deep. From the curatorial point of view, it was not what you would call best practice! He also had a pile of paintings underneath his bed – I remember he got down on his hands and knees and pulled them out. And they were primarily paintings by people with names like Colin McCahon and Toss Woollaston.[27]

Toss Woollaston, *Tasman Bay*, 1965
Oil on board
Te Manawa Museum of Art, Science and History

The Department of External Affairs (later the Ministry of Foreign Affairs and Trade) was crucial to Peter's project right from his early days as an art dealer.[28] Under the leadership of Alister McIntosh in the 1940s, the department began to purchase historical paintings for display in New Zealand's overseas posts. Younger diplomats pushed for a more contemporary presence, and from the early 1960s the department made a commitment to buying works by leading artists: McCahon, Woollaston, Mrkusich, Walters, Binney, Smither and others. In May 1966, the department bought two landscape paintings by Woollaston from Peter, and other purchases soon followed.[29] Quite apart from their practical value, these sales were significant on a symbolic level. 'Early on, this was very important to the artist,' Peter recalled, 'that one of the agencies of the government was buying work, and showing it internationally in our missions abroad.'[30]

As a self-styled missionary for New Zealand culture, Peter felt he had a lot in common with his new contacts at External Affairs: Alister McIntosh, Mervyn and Françoise Norrish, Paul Gabites, Douglas Zohrab, Frank and Lyn Corner, and Tim and Sherrah Francis. 'There was something in the air,' he recalled. 'There was a sense of excitement, a sense that things were changing. An indigenous school of art was emerging... something to be proud of. They wanted to commit themselves to that, they wanted to stand alongside those artists and help shape New Zealand.'[31] Some were already committed collectors. In 1960, for example, Frank and Lyn Corner – who first encountered New Zealand art at the home of John Beaglehole – had purchased a large Woollaston oil from the Centre Gallery. Two years later, they acquired another work by the artist, this time for External Affairs. Frank Corner had been posted to New York, and he chose the painting because it would stand up to the enormous panoramic view from his twenty-seventh-floor office.[32] As Peter noted, 'These mandarin figures, they wanted something that was uniquely of this place. Something a bit raw, not too polished... They were looking for icons of place that they could take away and hang in their rooms in Moscow, Brussels, London, that would remind them of where they came from.'[33]

In his first few months in business, Peter sold seven Woollastons – four oils and three drawings – including *Tasman Bay* to the Palmerston North Art Gallery (now Te Manawa). He was especially pleased with this sale, as he knew that inclusion in public collections would be most influential in promoting his artists.[34] In June, he sold his first Smither, to an Australian collector, and in August his first Mrkusich, a small drawing for £6. 'Dear Milan,' he wrote, '"From the small Acorn the mighty Oak doth grow." Enclosed is my cheque'.[35]

Peter was discovering that he was a natural salesman, reinforcing his belief in his new career. Even the sale of the smallest work produced a rush of adrenaline and a sense of achievement. 'I love selling,' he declared many years later. 'I sell, therefore I am.'[36] Peter brought his passion, his intelligence to each sale: 'You have to feel for the work. You have to love the work. You have to feel enthusiastic and you want to express that love to the public. So it's a very passionate and emotional business.'[37]

And yet there was nothing of the hard sell in his manner. Looking back in 2011, Sir David Gascoigne recalled: 'Peter was whimsical even then. He's got a very gentle whimsical nature and he's a very likeable person. You never get a big sales pitch with Peter. He's reflective, he's gentle and he's kindly humorous. He was like that then, and he's like that still.'[38]

For all his enthusiasm, Peter's first year as an art dealer could hardly be called a success financially. By the end of March 1967, his gross sales amounted to £836 and his commission of 25 percent to £209. His expenses – advertising, travel and telephone – came to £308, leaving a net loss of £99. Of course, his activities as an art dealer were subsidised by his job in insurance, where he was earning a salary of more than £1000, but the figures showed the very real difficulty in earning a living from the sale of contemporary art.

His next move is therefore all the more surprising. In late April, he told the Auckland artist Pat Hanly that he had handed in his notice: 'Things reached a head when I was promoted to a new job with considerable responsibility and found that I could not serve two masters. After reflection I decided to leave and concentrate on the dealing. It's a somewhat risky enterprise even at the best of times but still it is worth it. I will get a part time evening job somewhere just to pull in a few quid and I can now devote my energies to the "cultural revolution".'[39]

As part of his 'cultural revolution', Peter knew that he needed to build a greater audience for contemporary art in Wellington. He was aware of the lack of informed comment in the media: the *Evening Post* tended to dismiss modern art, while the *Dominion* had a weekly arts column, which focused on music and theatre.[40] There was clearly room for a column devoted to the visual arts that would inform the public and encourage interest in contemporary practice. Fired up by the challenge, he decided to take it on himself.

Peter had little experience in writing, but he had an excellent tutor in Gordon Walters' wife, Margaret Orbell. Every Tuesday evening he would visit their flat in Brougham Street and Orbell would set to work on his text: 'Sometimes she would quite radically rewrite, rephrase and repackage the whole thing... Through Margaret I learnt how to write, or how to polish my writing. She was a great help to me.'[41]

Beginning in June 1967, Peter chronicled the problems in the local art scene in a weekly column in the *Dominion*: the conservatism of the Academy of Fine Arts, the fustiness of the National Art Gallery and the need for a council-subsidised gallery. He noted the exciting developments at the Auckland City Art Gallery, and also in the regional centres. 'With cities like Palmerston North and New Plymouth forging ahead with their own civic art galleries,' he wrote, 'it is time that the question of financial priorities [for an art gallery in Wellington] was scrutinised. Particularly when the city council gave a subsidy of only $200 in 1966 to the capital's only dealing gallery, the Centre Gallery. This when the recent council estimates allocate $4600 for rat catching and dog control.'[42]

Peter also used his column to introduce local artists, including those he was now representing: Hanly, Smither, Woollaston, Walters and McCahon. He devoted an article to the expatriate film-maker and kinetic sculptor Len Lye, and mentioned a recent exhibition by another expatriate, Billy Apple, at the Howard Wise Gallery in New York. He wrote about international art stars, too – Marcel Duchamp, Andy Warhol and Francis Bacon – and the biennales, which were increasingly important in the global art world. 'New Zealand has artists whose work could be shown with confidence at international exhibitions,' he claimed. 'Now that we are trying to expand our trade both in South America and in Europe it is surely time for the Government to give serious consideration to New Zealand's participation at future biennales at both Sao Paulo and Venice.'[43]

Above all, Peter urged the need for more recognition of local artists. Reflecting on the New Zealand honours list of more than 2000 people, he noted that, with the exception of the Wellington watercolourist TA McCormack, 'there appears virtually no other present-day painter, writer, or poet. Men and women in the creative fields of art and letters are conspicuous by their absence ... The contributions of these people, who have helped establish some semblance of national or cultural identity, has apparently gone unnoticed.'[44]

Peter wrote with clarity and confidence, and his columns for the *Dominion* show how far he had come in a few years. By a diligent process of self-education, he had become, in his early thirties, an expert in the small New Zealand art world. He was increasingly focused on his mission – 'to keep plugging the art thing as hard as possible'.[45] As he wrote to Pat Hanly, 'I have got to work harder and build up all my contacts.'

——

During the late 1960s, Peter took a range of part time jobs to support his gallery, working as a 'general dogsbody' at Wakefield Motors, and a dishwasher at La Normandie and Orsini's restaurants.[46] He later described his brief career as a telephone directory checker as the most 'diabolical': 'It was a refined, sort of New Zealand version of the Chinese water torture ... The old hands who had done it for years were almost an alien race. A unique sub culture with attitudes towards the world that were pure Genghis Khan.'[47]

He was also looking for a financial investor for his gallery, and in 1967 he discussed the matter with three local men who had artistic interests: Ralph von Kohorn, an American industrialist who had come to New Zealand in the 1960s to establish a nylon factory at Shannon; businessman Fred Turnovsky; and Percy Young, who ran Websters' picture framers. All three had emigrated from Europe during the 1930s. They had been encouraging to Peter in his new venture, and he hoped they might assist him financially.

In May, he wrote a remarkably frank letter to von Kohorn, summing up their discussions to date:

> ...I have said that I *feel* I could make a success of this proposition. But I don't *know* if it will be a success. I cannot *guarantee* anything...
>
> The backing of a gallery can only be considered as a *highly speculative* investment. It requires backers who are prepared to take risks. It requires backers who are prepared to have their names associated with an economic failure. Backers who are prepared to lose their money...
>
> For my part you may think it is easy for me to talk as financially I have very little to lose and I am spending other people's money. To this I can only reply that I am only interested in developing the arts (visual) in this city and to do this well I will have to have money. If it is yours, marvellous, for I can assure you that I would work long and hard to make it a success. I believe that I have the ability and judgement to create both financially and artistically the best art gallery in the country. One day I will do it.[48]

Having failed to attract investors, Peter borrowed money from his mother and sold some paintings from his own collection to subsidise the gallery. Tim Beaglehole had the 'enormous good fortune', as he put it, to be offered two McCahons: he purchased an early watercolour of Mapua for his and his wife Helen's collection, and a large oil, *Agnus Dei, Donna Nobis Pacem*, for Victoria University.

Peter continued to attract new artists to his stable, and in May he sold his first work by Michael Illingworth. McCahon supplied some works on paper, including a Northland ink and brush drawing that was acquired by Ivan Bootham, but as he was working full time, now teaching at Elam School of Fine Arts, he was reluctant to release much more. 'The situation remains as it was,' McCahon told Peter. 'Were I to sell any of the paintings asked for I would be making a magnificent gift to the income tax people. It just doesn't do me any good selling now. Later – yes. I just don't want to give up the school at the moment and being taxed both ways is a bit tough. Sorry.'[49]

Writing to Mrkusich in September, Peter reflected on his progress. 'I am confident and have faith in the future but it will be a slow long slog. This feeling of faith and confidence is strange... Most of the time I am completely integrated, moving forward and my whole person seems to

Peter at 270 The Terrace with one of the first paintings he bought for his personal collection, Pat Hanly's *New order 28. Part I*, 1963, photographed by Marti Friedlander, 1967

be excited.'[50] Not for the last time, his account of his immersion in his new career suggests the fervour of a religious experience.

In June 1967, Marti Friedlander photographed Peter in his flat, surrounded by pictures, for an article in the *New Zealand Herald*. 'His figure is slight,' it began, 'his expression sensitive, his conversation is considered and precise ... He could be an academic, a boffin, a monk ... He gives the impression of being a "loner".'[51] Peter spoke of his trips to Auckland: 'He goes back with ideas, paintings, and a sense of envy that, in matters of art, Auckland is a swinging city and Wellington is not.' As Peter put it, 'What Auckland has and we lack is a vital and stimulating environment for painting, a place where people can see and be made aware of front-rank work.' The rookie art dealer evidently impressed his interviewer – the article was entitled, 'Young man on way to the top'.

Peter McLeavey
Gallery

FIVE

It was a Clark Kent sort of life.

Financially, Peter's second year as an art dealer was no better than his first. Yet again his expenses exceeded his commission on sales, and he was left with a loss of nearly $200 in the new decimal currency – the equivalent of just over $3000 today.[1]

But if sales were sluggish, life had never been more stimulating. Peter was in contact with influential New Yorkers, including William Rubin, a curator at the Museum of Modern Art, and high-profile collector Robert Scull, in an attempt to arrange an exhibition of American painting to tour the country.[2] 'We are very isolated here in New Zealand from the main scene,' he told Len Lye, 'and I think anything that can help activate and stimulate people to think about, and explore art, is a good thing.'

Peter had sent Lye a copy of the *Dominion* article in which he outlined the artist's achievements. 'Ironically,' he had written, 'this man and his work are virtually unknown in his own country.'[3] Lye replied, encouragingly, 'You seem pretty spazy on your stuff', and soon the two were corresponding regularly.[4] Peter told Lye about developments in his home town: 'The place is still conservative. The wind is always "fresh" and the hills you climbed as a kid delivering the "Dominion" are as steep as ever. However, the city has grown considerably with suburbia extending as far north as the paddocks north of Upper Hutt.'[5] He also raised the possibility of a visit: 'Have you ever thought of coming down here? … I know that there would be a number of people who would like to see you. If there was anything I could do to help you or facilitate your visit to New Zealand I would do all I could.'[6] Much to Peter's delight, Lye sent a package of invitations and ephemera from recent exhibitions in

Andrew Ross, *Approach to the Peter McLeavey Gallery (with original sign), 20/10/2001*, 2001
Toned gelatin silver print
Museum of New Zealand Te Papa Tongarewa, purchased 2009

New York. 'I am particularly impressed by Leo Castelli's invites,' Peter replied. 'We have the Don Judd poster hanging in the kitchen at present.'[7]

In January 1968, Peter contacted another expatriate, Billy Apple. 'I would very much like to run an article on you and your work,' he wrote. 'I know that it would be read with great interest and would be important for our younger painters… Your achievement in breaking in to the United States art world would be read with considerable interest, and I'm sure, pride.'[8] He asked Apple what advice he would offer a talented young New Zealander: 'should he get out and strive to make it in the international race or stay behind and toil away to try and change this country from within'? It was a question that he would often revisit, but for now he had no doubt: 'If I had talent I would try and prove myself at the highest international level.'

Back in Wellington, meanwhile, his work for the *Dominion* led to interesting contacts. Early in 1968 he interviewed a new acquaintance, Helen Hitchings, about her pioneering dealer gallery for modern art in Wellington. By providing a venue, he wrote, 'and by her encouragement and enthusiasm, Helen Hitchings helped to give our artists a sense of confidence. She also stimulated people to buy pictures and a number of fine collections owe their origin to her gallery.'[9] Peter could not resist taking a swipe at the National Art Gallery: 'It is a compliment to Helen Hitchings' eye and discrimination that she recognised the value of [McCahon and Woollaston] at a time when both artists were singularly misunderstood by the art establishment… Twenty years later, these two painters are widely recognised as being among the best in the country. However, the National Art Gallery still does not own a McCahon and its only Woollaston is a recent acquisition.' Such comments did not go unnoticed. After Peter gave a radio broadcast criticising the administration of the gallery, the Academy of Fine Arts threatened him with charges of libel.[10]

Early in 1968, Peter was invited to attend a seminar on art criticism in Sydney, where the guest speakers included the legendary American critic Clement Greenberg, best known as a champion of Jackson Pollock and the abstract expressionists. 'I have decided to accept,' Peter told Michael Smither, 'as it will give me an opportunity to meet a number of dealers, critics and collectors.'[11] He also contacted the arts council and persuaded officials to invite Greenberg to visit New Zealand after the seminar.

In mid-May, Peter flew to Sydney – his first international flight, and an experience that left him rather shaken. 'My heart is like a bird in a trap when I fly,' he confided to McCahon. 'It soars and drops with the great plane. I perspire a lot. And try not to look out of the window.'[12] But he was excited to be back in Sydney for such an important occasion. An ambitious seven-day event sponsored by UNESCO, the seminar considered criticism across the spectrum of the arts: literature, visual arts, music, theatre and film.[13] Apart from Gil Docking and his artist wife, Shay, Peter was the only New Zealand representative among the 144 participants. He was especially impressed by Greenberg, who spoke on 'Difficulties of criticism', and the English poet and critic Al Alvarez, who gave a sociological perspective on the critic's role.

It was Peter's exposure to the dealer galleries in Sydney, however, that was the most influential part of his trip. He was astounded by the price of Australian art: Sidney Nolan's *Burke and Wills leaving Melbourne* had recently sold for $35,000, setting a record for a painting by a contemporary Australian artist. The salesman was Barry Stern, an ambitious young dealer who had stunned the art world by taking out a full-page advertisement in the *Sydney Morning Herald*.[14] Peter took the opportunity to meet Stern and other dealers, including Rudy Komon and Kym Bonython, but it was the relatively new Central Street Gallery, opened in 1966, that he found most inspiring. Established by the charismatic Tony McGillick and initially run as an artists' cooperative, Central Street was Australia's first 'white cube' gallery – a modernist industrial space with exposed beams, concrete floors, and white-painted floors and ceiling.[15] Largely dedicated to hard-edged abstraction and minimalism, it was a catalyst for Peter: 'They were essentially students, it was a low rent thing. It gave me a bit of confidence.'[16]

Peter was also impressed by the public museums in Sydney. At the Art Gallery of New South Wales, he was able to see recent acquisitions, including *Ayin*, a large work by the American colour-field painter, Morris Louis.[17] Reporting back for the *Dominion*, he noted a bold new sculpture commission: Alexander Calder's *Crossed blades*, purchased for the forecourt of the Australia Square Tower for the hefty sum of $54,000. He suggested that New Zealand property developers could well take notice.[18] Peter also commented on the presence of New Zealand artists, just three years after Hamish Keith had curated the first collection of contemporary art to tour Australia:[19] Shay Docking and Suzanne Goldberg were exhibiting at the Rudy Komon Gallery; McCahon was soon to have a solo show at the Bonython Art Gallery; and Gordon Walters was to exhibit as part of a group show of New Zealand painters later in the year. For the moment at least, local artists seemed to be making some impression across the Tasman.

Back in Wellington, Peter had the stimulus of Clement Greenberg's visit in late June. The critic was impressed with the work of McCahon and Woollaston, among others: 'What a pity you're not in New York!' he told McCahon.[20] Lecturing in the three main centres, Greenberg caused a stir with a provocative remark: New Zealanders were unlikely to produce outstanding art, he claimed, because they were so isolated from the major international art centres. He also dismissed the local preoccupation with a distinctly 'New Zealand' art: 'Australian-ness or New Zealand-ness has nothing to do with quality.'[21] Peter found the critic likeable and engaging. 'He is a very nice chap,' he reported to Len Lye, 'and I was very knocked out by having the chance to speak to him.'[22]

Peter had returned home determined to step up his activities as a dealer. His flatmate was soon departing, and he decided to move into the back room and turn the front room into a dedicated gallery. He wrote to invite Woollaston to have the first exhibition in August, and received an immediate reply: 'Hooray! for the Peter McLeavey Gallery. I will come.'[23] Peter was buoyed by the response from artists.[24] 'Congratulations! That's the spirit!' wrote Len Lye. 'There's always someone to branch out; now it's your turn. I'm sure you'll start something, & wake things up.' Lye added a note of caution: 'You'll have the usual gallery headaches of stress between artist & gallery. Every artist thinks the sun shines out of all his orifices. It's a landlord & tenant, husband & wife, free-thinker v. establishment friction situation.'[25]

These were conflicts that Peter would come to know all too well, but for now he had his own 'landlord & tenant friction situation'. Despite his assurance that the gallery would be 'quiet and dignified', he was not allowed to install a discreet sign on the front of the building. In mid-July, he wrote to advise Woollaston that his exhibition would be delayed: 'The landlord is not happy with my ideas so it does seem that I will have to leave this flat.'[26] It was time to find new premises.

Aware that it would take years for his gallery to break even, let alone turn a profit, Peter was determined to keep his costs as low as possible. He had already canvassed potential spaces, and had seen a suite of rooms in a run-down three-storey building at 147 Cuba Street, just above the Ghuznee Street intersection. The rooms were on the first floor, above a fruit shop, and accessed by a narrow wooden stairway. The largest had good proportions, an elegant tin ceiling and, most important of all, excellent natural light from a semi-circular window overlooking the street.[27] Peter was also attracted to the faded, slightly seedy ambience of the neighbourhood, the heart of Wellington's red-light district, with its second-hand stores, tattoo parlours, cheap hotels and nightclubs. As he once remarked, 'Even its name, Cuba, has a slightly racy aspect compared to Lambton Quay and Willis Street, which sound quite Anglo.'[28]

Peter was careful not to commit himself in discussions with his new landlord. 'I said I'd like to try the space on a monthly rental. For many years I didn't even have a lease, I just paid from month to month.'[29] He started at a rental of $10 per week, the equivalent of $162 today, and kept the cost of outfitting the gallery to a minimum. Peter was now flatting in McDonald Crescent, just off The Terrace, with John Ganaway, a solitary, music-loving bachelor who had inherited 'a big old rambling Victorian villa like something out of Miss Havisham, full of thousands of records, and crammed with old furniture'.[30] When Ganaway invited him to take anything he needed for the gallery, he chose a single piece – an olive-green chaise longue, a link to his psychoanalysis sessions with Mario Fleischl.

Initially, Peter was going to move into his new space as it was, but Gordon Walters would have none of that. 'If you're going to show art, you must paint the walls white,' he declared.[31] The artist helped with the task, and in later years Peter liked to describe the gallery as 'Gordon Walters' largest painting'. 'That's a bit of myth making on Peter's behalf,' his friend Tim Curnow noted. 'There were a lot of us helping with the painting and I remember vividly the painting bee and lugging pieces of 4×2 timber up those stairs to build a two storey rack for pictures which was to go in the storeroom.' But then: 'Classic carpentry boofhead moment.' Someone realised that the rack would not fit through the door from the main gallery. 'We had to dismantle two hours of work and then try and re-assemble it into this tiny space of the storeroom.'[32]

Amid his preparations for the opening, Peter received good news: the National Art Gallery confirmed the purchase of a Woollaston landscape.[33] This was his first sale to the national institution and only the second Woollaston to enter the collection, but there was a tale behind it, as John Beaglehole reported to the artist Janet Paul.

> Toss rang up this afternoon, full of high spirits; he says the Nat. Gallery has bought a picture. A longish story: Reg Waghorn, nice dull fellow says Toss, told him they wanted to buy one; all right says Toss, Peter McLeavey is my Wellington agent; oh, we don't want to get it from him, we don't like his attitude: all right, says Toss, you'd better not get it at all, he's selling all my pictures in

> Wellington, anyway I don't want your money, I'm doing all right now... Toss then goes home & thinks Well maybe I was a bit rude, & writes to Reg & says sorry if I was a bit rude but Peter McLeavey & c.... Then he hears from Peter McL. that the Nat Gallery has bought a picture, & at a good price too.[34]

On the evening of 4 September 1968, the new Peter McLeavey Gallery opened with an exhibition of recent Woollaston paintings. Early that morning, the artist wrote home to his wife, Edith: 'Peter's gallery is small, but beautiful. Fifteen pictures, fastidiously hung. It's a new note in N.Z. Galleries.'[35]

Peter had arranged for John Beaglehole to open the exhibition, but illness kept the historian in bed, so he nervously said a few words instead. 'It was a big thing for me, the gallery opening, but I didn't want to push it as a big event. I was taking it one day at a time. I thought to myself, Don't pump it up too much because it might not last.'[36] Many friends and supporters attended, including Mario Fleischl, Gordon Walters, John Malcolm, secretary of the arts council, and representatives of Victoria University and External Affairs. The works – mainly landscapes of the Taranaki hill country where Woollaston had spent his childhood – were priced from $25 for a drawing to $240 for a large oil. The first purchase, a pen and ink sketch of Bayly's Hill, was made by Gordon Walters and Margaret Orbell.

Two weeks later, all but one work had sold for a total of $1384. The buyers were all private individuals: mainly academics from Victoria University (including James Bertram and Fred Page), professionals, and artists and writers.[37] Most were already known to Peter, but the exhibition also attracted a new audience. Neil McGrath was one of many young professionals who would discover New Zealand art through the Peter McLeavey Gallery. He saw a small advertisement in the *Dominion* and went to see the show on the final day. 'I'd never heard of Peter McLeavey,' he recalled, 'and I'd never heard of Woollaston. But as soon as I saw the paintings I was smitten. It was an immediate reaction. I remember most of them had sold; there was only one of the big ones left, and I bought it. It was my first original painting.'[38]

News of Peter's promising start made ripples further afield, even rating a mention in the *New Zealand Herald*, which noted the gallery's 'intimate atmosphere'.[39] 'It was good to hear the Woollaston show was a near sell out,' wrote Mrkusich. 'If sales keep up it could mean exhibiting

INVITATION

You are invited to attend the opening of the Peter McLeavey Gallery
147 Cuba Street (First floor), Wellington
at 6.00 p.m. on Wednesday the 4th of September, 1968.

The Peter McLeavey Gallery will open with
an exhibition
of paintings, drawings and watercolours
by the distinguished New Zealand painter Toss Woollaston.

This exhibition can be previewed from 2.00 p.m. on the same day.

Dr. J.C. Beaglehole will open the exhibition
and
Mr Woollaston will be present at the opening.

Invitation to the first exhibition at the Peter McLeavey Gallery,
MT Woollaston: Paintings, drawings and watercolours,
September 1968

MT Woollaston: Paintings, drawings and watercolours,
September 1968, photographed by John B Turner

in Wellington would be worthwhile for painters in other centres.'[40] The idea that it might be useful to have a dealer outside of Auckland, cultivating a more southern clientele, was still quite novel. But Peter himself had no illusions: he was aware that Woollaston, a well-established painter working in a landscape tradition, was hardly typical of the artists he would be representing. He wrote to Len Lye, 'While it is nice to start off with a sell out the going is going to be much harder as I move forward. People here are slow to respond and the whole history of art gallery management here in New Zealand is strewn with numerous financial wrecks. Still, I feel confident that if anybody can pull it off here in Wellington I can.'[41]

In fact, Peter was not yet convinced that his future lay in Wellington, and recent visitors – including the English art critic Robert Melville – had reminded him that New Zealand was very much the backblocks in the international art world.[42] He confided to Lye:

> I must confess that talking to men like [Melville and Greenberg] I get a little envious and I sort of question what I am doing here. The thought of going to live in Sydney or London often passes through my mind. In conversations with Melville he projected an encouraging view of the London scene. He thought that I could perhaps get a job … However, I have this feeling that I have got something which I can contribute to the development of art here. This probably sounds bloody big headed or idealistic or something but I feel this strongly, namely that I have a challenging and important job here which I must have a crack at.[43]

He certainly had a challenge with his next exhibition, which opened in late October. Peter was delighted to be showing Colin McCahon's *Northland panels*, an eight-piece work completed after a life-changing trip to the United States in 1958. McCahon saw a vast amount of art in America, but the works that most impressed him were large, wall-sized paintings by Jackson Pollock, Picasso and Diego Rivera.[44] After working on a domestic scale for more than twenty years, McCahon recognised 'the importance of pictures for people to walk past'.[45]

McCahon described his return home to the bush of Titirangi: 'It was cold and dripping and shut in – and I had seen deserts and tumbleweed in fences and Salt Lake Flats, and the Faulkner country with magnolias in bloom, cities – taller by far than kauri trees. My lovely kauris became too much for me. I fled north in memory and painted the *Northland panels*.'[46] The painting represented a breakthrough – in scale, format and media. McCahon abandoned the frame to work directly on strips of free-hanging canvas, and used commercial oil paint instead of traditional pigments. He also experimented with his technique, employing a bold, fluent style of brushwork to evoke the lush beauty of the northern landscape.

The importance of the *Northland panels* was acknowledged by local experts: Hamish Keith, for example, claimed that its place in the history of New Zealand art was comparable to that of Picasso's *Les demoiselles d'Avignon* in the development of cubism.[47] Even so, Peter knew that it would be difficult to find a buyer for the work, given its size and the

Colin McCahon, *Northland panels*, 1958
Alkyd on unstretched canvas
Museum of New Zealand Te Papa Tongarewa,
purchased 1978 with Ellen Eames Collection funds and
assistance from the New Zealand Lottery Board

a landscape
with too few
lovers.

TUI
TUI
T

oh yes it can
be dark here
and manuka
in bloom may
breed despair
NOV. 58.

Colin McCahon: The Northland panels, showing three of the eight panels, October–November 1968, photographed by John B Turner

price of $3000, the equivalent of $48,000 today.[48] Determined to do all he could to create publicity, he invited Keith to write an essay for the occasion, but the critic refused payment. 'Please use the four dollars for this article to keep me on your mailing list,' he requested. 'I don't want to be paid for it really since I feel like you that something needs to be said about the panels in Wellington and in fact in a kind of oblique way I have aimed some of my remarks at the new incumbent in the tomb on the hill.'[49] Keith was referring to Melvin Day, the young painter and art historian who had recently taken over from Stewart Maclennan as the director of the National Art Gallery.

The gallery was on Peter's mind; indeed, he hoped the *Northland panels* would find a home there. He wrote to Keith, 'There is interest here from a client of mine to buy the paintings and present them to the National Art Gallery. However, this is going to take considerable luck, tact, diplomacy and salesmanship on my behalf to pull it off.'[50] It was a generous gesture by Peter's client, Dr Ian Prior, but McCahon vetoed the proposal: 'I have already had bad dealings with the Nat. Gal. over a "presentation" & don't want the same to happen again.'[51] Just a few years earlier, the gallery had declined an offer from the arts council to gift *Landscape theme and variations (series B)* to the collection. To compound the insult, the gallery's representatives had also raised concerns about McCahon's materials, even suggesting he needed painting lessons to correct his supposed weaknesses.

With Wellington clearly out of the running, Peter's ambitions for McCahon knew no bounds. He contacted the National Gallery of Victoria in Australia, and the Museum of Modern Art in New York – then the most influential collection of twentieth-century art in the world. 'Normally,' he wrote to curator William Rubin, 'I would not bother the Museum of Modern Art ... However because this particular painting is so highly regarded – a New Zealand equivalent to Nolan's "Ned Kelly" series – I bring it to your attention.'[52] Rubin replied that the museum was unable to buy the painting, but ended on a positive note: 'I should like you to know how much we appreciate your continuing to bring works by artists from New Zealand to our attention.'[53] Peter may have failed to sell the *Northland panels*, but he felt privileged to display it, and was pleased by the many visitors to the gallery. He told McCahon, 'I am sorry that they were not sold but I guess one has to be philosophical about it.'[54]

By now Peter had established his daily routine at Cuba Street, having secured a part-time job nearby at Graur's Electrical and Battery Services. 'I was the dogsbody, packing parcels, stacking batteries, lamps, manual work, painting, sweeping.'[55] At midday he would duck around the corner, exchange his overall for a suit and tie, comb his hair and straighten his glasses, and become Peter McLeavey the art dealer: 'It was a Clark Kent sort of life.'[56]

He was also developing a very personal way of presenting art to his clients, and McCahon and Woollaston were central to his project. To him, the two painters represented the first wave of modern New Zealand art, in that they developed in this country, instead of training and spending much of their lives overseas. '[T]hese people essentially invented New Zealand as I know it,' he remarked. 'They looked at the landscape and from what they saw distilled a set of symbols that I could relate to and I sensed the wider community could relate to. It was strongly of this place but addressed to the wider world. The symbols they extracted from the landscape were so potent for me.'[57]

To this deeply held conviction about the importance of the work, Peter brought his considerable gifts as a storyteller. Unveiling a new painting by McCahon or Woollaston, he was able to transmit his own sense of excitement and discovery, and frame the work within the culture and history of New Zealand. 'I shared with them my dream. The paintings became the icons, the objects of this civilisation. We emphasised New Zealand, they were made here, they reflected aspects of this culture. It was a total culture. I would use my intelligence, my language, to sell.'[58]

Peter's final exhibition of 1968 was a show of ceramics: seventy-eight items of domestic ware by Juliet Peter, Roy Cowan and Peter Wilde. Prices ranged from $2 to $27, and total sales amounted to an impressive $580. It was one of Peter's few ventures into ceramics, however: apart from sporadic showings by the potter and environmentalist Barry Brickell at the gallery until 1992, he would henceforth concentrate on painting and sculpture.[59]

As the first dedicated art dealer in Wellington since Helen Hitchings, Peter had his pick of artists from all over the country. The only refusal came from the fiercely independent Rita Angus, who had already turned down a similar invitation from the Barry Lett Galleries. 'She wrote me a rather harsh letter,' Peter recalled. 'She didn't want to have anything to do with me. It shook me a bit.'[60] Angus belonged to an older amateur art culture in which commerce was viewed with suspicion, and Peter had to negotiate this attitude throughout his early years at the gallery.[61] It was his insistence on art *before* business that won over so many of Angus's contemporaries – including McCahon, who remained uneasy about the idea of commercial success and continued to gift paintings all his life.

Now that he was committed to the risky business of establishing a gallery, Peter was concerned by the Academy's move to improve its image by inviting leading young artists to show as guest exhibitors. He was dismayed when he learned that Pat Hanly – one of the first painters he had represented – was thinking of accepting. Writing to Hanly, he took aim at the Academy's amateurism, also revealing his own resentment towards the Wellington 'establishment':

> Considering this institution's reactionary, establishment attitude towards painting in this country and their various shenanigans in relation to people like me I find it curious that you are able to give them work before your Wellington dealer ... I hasten to add that I am not suffering from a persecution complex but that they have on several occasions tried to steam roll me ...
>
> All this will not make any difference to what I am doing, nor where I am going. The academic, establishment attitude toward art is always a safe one. Exhibiting at the Peter McLeavey Gallery will, I believe, in the future be of more importance than showing in any quasi-prestige New Zealand Academy of Fine Art Show. The gallery which I am building will, I hope, do more for art and artists in this country than the ingratiating aesthetic and cuisine refinements of *academic art moderne, 1969 variety* ...
>
> If my remarks seem a little harsh, well I must speak my mind. I am not slaving my guts out as a dishwasher for kicks.[62]

Peter's letter had no effect, and Hanly took part in the Academy's *Five guest artists* show in 1969.[63] Hanly went on to have seven solo exhibitions with Peter but, with the exception of his 'Golden age' paintings in 1981, his major shows tended to be with his Auckland dealers, Barry Lett and later Rodney Kirk Smith.

Not only was the Academy encroaching on his territory, but Peter now had competition next door. In September, the artist Elva Bett, who had been running the Centre Gallery, attended Peter's first opening and wondered, aloud, whether there was any vacant space in the building. Just weeks later, she and her business partner Catherine Duncan signed a lease for a room on the same floor, and in December the Bett-Duncan Studio Gallery opened, showing prints by young Christchurch artists and ceramics by Doreen Blumhardt.[64] Still nervous about his new venture, and deeply competitive by nature, Peter was initially rather resentful: 'I thought why couldn't Elva have found somewhere else. At first it was a bit awkward. But we formed a good relationship, and it worked well.'[65] In fact, the two galleries were complementary. Bett was a Wellington personality, with close ties to the Academy and the Centre Gallery, and although she later showed young painters such as Tony Fomison and Philip Clairmont, her gallery would retain a strong focus on local artists.[66]

In December 1968, Len Lye toured New Zealand with his wife Ann – his first visit in forty-six years. As part of his three-week trip, he lectured in Auckland on 'The art that moves', and spent two days in Wellington, where Peter hosted a party in his honour at the gallery.

Peter with Len Lye, photographed by
John B Turner, 1968

Lye had turned down the opportunity to lecture in the capital, citing the difficulties in organising equipment and the paltry payment. '[T]he stipend, though absolute tops in NZ is not worth it,' he informed Peter. 'If people are mean on the art stuff in N.Z. like they were when I left the place, they'd better begin to learn that it's not good enough. The place is marvellous, of course, & that's why we're making a visit; but I'm not educating anybody, nor bothering about TV & all that junk that I avoid like poison here, although they pay well. I don't want to depress you old boy. We can all get there in spite of the numb squares. And you will too.'[67]

Meeting Lye for the first time was 'terrifically exciting' for Peter.[68] He was impressed by the artist's intelligence, his extraordinary energy and 'his wonder at being alive ... [H]e seemed to confront the world with the eyes of a child.'[69] Lye's total commitment to art was a tonic: '[I] felt really inspired after talking to him,' Peter told the American painter Clyfford Still, with whom he had struck up a brief correspondence.[70]

Lye was similarly impressed by Peter: 'I think it is fabulous of Peter to stick it out and try to keep art moving in so meager an art collecting place as Wellington. It would break anyone else's heart.'[71] He wrote to thank Peter after his return home:

> Dear Peter
> Here's all WOWS and Oommms
> We're gradually back from the Pacific
> wavelets lapping at our toes
> We had a ball & you made it
> roll in Wellington; we love
> you for it. Keep well![72]

SIX

Those bedraggled students were the collectors of the future.

When Peter decided to open his gallery in Cuba Street, he had resigned as a columnist for the *Dominion* and recommended that Margaret Orbell take his place. Her first review, an appreciative account of the Woollaston exhibition, was published on 9 September 1968. One of those who read it with interest was the young Hilary Pitts-Brown, who had recently arrived in Wellington and taken a job at Cadeau, a gift shop in Lambton Quay. It was not until the last day of the exhibition, however, that she was able to catch a bus up to Cuba Street in her lunch hour and visit the gallery.

Hilary found Peter in the midst of taking down the exhibition and the paintings stacked against the walls. The two exchanged only a few words, but Peter was smitten – and he managed to find out where Hilary worked. A few days later, she caught sight of him loitering outside Cadeau, waiting for her employer to leave so that he could speak to her in private. Eventually he asked her out. 'Peter invited me to a concert of Maxwell Fernie's choir – thirteenth-century unaccompanied voices – and this was all terribly new to me. I was flatting with a friend who was quite musical and played the violin, so I took her along. I had a chaperone. Later we laughed about it.'[1]

Then in her late twenties, Hilary was a tall, elegant young woman with long blonde hair and a captivating smile. Temperamentally she was Peter's opposite: warm, open and practical, with a calm, unflappable quality. Like him, she had lived and worked overseas for several years, and visited the great art museums of England and Europe; on her return, she worked in Christchurch, first for Fisher Fine Arts and later for the Little Woodware Shop, an arts and crafts store. Hilary had similar interests to Peter, but she came from a very different, middle-class Anglican

Peter and Hilary at the gallery, photographed by John B Turner, 1969 milieu. Her father, Hilcote Pitts-Brown, had studied history at Oxford University before returning to run the family orchard in Nelson, while her mother, Jessica Thompson, came from a 'big, jolly' Timaru family who owned a department store. By Peter's standards, this was a privileged background. He had never met anyone quite like Hilary, and he was dazzled by her poise and sense of style in her leather miniskirts and colourful Marimekko print dresses.

The courtship continued in the spring of 1968. 'Another day he asked me out for tea. And I went to his flat and we had tea sitting on the edge of his bed ... a plate of green beans with two hard-boiled eggs on top. And I thought, Well this is really odd. This is different.' Hilary was attracted, nevertheless. 'I'd grown up in a small town, very conventional and insular. My mother's family were sporty, so we always had to be busy doing something, and although my father was quite intellectual – rather like Peter in some ways – we tended to live a very practical outdoor life. I didn't want to marry anyone from my background – that would have been too known, too familiar. Peter was very intelligent and unusual, and I was attracted by his difference.'

Hilary was not uncritical of her new suitor, however. 'He was a bit of a know-all when I met him. He was very driven and ambitious, and like a lot of young men, he wanted to change the world. And the culture of the time wasn't very responsive. In fact, he was battling against powerful reactionary forces. So there was a kind of defensiveness, an arrogance.' Hilary also noticed a vulnerability in Peter. 'He was quite a fragile personality as a young man, and rather eccentric. Very self-absorbed. He always did what was right for himself, whereas I had been brought up to think of everyone else. But he was witty and sharp, and so original in his thinking – that had enormous appeal for me.'[2]

While Hilary visited her family at Christmas, Peter went to stay with the Woollastons, who had recently moved from Greymouth to a dilapidated old farmhouse at Riwaka. The Woollastons were keen to meet the young woman Peter had mentioned, and invited her to come and stay – which she did. 'That sort of clinched the relationship,' Hilary reflected. 'We had a lovely time together, and Dad had lent me his little car and so we went off every day to places like Kaiteriteri and Collingwood.'

That summer, the young Laurence Aberhart – who had only recently discovered photography – was helping out on the Woollaston property. He took a photograph of Peter, Hilary, Toss and Edith lounging on the veranda with drinks at hand. Peter is barefoot, like Woollaston, and looks happy and relaxed. 'I think maybe we decided to live together

TOP: Peter and Hilary at Barrett's Hotel, 1968

BOTTOM: Toss and Edith Woollaston, Peter and Hilary, photographed by Laurence Aberhart, 1968

on that holiday,' Hilary recalled, 'because when we got back Peter said he'd start looking for a place.'

By mid-February, Peter and Hilary had taken a flat above a chemist's shop on the corner of Moxham Avenue and Waitoa Road in Hataitai. Hilary commented, 'At that stage living together wasn't very common, and it certainly wasn't the thing for our parents' generation. But Peter and I were a bit older, of course. I didn't actually tell my parents, but I didn't not tell them either. I told them I'd shifted, and if they wanted to connect the dots that was fine. It was the same for Peter's parents. I think they would have known, but they never made any comment.'

One of those who was informed about the new arrangement was Len Lye, who had met Hilary on his visit to Wellington. '[S]o glad you're tied in with Hilary,' he wrote to Peter. 'She was the outstanding gal of the whole scene, Ann liked her muchly too.'[3]

Peter waited until March 1969 to reopen the gallery so that he could work full time at the battery factory over the summer. When he assessed the year financially, it was clear that his sales were up: he had doubled his commission, earning nearly $1200. But running a full-time gallery had proved costly, and yet again his expenses exceeded his earnings. For the third year in a row, he made a loss – this time of $304.[4]

The first exhibition of 1969 was by Don Driver, a largely self-taught artist from New Plymouth who had made a formative trip to New York in 1965. Peter had admired his work for years, and had supported him in the *Dominion* in 1967 when one of his sculptures, installed at the New Plymouth War Memorial Library, was controversially removed at the insistence of the library's committee.[5] Driver exhibited eight large exuberant works, which combined aspects of painting and construction, including the eye-catchingly vibrant *Patmos shield* (since renamed *Zig zag-1*).[6] Peter had strong ideas about how to display such works. 'My main concern,' he wrote to Driver, 'is to give every piece plenty of room to "breathe". The presentation of the exhibition is most important, as you know. I am sure that your work will have a terrific impression when displayed in my gallery.'[7]

Peter sold three works from this exhibition, and was pleased to sell two to public collections. Tim Beaglehole purchased *Zig zag-1* for Victoria University, while the Palmerston North Art Gallery, under the directorship of Brian Muir, acquired *Saracen*.[8] The sale to Victoria led to further enquiries from university staff, as Peter informed Driver: 'Apparently your painting is very well hung and has created a great impression.'[9]

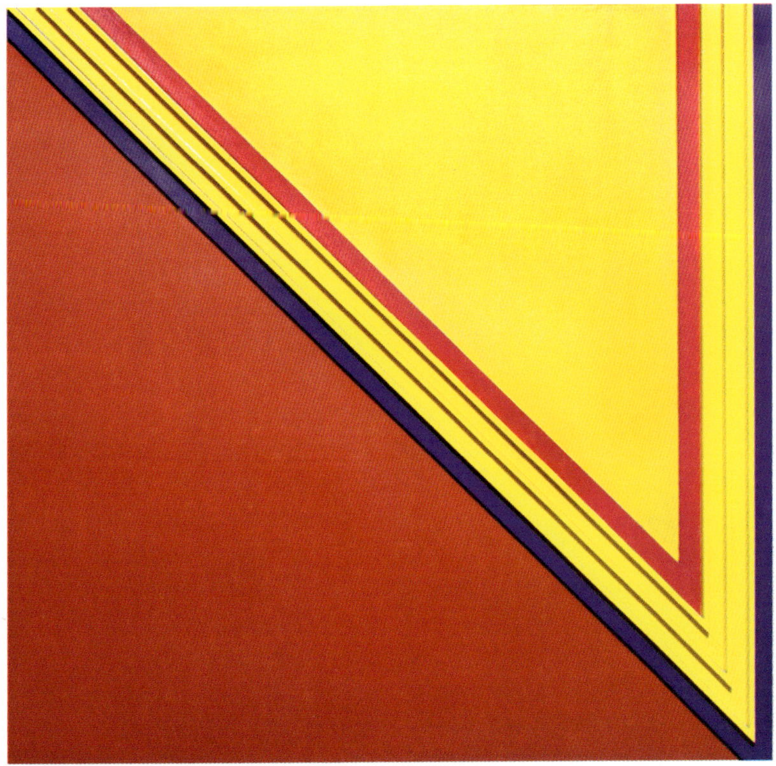

Don Driver, *Zig zag-1*, 1969
Acrylic on canvas and board
Victoria University of Wellington Art Collection, purchased 1969

Peter was still learning his new business and felt that he had underpriced the works at $150 to $240. Moreover, as he reported to Driver, he had a confession to make: 'When the Director of the Palmerston North Art Gallery requested me to send the painting up I did an extremely foolish thing. Observing that the outer frame of the painting had received a couple of small knicks I dabbed the offending spots with some black paint I had. Much to my horror I discovered that it was just a shade blacker than the paint you had used. Naturally I should never have touched the painting but I was just carried away and excited by the prospect of another sale ... I am very sorry and have learnt my lesson well.'[10]

In April, Peter opened an exhibition by Michael Smither: paintings of landscapes and domestic scenes featuring the artist's son Thomas, ranging from $100 to $400, as well as silkscreen prints priced at $6. Bill

Gordon Walters, *Tamatea*, 1968
Acrylic on canvas
Govett-Brewster Art Gallery, purchased with the assistance of the Queen Elizabeth II Arts Council of New Zealand in 1969

Emsley, who had taken over as the art critic for the *Dominion*, commented, 'The new Peter McLeavey Gallery is achieving a reputation for work of quality.'[11] Sales amounted to $1032, and Peter noted there had been multiple interest in some works. He was especially pleased that all the buyers were in their twenties – it seemed to promise well for the future.

Peter was aware that his next exhibition – Gordon Walters' first in Wellington since 1949 – was historically significant. Walters had been working intensively during those years, but he had refrained from exhibiting because he felt the climate was unsympathetic to abstraction.[12] As a result, Peter observed, Walters' art was 'almost unknown' in the capital: 'There are none of his paintings in the National Art Gallery yet the Art Gallery of New South Wales, Sydney, has a large oil by Walters in their permanent collection. He is only the second New Zealand painter to be included in this prestigious collection'.[13]

In an interview with Peter, Walters reflected on the challenge of working as an abstract artist in Wellington. 'There are advantages when one develops in relative isolation, one either sinks out of sight or becomes stronger, this has been the problem of almost all New Zealand artists. Wellington seems to me to be the ideal place to develop toughness in. The mass of non art produced here and displayed by the establishment each year, together with the disapproval of "modern art" means that one has to be really convinced to keep going.'[14]

Peter had another string to his publicity with this show. The English critic Robert Melville, who had recently visited the country, had praised Walters in the prestigious international magazine *Architectural Review*, discerning 'a hope for New Zealand painting' in his synthesis of Māori and European artistic traditions.[15] The koru motif, he wrote, 'is put to systematic use in Gordon Walters's restrained and beautifully executed contribution to Op painting. Walters is probably New Zealand's most distinguished modern painter'. Peter made sure Melville's comments were widely reported.[16]

The exhibition opened on 6 May 1969: five acrylic 'Koru' paintings, priced from $150 to $400, and four small works on paper. Tim Beaglehole secured one of the two largest works, *Kahukura*, for Victoria University, while the Govett-Brewster Gallery in New Plymouth bought the other, *Tamatea*.[17] Five sales to private collectors followed, suggesting that there was indeed a market for Walters' refined yet austere modernism in the capital.

At this show a discreet note appeared on the exhibition catalogue for the first time – 'Terms arranged on 20% deposit'. Peter's willingness to let buyers pay in monthly instalments would be crucial in broadening his client base, and it also helped to encourage a habit of collecting. Many clients would finish paying for a work and commit to another almost immediately, and some continued the practice for decades.[18]

By the end of the Walters show, it was clear that the gallery was breaking even at last, and Peter's accountant showed a glimmer of optimism: '[Y]ou will still find it necessary to have part time employment for your own living ... [but] the development of your activity is very promising and does show a good potential.'[19] After three years of subsidising the gallery, Peter was more confident about the way ahead.

In his personal life, too, he was happier and more settled. On 14 August, he wrote to Michael Smither, who was now working in Patearoa in Central Otago, 'I hope I can see you sometime soon. I had intended to pop down for a weekend but I've been so darn busy. For one thing I've decided to get married. Yes I know you think I'm playing silly buggers but I've really fallen for Hilary. After living together for six months we will be married on Thursday the 28th of August.'[20]

The weeks leading up to the wedding were not without incident. Peter was still seeing Mario Fleischl, who believed he was not yet ready for marriage, and advised him to reconsider. Hilary recalled, 'Just a few days before the wedding Peter came home from a visit to Mario and said, "Oh I can't marry you." I said, "Well, either we get married or I leave for good." And so – we proceeded.' Peter's appointments with Fleischl waned and eventually ceased after his wedding. With Hilary, he had found another source of strength and stability in his life.

On the day of the wedding, Peter worked in the gallery until 2.45 in the afternoon. Then, dressed in his best black corduroy suit, '[O]ff I went, down Cuba Street, to the building housing the Register of Births, Deaths and Marriages. I bought a bunch of daffodils on the way down and placed them in a vase just as we went in.'[21] Hilary was wearing an outfit made by a friend: an olive-green leather waistcoat with brass buckles and a matching miniskirt: 'It didn't cross my mind to have a white wedding.'

Peter was the first in his family to wed outside the Catholic faith, and for his parents – who had 'so much wanted me to marry a good Catholic girl blessed by the sacrament of God' – the ceremony in the registry office was 'just too much'. Les and Betty stayed away – but they did join the wedding party for a reception at the Royal Oak Hotel in Cuba Street. Later, the guests returned to the flat in Hataitai, where jazz musician Malcolm McNeill sang a few impromptu songs.[22] Peter and Hilary were delighted to find paintings among their wedding presents – gifts from Walters, Smither and Woollaston.

There was no honeymoon for the newlyweds, who went back to work the next day: Hilary to her new job as a postie, Peter to the battery factory and the gallery. Nor were there any official wedding photographs. A few days later, however, John B Turner (who was then working as a photographer at the Dominion Museum) took a series of portraits of the couple at the gallery as a wedding present (see page 88).[23] If it was an unconventional setting for such photographs, it was also quite appropriate, for the gallery was a third partner in this marriage – and, as it would prove in the following years, a very demanding one.

With the gallery breaking even for the first time, Peter was aware that the next year would be crucial: after four years as a dealer, could he finally turn the corner and show a profit? He knew he had an excellent programme lined up in 1970, with many well-established artists in his stable: McCahon, Woollaston, Smither, Walters, Mrkusich, Illingworth, Hanly and Binney. But he also had a number of young artists exhibiting for the first time.

Like any art dealer, Peter needed to find the right mix in his programme. He relied on the loyalty of the senior artists who lent credibility to his gallery, but his long-term survival depended on his ability to identify and nurture new talent. The young artist graduating from art school in 1970 was potentially the senior artist of the new century.

One of the striking things about Peter's line-up for 1970 was the relative youth of his artists. Woollaston, at sixty, was by far the oldest; next came Robert Ellis at forty-one and Pat Hanly at thirty-eight. The others were all in their early thirties or younger, with Ian Scott and Wong Sing Tai, the two youngest, just twenty-five and twenty-six respectively. Peter knew that the work of these emerging artists would not be easy to sell. As Tim Beaglehole commented, 'Peter clearly had a very good eye. But that didn't mean, in those days, that he had sales.'[24]

Peter began the year with an exhibition by Palmerston North artist Ray Thorburn: paintings from his 'Modular' series, which could be hung in different configurations. These large gleaming works offered a local take on op art and challenged traditional methods, as they were painted by a tradesman, with spray guns and automotive lacquer, to Thorburn's specifications. Peter sold three, including two to public collections in Victoria University and the Robert McDougall Art Gallery in Christchurch.

The next exhibition was even more bracing in its modernity. Carl Sydow had studied in England in the mid-1960s, a time of great upheaval

Carl Sydow: Sculpture, April–May 1970, showing *Floor piece* and *Wall sculpture*, both 1970

in contemporary sculpture. Under the influence of artists such as Anthony Caro, young sculptors brought a new experimentation to their work, employing everyday commercial materials and banishing the traditional pedestal. On his return home, Sydow's work underwent a gradual change, and he began to make assemblages using acrylic tubes and roofing sheet. Peter saw these works at The Group in Christchurch in November 1969 and invited him to have his first solo show at the gallery.

Sydow exhibited two large works in April: *Floor piece* and *Wall sculpture*, both made from colourful acrylic piping. Critic Stephen Green described the scene in the gallery: 'Leaning against one wall a collection of pipes of different diameters and colours, a few people standing in a rather dazed circle, looking down at a heap of pipes on the floor, and the voice of Peter McLeavey saying, 'yes, that's the exhibition'.[25] One visitor told a reporter he felt he had 'stumbled into a plumber's workshop'.[26] The staff at Auckland City Art Gallery showed some interest in acquiring a piece, but eventually withdrew their option. Peter was undaunted, however, telling Sydow he was delighted with the response: 'Your show was the most heavily patronised exhibition I have ever had. A number of prominent people in the art scene here saw it, including several art gallery directors.'[27]

Peter would go on to give Sydow three more solo exhibitions before the artist's untimely death in 1975, but the only sales he made were two works on paper.[28] 'That was typical,' Tim Beaglehole observed. 'He showed people like Sydow whose work was so unlikely to sell.'[29] Peter believed this was a vital part of his role as a dealer. How else would the public learn about new developments in contemporary art in New Zealand? There were so few resources available on the subject: only a handful of books, and no magazines or art history courses. Apart from EH McCormick's *Eric Lee-Johnson* (1956), and small gallery publications and periodicals, there was little of substance on contemporary artists until the early 1970s.[30]

To many, Peter's gallery opened a window on a new and fascinating world. Malcolm McNeill was one of those who regarded him as a mentor: 'He would haul things out of the storeroom in Cuba St that initially I might dislike – and then over a year or so – I would come to appreciate and see differently. He helped educate my eye and that was his intention, for I was only rarely a customer. That wasn't what it was about.'[31]

Sam Neill was working at the National Film Unit when he discovered the Peter McLeavey Gallery:

> Peter would invite us impoverished young people to his openings, and not only would he let us drink his wine, in the full knowledge that none of us could afford a painting, but he took us as seriously as anyone else. That's thinking ahead really, investing in the future. Those bedraggled students were the collectors of the future.
>
> There was a vaguely bohemian thread running through Wellington when I first got there – that gallery, in its dubious Cuba Street context, was decidedly part of that. At Peter's there were diplomats slumming it, junkies being difficult, nice girls that would go for a drink later, drunk painters that would offer offence, film makers and actors squeezed loudly into those two little rooms, senior writers in their best suits, hippies and hipsters. It was LIVELY.

And it's important to remember how radical what Peter showed seemed – what NZ produced above all at that time were nice landscapes that would go nicely with your three piece suite – fucking awful. What landscapes there were in Peter's gallery were 180 degrees from that tradition – so much so that you were *never able to see your own country the same way again.*[32]

For Peter, every visitor, young or old, rich or poor, was crucial in sustaining his sense of purpose – as were critics like Hamish Keith. In June 1970, Keith chronicled the problems in the Wellington art world in the *Auckland Star*, quoting Peter without revealing his identity:

> Of all the main New Zealand centres, Wellington looks most like a city, and as a city, it has quite a bit of style. But New Zealand art, though alive, is far from well in our capital...
>
> As one Wellington dealer put it, 'Contemporary New Zealand art in Wellington is a non-event.'
>
> Since Wellington is the home of the National Art Gallery, the Arts Council and all the bright young executives of head offices and Government departments, the situation is surprising to say the least. It has most of the ingredients for a rich art scene, including a handful of the country's best painters, but somehow the mixture just hasn't jelled.
>
> The capital's two dealer galleries, PETER MCLEAVEY'S and the BETT-DUNCAN STUDIO-GALLERY, bravely work in a climate of almost complete neglect, despite the quality of the shows they mount.
>
> Last week, McLeavey's was showing a fine collection of recent works by Aucklander Robert Ellis. This week, the gallery opens an eye-shattering collection of major works by Ian Scott. For all this, the shows will probably attract at the best, a couple of vague newspaper paragraphs, not even approximating criticism.
>
> One local painter commented that, for the capital, New Zealand art last happened in 1940. Over the whole thing, he said, hangs the ghost of the centennial exhibition of New Zealand painting, the New Zealand Academy and the almost complete neglect of contemporary New Zealand painting by the National Art Gallery.[33]

Though there had been some modest change at the National Art Gallery in recent months, it was not enough to satisfy its critics. Melvin Day had replaced the elderly Stewart Maclennan in 1968, returning from London to take up the position. Just a few months later, he organised an exhibition

Carl Sydow: Sculpture, August 1973, showing *Construction II*, 1973

of abstract art, and the media made much of the change in the gallery's image: 'Swinging London has enlivened our art gallery,' one reporter proclaimed, rather optimistically.[34]

Day would continue his efforts to bring a more contemporary focus to the gallery, but he remained hamstrung, and not just by the influence of the Academy on the council. Every year he reiterated the gallery's problems in his reports to Parliament: the sub-standard building, low staffing and sorely inadequate funding for acquisitions. Well into the 1970s, Wellington would be ill-served by its public gallery.

—

Peter (left), Gordon Walters and Wong Sing Tai outside the National Art Gallery, photographed by John B Turner for Hamish Keith's article, 'The art scene', in *Vogue New Zealand*, 1968

Throughout 1970, Peter kept Len Lye updated on the local art scene and the fortunes of his gallery. '[The] last six months have been good,' he noted in October.[35] In March, he had recorded a net profit for the year of $1414; in the following year, this figure would double. Lye continued to send ephemera from New York exhibitions, and Peter used an invitation from the gallery of André Emmerich, one of his heroes, as a model for a Don Binney show.

In 1970, Lye turned sixty-nine. He had a long career behind him as an experimental film-maker, painter and writer, but from the late 1950s he had focused on his 'tangible motion sculptures' – large-scale kinetic works, which were first exhibited at the Museum of Modern Art in 1961. Now, however, he had grown weary of the technical challenges they posed. Instead, he was increasingly absorbed by plans for utopian schemes such as temples of art in beautiful natural settings – projects that appealed to his long-held belief that 'art and happiness will be the basis of a final religion'.[36]

As the artist's Wellington agent, Peter hoped to bring Lye and his work to New Zealand for a major exhibition. The first step was to enlist the support of the arts council, and to this end he invited a group of officials – including Bill Sheat, Dr Ian Prior, John Malcolm and Melvin Day – to attend a meeting at the gallery on 8 December.[37] After viewing Lye's films and a documentary in which he featured, they agreed to support Peter's proposal. He was asked to draw up a draft itinerary programme and a budget for submission to the council.

So far so good; but Lye, who had been enthusiastic about the idea, was difficult to pin down on the details. He wrote to Peter in the new year, 'You certainly are to be congratulated on your entrepreneuring; great! ... I realise the N.Z. Govt must do the best it can on monies available, & much appreciate the "in depth" show offer; but I cannot get caught up in deadlines, mechanical problems, & that when my one concern is creative & *non-pressured* time.'[38] Rather than labour to get existing pieces exhibition-ready, Lye preferred to focus on new projects.

By March 1971, Lye seemed resigned to the fact that the exhibition was impossible, and offered to reimburse Peter for his time and expenses: 'As I see it now it may not come to anything – due to the obdurate unshowable nature of my technologically handicapped work.'[39] But Peter was undeterred. He was negotiating with the National Art Gallery over the possibility of a project, and was also in discussion with Gil Docking in Auckland. Eventually, in May, he heard that the National Art Gallery was unable to commit owing to the difficulty in assessing the financial implications. Peter wrote to Lye, 'I must say that I have found dealing with the Arts Council and the National Art Gallery a long frustrating experience. While the officers are pleasant and well meaning the lack of funds makes for a complicated set of checks and counter balances (committees, directors, secretaries et al). Still, one must stick with it.'[40]

In 1972, Ray Thorburn revived the idea of an exhibition and lobbied the arts council, but Peter remained critical of its attitude. He wrote to Lye:

> It's obvious that any official thing here involving you is geared where they want as much as they can get for as little financial involvement as possible. Instead of just giving you $3000.00 to do what you wish with they meanly insist on all manner of provisos ... The whole Government thing here is so depressing; invariably only promoting and buying what's 'safe'; taking the balls off anything that's got the juices of life. No, my vibes tell me forget about the

Len Lye exhibition at the Australian Centre for the Moving Image, 2009, showing *Fountain III*, 1976

> National Art Gallery, Queen Elizabeth Arts Council et al. Your work's too big, too good, too great to be fucked around by the whinging, mealy mouthed bunch of hicks.[41]

Lye suggested that if the arts council provided the funds, Thorburn could visit New York, note the technical requirements of the work and take it back to New Zealand – 'get it machined motorised & rigged up there. (God knows how much that would cost & I can't be bothered spending weeks & weeks lining such a thing up, & finding materials, wow wow, no sir.) But if a practical artist like Ray could spare time from his own career & get time off from teaching. Why it could work.'[42]

The matter dragged on until a New Zealand film crew visited Lye and made a documentary entitled *Len Who?*[43] After it was screened on television in 1973, Peter wrote to Lye:

The T.V. documentary was very, very good. And it made a lot of impact...

The result of all this has been another enquiry from an art gallery out here regarding your work. This time the Govett-Brewster Art Gallery, New Plymouth. It is run by a young American, Bob Ballard. He would like to enquire if you would be interested in coming out to New Plymouth and perhaps make a piece...

It would be of great importance to New Zealand today and in the future. An original Lye in our land; Wowweee.[44]

From there the project slowly gained momentum. Lye was impressed with Bob Ballard's idea, but did not feel able to undertake the technical challenges himself.

But to dream: Should a genius engineer designer and technical motion programmer (GEDTMP) fly over from N.Z. and scrape up the bits and pieces of my dismantled works called *Twisters* and *Cave Goddess* off the dusty cellar floor of my puny studio in NYC and resurrect them somewhere...

Mr. Ballard could then fly over to wherever the figures are set up and get their story and how it could be unfolded, i.e., spelt out or presented, displayed, observed, or recoiled from, as the case may be...[45]

Late in 1973, Bob Ballard wrote to offer Lye just such a 'GEDTMP': a young engineer from New Plymouth named John Matthews. In the following year, Matthews flew to New York to meet Lye, and the two began a highly productive phase of collaboration. Lye was so impressed by the quality of Matthews' work and the support of the Govett-Brewster that he eventually decided to leave his entire collection to New Zealand, with a non-profit foundation to administer it.

Peter continued to correspond with Lye in the following years, but he met the artist only once again. That was in March 1977, when Lye visited New Zealand for the long-awaited opening of his exhibition at the Govett-Brewster Art Gallery. '[H]e was sparkling,' Peter reported to Gordon Walters. 'He has got older though and now looks and acts his age.'[46]

Lye died in New York in 1980, but his reputation has continued to grow, and new technology and expertise has enabled the realisation of his ambitious kinetic sculptures. In 2015, the Len Lye Centre is scheduled to open in New Plymouth – the first public gallery to be devoted to a single New Zealand artist.

SEVEN

Painting is about people. It must be – else I die.

Despite the constraints of his day job, first as a curator at Auckland City Art Gallery and later as a lecturer at Elam School of Fine Arts, Colin McCahon was extremely productive in the 1960s. As he approached fifty, he looked forward to the day when he could retire from teaching and work as a full-time painter. He had recently established a studio at Muriwai, on Auckland's dramatic west coast, and was planning to divide his time between there and his home in the city.

Visiting McCahon and his wife Anne was always a highlight of Peter's trips to Auckland. He regarded McCahon as a visionary, and the artist appreciated what Peter was attempting to do, running a 'New York style gallery' in Wellington.[1] Both men viewed art as a spiritual quest, and held a passionate belief in its importance in society; they also shared a strong socialist bent and a keen sense of identification with New Zealand.[2]

Yet another bond was religion. McCahon had grown up in a Protestant family in Dunedin and was briefly involved with the Quakers as a young man. From the late 1950s, he took instruction with the Catholic Church, but he was unable to accept some aspects of its doctrine and his training consequently came to an end. He continued to be drawn to Catholicism, however, and as Peter recalled many years later, 'it was a fertile area we could talk in'.[3]

> I remember conversations about the Virgin, the Mysteries of the Faith, the Saints and their iconography, the power of the symbols, and the idealism of the many Saints, Martyrs, who 'lived the life'. Who loved.
>
> I can see the room in Partridge Street with the fire roaring. And, if I dig deep, very deep, I can taste the flagon sherry: a warming

Colin McCahon teaching at Elam, 1967

Peter at *Colin McCahon: A retrospective exhibition of paintings and watercolours from the collection of RN O'Reilly*, August 1969, showing *Kahikatea*, 1958, photographed by John B Turner

> brew, which, after the sharpness of the first sip, warms the cockles of the heart…
>
> And, an important skein in this friendship was my Catholicism. I was a believer. Colin liked that.

Like Peter, McCahon loved language and found a natural outlet in letter writing. By the late 1960s, he was writing long dispatches to his dealer – warm, direct letters, which are often playful, witty and revealing.

McCahon's letters are grounded in the domestic details of daily life: stories about his grandchildren, observations on the garden at Muriwai, and even occasional recipes (lentils with Marmite, and briar rose-bud soup).[4] But in the background there is the constant theme of painting, and the challenges of his vocation.

'I've not been painting so much as thinking about painting,' he wrote to Peter on one occasion. 'Meanwhile – I'm working something out – for myself – and not very helpful for dealers & public – but I feel I'm getting places very slowly.'[5] He described periods of stalled work, and even shock at the direction his work was taking: 'A lot of my painting scares me I must make the most ugly paintings ever.'[6] McCahon regarded his art as a conversation with his God, and his letters dramatise the search for insight and understanding and the daily struggle between doubt and faith. 'Nothing like painting,' he wrote. 'Months of terror opening to enlightenment or the very edge of disaster.'[7]

Although McCahon had always had a small core of supporters who championed his work, the public reaction to it, well into the 1970s, was often negative and even outright hostile. On good days he took pride in the fact that his work was controversial. 'I am delighted I can still upset people – if that were to stop I would be dead – at least my ideas on painting being revolutionary in its whole being would no longer work.'[8] But he was also dismayed at the way his art was misinterpreted. 'I got into a state of shock,' he wrote after one incident. 'I paint to tell people of the beauty of the land I love & of their relation to it and the God they all ask of for help.'[9]

For McCahon, painting was a means of communication, a way of exploring what he described as 'the human condition'.[10] In 1972, he underlined the challenge in a letter to Peter: 'What's the answer. Certainly not to try to make beauty, perfection and so on. Painting must operate on a most basic level, as I have said before but not to you, like pigs fucking. That's what it's all about. Hot, nasty, moist & lovely. A big roar of animal laughter comes in here. And the place we live in is suddenly clean & lovely, all the horror cleared away & my beloved and I touching hands. Painting is about people. It must be – else I die. Or am I a fool.'[11]

McCahon's second exhibition with Peter in July 1969 reflected his renewed interest in Māori culture – an interest fuelled by family developments. His daughter Victoria had recently married Ken Carr, a member of a prominent Māori family, and their son Matiu – McCahon's first grandchild – was a source of great joy to the artist. At the same time, his younger daughter Catherine had given him a book by Matire Kereama, an elder of Te Aupouri, entitled *The tail of the fish: Maori memories of the Far North.*[12] 'This is a personal and "family" exhibition,' McCahon told Peter. 'The paintings 1, 2, 3, 4, 5, 9, are all for Matiu Carr, our grandson (No 5, for his first birthday). His birth, and the discovery of Matire Kereama's book ... has made these paintings happen & become real to me.'[13]

Of the twelve works in the exhibition, priced from $60 to $550, the key painting was what McCahon described as 'an odd 2ft × 16ft genealogy of the Tainui Canoe (unsaleable)'.[14] This austere yet intensely lyrical work presents the whakapapa of his grandson's tribe, the white brushwork flickering and receding against a dark background. *The Canoe Tainui* was purchased at the opening; Peter informed McCahon, 'The buyers are a young married couple who just had to buy the painting.'[15]

Much to the artist's surprise, all but two works sold on opening night.[16] The *New Zealand Herald* reported, 'The rapidity with which the works were sold suggests that the art climate in Wellington is changing. A small group in the city has been buying contemporary New Zealand works for many years, but they have been mostly academic and intellectual people who have constituted a market nowhere as diverse as its Auckland counterpart.'[17] Peter told McCahon, '[I]t was a great thrill to see the show go off with such a bang. The first week the gallery was always full of a steady stream of people.'[18]

As a follow-up, Peter installed a retrospective of McCahon's work since the late 1930s – a rare opportunity to study his development, with key paintings such as *King of the Jews* and *Elias will he come to save him.*[19] All seventeen works, exhibited 'not for sale', were from the collection of McCahon's longtime friend and supporter, Ron O'Reilly, director of the New Zealand Library School.[20] By showing an impressive private collection, Peter was issuing a challenge: 'I wanted to say to everyone who came up the stairs, Look, this is what you can do.'[21] Bill Emsley commented in the *Dominion*, 'It is ironic that one of the best collections of one of the best artists in New Zealand has been bought by a private citizen over the years for a modest cost – while, one assumes, the National Gallery apparently ignored the artist.'[22] In fact, the National Art Gallery had purchased its first McCahon only weeks earlier from the Barry Lett Galleries.[23] He had by then been exhibiting for thirty years.

Peter wrote to McCahon in April 1970, 'My first full year of trading at 147 Cuba Street ended in March on a good note, however prudence dictates that I stick with my morning job in the battery factory. Hilary,

Colin McCahon: Paintings, July–August 1969, showing (top) *For Matiu: Muriwai*, and part of *The Canoe Tainui*, and (bottom, from left) *The Canoe Mamari*, *I know that whatever you ask of God* and *Mary went to the place where Jesus was*, all 1969, photographed by John B Turner

my wife, is currently working as a postie and she comes in to the gallery once a week to give me the afternoon off.'[24] McCahon, anticipating his retirement from Elam, was apprehensive about the prospect of earning a living from art. 'I'm doing winter gardening,' he told Peter in June. '[F]eel I won't ever paint again; I have to do better than the giant summer painting spree and find I'm just scared to be as banal as I know I'm going to be. Seed packets & nurseries of little trees get me – today I planted an aster ... Have hundreds of jonquils out ... Should any client prefer a garden done please put them onto me – I'm a past master at JUNGLES – but seriously. It is so. And as I'm leaving the school either at the end of this year (or next June) I'll be looking for jungles to create.'[25]

McCahon resigned from Elam early in 1971. Liberated from the city, he was able to spend more time at Muriwai, sowing grass seed and blue lupin, and watching his garden grow. Enchanted by the coastal environment with its dramatic cliffs, bird life and windswept vegetation, he began a series of lyrical, exuberant watercolours and acrylics entitled 'View from the top of the cliff'. 'All this colour & fun is a direct result of leaving the school,' he wrote.[26]

Peter opened an exhibition of these works in April: twenty-four watercolours priced from $50 to $65, plus an oil of 1963, *Pink, blue and white painting*, marked 'not for sale'.[27] 'The show looked great,' he reported, 'the colours just sang out and filled the room. Heavens! When the sun moved in through the nylon curtains the whole room was diffused with colour'.[28] Some seventeen works sold on the first day of the exhibition, many to regular visitors, including Tim and Helen Beaglehole, Ron O'Reilly, Elva Bett, Janet Paul, and the architect Martin Hill.

In the winter, McCahon wrote to Peter about a new series, entitled 'Necessary protection' – 'these about the Almighty looking after us ... All very formal & I think good. But probably hard to take ... This business of living off painting is tough. So far – so good – but I've got to keep it up or Anne & I starve.'[29] He congratulated Peter on the impending arrival of his first child, due in July. 'I am so glad for you ... Children are wonderful & make you happy. Our last is about to go & I just don't know how we will get on in our empty house. It is most right & proper that the children do go but it is – in the end – that you stand alone as before.'

Peter and Hilary had recently purchased their first property in Dixon Street in central Wellington – 'an old house, small but cosy' – which needed extensive renovations.[30] Peter, who had not the slightest interest in gardening, was cajoled into helping to clear the section. 'Last

Colin McCahon: View from the top of the cliff – watercolours, April 1971, showing (left) *Pink, blue and white painting*, 1963

weekend I filled a 10 square yard dump truck with rubbish; could hardly stand up on Monday morning with stiffness.'

Catherine Anne McLeavey was born on 14 July 1971 – 'a bonny child. Big for her age.'[31] But the stress of becoming a father and moving house had left Peter rather unsettled, as he reported to McCahon. 'Sometimes I think that I would like to shift north. Not as an art dealer or anything but just to live in a city where there was more things that interest me… the lack of stimulus does get me down sometimes. However, I do seem to have a strong inner life which sustains me and helps at times of loneliness. Perhaps I'm a bit negative at the moment; a dose of the post-natal blues.'

McCahon, who shared Peter's tendency towards introspection, was always sympathetic to his bouts of despondency. On this occasion he wrote encouragingly, '[Y]ou do sound depressed & sad. If you didn't exist in Wellington – I'd have to go out of business.'[32] McCahon suggested that Peter might apply for the position of curator at Auckland City Art Gallery: '[S]ome good & thoughtful person is badly wanted. If you do want to come to Auckland this could be the way. It's a lovely job &

Peter and Hilary with Catherine, Nelson Airport, 1971–72

the whole place needs a shake-up.'[33] Of course, McCahon continued, 'I shouldn't be telling you this as it cuts against my own financial interests.' The crisis blew over, but it was part of Peter's temperament to be constantly questioning what he was doing, and considering the alternatives. The prospect of moving to Auckland or Sydney would linger in his mind for decades.

—

In the last weeks of 1970, McCahon had completed his largest work to date. Over 3 metres high and 10.5 metres long, *Gate III* (often described by McCahon as 'the I AM') was commissioned by the Auckland City Art Gallery for the exhibition *Ten big paintings*, which opened in February 1971. McCahon intended this work as a major public statement – a protest against the proliferation of nuclear arms in

Gate III, 1970, on display at Victoria University, Wellington, 1978

Europe and America – and used texts drawn from the Old Testament that foretold the end of the world. The painting can also be seen as a comment on the threat of spiritual desolation in an increasingly secular and commercialised world.

Tim Beaglehole saw *Gate III* at the gallery and was struck by its power. 'When I first saw it I thought, We've got to have that. It seemed to me to be particularly appropriate for the university.'[34] But there was no precedent for Victoria to buy such a large and costly work, and it took time for Beaglehole to lay the groundwork. A year later, when Peter wrote to tell McCahon about the possibility of a sale, he replied, 'Your letter astounds me & I am delighted... But get rid of the thing – I can't have it here.'[35]

10, Partridge St., Auckland 2. Aug 4 '72

Dear Peter,

Have had a lovely letter today from Tim Beaglehole about the I AM. I have just written to him. And now, what I didn't really say on the 'phone the other afternoon, ~~my~~ thanks to you for your faith & care in what you have done for me.

Can I let it go at that please.

I can't say more but am, as ever,

Colin McCahon

Greetings & love &

THANK YOU.

THIS IS A FIRST. I'LL COME TO WELLINGTON & LICK YOUR BOOTS.

Horrid thought really, & one I probably wouldn't carry out in actual performance. It would, of course, make a wonderful happening at the unveiling ~~[illegible]~~ at the university

Please forgive this letter, I'm just happy. Anne & I need money. Not at the final drop but getting near.

In the following months, Beaglehole applied for a grant of $2000 – half the asking price – from the arts council.[36] Peter kept McCahon informed about progress. 'There is still nothing definite regarding the large "I am",' he wrote, 'however I am confident that it will go through. I can just see it now on the large spacious wall in the new lecture block at Vic.'[37] In July 1971, the arts council agreed to the grant and the purchase was confirmed. It was by far the biggest sale of Peter's career to date; indeed, as the *Evening Post* reported, the price was the highest ever paid for a work by a living New Zealand artist.[38]

McCahon wrote to Peter in early August:

> Dear Peter,
>
> Have had a lovely letter today from Tim Beaglehole about the I AM. I have just written to him. And now, what I didn't really say on the 'phone the other afternoon, my thanks to you for your faith & care in what you have done for me.
>
> Can I let it go at that please. I can't say more but am, as ever,
> Colin McCahon
> Greetings & love &
> THANK YOU.
> THIS IS A FIRST. I'LL COME TO WELLINGTON & LICK YOUR BOOTS.
>
> Horrid thought really, & one I probably wouldn't carry out in actual performance. It would, of course, make a wonderful happening at the university.
>
> Please forgive this letter, I'm just happy. Anne & I need money...[39]

After his success with *Gate III*, Peter wrote to enquire about the possibility of selling another large work, such as *The Second Gate Series* of 1962 or *Numerals* of 1965. The artist was surprised and a little taken aback. 'I've never regarded these very large works as saleable,' he replied.

> I certainly would like them to be places where they could be used – by being seen. I should hate them [to] be divided up into individual items. I would most certainly put them on a long term loan to the right place. I can't define this right place as yet. The lateness of my reply is the result of my wanting to talk over this with William [McCahon, his son] who has long been my friend & advisor about my paintings. He is against a sale unless to [a] well controlled gallery, or institution where they would be looked after.[40]

Letter from Colin McCahon to Peter, 4 August 1972

It was not until later in the decade that McCahon would revisit this question.

In March 1972, the retrospective *Colin McCahon/A survey exhibition* opened at the Auckland City Art Gallery before touring the country. It confirmed McCahon's status as New Zealand's leading contemporary artist, but his growing reputation brought new demands. He was now under pressure from a variety of sources to supply paintings, and to lessen his administrative workload he appointed Barry Lett his principal dealer, responsible for organising exhibitions in other centres. Lett wrote to Peter, 'He is very happy with the association he has with you and does not want the new arrangement to be interpreted as anything other than a centralising of activity and a way of freeing himself of extraneous time consuming correspondence etc. You will continue to have access to his work and your requirements for individual works or exhibitions will be met of course.'[41]

The new arrangement was not ideal: it meant Peter would have to work through Lett, and it concerned him that the Auckland dealer would have first pick of McCahon's output. Peter needed to feel that he was getting the best for his gallery, and it was vital for him to have a say in the selection of work, rather than simply waiting for what an artist cared to send him. Later, his need to control what was exhibited would create tension with some artists, but with McCahon the potential for conflict was alleviated by his rapport with the painter and his absolute confidence in his work.

In March 1973, McCahon wrote to Peter:

> I've made a mighty purchase of a bolt of canvas yesterday, picked it up today we cut it up into lengths on the road – it was far too heavy to get out to Muriwai as it was. 180 yards in all, this lot. And I know what I'm going to put on a lot of it. The divine smell of raw canvas. I bought it for a very special job. You will get some later. I'm not talking yet. I might laugh at my own ideas, I often do now. It's a good way to be really – these will be a kind of poster I think – I've not seen them yet but I do know what they must look like. I think the title for the whole series will be 'Little poems for large walls'.
>
> When I painted the small painting for Hilary Baxter I opened up a new way of thinking about painting I'd been working on for a long time. I've hardly painted for 3 months now. I'm doing a big

> rethink on all sorts of things. I've been walking & looking. Not, really, not working.[42]

McCahon's painting for his godchild Hilary Baxter was *Jim passes the northern beaches*, marking the death of her father, the poet James K Baxter, in October the previous year.[43] In this radiant sketch on unstretched canvas, McCahon imagined the spirit of his old friend flying north over the landscape towards Cape Reinga.

By July, he had further progress to report:

> Things are going good for me – now. I've got work done – digging at Muriwai & making canvases. I might turn up with a 96 yard canvas soon – twice around your gallery & up the walls to the roof. It won't be like that. I wish it could, & will do it sometime. I saw the direction over the weekend and being of little faith turned it down: now I know I was right in my forty days in the wilderness – we must have a place to wander – to find the narrow path. Please send me your gallery wall sizes – a wee plan. I have no intention to embarrass you with an impossible monster.[44]

Looking for a public way to honour Baxter – whom he had met in 1943, when the poet was a seventeen-year-old schoolboy – McCahon turned to the Muriwai landscape. 'This beach,' he informed Peter, 'is a part of the long road that Maori spirits travel on their way to Te Rerenga Wairua [Cape Reinga]'.[45] He described the work for his forthcoming exhibition in Wellington:

> Your lot have numerals painted on them – are really Stations of the Cross & are painted in memory of Baxter. They could be used for a church, but it would be a most adventurous one to use them…
>
> People should know perhaps that I don't regard these canvases as 'paintings', they shouldn't be enclosed in frames, they are just bits of a place I love and painted in memory of a friend who now – in spirit – has walked this same beach. The intention is not realist but an abstraction of the final walk up the beach. The Christian 'walk' & the Maori 'walk' have a lot in common.[46]

The exhibition consisted of two paintings: an eleven-piece work entitled *Walk (Series C)*, and the six-piece *Series D (Ahipara)*.[47] On the day after the opening on 11 September, Peter wrote to McCahon:

> They look fantastic; they're beautiful. The white walls. The paintings move across them like Moby Dick…
>
> The Ahipara series hangs alone; the wall along side it is bare. The painting moves like a big fish; silently…

Colin McCahon: Recent works, September 1973, showing part of *Walk (Series C)*, 1973

> The quality of Series 'C' is outstanding. It's a beauty. WHAT can one say: just 'thank you' and a hug. Yes. 'Thank you' from all those who have seen them and who will see them.[48]

Numbered in sections representing the Stations of the Cross, *Walk (Series C)* is painted in thin washes of black and white acrylic that allow the warm ochre of the rough jute canvas to show through. Each panel presents a 'slice' of Muriwai Beach: the tide receding across the sand, the sombre line of a darkening horizon, a burst of light illuminating a squall at sea. Against this luminous, moody backdrop, McCahon imagines a long walk with his old friend, a walk that parallels the journey of Baxter's departing spirit. Lyrical, meditative and deeply moving, this painting brings together some of McCahon's key themes – the transience of life, landscape and memory, Christian and Māori spirituality.

Walk (Series C) was priced at $2800, the equivalent of $31,500 today, and exhibited with a note: 'It is hoped to sell the eleven panel series as a unit.' If not, McCahon had instructed Peter, 'I don't mind if the series is broken up. We can't house any more large works here.'[49] Peter recognised the importance of the work and the merit in keeping the panels together, but there was little market for such a large painting and he was delighted to find a buyer, who later recalled, 'I was immediately attracted to it. But I had to think about that one, it was a lot of money for us at the time. And I didn't have anywhere at home I could hang it – at that stage we were living in quite a small 1960s house. I ended up hanging it all the way up the stairs, where it still looked splendid, and there it stayed for many years.'[50] In 2004, the Museum of New Zealand Te Papa Tongarewa (which subsumed the National Art Gallery) acquired the painting for $3.1 million, a record for a New Zealand work.

In July 1973, McCahon's mother Ethel died, and the elegiac tone of the 'Walk' paintings lingered well into the following year. In October 1974, he wrote to tell Peter about a new work, inspired by the artist Ralph Hotere sending him a poem entitled 'Song of the shining cuckoo'.

> I don't think I sounded very good when you phoned. Back here I came right again & have been at work. Digging, mowing lawns & painting & what was so wrong with my work has come better. It could be good. Five panels each 3ft × 10ft. A poem by Tangirau Hotere (Ralph's father). He uses the word song – either the song –

> or the grief of – the shining Cuckoo: Tangi. It's most beautiful & Ralph sent it to me to be used & it's been on my mind for a time now…
>
> I've put this poem in relation to the Stations of the Cross & the Spirit Path to the North – two migrations (both ways). It's very wild & tough & I feel much more happy.[51]

McCahon had just learnt that Peter had been ill with a serious ear infection, which had required an operation and two months off work. He wrote, 'I have been in pain, on my feet at least, you in Hospital:

Colin McCahon: Recent paintings, November 1974, showing *The Song of the Shining Cuckoo*, 1974

I think I would die rather than be captive… I am a coward before canvas & paint & people; your awful time in Hospital & me, only thinking of canvas & paint & my subject & myself in no way knowing. Forgive me.'

Peter was back at work just in time for McCahon's exhibition in November, which featured *The Song of the Shining Cuckoo*. The artist had completed the other works only hours before they were due to be dispatched to Wellington. 'This lot goes under the name BLIND,' he informed Peter.[52] The five panels, each divided into vertical sections, feature a sombre yet evocative landscape of delicate greys and silvers – a narrow tonal range occasionally alleviated by a sliver of yellow at the top. Painted on window blinds, the panels play on a key McCahon theme: the lack of vision in contemporary society, and the failure of New Zealanders to see and appreciate their natural and cultural heritage. The artist acknowledged their austerity in a letter to Peter: 'You are getting some of [the] most brutal paintings in this lot'.

There were only a handful of sales from this exhibition. *The Song of the Shining Cuckoo*, priced at $3000, remained unsold, and McCahon later gifted it to the Hocken Library in memory of three poets: RAK Mason, James K Baxter and Charles Brasch.[53] The 'Blind' panels were dispersed, a reflection of the limited market for major McCahons at the time. One sold to the Robert McDougall Art Gallery; much later, in 1980, the Ministry of Foreign Affairs purchased panels three and four.[54]

Meanwhile, McCahon was looking forward to a break:

> I'm going to close down & do some gardening for a few weeks. I've painted so much this year I need a rest. Anne & [I] haven't had a holiday for months, really years. We get around & go places but to work and want to go somewhere & sit. I think sitting must be great. Anne & I remember your sitting on the Muriwai cliffs – I must say I was a bit scared but you did see the joy of the place. You know, you came home & sat on our double yellow gasania (that is really gazania). Really, my friend, you are a bit of a menace but a friend ...[55]

McCahon had commemorated this occasion, when Peter alarmed him by sitting too close to the edge of the cliff, in a drawing entitled *McLeavey sat here*, a schematic rendering of the Muriwai landscape that appears in so many of the 'Necessary protection' works. The landscape is reduced to essentials: a vertical form suggesting the steep cliff, and another representing Moturoa, the rocky protrusion just offshore where the gannets nest. Oaia Island ('Moby Dick') is visible in the distance, and a loop of rosary beads stands in for the sun. McCahon later gave the drawing to Peter.[56]

McLeavey sat here can be seen as a gesture of appreciation and an affirmation of the friendship between artist and dealer. It was a bond that would deepen in the following years as Peter assumed an increasingly important role in McCahon's life.

Colin McCahon, *McLeavey sat here*, 1975
Pen and ink
Museum of New Zealand Te Papa Tongarewa, gift of Peter and Hilary McLeavey, 1986

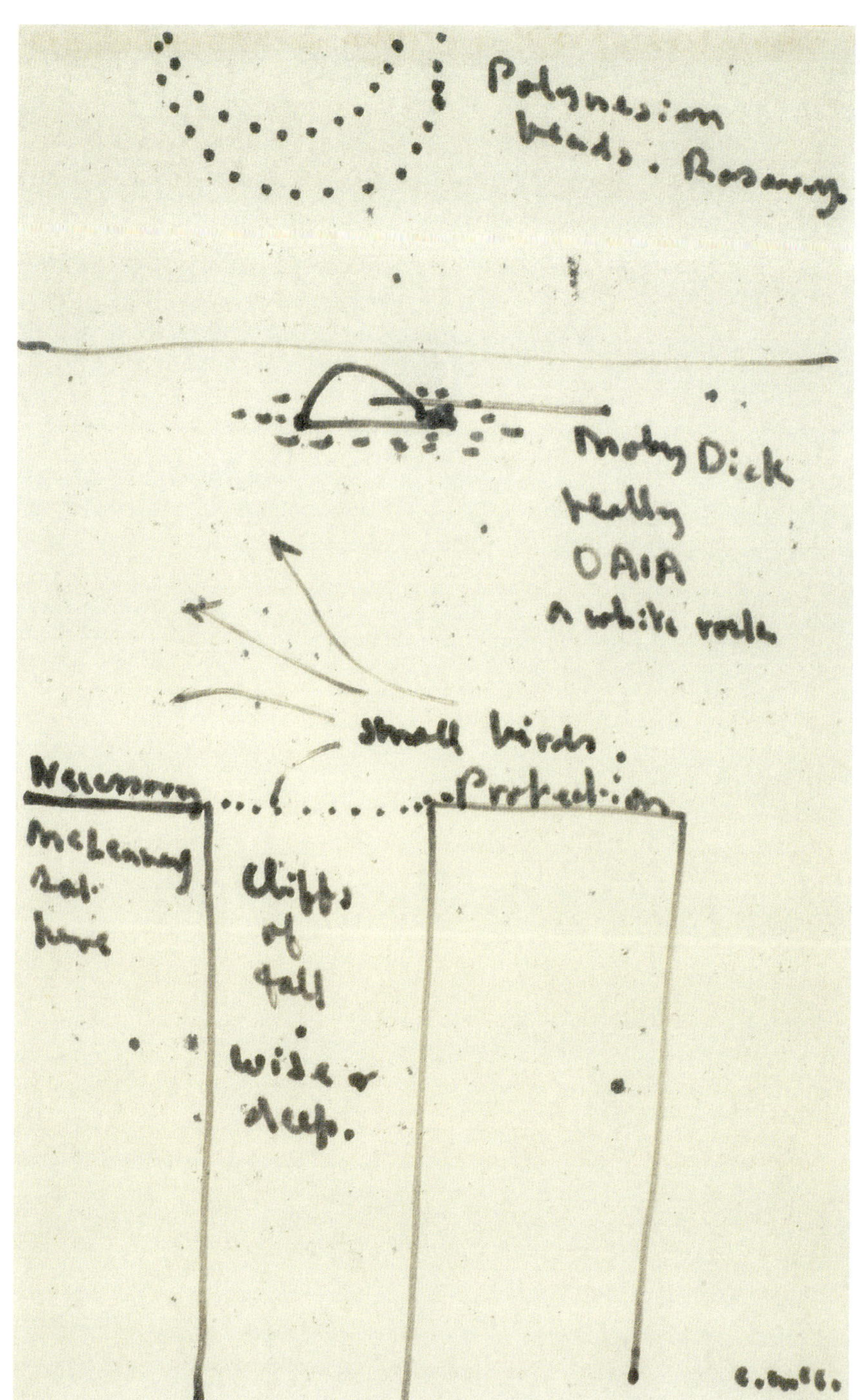
Polynesian
beads. Rosary.
Moby Dick
OAIA
a white whale
small birds.
Necessary
Protection
Cliffs
of
fall
wise or
deep.

The C&A ODLIN TIMBER&HARDWARE Co Ltd

EIGHT

The revelation that pictures are worth as much as fridges, television sets, or pleasure boats, seems a hard one for most people to accept.

When Peter started his business, there was little understanding in Wellington of the art dealer's role. As Hilary recalled, 'There was the idea that the dealer was "taking" money from the artist, and that the art would become so much more expensive and unaffordable.'[1] The situation was quite different in Auckland, where dealer galleries were an accepted part of the art scene. 'Peter was very much on his own in Wellington,' Hamish Keith observed. 'He was dealing with the same kind of closed society that Auckland had been twenty years earlier, when a little cabal of people had their hands on everything and they could run it their way and they didn't like change.'[2]

Among the first to appreciate the importance of good dealers were the artists, and for some, such as Toss Woollaston, their emergence was life-changing. Prior to the mid-1960s, Woollaston had organised his own exhibitions, taking time off from his day job to 'mind' his shows at the Centre Gallery and other venues.[3] Looking back in 1977, he commented:

> [F]or ten years or more, I have had a dealer who makes me a living, relieves me of the burden of hawking my own wares, the exhausting bustle and hassle of running my own one-man shows – or the being submerged twice annually in the two-hundred-artist exhibition of the Art Society – and all for no more than it would cost me to do it myself…
>
> I know there are those who think dealers are necessarily rogues, battening on artists to fatten themselves. I can assure them that not all are like that. Remarks like 'the dealers have got him, alas', come from people who wish, impracticably, that it was still as it was in the good old days, when artists still got no income worth the name…

Peter and Don Binney with Toss Woollaston's *Mapua*, 1971

The revelation that pictures are worth as much as fridges, television sets, or pleasure boats, seems a hard one for most people to accept.[4]

In the early years of their marriage, Peter and Hilary often stayed with the Woollastons over the summer, and the friendship was one they both found deeply sustaining. For Hilary, Edith was something of a role model. Both Toss and Peter were driven, single-minded, completely absorbed in their work; neither was a conventional husband and father. 'Edith was a wonderful woman,' Hilary remarked. 'She had such a sense of strength and calm. She made allowances for Toss, who mostly did whatever he pleased, and yet the two of them had such a close and loving relationship. In the early days of my marriage, when the children were young and demanding and Peter was so totally preoccupied with the gallery, I would often think, How would Edith deal with this?'[5]

For Peter, Woollaston was a mentor and even to some extent a father figure. 'The more I think about it,' he wrote in 1978, 'the more I feel that we have a most special relationship. And I give my thanks for that. You have been so central to me in my development, both personal and in my drive to make my gallery live. I often think that it is your gallery too. For you have played such an important role in its birth, growth, and survival.'[6] Temperamentally the two men were opposites – Woollaston direct, outspoken and sunny-natured; Peter guarded and introspective – but they appreciated each other and formed an unshakeable bond. With some artists, Peter had a very hands-off approach, but with Woollaston he acted as a critic, reviewing the work as it was made, evaluating whether it was of exhibition standard, arranging commissions and suggesting subjects. As Woollaston told the Auckland dealer Rodney Kirk Smith, 'I depend on his judgment rather more than my own.'[7]

Even before he opened his gallery in Cuba Street, Peter had commissioned the artist to paint his parents. Woollaston visited the couple at Riverside Drive during the winter of 1968, and as Peter's sister Marie relates, 'They were rather self-conscious about the idea of being painted and it took a while for Toss to win them round.'[8] Later Peter reflected, 'My father, I gather, didn't like Toss and I suspect he felt threatened. My father is a conservative type of working man and I think he found Toss's more liberal ideas unacceptable.'[9]

Peter's initial response to the portrait, *Mr and Mrs L.F.M.*, was one of shock – and recognition. 'Toss had captured something of the dynamic in their marriage. The painting is dominated by my father's presence, his big head, but it's my mother with her downcast face who

Peter with Toss Woollaston's painting of his parents, *Mr and Mrs L.F.M.*, 1968–70, in *MT Woollaston: A retrospective exhibition of portraits*, October 1970, photographed by John B Turner

is the powerful one.'[10] In 1970, Peter included this painting in an exhibition of Woollaston's portraits, all drawn from private and public collections and therefore not for sale.[11] He hoped the show might prompt some portrait commissions, as it eventually did.

By the early 1970s, Woollaston, like McCahon, was becoming overwhelmed by correspondence about his work. He arranged for Peter to become his national agent, liaising with dealers throughout the country and organising exhibitions in other centres. As part of the new agreement, which took force from August 1971, Peter increased his commission on sales from 33 percent to 43 percent and assumed responsibility for all associated costs: mounting and framing, freight and exhibition expenses. 'I am entirely in agreement with all you propose,' Woollaston wrote. 'I hope the increase to 43% will be enough for your trouble and expenses.'[12]

Visiting Woollaston at Riwaka over the summer of 1970–71, Peter felt the artist had reached a plateau in his work and needed a new challenge. 'We went up to Britannia Heights together,' Peter recalled. 'And we looked out at the view and I said, "Look, Toss, why don't you increase the size? You could do a big four by nine foot painting of Nelson, a real panorama."'[13]

Until then Woollaston's largest work had been just over a metre in width, and he was initially a little uncertain about such a dramatic increase in scale.[14] He wrote to a friend, 'I'm beginning a new attempt, inspired by Peter, to paint pictures on whole sheets of hardboard 9'×4' – it feels more like labour than inspiration as yet. What is he trying to do to me? Make me conform to modern standard sizes? Release my potential? Anyway, it might be an interesting experiment.'[15] Two weeks later, he was much more positive. 'This size has a curious effect on my feelings about other work,' he told Charles Brasch. 'Peter perhaps knew what he was about. I feel stimulated. He is comforting about crates and transport problems – and that he will sell such pictures.'[16]

Peter's 'interesting experiment' was a great success, leading to some of the finest works in Woollaston's long career. Working on a panoramic scale was both challenging and liberating, enabling him to create majestic paintings of tremendous energy and vitality. One of the first was *West from Nelson*, which was shown at the gallery in September 1971 along with two more of the same size: *Motueka mountains* and *Mapua*.[17] Peter contrived a striking photo opportunity for this exhibition, enlisting Don Binney to help carry *Mapua* across a busy downtown intersection: 'We were taking it to show an interested party,' he told a reporter.[18] Meanwhile, the journalist Peter Cape had recently started an art column in the *National Business Review* – a sure sign that a corporate class was emerging with an interest in the visual arts – and his response could hardly have been bettered. 'The pick of the fortnight,' Cape wrote, 'is the Woollaston exhibition at Peter McLeavey. Three 9×4 feet oils at $1000... It would be worthwhile to fly from anywhere to buy one of these oils for the boardroom or the entrance foyer.'[19]

Two weeks into the exhibition, Peter told Woollaston that he had sold *West from Nelson* and had an option on the other works. 'I don't know how you feel about painting further large ones. All I know is that there is great interest in them and it appears that the price of $1000 is no hindrance to sales. Perhaps we will talk about sites or views to paint... I can visualise a view of Wellington from the back of Brooklyn for example.'[20] Days later, Peter had second thoughts. 'I don't want you to feel any pressure,' he wrote. 'My main concern is that you don't feel that you are pushed to paint these larger works. I guess I must feel this because of their very size and scale; they just appear (to my mind) hard physical labour.'[21]

Woollaston, now in his early sixties, was not at all daunted: 'I will be happy – and even excited – to paint some more nine-by-fours … I have one board ready primed now, and a subject – Mount Malita from across the Waimea Plains. I was intending to paint this subject, and am just waiting for a fine day now to go and do some watercolours.'[22] Woollaston had enjoyed the stimulus of responding to Peter's challenge and was pleased at his proposal for a Wellington landscape. Writing to Charles Brasch, he commented, 'I find it wonderful, to work in with somebody else like that … Like the old painters'.[23]

Mapua had been purchased by Peter's friend, John Casserley, a pioneer of modern dance who was now based in the United States. Every year, Casserley returned home to work with the New Zealand Ballet and other companies, and he wanted to take something back as a tangible reminder of his country. 'I missed New Zealand so much,' he recalled. 'The first year I bought some pottery, but it broke. So I thought maybe I could get a painting. It would be something I could treasure, something to look at every day.'[24] In the early 1970s, Casserley often used his fee from the ballet to buy a painting from Peter. 'It was all so affordable then. I met some of the artists, extraordinary people like Toss Woollaston. It was a rite of passage really. I was so lucky.'

The 1970s was an era in which a new generation of well-educated, sophisticated and internationally aware New Zealanders discovered the art of their own country.[25] In not much more than a decade, art had moved from being a virtually underground activity to one that had cachet in the wider culture. As Tim Curnow observed, '[P]rofessional people, businesses, Govt Depts and younger people like myself were prepared to write a cheque and buy a McCahon, a Woollaston, a Binney.'[26] Peter sold Curnow several works after he moved to Sydney in 1970. '[H]e'd come for dinner and bring, largely, works on paper to show us … [P]ayment was made by me sending over a cheque for $100 or $200 when I could afford it. Usually it took 12–18 months to pay it off and Peter was happy with this knowing that the work had gone to a good home … [W]e certainly couldn't afford Australian art and if we could we wouldn't have been able to pay it off in this way.'[27]

For Curnow and others, acquiring New Zealand art was a rewarding experience, 'especially if you'd been sold a work by someone like McLeavey who'd explain the work, give the purchaser the keys to it and put it in a context of art generally'.[28]

Toss Woollaston, *Tasman Bay, 1928*, 1974–75
Oil on board
Tim and Helen Beaglehole collection

In 1973, Luit Bieringa, the director of the Manawatu Art Gallery, curated a major touring exhibition of Woollaston's work.[29] It included four of his new panoramic paintings, including two from Woollaston's second show of large works at the Peter McLeavey Gallery in September 1972.[30] For his third exhibition of panoramas in May 1976, Woollaston painted a landscape with a deeply personal resonance. *Tasman Bay, 1928* was inspired by a drawing that his daughter, the artist Anna Caselberg, had made of the same subject. It evoked a key memory – that of Woollaston's first sighting of Tasman Bay as a romantic eighteen-year-old with a book of Shelley's poems in his haversack. Nearly fifty years later he looked back, recalling his youthful emotion, and *Tasman Bay, 1928* is one of his most radiant and ethereal paintings. Peter was quick to appreciate its significance, writing to McCahon, '[A]ll those shadows that made Toss are evoked in this large work. The view is of a sheet of water; the hills behind Nelson and the pearly, milk blue sky. It's a fine work that resonates within my heart.'[31]

Tim Beaglehole recalled his response to the painting:

> When it was first shown it bowled me over. It struck me that there was a kind of mood, almost a sort of nostalgia about it, which I found tremendously powerful. But even then, when it was first shown, it was quite expensive, and I thought, Oh, I'd love to have it, but we can't starve the children.
>
> But then a few years later an aunt of mine died and left me a few thousand dollars and my immediate thought was, Ah, Tasman Bay – it's possible. I thought it would be nice to do something definite and say, That's Aunty Edith's money. And I went back to Peter and said I was interested in Tasman Bay and he said, 'Oh. Oh. I don't know. I'll have to consult Toss.' And I wasn't quite sure what that was about ... But Peter went off and consulted Toss and eventually the work came through.[32]

In fact, Woollaston had been reluctant to sell the work. He wrote to Peter, 'I am amazed, startled, upset, at anyone wanting to buy Tasman Bay in 1928. The price will be some compensation; but I hope I may get to know the owners (if they become its owners) and be able to go and look at it sometimes. For your sake, I am pleased, thrilled even, if it sells. I am a mixture of many feelings.'[33]

Michael Smither was another of the stalwarts of the Peter McLeavey Gallery in its early years. Taranaki born, he studied at Elam School of

Peter at *Michael Smither: Paintings (14 Stations of the Cross, in memory of Rita Angus)*, September–October 1970, photographed by John B Turner

Fine Arts and began exhibiting in 1961. Just three years later, back in New Plymouth, he painted the first of his now-celebrated rock pool works. Peter greatly admired Smither and felt he owed him a good deal. 'This year has developed up to my expectations,' he wrote late in 1969, 'and I am hopeful about next year. Actually in some ways it seems remarkable to me how things have gone so well. Part is due to my own drive and enthusiasm but mainly it has been due to the help and encouragement I have received from the painters. In particular, you and Toss whose work I have sold right from the beginning.'[34]

Peter and Smither were contemporaries, both formed by a strict Catholic upbringing in small-town New Zealand, but Peter saw Smither, in many ways, as his opposite. He admired the artist's easy-going, sociable nature: 'The fact that you are so open and "take risks" in every way is something so special. It's something I aspire to. That freedom, that ease, that life.'[35] By contrast, Peter confided, 'I've got to make an effort and just relax. Take it easy. Not to be so regimented and unflexible. In so many ways I make rods to beat my own back with.'

Smither's second show with Peter in 1970 was something of a departure from his previous work, consisting of fourteen canvases in the shape of a cross and painted with details from the Central Otago landscape. As the Frances Hodgkins Fellow at the University of Otago that year, he had been captivated by the local landscape with its soft, clear light. He had also been reflecting on the death of Rita Angus in January. As he explained, 'Rita Angus was a painter I could relate to. I felt very close to her and when she died I was very sad. I felt that I had lost something. And I painted this personal memorial to her in the shape of a cross. It had a landscape inside it, a part of Central Otago, a part of New Zealand that she used to love painting.'[36]

At the opening in September, Smither's exhibition attracted a rush of sales. Neil Robertson, one of the young diplomats who visited Peter regularly, had already had a good look at the works.

> Late one Friday evening we tripped up Cuba Street to see Peter, and he had a great packing crate there, full of Michael Smithers for the next show. He invited us to help unpack them and we stacked them all around the room. And my wife and I were very taken by them, and we worked out which one we wanted.
>
> Then when the exhibition actually opened I was waiting at the door along with four or five other art lovers, and when the door opened in we swept. I waited all of 30 seconds before I said to Peter, 'That's the one I want.' And almost immediately someone else came up and wanted it too. You had to be quick![37]

As one of the new talents to emerge in the 1960s, Smither had enjoyed a degree of critical acclaim at an early age. By 1970, however, he was wary of the pressure that came with success: 'Many young painters go under because they have to perform. They get stuck with an acceptable style and stop developing. They freeze – and that's bad. This happened to me with rocks. If you change and want to paint something else, people say, "that's not your style". But I didn't want to be lumped with painting stones all my life.'[38]

Michael Smither, *Joseph with bear and bottle*, 1973
Oil on board
Private collection

After successful exhibitions of landscapes in 1971 and 1972, Smither's major shows at the Peter McLeavey Gallery focused on portraits and family groups. One of the most significant was his *Domestic paintings* show of 1973. Martin Hill, who reviewed the exhibition, observed, 'The artist's children are in all sorts of unloveable situations such as annoying cats, teasing fleas, demanding things from mother and usually with nappies around their knees.'[39]

Wellington collectors Les and Milly Paris bought their first Smither from this show. The couple had become 'hooked on art' soon after their marriage in 1963; as Milly recalled, 'We had paintings on our walls even before we owned a dining-room table.'[40] They began collecting in earnest in the late 1960s, driving to Auckland every year to visit the dealer galleries. Les made his first purchase from Peter – a Barry Brickell ceramic – while he was still at The Terrace. When Peter moved to Cuba Street, Les, who worked as a lawyer in Manners Street, often called in at lunchtime to have a chat and see what was new.

Milly Paris recalled her husband coming home and telling her about a Smither painting he was greatly taken by:

> Les asked if I could come in and have a quick look, and when I walked in to the gallery there it was, *Joseph with bear and bottle* – the little boy in the nappies, pointing. And I said, 'Yes Les, I could live with that one.' And so he went up to Peter, and Peter said, 'Oh, there are three options on that painting already.' So Les said, 'Put me down as another interested party and if no one takes up on their option, then let me know.' Well, after a while, a few weeks, Peter rang him up. And he said, 'If you still want that painting, it's yours.' So three people did not take up their option. And I thought, Well, that painting was meant to come to us. And how incredible is that?

Smither continued to develop the domestic theme, and in 1978 he exhibited seven large paintings with a more sinister undercurrent. The art critic Neil Rowe commented: 'Each of the paintings is concerned with some aspect of violence, war, or man's inhumanity to man and the environment. The most impressive painting here, entitled *Gifts*, portrays an old man giving presents to two small boys. In the foreground one of the boys has unwrapped his gift to discover a bright pink machine gun'. Rowe concluded, 'These are remarkable paintings and show Smither at his strongest, as a toughly unsentimental painter of people.'[41]

In the following year, Peter wrote to the artist:

> Dear Michael
>
> I had some good fun this morning.
>
> I went through all the colour slides of the various artworks that had passed through my hands over the last 12 years. It was, in a funny way, a very 'particular' experience.
>
> In particular, it made me realise how good you had been to me. How many fine paintings by you had passed through my hands. I felt touched and most warm towards you; and to the time we have shared.
>
> Michael, look: this letter is to say 'thank you'. That is all that's needed.

A big 'thanks' for your help, support, friendship.
Best wishes
Peter.[42]

Don Binney had been a contemporary of Michael Smither at Elam in the late 1950s, when it was 'the most dowdy, bigoted, backward-looking, motheaten, obscurantist dump you could ever imagine'.[43] Like Smither, he developed early, finding his mature style when he was just a few years out of art school.

Binney's art was informed by his fascination with ornithology and bird-watching, and his concern for environmental issues. As he explained to Peter in 1975:

> You understand how much my involvement with Birds has contributed to my development, not necessarily as a painter, but generally? You know my very first exhibited work, 'Pipiwharauroa Late Summer' was first shown Auck. Art Gallery in November 1962. But I went on my first fully-fledged adult bird-watching expedition, with binoculars & grown company, in November 1950. With or without the appearance of a bird image in my work at any given stage, my response to the whole landscape idea has been essentially related to such sorties, and to the responses to places seen or found or revisited in the pursuit of the Bird.[44]

From 1963, when he first exhibited his bird-in-landscape paintings at the Ikon Gallery, Binney's reputation soared. He later described this period as 'my seven fat years'.[45]

During the 1960s, a new generation of critics had begun to piece together a history of New Zealand art for the first time. Searching for themes and connections, they saw a link between the art of Binney and Smither and that of a previous generation – the realist landscape painters of the 1930s and 1940s, such as Rita Angus and Christopher Perkins. According to this narrative, Binney's art was the latest development in a quintessentially New Zealand artistic tradition, featuring crisp drawing, bold colour and hard clear light. As one critic noted in 1964, 'The search for a national identity is something that is now influencing all the arts in this country. It is evident in our prose and poetry ... In the realm of painting however, it is hard to define and much harder to express ... Exhibitions of their work last year showed that Toss Woollaston and Colin McCahon continue to contribute to it, but after them, who else? My choice would be Don Binney, whose first

Marti Friedlander, *Don Binney*, 1977–79
Gelatin silver print
Museum of New Zealand Te Papa Tongarewa, purchased 2007

one-man show showed an understanding of the peculiar rhythms that go to make the New Zealand landscape.'[46]

In time, as the critical concern with regionalist landscape painting waned, Binney would come to rue the fact that his work had ever been linked to the 'national identity' project that pigeonholed it in a particular timeframe. In the 1960s, however, it was a key factor in his success, both critical and commercial.

Binney met Peter at the Barry Lett Galleries in 1965: 'I remember a strange, odd, timid yet persistent sort of McLeavey character making an oblique orbit around the Auckland arts scene.'[47] In the following year, Peter wrote to him: 'I would now very much like to be able to get 3 or 4 of your recent paintings and "have a bash" in selling them to some of our Wellington and South Island collectors, but I have been rather "affrighted" when I read this afternoon that there was a waiting list of some 3 dozen human beings all insisting on buying a Binney. Well I don't know quite what to do as I would like to get 3 or 4?'[48]

Binney's work was in demand – an unusual situation for a New Zealand artist, and one which brought its own pressures. When Peter opened in Cuba Street, he scheduled an exhibition for March 1970, but Binney asked for an extension. 'I hope this does not upset your no doubt well-laid-out plans,' he wrote. 'I am a slow worker: I have been under some pressures this year already, and while things are really working out pretty well now, I feel obliged to let you know how my affairs stand... Naturally I don't like having to write to you in this way, like an old bum, cadging a handout of more time to spend.'[49]

The exhibition eventually opened in July. It comprised twenty-two works, with a top price of $600: one series on the landscape of Te Henga, on Auckland's rugged west coast, and another on Mana Island near Wellington, and the islands of the Hauraki Gulf. The American ambassador's wife had already contacted Binney to enquire about buying a work, as he informed Peter: 'If diplomatic kidnapping breaks out in NZ, then maybe future desperadoes will swipe a Binney for ransom instead of her old man.'[50] The *Evening Post* noted 'a record flurry of keen buying' at the opening: 'more than $2000-worth of contemporary paintings by the young Auckland artist Don Binney were sold or taken on short option'.[51] When Peter assessed his accounts at the end of the financial year, he learned that nearly half his annual commission had come from this show.

Despite the commercial success of the exhibition, there was a note of dissent from critic Stephen Green: 'Don Binney is obviously gifted and intelligent, and yet most of these paintings repeat a formula that is becoming monotonous.'[52] It was a comment that would be repeated in the following years.[53] Binney soon came to feel that Peter, too, had reservations about his work: 'In a way, there was always a bit of a downhill toboggan ride right from the rich beginning.'[54]

Prior to his second exhibition with Peter in 1973, Binney recalled, 'McLeavey came up to Auckland, saw the work, and I remember he had coffee with me in lower Parnell one morning and he just did a dump.

He did a dump on what I was doing. He said my big black and whites just looked like Rei Hamon. He said, "You ought to just stop painting for a few years and get a job as a barman. And sort your ideas out."'[55]

Peter could be brusque and tactless on occasion, but he felt that Binney was at risk of burnout. In 1974, he counselled him to husband his energies: 'The main thing is for you to protect and develop your talent and not to be worried about all the pressure. Grow as an artist; plumb those seas and bring up those good, and possibly great paintings, that are there, within you.'[56]

In 1976, Peter negotiated a commission for Binney – a painting of the synagogue on The Terrace for Les and Milly Paris. The building, soon to be demolished to make way for a new motorway, had special significance for them: as Les noted, 'We were married there. I was barmitzvah'd there, my three brothers were barmitzvah'd there also.'[57] Milly recalled, 'At that particular time there was a lot going on in the Middle East, and the dove is a symbol of peace and that's why we asked Don to paint a dove in there, rather than a New Zealand bird.' She showed Binney how to do the Hebrew lettering on the building – 'I lent him one of my children's primers' – and the large work that resulted, *Old Wellington synagogue*, became one of their most cherished possessions.[58]

Two years later, Peter arranged another commission for the Parises – a family portrait by Toss Woollaston. When Milly first suggested the idea, Les was reluctant: 'He said, "Oh no, that's far too ostentatious." But then he must have talked to Jim Barr or Peter because the next thing it was all on.'[59] Woollaston flew up from Nelson several times to make sketches, arriving as the children came home from school. 'Our son Zalman asked, "How much longer, Mr Woollaston?" He wanted to be out, playing with his new bike! And Toss said, "Ten minutes" – and then Zalman started timing him.' Woollaston eventually painted two versions of the Paris family portrait, both of which they purchased.

On one occasion, Les took Milly to the gallery to see a Gordon Walters at lunchtime.

> We sat there on the chaise longue, and Peter said, 'I've got something to show you.' So he went into his storeroom (you were never allowed to go in there – never!) and he brought out three works on paper by Allen Maddox. And I looked at Les – I said, 'Oh I like that one!' We both loved it, and we said we would take it. And Peter said, 'Well, you've made history today!' And he explained: Maddox had painted the works in the early hours of the morning and brought them in

Peter at *Don Binney: Paintings and drawings*, July–August 1970, photographed by John B Turner

when he opened the gallery. Then we had come in and bought one. So the work had been created, shown and sold all in the same day!

Like other collectors, Milly noticed Peter's eccentricities. Often he seemed reluctant to part with a particular work, and sometimes he even tried to talk a client out of a purchase. He could be disconcerted by a buyer who pulled out their chequebook before he was ready to give his blessing to a sale. And his evasiveness was legendary. As Milly put it, 'Peter chose what you could buy, and when. Oh yes, he liked to

בית אל

have control and he wanted his works to go to good homes. Many times Les would ask him, "Is that painting for sale, Peter?" "Oh, I'm not sure," he'd say. He wouldn't give a definite yes or a no, he just left Les dangling.'

It's possible to see Peter's prevarication as a dogged attempt to retain control in a business in which buying power is generally the ultimate decider. In his world, money could *not* buy anything. Each artwork was special, a unique work by a gifted human being, and it deserved respect. Peter believed it was a privilege to own a work of art, and he reinforced that in his dealings with clients. It was a deeply held conviction that dated back to his early days as a collector.

But there is another explanation for Peter's behaviour. His very evasiveness, his apparent reluctance to sell – as if in defiance of his role – were also highly effective strategies. They enhanced the mystique of the works he proffered. Peter was nothing if not shrewd. Like any salesman, he was in the business of exciting desire, and he used all his skill, all his intelligence, all his theatricality in that quest.

Don Binney, *Old Wellington synagogue*, 1976
Acrylic on canvas
Private collection

NINE

Those koru works will be much sought after.

In 1971, Peter was dismayed to learn that Gordon Walters and his family were relocating to Auckland. Walters cited his dissatisfaction with the National Art Gallery and the lack of good touring exhibitions in Wellington as key reasons for the move. He felt he needed a more stimulating environment.

Peter felt the loss acutely, especially since his other artists were so dispersed around the country. Walters had been a mentor since Peter's early days on The Terrace – someone deeply versed in art with whom he could air his professional concerns. He often remarked on the debt he owed Walters: 'without his good advice I don't think I'd have got my act together'.[1]

There was a link on the domestic front as well. Although Walters was seventeen years Peter's senior, the two men had young families in the same decade, and baby clothes were often exchanged in the post, along with art books and magazines. Walters' first child was born in 1969 when he was nearly fifty, and a son followed in 1976; Peter's second daughter Olivia was born in 1974 and his son Dominic three years later. Neither man was a natural with small children. 'I don't think the child rearing role is really for me,' Walters wrote in 1974, 'and while I enjoy kids occasionally I am happy to see them grow up.'[2] Peter offered sympathy when Walters was on child-minding duty. 'I hope the "Batching" is not trying... I know what it is like when I have to do some "baby sitting" at home. After three hours I'm a bit of a cot case.'[3]

Walters was a meticulous and exacting artist, a ruthless editor of his own work who often destroyed paintings that left him unsatisfied. In person he was gentle, calm and modest, yet 'he was a very passionate

Gordon Walters, *Hautana*, 1970
PVA and acrylic on canvas
Auckland Art Gallery Toi o Tāmaki, purchased 1976

man'.[4] Peter saw him as a model of integrity and commitment, and a greatly underrated painter. 'Gordon is a very important artist,' he commented in the mid-1970s, 'whose real value is not even remotely appreciated here, yet. However, one day that will change. And those koru works will be much sought after.'[5]

Walters' second show at the Peter McLeavey Gallery in August 1971, just after his move to Auckland, comprised five large works priced from $500 to $600; three 'Koru' paintings and two based on a new motif derived from the Māori carving pattern, rau-ponga. 'They are all very good paintings,' Peter wrote to McCahon, 'difficult to sell, but I think I have a couple of people interested.'[6] Walters' own expectations were typically modest: 'I hope you can manage to shift one of them but it's not really a disaster if you don't manage it.'[7]

In fact, Peter sold three works: one to his friend in California, John Casserley, who bought it after seeing a colour slide; and another to some clients who took a long time to confirm the sale – as Peter noted, 'They spent some 2 months humming and hahhing; eventually hahhing the right way.'[8] The third was purchased by the young painter Ian Scott, who had begun to exhibit at the gallery in the previous year. 'It was a lot of money, 500 bucks – about a third of my salary as a teacher. But I felt Walters was the best artist in the country. My father thought I was mad. He said, "Why didn't you buy a section? You could have done something with that money."'[9]

After the show closed, Walters wrote to Peter, 'I am surprised that you sold so well. Would it be an impertinence at this stage to ask you *not* to sell the pale mauve painting with the new motif [*Hautana*, 1970; see page 146]. It does not sound as if you have anyone interested in it and as the painting is a particular favourite of mine I would like to keep it for the time being.'[10] It was not unusual for Walters to wish to keep works, or even change his mind about which could be sold. Meditating on his paintings was a part of his practice, and he was especially reluctant to release those that seemed to point the way to a new development.[11]

Walters' move to Auckland coincided with a period of change in the dealer-gallery world, and he soon became Peter's chief informant on his northern counterparts.

Since the mid-1960s, the Auckland scene had been dominated by two galleries: Barry Lett, which now had a wide-ranging stable of nearly sixty artists; and New Vision, run by Kees and Tine Hos, which

Peter at *Gordon Walters: Paintings*, August–September 1971

had started as a craft store in Takapuna before moving to His Majesty's Arcade in Queen Street.[12] In June 1972, the young Petar Vuletic, a collector and champion of abstract art, opened the Petar/James Gallery on the corner of O'Connell and Shortland streets.[13] His first show included the work of Walters, Milan Mrkusich and Richard Killeen – artists he felt had been marginalised by a critical preoccupation with issues of national identity. Vuletic described the local art scene as 'smug and complacent'[14] and, following the lead of the American critic Clement Greenberg, dismissed the idea that New Zealand art should have an identifiable character. Instead, he urged artists to become more aware of international developments. Vuletic and his gallery would become part of a wider critical reversal as the focus shifted from the inward-looking regionalism of the 1960s towards a greater engagement with contemporary art practice in the world beyond.

Peter followed the changes in Auckland with keen interest. To Don Binney, who was overseas, he reported, '[Vuletic] has taken Walters from New Vision, Mrkusich off Letts, Killeen off Letts; and in all cases he has exclusive Auckland rights... The whole operation has rocked a few boats. Still, while he is competition for me I feel that it is good – it will sharpen us all up. He has drive, charm, and a quality of business which should make him a success.'[15] Peter was a little disconcerted, however, by Walters' review of Vuletic's sleek, up-market premises:

> I have just come back from viewing the new gallery and am still feeling bowled over, it's a beaut! It is not an exaggeration to say that there is no better private gallery in N.Z. or Australia. It would be an understatement to say that it leaves the Barry Lett Gallery about 10 years out of date...
>
> I don't know what your orientation is going to be to this outfit, but it needs some careful thought. Work will be shown here in a style completely new to Auckland gallery goers, and the emphasis is going to be solidly on class.[16]

With competition increasing from Auckland, Peter was aware of the need to foster new markets in Australia. He had already sold a number of works to clients in Sydney and Melbourne, and was quietly cultivating a small network across the Tasman. Among them was an Anglican minister from Melbourne, Ian Brown, who met Peter when he visited Lower Hutt to stay with his sister in 1971. 'Wellington in those days was smaller and quieter and more like Australia was thirty years ago. I'd become obsessed by art by that time so I wanted to hunt it out, and I heard that a new gallery had opened in Cuba Street.'[17] Brown recalled his first impressions of Peter: 'At that time he was asthmatic, rather breathless, a trifle nervous, and I felt he was a bit out of place in New Zealand. Everything seemed to be rugby and sport, and I thought, You're a loner, you're the petunia in the onion patch.'

In June 1972, Peter flew to Sydney, staying with Tim Curnow, who was now managing the literary agency Curtis Brown. 'He is doing so well,' Peter reported back to Binney, 'and fits well into the Sydney culturati: afternoon tea with Patrick White, drinks on the lawn at Harry Miller's palatial Bellevue Hill duplex'.[18] Visiting the local galleries, he was taken aback at the prices – $12,000 for a painting by Fred Williams at the Rudy Komon Gallery; $13,500 for an Arthur Boyd at Barry Stern – and wondered if 'an anti-dealer backlash' was developing. Peter found the more contemporary work 'sterile and academic' and responded best to what he described as 'middle period stuff' – Godfrey Miller, Grace Cossington Smith, Arthur Boyd, Sidney Nolan ('his 40s stuff usually wears well') and Ralph Balson. He also spent a 'pleasant evening' with Brett Whiteley, one of Australia's young art stars, although he was unimpressed with Whiteley's exhibition at the Bonython Art Gallery.

In Melbourne, Peter stayed with an old flatmate and had an enjoyable week visiting galleries and seeing clients. He was even offered a partnership in the Rosalind Humphries Galleries: a good wage, a one-third share in the business, plus a commission on sales.[19] 'Interesting,' he told Binney on his return home, 'but the old pioneering spirit keeps me in Godzone. I love Toss and Colin and the other work too much. It's harder here; but those intangible rewards (of the spirit) are far more satisfying than those of flogging Sid Nolan out of South Yarra.'

Financially, Peter's trip was only a modest success, but its value lay in establishing the groundwork for future business. Interviewed for an article entitled 'Eyes opened in Sydney', he reported 'developing interest' in New Zealand artists. 'And he comes back open-mouthed at the success and salesmanship of dealers there – men like RUDY KOMON who have made a fortune for their artists and themselves.'[20]

Peter was still a long way from making a fortune. By 1973 he was able to support his small family from the commission on sales, but business remained unpredictable and his income fluctuated from year to year. He was encouraged, however, by the growing number of young people who trekked up the stairs at Cuba Street, and his ambitions were by no means limited to the capital. 'I've been down south visiting clients in Dunedin and Christchurch recently,' he informed Walters in 1975. 'It is becoming more and more apparent to me that I've got to travel more and more. The last two years I've managed to build up some good clients in Auckland, Christchurch and Dunedin and they are keen.'[21]

His time and energy were now stretched to the limit. 'It's jolly hard at times, just to keep "spiritually" and "emotionally" going,' he told Walters later in the year. 'The wear and tear; just the isolation of a man in a room selling dreams and the ups and downs that that entails. Sometimes I feel like a madam at a high class brothel. I make sure the girls sit and look good in an unstudied elegant way… It's a sort of private joke; a "tick" that keeps me from (sometimes) assaulting some poor unfortunate with a Killeen; something that keeps me sane.'[22]

The price of New Zealand art rose steadily during this period. In 1971, sales exceeding $500 accounted for just 18 percent of Peter's total; two years later, that figure had more than doubled. In 1972–73 he sold thirty-four works priced at more than $500: Woollaston was by far the top earner, with twelve, followed by Smither, Mrkusich, Binney and McCahon.[23] In the five years to 1976, Peter's income from the gallery doubled, but at the same time his overheads soared owing to inflation, his rent increasing by more than 300 per cent and the cost of advertising rising tenfold.

Among Peter's clients, Foreign Affairs and Victoria University continued to be key supporters, and corporate collectors were on the rise. Fletcher Holdings Limited in Auckland was the earliest corporate collector, buying colonial paintings in the early 1960s and moving into contemporary art later in the decade. Peter sold a few paintings to Fletchers, but his most important corporate client was closer to home – John Todd of Todd Motors.[24] Todd recalled, 'I was interested in trying to build up a collection of young New Zealand artists who were doing contemporary themes rather than an old-fashioned style of art. And Peter really educated me; he introduced me to so many of the artists. He'd ring up and say, "Come in, I've got something to show you." He'd persuade me that some of the things he was showing were good, even though it took a lot of self-persuasion to believe they were good.'[25]

One day, Peter offered McCahon's *Northland panels* to Todd. 'I thought they were wonderful, but I'd already bought a couple of paintings that year and I don't think we were making much money at the time. And we didn't really have a wall big enough to show them. I thought, Well, I'd better turn them down. And you know, I could have bought them for $16,000 – $16,000 for the lot!'

Todd supervised the installation of paintings in the company offices, but initially he met with a mixed reception. 'Oh, the response was terrible. I used to get groans: they'd say, "Oh no, what's he bought this time! That's terrible, that's not art." And I'd say, "Well, it's wonderful art and you're just going to have to have it." And I'd go back six months later to move the pictures around, and by that time the staff would be saying, "Oh, you can't take that, that's our painting!" They'd become attached to it.'[26]

The 1970s saw a growth in infrastructure for the arts, a development that owed a great deal to the third Labour Government, elected in a landslide victory under Norman Kirk in 1972. Kirk claimed that New

Zealand had come of age as a nation, and needed to cut its economic and cultural dependence on Britain. His government introduced new social legislation, promoted biculturalism and supported a more independent foreign policy; it also injected money into the arts as part of a strategy to strengthen national identity.[27] After years of underfunding, the arts council became a credible institution and a vital part of the local arts network.

Even more important for the growing profile of New Zealand art – and its market potential – was the rise of public galleries. 'The art gallery movement of this country is going through an unparalleled renascence,' the director of the Dowse Art Gallery David Millar claimed in 1972. 'Public support is snowballing, morale is high and professionalism has become its hallmark.'[28] Across the country, a new crop of energetic directors organised touring exhibitions by leading artists, and made the acquisition of contemporary art a priority. In the lower North Island, the regional galleries took the lead, notably the Govett-Brewster under directors John Maynard, Robert (Bob) Ballard and Ron O'Reilly; the Manawatu Art Gallery under Luit Bieringa; the Sarjeant in Whanganui under Gordon H Brown and Bill Milbank; and the Dowse under Millar and Jim Barr.[29]

The 1970s was also a crucial period for the National Art Gallery. In 1972, its funding for acquisitions was increased, and in the same year an Act of Parliament reduced the influence of the Academy of Fine Arts.[30] Young staff, such as artist Ian Hunter, helped to revitalise the programme, and a new National Art Gallery Council was invigorated by the appointment of Hamish Keith, Janet Paul and others.[31] It was not until later in the decade, however, that the gallery would become a truly vital force in the local art world.

In the commercial field, a new crop of galleries emerged, including the Brooke Gifford in Christchurch and the Bosshard in Dunedin.[32] Harry Seresin opened the Wellington Settlement Trading Company in Willis Street in 1973; it included a gallery, but like the Antipodes Gallery, established in 1970, it focused on pottery and crafts. Other venues in Wellington included the Osborne Gallery and McGregor Wright, both specialising in early New Zealand painting. Peter McLeavey and Elva Bett remained the only dealers for modern painting and sculpture.

In Auckland, meanwhile, Barry Lett left his gallery in 1975 to paint full time. Kim Wright and Rodney Kirk Smith took charge, and in 1976 the gallery was renamed RKS Art.[33] In the spring of 1974, Peter heard that a new gallery was to open in Auckland, backed by investor Barry Cramp and managed by Peter Webb in partnership with Bob Ballard, formerly of the Govett-Brewster.[34] The Barrington Gallery in Customs Street had four staff, spacious premises and the latest in luxury living – a shagpile carpet. It caused Peter some trepidation, as he confided to McCahon: 'It scares me a bit; way down here in Wellington I think that eventually I'll be put out of business by the "big boys".'[35]

Six months later he wrote again:

> Yes, the new Webb/Ballard Gallery certainly sounds flash. Elva Bett went to the opening and came back with the catalogue *Figurative Art Now*. Very impressive but I can't help thinking 'so what'; it's just a bit of window dressing. Very nice window dressing I must admit but surely when the chips are down it's the quality of the work that counts and for my money most of the stuff they have is rather thin. Still, good luck to them.
>
> One final point: I do think their heavy handed emphasis on the 'investment' angle can only backfire. Trying to sell art as an investment strikes me as against the whole spirit of art, and authentic art dealing. The *wanna make a buck* crowd are apt to vanish overnight as has happened in Aussie of recent times. There, investment only dealers and investment only buyers have come a real cropper and the Sid Nolans that they were selling at inflated prices have bottomed.[36]

Writing to Walters about the new gallery, Peter reflected on the modest scale of his own venture:

> With all that money muscle and the clout of Webb/Ballard it's going to put a new dimension into art dealing here.
>
> As I sit here, at 147 Cuba Street, typing this letter I can't help thinking that this is very much a third rate set-up. Mind you, I suppose when the chips are down a gallery is only as good as its stock; what's hanging on the walls.
>
> At present I have a 1965 McCahon; two superb 1974 Mrkusich Corner works; a cracking '68 Smither domestic; an elegant 'slip of an Ian Scott'; and two '74 McCahon landscape panels. It's a damn good show and looks great. Sales? Well not bad. A 1961 Mrkusich work on paper flitted out the door last Thursday; $420. It all helps.
>
> How are sales in the big smoke? Sort of curious. Actually, things are not bad here. It's always sort of slow but it is consistent and currently I've several good (hopefully) sales in the pipeline.[37]

Walters took Peter's query seriously, visiting the Barrington Gallery and noting all the sales, which he listed in his next letter. 'The whole show is booming with an unprecedented number of visitors. I think that

Gordon Walters, *Untitled*, c.1955
Gouache
Tim and Helen Beaglehole collection

Barrington will have their pick of NZ artists within 6 months if this keeps up. I think you will have to upgrade your gallery to cope with this sort of thing. But I am sure you can do it. This marks the beginning of a new era in art dealing. There is greater potential here than I had realised. These boys are pretty smooth and really mean business.'[38]

Ever cautious about expenditure, Peter replied, 'Yes, you are right about my upgrading this gallery. It needs a better address and more polished "gung ho" as they say. It will come. However, not just yet as the time is not right. The economic indicators suggest that prudence should be the rule.'[39]

Peter continued to watch the Barrington Gallery with some concern, and it did indeed make a mark on the local art scene for a short while. It was ahead of its time in sourcing exhibitions from overseas, such as *Jim Dine, works on paper*, but by the end of 1975 Barry Cramp had withdrawn his support and it closed in the following year.

Gordon Walters, *Study*, 1956
Gouache
Hocken Collections Uare Taoka o Hākena,
University of Otago

The Barrington Gallery was not the only casualty; in 1976 Petar Vuletic closed his doors, though he later reopened and held a number of important shows.[40] New Auckland galleries filled the gap: Peter Webb opened his own venue in 1976; Denis Cohn followed suit in 1977; and in that year a group of ex-Vuletic artists including Mrkusich, Geoff Thornley and Stephen Bambury established the Data Gallery as a cooperative. Walters was not involved with this venture and wrote to Peter, 'I'm sorry that Milan is going ahead with his gallery idea, I don't think it has much chance of success. My feeling is that Peter Webb is the best bet in Auckland.'[41]

Gordon Walters was never prolific and his output was limited during the early 1970s, especially in 1972, when he was a visiting lecturer at Elam. His third solo exhibition at the Peter McLeavey Gallery was not until 1974, and it was devoted to an exceptional series of gouaches produced during the 1950s. These were mainly preliminary studies for paintings, incorporating a wide range of stylistic influences from Oceanic art to European abstraction. As Walters noted, 'They were not shown at the time I did them because I considered the artistic climate to be too unsympathetic, if not downright hostile to abstraction.'[42]

Peter was aware of the historical importance of this show and wrote to alert key clients:

> These [gouaches] represent about 50% of the works that survived from the fifties. Gordon is a rigorous editor of his own work and some years ago he had a big clean out and destroyed a number of inferior works of the period. Recently he showed half the surviving works in Auckland and now we have the other half here. Only 10 of the works are to be sold. Any ten, but after we reach our 'budget' he will place the balance in safe keeping in his studio and hold them as a form of 'superannuation' for his future.
>
> All this suffice to say that they are collectors' items. Works of a period when the artist was working toward his present refined abstraction. They are of the highest quality. I can totally recommend them; they are *all* so good.[43]

Peter bought a work from this exhibition himself, and sold several to his regular clients, including *Study* to the Hocken Library and *Untitled* to Tim and Helen Beaglehole. His friend, the artist Peter Ireland, attended the opening. 'I was lucky to get one,' he recalled, 'but the work I bought was my third choice. It was $190, two weeks' salary for me at the time. My first choice was a "Koru" and I knew that was for sale only to a public gallery. Michael Hitchings at the Hocken snapped that up.'[44] Interest was so keen that Peter oversold his allocation and wrote to reassure Walters, 'I will try to keep the lid on it'.[45] He reported that the exhibition had made a considerable impact: 'Many clients suggesting to me that it was perhaps the best show I'd had this year. One went completely overboard; he felt it was the best show I'd ever had, period.' Walters was delighted.

Gordon Walters, *Painting J*, c.1974
Acrylic on canvas
Museum of New Zealand Te Papa Tongarewa, purchased 2006

In 1975, Ron O'Reilly, the new director of the Govett-Brewster, wrote to Walters to propose a national touring exhibition of his work. This institutional validation would have enhanced the artist's reputation, but he was reluctant, as he explained to O'Reilly:

> My real objections still concern the physical risk to my work in being shifted about the country. Granted that it would be well packed and insured, the fact still remains that even slight damage to an acrylic painting cannot be put right, and insurance does not bring back my painting... One only has to look at the condition of paintings of mine in public collections; with the possible exception of the Govett-Brewster Gallery, all of them are damaged or displayed in a dirty condition... As well as this, I question the value of touring an exhibition of my work. Outside of Auckland and Wellington, there is almost no interest, in fact often hostility to this sort of painting, and a temptation for the doodler to mark up the work.[46]

Early in 1976, Walters and his family moved to Christchurch so that Margaret Orbell could take up a position as a lecturer in Māori at the

Gordon Walters: Recent paintings, April–May 1976, showing (foreground) *Mokoia*, 1975, and *Maho*, 1973

University of Canterbury. In April, Walters held his fourth solo show with Peter, and all but two of the works represented a departure from his 'Koru' paintings. *Painting J*, for example, is constructed from carefully calibrated rectangular forms, which play on the opposition between positive and negative, figure and ground. In its economy and restraint it recalls Walters' early interest in European abstraction, but the image is in fact derived from a motif in Marquesan art.

Peter sold several works from this show, including *Mokoia* to Les and Milly Paris, but Walters vetoed the sale of *Maho*, a radically simplified 'Koru' painting, to Foreign Affairs. 'I like the work enough to want it to stay in the country where it can be referred to if the need arises. I'd let it go to a public gallery where it was looked after, but as this does not seem possible at present I prefer to keep the work. I hope this doesn't sound like megalomania but I consider the painting to be one of my best. You will still have the chance to sell the painting in the

The Walters family (from left) David, Gordon, Margaret and Anna at Camrose Place, Christchurch, photographed by Peter McLeavey, 1985

future and I won't turn down an offer that fulfils my condition.'[47] Soon afterwards he gifted the work to his wife.[48]

On the domestic front, Walters was occupied with house-hunting, as well as a new baby. '[I] have now almost decided to buy a builder's "spec" home modified to give me good studio space,' he wrote.[49] With the upheaval of moving and the building project, his output slowed. 'I don't know whether I can manage a show this year,' he informed Peter in March 1977. 'It depends on how much work I can produce. I would I think, prefer to wait until early next year.'[50] In July he sent an update: 'Lots of minor irritations going on here since you were down. The car has been giving trouble, the plumbing and other things in the house need attention and it's difficult to get people to do anything. I feel like blowing my top. However I suppose I should be thankful that my work is going reasonably well.'[51]

Walters was waiting for the release of a new print, *Tama*, commissioned by Peter Webb and produced by the artist and professional screenprinter Mervyn Williams at Helensville. 'Mervyn made a good job of the print,' he wrote in August, 'and I was pleased to have a reasonably good one at last.'[52] The edition sold out quickly, and Walters produced a number of prints in the following years. 'There is a big potential for good prints,' he told Peter, 'but the problem is to get a good professional printer to do the job and take the necessary pains. Otherwise one ends up with the usual rather crude artist produced job which is not good enough for me. Not after seeing the good American & British stuff.'[53]

Like Mrkusich, Walters generally set his own prices, with some input from Peter. After Peter wrote to tell him about his latest Mrkusich show in 1977 – 'Four biggies at $2700.00' – Walters decided that his prices should go up.[54] 'I want you to increase everything of mine you have in the gallery by 50% ... This is getting closer to a realistic price for my work; compared with almost anybody else my work has been ridiculously cheap and I have to do something about it ... I hope you don't find this too devastating but the days of cheap Walters are definitely over.'[55]

The success of Walters' next show, at the Peter Webb Galleries in April 1978, suggested that the new prices were no deterrent to sales. He reported to Peter:

> I thoroughly detest the whole business of exhibitions. Not that this one was so unpleasant, after deciding with Peter Webb to do the thing on a fairly modest scale it ended up as a rather lavish event, or so

it seemed to me. The trouble is that Peter and his cobbers are fairly lavish livers, given the slightest excuse ... I can't help feeling that one reason for the economic difficulties faced by Peter's outfit is his tendency to 'live it up' if one may use such a dated expression.

Anyway, I had a good time in Auckland, the show looked fairly good ... and just about everything has been sold. So this starts a new chain of worries ... I had intended to have unsold work sent down to you for my show in June but unless sales fall through there won't be anything to send ... Perhaps you would be happy with a show of only three paintings? This is actually all I have at the moment, but I am busy now on new work and it is going well ...[56]

Back in his studio, Walters made good progress, reporting in May: 'I'm hard at work on a new koru for my show with you. It shd be a good one. One more after this and I'll have enough ... I want the show to look good.'[57]

Walters exhibited eight works at the Peter McLeavey Gallery in July, including three large 'Koru' paintings – 'probably the best korus I have done,' he noted.[58] They were priced at $1800, a threefold increase since 1971, and all three sold to public collections: *Karakia* to the National Art Gallery, *Patere* to Foreign Affairs, and *Waiata* to the Dowse Art Gallery.[59] Neil Rowe acknowledged the importance of this show in a glowing review: 'Whatever direction Gordon Walters takes in the future, his achievement at this time is immense. He is the single most important formal abstract painter in New Zealand. It is high time we saw a retrospective exhibition of his work. The lack of such an exhibition has became a matter of serious neglect.'[60]

While grateful for the generous review, Walters was disconcerted by Rowe's suggestion. 'I hope nobody is going to take him up on the idea of a retrospective,' he told Peter. 'As you know I am at present much more interested in producing new work than in getting bogged down with that sort of nonsense. I am pleased with the way the show went and very much so with your efforts on my behalf. It was a thoroughly professional presentation of the work and as usual it was a pleasure to work with you. The gallery showed the paintings off to perfection.'[61]

Peter confirmed that he too was 'thrilled to bits' with the show. 'The quality was just so high. Yes, it was nice to sell, too. And, I agree with your remarks about the gallery ... These walls have been good to me, Gordon. It's 10 years now. Remember painting them, when we started? 10 years ago.'[62]

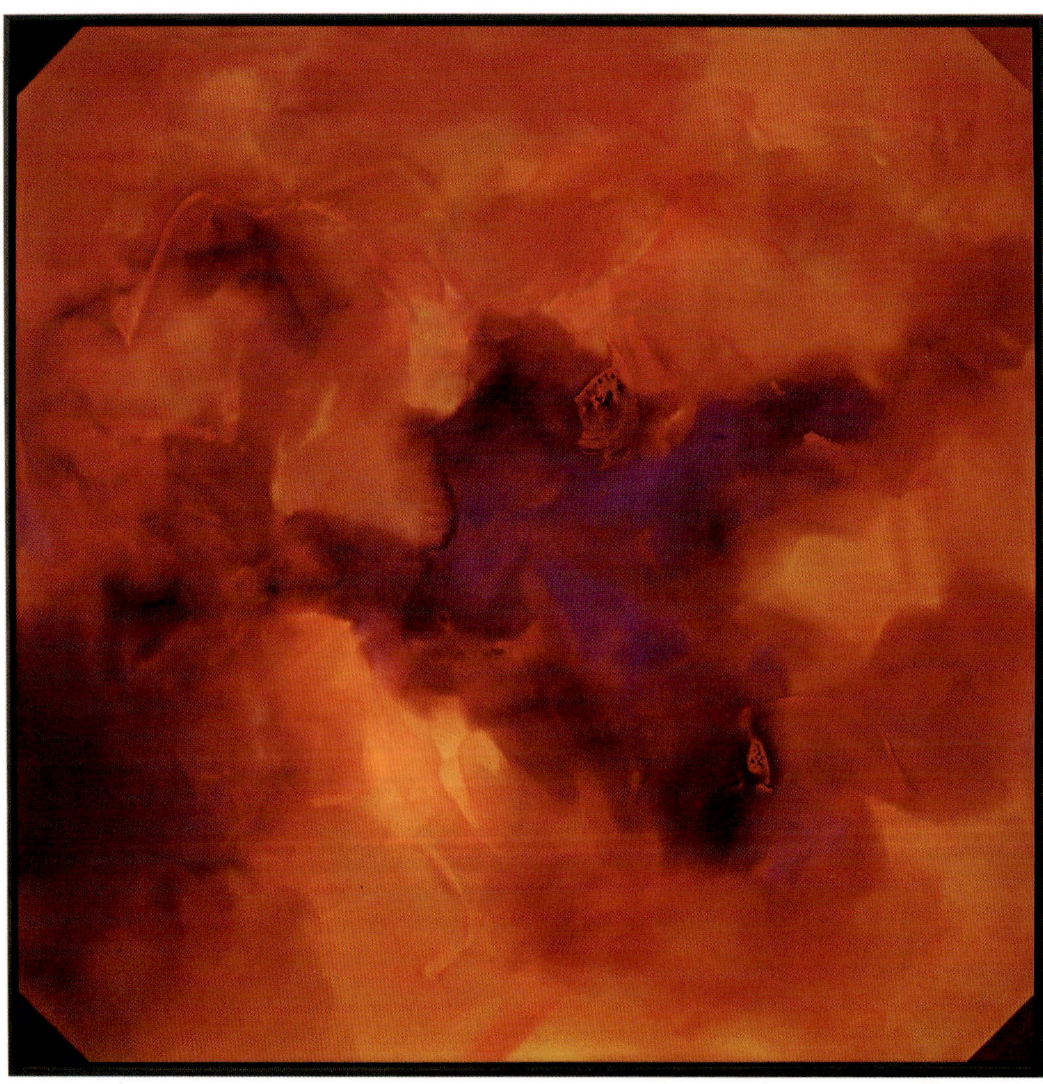

TEN

You want a landscape? Take a drive in the country.

Like his contemporary Gordon Walters, Milan Mrkusich made an early commitment to abstract art during the 1940s. He held his first solo show at the School of Architecture at the University of Auckland in 1949, and later became a full-time painter, supplementing his income with design commissions. As an uncompromising modernist, he worked in isolation from the main currents in New Zealand art and weathered a good deal of hostility as a result. Over time, this formal, courteous and self-contained man developed a certain prickliness. 'You want a landscape?' he asked an interviewer in 1969. 'Take a drive in the country.'[1]

Peter saw Mrkusich as a model of long-term commitment. '[He is] a very brave man who struggles on with virtually no encouragement. He is tough; you have to be. And he is bloody-minded.'[2] He once described Mrkusich as the most businesslike artist in his stable, but the two never developed a close personal relationship.[3] Partly this was a matter of circumstance: Mrkusich lived in Auckland and disliked flying, so he seldom attended his openings in the capital. Peter visited him several times a year, but that was generally the extent of their meetings. Nor did they write regularly: Mrkusich was not a prolific correspondent, and his letters are limited mainly to neatly typed lists of paintings.

Mrkusich's first show with Peter in September 1969 comprised a series of recent 'Corner' paintings: fields of saturated, luminous colour, with four small triangles sectioned off in each corner. These works signalled a more minimalist approach than his previous 'Emblems' and 'Elements' series, but they were also, in their subtle surfaces and quiet authority, among his finest paintings to date. 'I am sure you will

Milan Mrkusich, *Painting 1972*, 1972
Acrylic on canvas, 68 × 68"
Christchurch Art Gallery Te Puna o Waiwhetu, gift of the Ministry of Foreign Affairs and Trade, 2004

MILAN MRKUSICH
PAINTINGS

You are invited to attend
the opening of this exhibition at the
PETER McLEAVEY GALLERY, 147 Cuba St
at 6.00 pm on Tuesday
the 2nd of September 1969.

The exhibition can be previewed
from 1.00 pm on the same day.

Invitation to *Milan Mrkusich: Paintings*, September 1969

approve of the *look* of the exhibition,' Peter wrote. 'The complete whiteness of the gallery really makes the paintings sing.'[4] There was just one sale, but as he noted, 'your work is not very well known here and it does take a while'.[5] In fact, it would take some time to build an audience for such contemplative abstract painting in Wellington. Critic Gerda Bell summed up the general response in a largely negative review: 'The Peter McLeavey Gallery where the most advanced art is always encouraged probably "shocked" the ordinary visitor with the totally uncompromising "Paintings" by Milan Mrkusich.'[6]

In May 1971, at his second Mrkusich exhibition, Peter reported to McCahon, 'My gosh, I have had a lot of luck … On Friday a chap came in and purchased the large *Meta Grey No 3*, $900'.[7] This was the most expensive painting on display – the equivalent of nearly $12,000 today. At Mrkusich's exhibition of 'Corner' paintings a year later, Peter once again sold the top-priced work, *Painting orange*, this time to John Casserley. Aware of the value of overseas validation in a youthful market, he sent out a press release – omitting to mention that the buyer was actually a New Zealander. The *Evening Post* reported:

> A top price for a New Zealand abstract painting – $1050 – had been paid this week by an American collector, said a Wellington gallery manager, Mr Peter McLeavey, today …
>
> The overseas sale was part of an increasing trend by discriminating buyers to buy top New Zealand painters, said Mr McLeavey. Local prices, while increasing rapidly, were still far below those for comparable quality work overseas.
>
> 'It is part of an increasing recognition of the worth of our New Zealand artists overseas', he said.[8]

According to Hamish Keith, who noted the sale in the *Auckland Star*, it set a record for an abstract painting sold in New Zealand.[9]

It was in fact an excellent year for Mrkusich, capped by a major retrospective exhibition at the Auckland City Art Gallery.[10] In July, Peter sold *Painting 1972* (see page 164), a work closely linked to *Painting orange*, with thin washes of paint and radiant, atmospheric colour, to Foreign Affairs for $900. Other sales soon followed – to the Robert McDougall, the Govett-Brewster, Victoria University and private collectors.[11] In 1973, Peter reflected on the artist's fortunes in a letter to Philip Trusttum. 'I suppose every painter has his day; or time. As I think I have told you it was only two years ago that Mrkusich started to move. Until then his paintings had sold very slowly. Now it's a different story. There is a regular and consistent demand for his work, right across the board. It's terribly gratifying for Milan.'[12]

Mrkusich had nine solo shows with Peter during the 1970s, making him, along with Smither, the gallery's most frequently exhibiting artist. Sometimes he would show recent works alongside earlier ones from the same series; in 1975, for example, he exhibited a selection of 'Corner' paintings spanning the last seven years. Peter also held two exhibitions devoted to the artist's early work. In 1976, he showed *Collages and*

reliefs, 1959–1963; in 1979, he recreated Mrkusich's very first solo exhibition of June 1949.[13] It included his *Letter to the world manifesto* – a piece of avant-garde photomontage, which spelt out his convictions about the role and significance of art in society.

Peter regarded this show as a highlight of his programme to date. 'It is a real knockout,' he told Richard Killeen.[14] But apart from an extremely appreciative review by Neil Rowe,[15] he was rather disappointed by the response, as he reported to the young painter Jeffrey Harris:

> I wonder who I'm addressing with my gallery… A bit like an artist, I suppose. I mean I have this beautiful show of the first Mrkusich exhibition of 1949. And it is something; I tell you. But the whole thing is really just aimed at about 10 people. I mean that is the reaction. About 10 souls understand it and like it. Nothing is for sale; I put it up just for the fun of it. Or for the hell of it. I wanted to do it for Milan who needs all the encouragement and help he can get these days…
>
> Anyway, the point of this epistle, is just a wondering about what we do and why we do it and who we address. I sit here. The only thing that keeps me going is my deep belief in what I do. In the artists and the culture we have put down here, in these isolated shores.[16]

The exhibition was billed as an historical show rather than a selling exhibition, yet a note on the catalogue informed viewers: 'A number of these works are for sale. Prices are available on request.' At its conclusion, Peter wrote to Mrkusich, 'I'm sorry that nothing sold. There was a lot of interest but nothing came of it all in the end. I was tempted to hold several of the works back, for a couple of weeks (just to see if something would go), but, in the end, decided against that… I'm sure the show did a lot of good. Seeds were planted that will bear fruit, later. Several art gallery (public) directors viewed the exhibition. They were tempted, but didn't buy.'[17]

Indeed, seeds had been planted. Jeffrey Harris reported that Luit Bieringa, director of the Manawatu Art Gallery, had 'raved' about the exhibition: '[He] said the National Gallery should buy the whole show, lock, stock and catalogue.'[18]

Peter generally found it challenging to sell Mrkusich's work during the late 1970s. Partly this was because the artist set the prices at the

Milan Mrkusich: The first one man exhibition, June–July 1979 (a recreation of the 1949 exhibition), showing (top) *Letter to the world manifesto*, 1949, and (bottom, from left) *Constellation with Red*, 1946, *Constellation with Yellow*, 1946, and *Constellation with Blue and Yellow*, 1946

Milan Mrkusich in his studio, photographed by Marti Friedlander, 1978

upper end of the range – they were consistently higher than those of Gordon Walters, for example. But Mrkusich believed there was far too little compensation for the time and effort that went into his work. 'The situation is bad for artists,' he noted. '[T]he values for paintings in this country are very low. At most they are ten times lower than in the rest of the world. Every artist has his price and I don't think people should criticise him for the prices he asks. If a plumber can get $100 for putting in five feet of copper pipe, there should be relativity somewhere.'[19]

In 1977, Peter wrote to Michael Smither, 'I've a Mrkusich show on at present. It looks very good. The problem is the prices: $2700 a throw, just too high, I think. But it's a lovely show to have.'[20] To Mrkusich, he was more circumspect:

Milan Mrkusich, *Painting (blue)*, 1976
Acrylic on canvas, 71 × 68″
Museum of New Zealand Te Papa Tongarewa, purchased 1977 with Harold Beauchamp Collection funds

The exhibition looks beautiful. I've already had a number of people in and I have one of the works on paper ($390.00) under option. I know it's not that fantastic but it's a start. And, considering the present economic climate and the tightening liquidity situation I guess it's something.

Yes, things are getting very tight down here. The people look thrashed. The squeeze is on…

You have not heard much from me of late. Rest assured that I've been doing my best. It does seem that the more highly priced works (right across the board) are difficult to sell. But then it has always been the way. I'm doing my best.[21]

Peter's philosophy was to try to keep positive, to focus on his next opportunity to make a sale. 'That is the thing about this game, you always have to be thinking of next time. You always have to be optimistic and hopeful. And somehow keep the show on the road. Not only financially, but, perhaps more importantly, spiritually. Keeping the pecker up.'[22]

In 1979, he described a day at the office to Jeffrey Harris:

> I've had a busy time recently. I was here until 8.00 last evening with a client. Nothing resolved but he is interested in a couple of Mrkusich's I've in stock … I must now wait until Saturday week when he will come in again and we will sit and talk and then he will decide. Perhaps one; perhaps two; perhaps none. You just never know which way they are going to jump in this game. Yes, you need patience and, I hasten to add, nerves of steel. It's a bit like the shootout at OK corral; not a flicker of emotion or feeling must be shown when they are lining the art works up in their minds.
>
> And then, you let them have both barrels. You boot it home; you've made a sale.[23]

Peter often reflected on the essential vulnerability of the salesman, waiting for an opportunity to do business and wondering where the next cheque was coming from. He knew the highs and lows of the salesman's lot, and the way a sense of confidence, and even bravado, could dissolve in an instant. Many years later, he copied an excerpt from Arthur Miller's play, *Death of a salesman*, in his diary.[24] After Willy Loman commits suicide, his friend Charley tries to explain his death to his bewildered family:

> Nobody dast blame this man. You don't understand; Willy was a salesman. And for a salesman, there is no rock bottom to the life. He don't put a bolt to a nut, he don't tell you the law or give you medicine. He's a man way out there in the blue, riding on a smile and a shoeshine. And when they start not smiling back – that's an earthquake. And then you get yourself a couple of spots on your hat, and you're finished. Nobody dast blame this man. A salesman is got to dream, boy. It comes with the territory.

Writing to friends, Peter often compared himself to Willy Loman.[25] '[L]ife is never tranquil with me,' he remarked to John Casserley in 1978, 'and this year has proved to be more "animated" than most but out of it all I am still standing up, and, like our friend Willy Loman, I'm still out there working the block.'[26]

The financial demands of the mid-1970s became all the more acute for Peter as his family grew. After the birth of their daughter Olivia in December 1974, he and Hilary purchased a house in Hill Street in Thorndon, a short walk from the central city. Their new home was an elegant two-storey villa, just like the properties he had admired as a young man, but there was one crucial difference – this place was a wreck. The departing tenants, upset with the landlord, had gone on a rampage, smashing the gas heaters, breaking floorboards, even wrenching out the electric wiring. 'We moved into our new place last weekend,' Peter told Philip Trusttum in May 1975. 'My God, I thought as I surveyed the hovel, there is just so much work to do. Can I cope at this stage. Well, I guess I can. So we are in and are busy getting repiling quotes.'[27]

In the following months the bills accumulated, leaving Peter stretched to the limit. 'The last three months have been fraught with worry,' he told Woollaston in September. 'The house and all the money it has bled from my account has been a problem. And we are not out of the wood yet ... The general economic situation seems gloomy with people uncertain about things. I suppose the forthcoming election has also served to make people uncertain.'[28]

On 29 November 1975, the National Party, led by Robert Muldoon, came to power with an overwhelming majority – a great shock for Peter and Hilary. The third National Government was economically and socially conservative, and Peter had no time for its abrasive leader. 'We have a new P.M.,' he wrote to friends in England. 'A curious fellow, not only wants to take the bikes off the bikies but wants to send the Maoris back to their pahs. That is, if they are "stirrers and troublemakers". I suppose we will muddle through and survive. I don't know however for his attitude just seems so wrong.'[29]

In 1975, Peter became the sole dealer for Michael Illingworth, an artist who shared his disillusion with New Zealand politics. Outspoken and provocative, Illingworth was closely involved with the 1970s counter-culture and its philosophy of self-sufficiency and environmental conservation. 'I am painting a little world of my own in a little world of my own,' he commented. 'I am building a facade against the Established facade, the facade of hypocritical suburbia'.[30] Like Peter, he saw himself as an outsider and trailblazer, paving the way for the next generation. '[K]eep with it you are on the right track,' he advised Peter. 'The real dealer like the real painter has a hard climb but keep with it for the going gets better. The climb in this land is most hard as the track has never been explored before. We are explorers-pioneers.'[31]

Illingworth was vociferous in his demand for a better deal for artists and took every opportunity to air his views. In 1972, for example, he made a strong impression on a reporter from the *Dominion*.

> [Illingworth] wore new sandals. The rest of his clothes including his underwear had been given to him. He has no brushes, no canvas.
>
> He still has some paint.
>
> He is not destitute. Not quite. He is 40 – the age, he says, of hindsight and foresight – is married and has two young children. There is no vacuum cleaner in their Puhoi cottage, the sheets and towels are threadbare.
>
> He is quietly angry.
>
> He is an artist who has won the Frances Hodgkins Fellowship but he struggles to exist 'in a society in which the creative artist is given crumbs'.
>
> 'I am doing something which requires a high degree of aesthetic concentration but I am living in virtual squalor,' he said.
>
> 'I want to build an environment, my living must be like my work. They're inseparable ... But no one will give me mortgage money. Good God no. But if I were a plumber or a drainlayer it would be easy.
>
> 'I'm not an inveterate bum. It gets wearying ...'
>
> Illingworth's message is a cry from the heart of all artists:
>
> 'Professionalism in art is not tenable in New Zealand. The nation must pay the price for its culture; it has to learn that culture is a necessary part of the national life.' ...
>
> He says the Government and the Arts Council should get into tune with the creative endeavour in this country so that resources could be channelled in the right direction.[32]

Always ready with a scheme to promote the arts, Illingworth's ambitions often had a utopian quality. In 1972, he had written to the chairman of the arts council, Bill Sheat, with a vision for a national art centre – something 'vastly superior' to the soon-to-be-completed Sydney Opera House. 'I know a new National Library is to be built. Such a complex could be expanded to include future concert halls, theatres, art museums and halls where philosophers, poets, mathematicians, actors, painters, musicians, scholars and intellectuals can mingle at need or will. The footballers have their football fields, the racing men their turf so why not we our School of Wellington'.[33]

Michael Illingworth at work on *Painting*, 1979,
photographed by Marti Friedlander, c.1978

Illingworth had begun to exhibit in 1961, after a period of informal study in London. He went on to become one of the mainstays of the Barry Lett Galleries – and to earn himself a certain notoriety. In 1965, his painting of a naked Adam and Eve sparked a complaint of obscenity, and the publicity continued for months.[34] Then, at his 1967 exhibition at Barry Lett, a single collector purchased nearly all the paintings at the opening – an unprecedented event in the New Zealand art world.[35] 'It seems marvellous that you had such a wonderful stroke of luck,' Peter wrote. 'The publicity angle was well handled and the country was completely covered with it making the National news at 11.15 the same night. It seems that everyone from Kaitaia to Invercargill is talking and the consensus of opinion is that it is the biggest thing that has ever hit the local art world'.[36]

Peter showed Illingworth for the first time in June 1969, by arrangement with Barry Lett: eleven works, priced at $95 to $450, including landscapes, still lifes, and portraits with a strong sense of social satire.[37] Peter was pleased to sell six, and delighted to make a sale to a visiting Australian, Robert Ypres, the director of the Native Art Gallery in Sydney.

By the time Illingworth exhibited again three years later, the works – priced by him and Barry Lett – were much more expensive, with a top figure of $2000. Peter managed to sell only one, much to Illingworth's disappointment. He and his family had been evicted from their rented cottage at Puhoi, and he had hoped a successful show would enable him to buy some land of his own. He wrote to Peter, 'It's that European thing I can't get out of my veins that an artist who paints well can expect to sell well ... This of course will come about in this land one day and I suppose we must console ourselves by the realisation that we are helping bring this about. In my case it is a poor consolation at the moment'.[38]

By the autumn of 1973, Illingworth had found a property at Coroglen on the eastern side of the Coromandel ranges – 'the place of my dreams', as he reported to Peter.[39]

> Let me describe the block. 250 acres 50 only cleared ... with 2 boundaries being rivers clear and stony that one can put one's head into and drink as they flow only from unsullied native bush ... The property is right at the foot hills of the range and is absolutely safe from the progress vandals as all surrounding land is owned by state and is mostly Nat. Forest park ... The river flats and house area have sun all day and both valleys get plenty. I could go on for pages but let me say it's a bit of unspoilt N.Z. and seems totally unspoilable in the future and all for the price of $18,000.

Illingworth had purchased the land with two investors, one of whom was Barry Lett, but by the end of the year he had bought them out – 'skinned me of my last cent', he informed Peter.[40] He was now burdened by a hefty mortgage, though for the moment the situation seemed positive. Peter wrote encouragingly, 'My feeling is once you have this farm question settled we are going to see some very fine work coming from you. And don't be over concerned about marketing. I'm confident that our star is coming. You are one of the best painters we have and I know that the tide is shortly going to run in your direction.'[41]

Initially, Illingworth was delighted by his new life. 'The farm is going very well,' he told Peter late in 1974. 'I got a very high lambing for this area 100% and have a fine flock according to expert eyes.'[42] A year later, however, he was becoming frustrated by the constant grind. 'I found my eyes wandering to a half finished work the other day and a great burst of anguish welled up in me and I actually cried out "God I wish I could paint". I manage to displace such bouts of anguish with hope. There is not a place here suitable for me to set out my gear even to work on little things but I know that a studio will come.'[43] Illingworth had longed for the security of a settled home for himself and his family, but it had come at a high price. In the following years, his struggle to make the farm viable would consume his energy and leave little time for his meticulous, labour-intensive painting.

In September 1975, Peter wrote to Walters, 'I've got a lovely Illingworth show coming up next week. Some crackers.'[44] The artist had produced very little in the previous years, so the show consisted of eight paintings dating from 1962 to 1971, including *As Adam and Eve* – the work that had caused a brouhaha a decade earlier. Peter described the opening: 'It was really very pleasant with Mike being the perfect artist; moving around making sure everyone spent some time with him. He is 101% professional in that way ... The result, 5 paintings sold.'[45]

Illingworth's exhibition coincided with a visit by the celebrated American artist Kenneth Noland, as Peter reported to Walters:

> Yes, I met Mr Noland. Unfortunately, I did not see him for nearly as long as I would have liked. It seems that he knew of Ray Thorburn and Ray 'collared' his eminence with the result that I only saw him for a couple of minutes late on Friday.
>
> The whole business was further complicated by the fact that Thorburn and Noland ... walked in right in the middle of a 'transaction' ... Perhaps my most valued client was shaping up to a $1600 Illingworth. Well I couldn't chat with the two artists. It was business as usual. I missed a Noland but sold an Illingworth.

The valued client was Les Paris; the painting was *As Adam and Eve*, which again attracted attention, provoking a spate of angry letters to the editor when it was reproduced in the *Listener*. Illingworth defended his painting: 'The naked and unashamed Adam and Eve are beyond the comprehension of people with clothes hang-ups.'[46] He also explained that 'each and every one of our ancestors' was the product of phallic energy – but that observation was cut from the published letter, much to his disgust.[47]

The Parises were unfazed by the fuss over their new painting. Milly recalled, 'We had it in our bedroom for a long time because we thought

Michael Illingworth, *As Adam and Eve*, 1965
Oil on canvas
Museum of New Zealand Te Papa Tongarewa, purchased 2012

it might offend someone. But when the 1990s came, I said to Les, "Come on, it's got to come out. I think people are more broadminded now."'[48]

From his early days in business, Peter was active in selecting work for his gallery. Rather than waiting for the artists to send their latest work, he preferred to travel the country, checking on how it was developing. This was important in controlling the quality of his stock, but it was also a means of building relationships with his artists, and fostering mutual trust and confidence. 'I wanted to make sure I was getting the good stuff and I also needed to have meat and potatoes with the artist, I needed to feed from them, talk to them.'[49]

Peter always found his visits to Illingworth particularly sustaining, and in 1977 he described a trip to Coroglen for Gordon Walters:

> Wednesday will see me on a NZR bus Coroglen bound. I'll change at Thames. Usually 40 minutes to kill which is just about long enough to go up, and down, the main drag. From memory, Pollen Avenue.
>
> At 2 o'clock it's all aboard the Whitianga bus which then zig zags its way across and through and around the peninsula. At 5 it's downtown Coroglen where Michael will meet me and we will nick into the pub for a quick one before we head out on the Tapu Road.
>
> The Illingworth compound is at the base of the hill and, in fact, it's the last farm house before you climb to nowhere. He always has a good fire and the logs burn hot and bright and we have a seat and drink cider.
>
> Dene, his wife, is a good cook and the food is good solid country fare: venison, wild pig, kumaras, silver beet, mushrooms, and sometimes pauas. Michael likes to talk long into the night. His cheery nature and warmth is good to be with.
>
> Sometimes he rages against the slings and arrows of fortune but usually his pet 'hates' are dispatched with a gentle irony.[50]

By now Illingworth had begun to build his long-awaited studio and had high hopes of being able to paint again. In 1976, he had written to Peter: 'I work 18 hours a day and my studio has a roof on. I sleep inside the poles beneath the roof on a temporary floor when the night is fine... It is like it would be sleeping in some of the small temples I have seen in Greece.'[51] But as the months passed, he was unable to marshal the money and time required to finish it. The project lagged on, half-completed, and he dubbed it the 'Monument to Frustration'.[52]

By the late 1970s, New Zealand was experiencing the worst recession since the Great Depression, fuelled by the oil crisis of 1973 and Britain's entry into the European Economic Community. Illingworth's situation was increasingly difficult: 'I have to have a sale my position is desperate,' he wrote in the autumn of 1977. Peter sent an advance against future sales and tried to reassure him: 'I do my best to sell your work. Believe me and don't judge me too harshly if, sometimes, things are slow. I love your work. And want others to share its mystery; its magic.'[53] Above all, Peter cautioned him, 'You must not let the Monument to Frustration destroy your spirit. I know it galls you to see it flapping in the cold north wind but we will get it built. One day. I pray for that day. When you are properly housed and your belly and heart are not ground down by the pedestrian. We want that Illingworth spirit to hum its song again. And whistle, too. A song that unifies us with that lifeforce'.[54]

On 3 August – his birthday – Illingworth was much relieved by a cheque for the sale of a painting, *A gent of consequence*. 'I was away with dawn on my lamb beat,' he told Peter:

> Stars clear over the ranges and a yellowing of the sky's base down the valley. Each paddock I visited had a new crop of lambs – fine – fit – newborn. The sun vanquished the bright frost by breakfast time and the bellbirds sung. My kids gave me presents of stones from the river wrapped up with lots of little pieces of paper into mummies. We missed the school bus and I had to drive them down so I got my mail and a letter from you and news of the sale of Gent of C. I faced toward Wellington, and offered you my 'thank you' loud and clear.[55]

Illingworth had begun to paint again, and one of his new works was included in his fourth exhibition with Peter in April 1978.[56] Reviewing the eleven works, most of which were from the late 1960s and early 1970s, Neil Rowe posed a question: 'How are we to consider the work of a painter who to all intents and purposes stopped painting several years ago? Will he start painting again? … The most recent work … does nothing to persuade me that Michael Illingworth has anything new to say.'[57] Peter was disappointed to sell only two works from the show.

By August 1978, Illingworth's studio was nearly finished, as he reported to Peter. 'It is a splendid building and fulfils all the hopes I had of it when I drew the plans. Light is first rate – spatial quality fine and we have added an annexe with a sleeping dreaming loft. That can be your bedroom. It is a most satisfying feeling after so many months to have the reality in place of the dream.'[58]

Soon Illingworth was in full flow, working on pictures that had remained unfinished since the early 1970s. 'I have one picture under way in front of me now I am thrilling myself with brush and colour in fine light and functional surroundings … I work long hours with joy with my hand and eye ever more sure day by day. I go through my days and have the thrill of a satisfied man at the end of each.'[59]

Two weeks later he wrote again:

> I have resurrected a large unfinished canvas from those Puhoi days. It goes well and caused a visiting stock agent who viewed it to

Michael Illingworth, *Taniwha*, 1984
Oil on board
The James Wallace Arts Trust, purchased from Illingworth's solo exhibition at the Peter McLeavey Gallery, 1984

> quiver with excitement. I work on small new pictures also. I neglect the farm. I have little enthusiasm for my sheep...
>
> I started this letter in morning – it is now late of night. I have worked steadily at my picture this day and with a mind full of things to write to you of my appreciation of the way you handle my work, of the good feeling it is to have new pictures for you, of Sir Charles Lock Eastlake, of the Tui song and the sunset, of the loneliness that is much my lot, of music and many things.[60]

Peter replied in early November:

> I'm so excited to know that you are painting. I have even pencilled a spot in for you at the latter part of next year.
>
> People have not forgotten you. If anything, they are acutely interested in what you are doing. The potency of your art is such that it can carry so deeply into their hearts and minds.
>
> It is probably best to hold the works there. Wait; wait; until I come and visit you in February... I look forward to then. My heart leaps with excitement.
>
> Love to you all
> Peter.[61]

ELEVEN

One day, they will eat their hats that they didn't buy.

While Illingworth was dogged by critical uncertainty, the late 1970s was a time of increasing recognition for another artist in Peter's stable, Ian Scott. Peter had first encountered his work at the Barry Lett Galleries in 1969 when his paintings were showing alongside those of his friend and fellow Elam graduate, Richard Killeen. He visited Scott soon afterwards and scheduled an exhibition for the following year. Open and affable, Scott soon established a rapport with Peter. 'As soon as I met him I realised he was a totally eccentric guy. But we got on really well.'[1]

Scott exhibited six large, eye-catching paintings in June 1970 – pop-art-inspired images of leggy bikini-clad girls cavorting in a stylised Auckland landscape. It was his first solo show in a dealer gallery, and he was apprehensive and exhausted. 'Those paintings were a massive amount of work. We didn't learn how to paint in a realist style at art school, and I had a real job, trying to figure it out for myself. I was young and fit, but it was a huge psychological strain doing them – my whole life was devoted to it.'

Peter sold three works from the show, much to Scott's surprise, and Tim Beaglehole purchased one of the finest, *Jump over girl*, for Victoria University.[2] Colin McCahon, who was taking an interest in his former student, commented, '[D]elighted about Scott, I think him very good also the tougher proposition, Killeen.'[3] Killeen had driven Scott to Wellington for his opening, and both men had stayed with the McLeaveys in their flat in Hataitai. On the first evening, Peter took them to meet Gordon Walters – the beginning of a long and important friendship between the three artists.

Ian Scott, *Jump over girl*, 1969
Oil on canvas
Victoria University of Wellington Art Collection

It took some time for Peter's relationship with Killeen to become established. 'I didn't know what to do about Killeen at first,' he remarked much later.[4] It was not unusual for Peter to take years to consider showing an artist, visiting their studio every few months and maintaining a lengthy correspondence before finally making a decision. For the artists, the long wait could be unsettling and even disturbing – and some never got the shows they had hoped for. Peter has described the process like a courtship:

> You go to a party one night. You notice a lovely woman over the other side of the room. You meet her. You have a fag together outside. You find out she likes Debussy. You like Debussy. How about we go out next Friday after work for a drink? You go to the pub. She has a Guinness, you have a Pimms... You book the classiest restaurant in town. And so on.
>
> But then sometimes it doesn't work. You think, oh gosh, I didn't realise her skin had that problem. And why does she rave on about Rodney Hide? And then there's the painful parting of the ways. But if the courting process goes well, you commit. Wedding bells.[5]

Peter liked to play up the image of a marriage for journalists, but the analogy gives an insight into how he saw his role. Like any dealer he expected his artists to abide by certain rules: no studio sales or sending works to auction, and all commissions to be passed through the gallery. But he never had a formal contract with anyone he represented, and business, while important, was just one aspect of the relationship.[6] Peter needed to feel a personal connection to the artist and excited about their work; indeed, it was his ability to remain alert and engaged that was the key to his gallery's longevity. 'He's like an artist in that respect,' Killeen noted. 'It's about keeping yourself interested; that's the most important thing.'[7]

It was not until 1972 that Peter began to represent Killeen, including two works in a group show in January. He reported that they had created a good deal of interest, and Tim and Helen Beaglehole had bought one for their collection. So far, so good – but later in the year he learnt that Killeen had reached an agreement with Petar Vuletic, who would have exclusive rights over his work. 'This would mean I'd be unable to obtain work from your studio,' Peter wrote. 'I'd have to go through a middleman; a fellow art dealer who would naturally want to hold your best work in his stock. My freedom of selection would be lost. From all this discontents would spring.'[8] Because of these difficulties, he continued, he felt he could no longer represent Killeen. But he ended his letter on a

Ian Scott at Marsden Avenue, Balmoral, Auckland, with (in background) *Sky dash*, 1969–70, photographed by Peter McLeavey, 1984

positive note: 'Thank you for letting me handle your work over the last year. I will be in touch when next I'm in Auckland.'

By 1974, Killeen had ended his exclusive agreement with Vuletic, and in March he wrote to ask if Peter was interested in showing his work.[9] The reply came immediately: 'I would love to handle it and exhibit it.'[10] Peter wasted no time in getting works into stock, and by June he had sold Killeen's *Blue panel* to Todd Motors. He told the artist that this sale was a 'good one', as the painting would be reproduced in the company's magazine, *Network*, and a reproduction fee paid.[11]

Killeen held his first solo exhibition with Peter in April 1975. The twelve works, priced from $75 to $600, were mainly from the 'Comb'

Richard Killeen: Recent paintings, April 1975, showing works from the 'Comb' series, 1973–74

series, in which a delicate zig-zag motif creates an optical 'shimmer' not dissimilar to that of Gordon Walters' 'Koru' paintings. Refined and highly sophisticated, they also had a local reference, as the motif was derived from traditional Polynesian combs.[12] Killeen exhibited works from his 'Constructivist grid' series as well, one of which was purchased by Les and Milly Paris and another, *Tukutuku*, by the Manawatu Art Gallery.[13] 'I am very pleased with the way that the exhibition has gone,' he told Peter. 'You hung the whole thing very well. I don't gauge an exhibition's success on the number of sales but more on my own feelings about it. To sell something though is so much the better as I can certainly do with the money.'[14] Killeen had at that time no real prospect of earning a living from art, and supplemented his income with a part-time job working for his father's sign-writing business.[15]

Like many of Peter's artists, Killeen usually stayed with the McLeaveys when he visited Wellington, and he was struck by Peter's knowledge of artistic and literary events abroad. 'When I first started going there he was getting the *New Yorker* and the *New York Review of Books* and I started getting them too. His library was incredible, he was always sending overseas for books. It was always interesting to see what was new.'[16] The two men formed a strong and long-lasting relationship – but it took time, as Killeen recalled. 'One of the things you learnt was that if you wanted to get on, then you let him do his thing, and he would let you do yours. He hung the shows, for instance, that was his area, but he didn't interfere with what you were doing. He never interfered. I mean some dealers would say, "Oh, do some small ones, because I can't sell the big ones". He would never do anything like that. So you really learnt early on that, okay, this is what he does, this is what I do.'

Over the years, Killeen came to appreciate Peter's attitude towards business. 'It's not about the money, it's sort of like, if you take care of the whole art thing, and the attitude, then the money will take care of itself.' He also appreciated Peter's unstinting support. 'I can remember talking to him on the phone and saying, "No one's going to like what I'm doing at the moment. No one will get it." And he said, "I will." He was always supportive. I mean, you need those people. He was really acting out the part that the culture, in theory, would play. He was like one of those people you get overseas, the Leo Castellis [the New York art dealer] or whatever, who played that crucial role... he was behind it all, with that drive.'

By the 1970s the critical preoccupation with 'New Zealandness' in local art was on the wane but, even more significantly, painting was now only one of a range of art forms. This was the decade of post-object art, which focused on environments, installation and performance, and at Elam a new group of artists was emerging in the hothouse atmosphere fostered by the influential head of sculpture, Jim Allen.

With so little opportunity to see contemporary international art in New Zealand, the exhibition *Some recent American art* at the Auckland City Art Gallery in 1974 was much anticipated. It showcased the work of those who were known locally through art magazines and had already been highly influential: Robert Morris, Carl André, Donald Judd, Sol LeWitt, Robert Irwin and others. Ian Scott reported to Peter, 'Of course up here everyone has been knocked out by this American show, it's unbelievable really seeing a lot of the best stuff from the last few years, all at once!... [T]o me at the moment it seems to make painting images look like a pointless activity. It makes you realise,

Ian Scott, *Auckland morning*, 1974
Acrylic and enamel on canvas
The James Wallace Arts Trust

also, the vast range and strength of American Art… Anyway I suppose we just have to plod on here and hope for the best.'[17]

The questions that occupied young painters such as Scott and Killeen were not easy ones. In a time of rapidly proliferating art movements, how to make paintings that were 'contemporary' in an international sense, yet went beyond slavish dependence on American models? And how to make contemporary painting that took account of local conditions – an art that was relevant in New Zealand? In some ways, this generation had an advantage, as Scott was aware. 'Milan [Mrkusich] always said to me, "You boys had it easy. When I was starting out there were no dealer galleries and hardly any buyers." Rick and I were ambitious, we had lots of energy, we were obsessed about art, but we had a different set of problems.'[18]

For Scott, the very qualities of American abstraction posed a challenge. 'It was so highly controlled and formally sophisticated – I wanted to loosen it up, to find a way through that.'[19] In his 'Sprayed stripe' works of 1973–75, he adopted a spray can – a commercial artist's tool – to paint a series of parallel coloured stripes on an off-white ground. The method sounds precise and deliberate, yet works like *Auckland morning* are luminous and delicately beautiful. The titles refer to the landscape of west Auckland, and the paintings, although uncompromisingly abstract, can be read as a distillation of its colours and forms. As Scott remarked, 'I'm influenced by the things I see and experience around me every day... I happen to like the suburban landscape, with its neatness, bright colours, clean edges – an area of white weatherboards, a touch of bright red curtain to one side, green hedge in front and blue sky above'.[20]

Peter had great confidence in Scott's new work, and was pleased with his exhibition in July 1974 – the first showing of the 'Sprayed stripe' paintings. The six works were priced from $350 to $500, but there were no sales, much to his disappointment. He wrote to the artist, 'I would like to put on another show next year. I think that it's important to keep the continuity and to keep letting people see what you are doing.'[21]

In April 1975, Scott exhibited twelve small oils on paper in a joint exhibition with Woollaston, but again there were no sales. 'I'm afraid one becomes pretty philosophical after a time in art,' Peter reported. 'Not cynical, not despondent. No, just acceptance... One day, they will eat their hats that they didn't buy. It will be like the early McCahon shows. During the 40s just nothing sold. All those works that today one could get several thousand dollars for just sat on the walls, unsold. Unsold at 5, 10, and 15 guineas.'[22]

Scott replied:

> [Y]ou're right of course about needing to be philosophical in connection with art, but I think one can be philosophical & objective about the whole business and at the same time tired & fed up with the whole thing...
>
> I haven't really done much painting this year yet... I can't really see that it's much use doing more sprayed stripe ones, and am a little tired of being under American modernism. There's just got to be some basic answer to the problem of our relation to world art.

> I suppose it will only be solved when a lot more people do a hell of a lot more painting.[23]

Killeen was also reviewing his work and his relationship to contemporary American practice. 'I've done a number of large new paintings (approx 6'×6'),' he wrote, 'although I feel that I am only beginning to get back into it. I am trying to widen my horizons beyond the cool American formalist abstraction that everybody seems to be preoccupied with.'[24] In September 1975, he reported on the visit of Kenneth Noland, whom Peter briefly encountered in Wellington:

> Nice guy – seemed to quite like our painting... It doesn't matter what he thought anyway, just to see him & find that he too was quite ordinary & limited like everyone else was good for morale. We knew as much of what was going on in the 'Art World' as he did which was interesting. There was a bit of political shuffling and jostling for position on art ideologies, but apart from that it was all rather pleasant...
>
> We told Noland about you, but he already had your address from [Clement] Greenberg which, as far as Noland is concerned is about as good a testimonial as you can get.[25]

In December, Killeen was awarded an arts council grant, enabling him to visit galleries in the United States, and Peter wrote to Greenberg in New York to provide an introduction.[26] After describing a recent touring exhibition by the American photographer Edward Weston, he moved on to a subject of mutual interest – popular television shows:

> Actually I'm someone who spends more time than I should watching TV. Programmes like Hawaii Five O and Mary Tyler Moore and Sonny and Cher are my favourites. It's the fantasy, the slick scripts, and the music that gets me...
>
> It's an interesting thought actually when you compare the penetration of music and art (respectively) here in New Zealand. For musically we get the best of artists touring... this year we have musical performers as diverse as Neil Diamond, the Kontarsky brothers, the Stuttgart Chamber Orchestra, Cleo Laine, and Roxy Music, and a visit threatened by Alice Cooper. But when it comes to art we are virtually starved...
>
> The only way out is for more Government help in importing and touring shows. And that is unlikely. We have just elected a new Government that is of the right, and they are pretty hard nosed when it comes to expenditure on the arts.

The only way for painters here to see the best art is to travel out of New Zealand. Later this year a young painter and friend of mine is travelling to the United States ... I normally would not presume to suggest that he call on you as I am conscious of the demanding life you must lead. However, if you will be in the United States during July/August/September, and would be happy to meet Richard Killeen I'd appreciate it.

And one day I'll visit America. When, God knows. The demands of running my gallery and family seem to prevent the accumulation of any excess cash to enable travel that far.[27]

Killeen exhibited with Peter in July 1976, just before he and his partner Margreta Chance left for New York. He had recently won the prestigious Benson and Hedges Art Award, judged by the Australian curator Daniel Thomas, for his painting *Frog shooter*, and this fuelled publicity for Peter's show.[28] Like *Frog shooter*, the eight works in the exhibition marked a shift from the cool and restrained 'Comb' paintings to a more exuberant and playful style. In the witty *Some of his parts*, Killeen toys with the conventions of painting, arranging 'mini-Killeens' – pictures-within-pictures – as well as insects and other motifs on canvas.[29] This was one of Peter's most successful shows in an excellent year, with eight sales: buyers included the National Art Gallery, Foreign Affairs, Victoria University and private collectors. In a rave review, Neil Rowe described Killeen as 'one of the more exciting and original painters to have emerged in the last ten years'.[30]

After Killeen's departure, Ian Scott moved into his house in Epsom. Peter had enquired about another show in 1977, but Scott was unsure if he could fully commit himself:

I've done very little painting this year, and am having a hell of a struggle getting going again ... Also April is likely to be a difficult time, because that's when Rick is due back more or less, so I might find myself out in the cold with all my paintings. Another problem is that the cost of putting on shows, the price of canvas – paint – framing materials, timber for stretchers etc has risen so much ... I just can't see quite how I'm going to manage a show. Still – Peter, I guess I shouldn't grumble about these things to you, as you've helped me so much with freight & framing bills ...[31]

A few weeks later, he reported on Killeen's travels: '[Rick] mentioned that he hadn't seen a single stripe or pattern making exhibition in N.Y. – shows just how far out of it we are – and also that if he lived & worked there he'd feel much more pressure to work in the present styles.'[32]

Richard Killeen, *Some of his parts*, 1976
Acrylic on canvas
Tim and Helen Beaglehole collection

Writing to Killeen, Peter reported on the local art scene, mutual friends and recent sales. The passing of his fortieth birthday in September 1976 had sparked a period of depression and soul-searching, as he confided: 'I made a sort of resolution to enjoy life more and not take myself so darn seriously. Someone said to me I took *things too seriously*. And I do. Well from now on I am going to have fun.'[33] He elaborated on the theme in a letter to John Casserley:

I haven't yet quite decided what fun is, but I'm trying. I'm such a stick in the mud. So serious. I want to be able to tell a few jokes. Tickle a few ribs. Know what I mean? No? Well I guess it must be something to do with reaching forty because all these thoughts have been skedaddling around inside since 21st September…

Another spin off from the new fun loving me is my desire to buy a nice T shirt and perhaps wear jeans. I saw a beaut in the shop the other day. It was a dark blue/green job with the words SUPERBITCH… I'm going to buy one. I guess you must have some beauts over in the US. Something that combines I CHOKED LINDA LOVELACE with the mean polish of DANIEL PATRICK MOYNIHAN IS A FAIRY. Know what I mean?[34]

While Killeen travelled on to England and Europe, Scott worked on his new 'Lattice' paintings in his friend's studio. He was relieved to hear that Killeen's trip might be extended – 'this will give me time to clean the place up a bit – & get the Bosshard show prepared & off – after that I just don't know!'[35]

Scott had begun to develop his 'Lattice' series, based on interweaving colour bands, early in 1975.[36] Taut and dynamic, these works play on the ambiguities of flatness and depth, figure and ground, positive and negative space. A development from the 'Sprayed stripes', they represent a high point in 1970s abstraction in New Zealand, and Peter was quick to appreciate their significance.

Scott first exhibited his 'Lattice' paintings in June 1977: six works, priced from $400 to $800. He wrote to Peter after the opening, 'Thanks for putting me up & everything… Of course I've just gone straight back into the studio to try & resolve some of the difficulties & problems that occurred to me upon seeing the work in the gallery.'[37]

Despite a positive review by Neil Rowe – 'This is formal abstract painting of a high order' – there were no sales.[38] Peter noticed, however, that Gordon Walters was enthusiastic about Scott's new paintings. 'I was very impressed with what I saw of Ian Scott's work in Auckland,' he informed Peter. 'He has really come on well and is doing big canvases with a lot of authority.'[39]

Others were impressed, too. In 1978, Scott won the Benson and Hedges Art Award, judged by the influential director of the Australian National Gallery, James Mollison, for *Lattice no. 45*.[40] That year he was awarded an arts council grant, and a second in 1979 enabled him to travel overseas with his partner Nan Corson. Meanwhile, the

Ian Scott, *Lattice no. 58*, 1979
Acrylic on canvas
Museum of New Zealand Te Papa Tongarewa, purchased 1980

'Lattice' works began to sell, and the market for them strengthened dramatically in the following years.[41]

But Peter was never quite satisfied with his efforts as a dealer. '[I]t is a tough game,' he told Scott, 'and you have to just keep pushing and thinking and planning all the time. In my case, the problem is also compounded as I do not have any assistance. I do everything from sweeping the place out to selecting and selling. Sometimes I think I might blow up. Still, I love it. It is my life. And I do, so much, want to do better for you. You are one of the very best of your time.'[42]

On the home front, too, Peter was feeling the pressure. He and Hilary were upgrading the house at Hill Street room by room, and in 1978 they began the project of building a new kitchen. 'We are still in a state of chaos,' he reported to Scott.

> And now the drains have gone by the look of it, as water or something is seeping out into Hill Street. I'll ring a plumber tonight. God knows what that will cost, or what he will find.
>
> And the place has got to be rewired.
>
> Problems, problems, problems. The everyday hassle of surviving with three young children even makes art seem irrelevant, at times. I know that probably sounds like heresy to you but it has an element of truth in it. You will probably find out what I mean one of these days.[43]

The cost of running the gallery rose sharply during this period too. 'Printing, wine, electricity, telephone, tolls, advertising; they have all gone up with a thump,' Peter noted in July 1979.[44] 'The cost of living – the cost of keeping this place open – the cost of working alone, without the Arts Council handouts ... Is it too high? Can I keep this small craft upright?'[45]

In 1976, the arts council had acknowledged the crucial role that dealer galleries played in presenting contemporary art by initiating a series of modest grants to assist with exhibition costs. Peter refused to apply. Fiercely protective of his independence, he rather perversely equated government support with selling out. 'I will not end up a vanity gallery subsidised by the Arts Council,' he maintained. 'I'd rather pull the plug out and walk away from the whole thing than end up the lap dog of the (cultural) agency of the state.'[46]

Peter's attitude towards the arts council was part of a deep-seated mistrust of authority in any form. Like his father, the railwayman – now retired but still living with Betty in the same house in Lower Hutt – Peter retained a strong sense of 'us and them', and an antagonism towards 'the powers that be, the bosses, the establishment'.[47] Even as he sold art to the middle classes, he retained the stubborn insistence on independence that was so much a part of his working-class background.

—

Soon after his return to Auckland in the spring of 1977, Killeen wrote to Peter, 'I am working away as hard as I can at the moment – I started painting almost as soon as I got back.'[48] Peter reassured him that there was no hurry to exhibit – 'just when you are ready'.[49]

Killeen was now working on sheets of aluminium rather than canvas, and had begun a series of triangulated grid paintings, using sprayed lacquer. He had also started to use stencils to spray motifs such as animals, birds and fish onto aluminium, and works from both series were exhibited at the Data Gallery in Auckland in April 1978. In early August, he wrote to Peter about his forthcoming show in Wellington: '[C]ould be that I will have something different besides the type of work I showed at Data'.[50]

His casual comment gives little hint that Killeen was on the verge of a breakthrough. Experimenting with stencils, he had hit on the idea of cutting out the shapes he had spray-painted on aluminium, and then assembling the pieces on the wall – thus dispensing with a frame and blurring the boundaries between painting and sculpture. His second innovation was in the way these 'cut-outs' were to be displayed. The instructions for their first showing read: 'Hang cut-outs five to six inches apart, in any order.' In other words, the 'composition' of the work was up to the person who installed it.

Killeen wrote to advise Peter about the two 'totally new' works he was sending for his September show. 'One of these is made up of 30 pieces the other of nine. Each piece hangs from a small nail. Quite easy to hang but just a bit different – they must be spaced out by eye ... The new works are very interesting & strong – people will probably find them difficult, but they are the realisation of something I have worked on for a long time.'[51]

Peter recalled the excitement of unpacking and hanging the first cut-outs: 'I thought they were fantastic.'[52] The two works in the show were the thirty-piece *Collection from a Japanese garden 1937*[53] and the nine-piece *2 black dogs*. Neil Rowe was impressed: 'In both these works [Killeen] has collated a private alphabet of pictograms, logos and motifs like road-signs marking an inner journey. His concern with signs and symbols and his experience earning a living as a sign-writer, combine with a composite of signs seen around the world in two remarkable documents which chart his artistic growth.'[54] Killeen, he said, was the 'most brilliantly innovative' young artist in New Zealand, and this was his most important exhibition to date: 'Richard Killeen is a formidable talent.'

One of Peter's regular Wellington clients was the first to buy a cut-out – *2 black dogs*, for $600. Six works sold during the exhibition, including

Peter installing *2 black dogs* (left) and *Collection from a Japanese garden 1937*, both 1978, in *Richard Killeen: Recent paintings*, September–October 1978

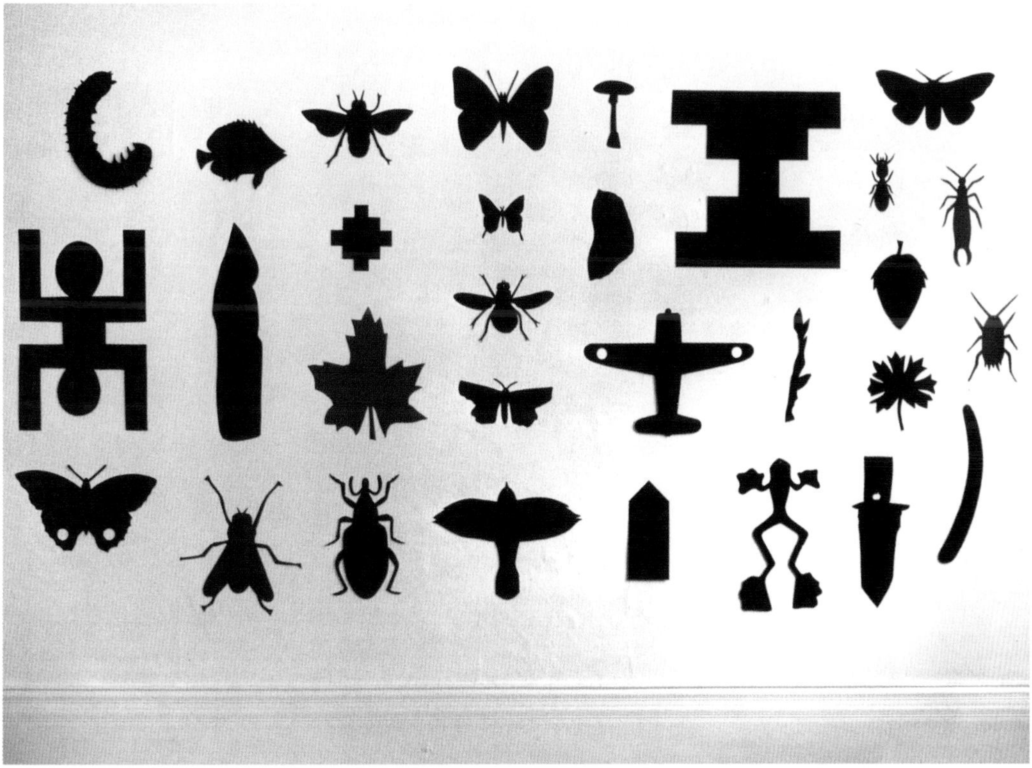

Richard Killeen, *Interpretation*, 1979
Acrylic on aluminium
Museum of New Zealand Te Papa Tongarewa, purchased 1979 with Queen Elizabeth II Arts Council of New Zealand funds and Harold Beauchamp Collection funds

a small watercolour to the National Art Gallery, and in late October, Peter confirmed a seventh.[55] 'Great news,' Killeen wrote. 'The whole show has given me a great lift after the long hard winter.'[56]

Killeen was now exploring new ideas for cut-outs, and in March 1979 he told Peter he had nearly completed two more: '[T]hey take some time to think out & get all the right pieces together. For once I do not feel as constricted or conscious of style problems as the cut outs solve the difficulties I have had in the past in reconciling the difference between painting & the way I see & feel things.'[57] In the winter he mentioned a series of lectures by artists at the community arts centre Outreach in Auckland: 'I turned it down as I could not face it at the time. Art is a terrible business in that so much public relations is involved if you want people to buy what you do. I should make more effort in that direction.'[58] Peter reassured him, 'Don't make any concessions to your feelings about what you "should" be doing regarding the public relations of art. If you feel that it is OK and comfortable then that is fine. But don't force yourself into becoming a performing seal for "business". It's not worth it. You're doing just fine the way you are.'[59]

In fact, Killeen's next exhibition in Wellington was eagerly anticipated. 'I'm really excited about your forthcoming show,' Peter wrote.

> I've got a couple of pots on the boil; just got to make sure that I don't over cook; and mustn't forget to 'strain' them, either...
>
> Yes, the second generation collectors are emerging... I've had good feelings from some of them. The future is indeed exciting; it's going to be good to you. It might take a bit of a haul but it will be a good time for the artists of your age. The people who buy art will still be there and they are growing.
>
> They are informed, and have good eyes. They also feel something about what it is to live here.[60]

At his second exhibition of cut-outs in September, Killeen showed ten works, including the twenty-eight-piece *Interpretation*, priced at $2100, which was purchased by the National Art Gallery. Peter and Hilary acquired *Seeds across the land*, while a smaller work, *North star*, was bought by Bill Milbank for the Sarjeant Gallery. Killeen wrote to Peter after the show, 'You are doing wonderfully well sales-wise. 5 of the 7 works in the show is incredibly good.'[61]

In reply, Peter thanked Killeen for his support and loyalty:

> It is something I do appreciate. I realise that some are critical of me and my 'method' of showing and selling the works I handle. I'm often accused (behind my back, I gather) of being too much of an 'antique dealer'; too 'precious'; too 'serious'. Well, perhaps there is some truth in that but often I think people are more motivated by envy. Many don't realise the role of a dealer, anyway. Nobody's perfect and I would like to think that, irrespective of my flaws and weakness, I've had a modicum of consistency. I've done my best...[62]

TUHOE
are the
People.
RUA is the
PROPHET

TWELVE

People still find the work 'Difficult'.

In October 1974, Colin McCahon had been commissioned to paint a mural for a new Visitor Centre at Aniwaniwa, designed by the architect John Scott. The theme specified by the Urewera National Park Board was 'the mystery of Man in the Urewera' – a compelling brief for McCahon, given his keen interest in Māori spirituality and conservation issues. Soon he was under way, preparing the canvas: 'I want to get the image down, go away, and come back to apply reason & not just brutish feeling to it. I know what it's going to look like'.[1]

In the new year, Peter asked how the mural was progressing and offered to show it – 'I could slot it in almost anytime.'[2] McCahon announced that he was having problems with the canvas: it would not lie flat, and he was anxious that he might have to start again. 'The painting is very largely on it & I am pleased with it. I don't want to lose what I've got.'[3] Difficulties had also emerged with the commissioners: 'My usual – people get scared.' McCahon was concerned that the finished work would not be acceptable, though he was determined to complete it anyway. 'I don't want them to pay for what they hate & the chances are they will hate this: Urewera is a bit buried under a cloud of pakeha emotion – the spirit of the mist & the lady of the lake thing.' He described the composition: 'Tane in the middle, the Tuhoe People on the left & Rua & Te Kooti on the right – and the Tuhoe who continue.'

In the winter of 1975, Peter reported an unusual sale: Television One had purchased a work from the 'Necessary protection' series to be displayed on the set of a new soap opera, *Close to home*. 'I am most intrigued,' McCahon replied. '[H]ow will the painting be used. Suggest to them a series on whales for All Whales year – I could help them out

Lionel and Ray Skipper with Colin McCahon's *A poster for the Urewera no. 2*, 1975, in the *Watercolours, drawings and prints* group exhibition, December 1975, photographed by Don Roy

– and one on the Urewera'.[4] Peter confirmed that the work was well lit and well presented on the show. 'They also have a Robin White print, a Hanly and Smither print and a rather nice oil on paper by Jeffrey Harris. The character is a school teacher in his early thirties. His marriage is in trouble. He has a rather attractive flat... The programme is a sort of Coronation Street affair; the Kiwi version.'[5]

McCahon was grateful for the cheque – and for another, for a work purchased by Ron O'Reilly. 'How does the money roll in. And I thinking I was broke & I nearly was... I saw myself in prison in a gloomy dungeon. Water, probably without bread. This to pay back all sorts of monies owing... And now my car has been stolen. It went last night. I must get to Muriwai to finish the Urewera mural. See, my friend, I live a very usual life.'[6]

In July, members of the park board travelled to Auckland to inspect the completed painting. 'I got scared,' McCahon told Peter. 'I couldn't take it. I'll tell you sometime. But they are buying it, it actually got them pinned to the wall.'[7] Absorbed in the Urewera project, McCahon had also produced a number of related works – 'Am painting a series of "Posters" about the famous people of the Urewera both to define the mural & also for fun'.[8]

Peter included two of these in a group exhibition featuring work by Hanly, McCahon, Smither, Robin White and others in December. 'The show is going to be a very good one,' he informed White. 'Colin has just sent me two marvellous gouaches on paper... A couple of humdingers.'[9]

Early in 1976, McCahon summoned Peter to Auckland for discussions. In the months since Barry Lett's departure, he had become dissatisfied with his Auckland gallery and he now invited Peter to become his main dealer. In the following year, Peter increased his commission on McCahon sales from 33.3 percent to 38 percent to cover his extra expenses, which now included framing and freight. He also took responsibility for liaising with dealers in other centres (as Barry Lett had done previously), and shared in the commission on their sales.

The new agreement between artist and dealer coincided with a period of growing acclaim for McCahon. In 1975, Luit Bieringa's survey of his early 'religious' works had toured the country; two years later, Ron O'Reilly's *Necessary protection* exhibition followed suit.[10] Late in 1977, Peter Webb devoted a special issue of his new journal *Art New Zealand* to McCahon's work, making him the first to receive such a tribute.[11]

McCahon's growing profile had an impact on sales, and he was disconcerted to find his work selling so readily. He told Peter:

Colin McCahon, *A poster for the Urewera no. 2*, 1975
Acrylic on paper
Aratoi Wairarapa Museum of Art and History,
gift of Ian Prior

> You keep piling in the loot. I must be the wealthiest man I know. Funny this when the family *did* starve & not really suffer though & we ate meals of parsley & mince – for weeks & never saw the lavish splendour of now – nor really wished it either. I bought a motor scooter to be cheaper than bus fares & roared around the country teaching to bring in the cash for winter woollies & build a house for my small flock. And now I'm rich ... money spinning out my ears, my eyes & nose. God forgive me ...[12]

But Peter's cheques were no use in McCahon's quest for an essential material, and he asked for help:

> Peter – my dear & lovely Peter
>
> Soft words to cage a hard request.
>
> Can you find me 100 sheets of Grumbacher or Steinbach HOT PRESSED paper in Wellington – the big ones – Not the do it yourself sketch pads. I'm desperate. I've been around & nothing coming in for 2 months ...
>
> Oh how I love the guy who sends me paper. I'm lost.
> Darkness hangs about my skinny neck ...
>
> Today has been blowing hard
> Wind blowing no paper to me ...

Peter came to the rescue with a gift of some seventy sheets of Steinbach paper, sourced in Wellington. He also sent the artist a photograph taken at his end-of-year show: Don Roy from the *Dominion* had caught two young Māori, Lionel and Ray Skipper, standing apprehensively in the doorway to the gallery, flanked by McCahon's *A poster for the Urewera no. 2* (see page 200). McCahon was moved by the photograph: 'That boy to the right going to unexplored land & the smaller fellow in the middle & me pushing a message neither of them have seen yet. I put my head between my knees'.[13] This photograph was the genesis of a new group of five works on Steinbach paper – the 'Scared' series. Peter told Gordon Walters they were 'crackers': 'Lovely things to have in stock to whip out and tempt the jaded palate'.[14]

In August 1976, the series was shown in McCahon's ninth solo exhibition at the gallery. Among the works was *Scared*, an austere, blackboard-like image with an inscription scrawled in white: 'I am scared. I STAND UP.' This deceptively simple painting with its two brief phrases goes to the heart of McCahon's concerns: a confession of existential anxiety, couched in the most direct and urgent language, followed by a resounding declaration of courage and faith. Also included

Colin McCahon, *Scared*, 1976
Acrylic on paper
Museum of New Zealand Te Papa Tongarewa, purchased 2008

in the show were works on paper from recent series, including eight 'Clouds' paintings from 1975, inspired by the view from the Muriwai cliff top. Peter sold seven works, priced from $400 to $500, and reported back to the artist:

> It's funny even after the long career you have had people still find the work '*Difficult*'. And in fact, unlike any other painter I exhibit, your works are the ones that spark the most positive reaction in people. They react. Either Yes or No. There is no halfway house. No inbetween.
>
> This is what I always find exciting about your work. It engenders so much feedback. And it makes people think. Even some of my best clients, they look and come over to me and say, 'Yes, but why isn't he painting like he used to.' Why, Why, Why, is what so many of them say. They can't see the beauty yet. But they will.
>
> Others are just 'knocked out'. They feel the directness. They see. And go out animated and talking... There is no in-between. No twilight zone here for the next two weeks.[15]

Colin McCahon, *Clouds 4*, 1975
Acrylic on paper
Auckland Art Gallery Toi o Tāmaki, on loan from a private collection, London

By now, Peter had renewed his efforts to sell one of McCahon's large paintings to the National Art Gallery. He had been encouraged by the appointment of Janet Paul and Hamish Keith to the gallery council, aware that they wanted to rectify McCahon's lack of representation in the collection. Janet Paul was keen on the massive *Practical religion*, a work that Peter had dubbed 'The Thunderer', but McCahon was ambivalent about letting it go: 'I would really not sell yet. My best for a long time – I could say, yet. I sort of treasure it'.[16]

In November, Peter heard back from the council: they had rejected his advice to buy recent paintings and planned to visit McCahon with a view to purchasing early works instead. 'The whole business was a bit disappointing,' he admitted.[17] McCahon replied, 'I'm a bit sad for us both and the Nation. But courage is a rare virtue that brings sadness with it. We both have courage & sadness. I don't really want to see the select committee … I'm not flattered by the Nat Gal's earlier neglect.'[18]

It was not the first time McCahon had commented on the traits he shared with his dealer. Both men were independent thinkers, sceptical of authority, a 'bit cranky'; both saw themselves as outsiders.[19] Also, and perhaps most importantly, both had a keen sense of serving a cause. In 1977, McCahon reflected on his early ambitions: 'I wanted to be a missionary & go to the Islands. I think that for a child was an honest deception … In a way I have been a missionary & so have you.'[20]

McCahon continued to write long sprawling letters to Peter, about his family, his art and his garden ('When I can no longer crawl around a garden I'll be finished – real proper. Lay me down & die in the Stoke Lavender I think would be right'.)[21] He also indulged his dry wit, spinning yarns for his dealer. In 1977, for example, he extolled the glories of Helensville: 'Look Peter, how about us buying God's ¼ acre on the main drag & building – you see down to the "river" & mangroves & the Kaipara & the flats & the beachedge hills. We could sit there & laugh at our stupidity … We could build the greatest – the McLeavey McCahon old men's retirement centre (we would take the ladies to do the work) & watch the fishing boats & the trains'. McCahon annotated this letter: 'These remarkable lines were written in a state of intoxication with the beauty of the land.'[22]

In April 1977, Peter made a sixteen-day business trip to Australia. 'I am going to have a good look around Sydney and Melbourne to keep up with what is happening,' he informed his old friend Wilson Buchanan.[23] He was aware that there was interest in McCahon, who had held two solo exhibitions in Australia, and felt it was time to promote his work more vigorously across the Tasman.[24]

Peter planned the trip carefully, contacting museum staff in advance, and Daniel Thomas, the curator of Australian art at the Art Gallery of New South Wales, sent an encouraging response. 'By all means telephone me … to fix a time for viewing McCahon,' he wrote. 'We all greatly admire his work and although we have no money until next financial year let's start considering the stuff.'[25] Meanwhile, the New Zealand expatriate

Ian North, a curator at the Art Gallery of South Australia, sounded a more cautionary note: 'As you probably know, the general feeling in Australia is that … New Zealand art is best looked after by New Zealanders. This view has some logic. But it must be admitted, too, that this attitude is fuelled by the legendary chauvinistic provincialism of many Australians.'[26]

In Sydney, Peter stayed in an apartment at Darling Point provided by a client, the businessman Robert Jones. He spent the days visiting galleries and the evenings having dinner with collectors, and was delighted with the response from Daniel Thomas – 'a great chap' – who reiterated his gallery's interest in acquiring a major work by McCahon.[27] Peter also visited Mervyn Horton, the owner-editor of the influential journal *Art & Australia*, to try to persuade him to feature more articles on New Zealand art.[28]

Ten days into his trip, Peter flew to Canberra to meet James Mollison, the director of the new Australian National Gallery, which was still under construction. 'Again,' he informed McCahon, 'it was a really great reception … For after me showing him the slides and works on paper that I'd taken trans-tasman he too said that they wished to have 5 paintings and fifteen works on paper by you. I was thunderstruck. Again I made great personal contact with James. (By this time we were on first name terms.)'[29] Mollison took Peter on a tour of some of the highlights in the collection: 'A Hans Hofmann he had knocked me out. Marvellous.'[30]

That evening Peter arrived in Melbourne, where he was met by his friend and client, Reverend Ian Brown. Staying with Brown at his vicarage in Eltham, he was astonished by his host's collection, which was particularly strong in works on paper – 'lovely watercolours by Rodin, Picasso, Ernst, and Ian Fairweather … Beautiful lithographs by Jasper Johns, Andy Warhol'.[31] Peter was particularly gratified to see the New Zealand art that he had sold Brown in such company. He informed McCahon, '[He] had "The Canoe Mamari" hanging in his bedroom accompanied by two Picasso pastels. And in the front room (or the lounge) he has a set of Muriwai panels … All very exciting.'[32]

After a weekend of visiting local galleries with his host, Peter called on Patrick McCaughey, the professor of visual art at Monash University, who expressed 'great admiration' for McCahon and urged him to send works for the Australian National Gallery to consider. 'He is the most influential member of the purchasing committee,' Peter noted later. 'Young, well connected, driven.'[33]

Back home, Peter received good news: Daniel Thomas had asked for a major McCahon, *Through the Wall of Death: A Banner*, to be sent to the gallery on consideration. 'They are pretty well committed to buying a work by you,' he told the artist, 'and it's just a matter of my keeping at them... I was so proud to represent you. To hear how high they regard your work in Australia. And to initiate plans to include your works in those two institutions.'[34]

Peter was well satisfied with his efforts. He had sold works by McCahon, Mrkusich, Woollaston and Allen Maddox in Australia, but even more importantly he had formed a link with several key curators and directors, which would advance the profile of New Zealand art across the Tasman.

A month after his visit to Australia, Peter wrote to tell Gordon Walters about another forthcoming trip:

> I'm off to Auckland tonight on the '*Silver Star*' for six days. I will go out to Colin's place at Muriwai tomorrow morning and will stay overnight returning to Auckland late Sunday.
>
> He has been writing a lot lately (two or three times a week) about his new work and seems very excited about it. They are called *Angels and Bed* and are, in fact, a development of three small works he did last year.
>
> It will be good to see him and we will go for walks across the great plain. On Sunday morning the three of us (Colin, Anne and me) usually hike across the top of the cliff and look down at the sea and the large citadel like rock where the sea birds nest. This lies about 30 feet off the coast and it has served as the trigger for Colin's Necessary Protection. Some opus, that one.
>
> Saturday night we will talk about things and have some of that 'Dally plonk' or sherry that is popular in those parts. It will be cold so he will light the fire and we will all warm ourselves like turtles; backs to the heat. Good times as the moon comes up.[35]

McCahon had begun his 'Angels and bed' series in June 1976, when he learned that his old friend Rodney Kennedy – one of the first collectors of his work – had been seriously injured in a fall from a ladder. Imagining his friend confined to bed and unable to move, McCahon painted a highly abstracted image of Kennedy's sickbed surrounded by protective 'angels' – a series of luminous white rectangles. He informed Peter, '[This work is] based on Rodney K's broken ribs & awful operations and a letter from him – nights of pain & driving the bed to eternity – all "Peer Gynt" mythology'.[36] Reflecting on one of his constant themes, the precariousness of life and the need for protection, McCahon painted two more works in sympathy for friends who had recently been ill: Dr Walter Auburn, an honorary curator at the Auckland City Art Gallery, and Peter himself, who had recently had his second operation on his inner ear in two years. All three works were exhibited 'not for sale' at the Peter McLeavey Gallery in August 1976.

Intrigued by the possibilities of the 'Angels and bed' theme, McCahon had also begun a large oil, and in March 1977 he sent Peter an update: 'The huge painting is good it's great I think. We get to Muriwai at about 5 p.m. today. I've got to see it. Looking is about the most time of painting.'[37] But he remained dissatisfied and continued his scrutiny: 'I keep seeing faults in my thinking and I want this right. I want it to tell me & not me it. Painting is pain: I cry. It's very much a sexual experience & it lives with God: Without, never.'[38]

McCahon was also working on a set of smaller 'Angels and bed' works – 'all children of the big one & grandchildren of Nos. 1, 2 & 3'.[39] In May he reported, 'I'm struggling with the final 4 paintings in the "Angels & Bed" things – there are now 14 of them ... The last four are bastards who want to join the family with clean faces. I looked them in the eye this morning and said "now" – they said "no" so I went out to the garden & left them alone for the day. I looked at them later & saw how I could help – but refrained. 4 to 14 have been probably the most difficult things I've done for years. I've been applying more discipline.'[40] The series had left McCahon exhausted. 'I feel smashed when I come to the end of a series of painting,' he told Peter. 'It always seems the end and then it's just a matter of waiting.'[41]

Peter unpacked the works for the *Angels and bed* show in some excitement. 'They look just so strong; monumental,' he wrote.[42] Aware of the effort these works had cost McCahon, he continued:

> I hope you don't get too sad after finishing a series of paintings.
>
> I think I know what you are saying for I've at times sensed a feeling about you. I was thinking the other day of my visit to you at Muriwai last. Thinking particularly about my conversations about business and the works I'd like and the prices etc. I do hope that I don't lose a reverence for all creative process; all growth.
>
> I know the feeling that must haunt you after you have done paintings and the Peter McLeaveys of the world come and examine them and take them and sell them. You have the gift. Like a hedgehog you must stay close to the root of the fern and the hedge and avoid the torch of the boy. At night the light picks up the creature's eye.

Colin McCahon, *Angels and bed no. 4: Hi-fi*, 1976–77
Acrylic on unstretched canvas
Auckland Art Gallery Toi o Tāmaki, purchased with assistance from the Friends of the Auckland Art Gallery, 1977

> The eye; the hand; the heart. Stay close to the fern. Snuggle up to the root and burrow deep amongst the leaves and fern to keep warm. Feel your heart beat, and smile, brave soldier.

Angels and bed opened in early July, comprising ten works on paper and the large oil. Two days later, Peter wrote to Walters, 'I now have my McCahon show hanging and it looks great. I have put $700.00 on each work. So far I've not sold any but I do have a couple swinging and I'm confident that they will, at least, go.'[43] By the following day, however, his mood had darkened:

> Friday. It's overcast and a cold wind is lifting coats, and hats, down Courtenay Place. I've had a few in and almost blew my top at a dozy bitch who bad mouthed my McCahon. Homicide stormed through the air. I bit my tongue (and, taking Keith Holyoake's advice) counted to ten. Thoughts of homicide abated.

Still, it does shake me and usually leaves the day a wreck. The envy and negativeness and blindness of people who one would think would have a bit of art. Particularly when they are clutching a Charles Jourdan bag and reeking of 'My Sin'. Still, I let fire with both barrels and she fled from this place stammering rubbish about 'some people' and 'rudeness'. Who cares.[44]

Peter sold two works, including one to Ron O'Reilly, and at the end of the show sent the collection to Auckland for a viewing at the Peter Webb Gallery. In August, the Auckland City Art Gallery purchased the work that McCahon called 'The Big One' – *Angels and bed no. 4: Hi-fi.*[45] Reflecting on the series, McCahon informed Peter, 'These last paintings do something I've worked for for years'.[46]

McCahon was now in his late fifties, and he and Anne had recently moved to escape the noise from the construction of a new motorway through Newton Gully. Their new city base was an old villa in Ponsonby, while at Muriwai, their second home, McCahon's son-in-law Ken Carr was converting a wash-house to a studio. Absorbed in painting and his domestic life, McCahon was increasingly reluctant to attend art world events: 'We don't appear, we go out hardly at all apart from Muriwai & long city walks. I can't go to exhibition openings – I get chased by cameras & fools who want rundowns on my work. No more, no more. I will crawl into my cave & wrap my bear skin about me and be ill if I like. I'm supposed to be a bit off my rocker – O.K. perhaps I am, I don't know – I don't want to.'

Peter replied sympathetically:

> You're off your rocker. Me too … [N]ow and again a passion grips me and I see things in a direct, unequivocal way. Things become just black and white. They can become too black and white, sometimes. Too narrow.
>
> I walk the streets and am harsh. I shake my fist at the sky. Too much I. Too much me. I have to learn to Love and be Warm and not expect too much. Have Grace …
>
> The old discontent still seems to whisper to me but its calls are more distant, now. Over the weekend something 'threw' me and I got a bit upset. It's then that the calls come. Go away; Move; drop this burden; become unknown; hide. Australia, they call. Happily I now 'right' myself very quickly and move on through the swell and mist & storm. Auckland does not hold any attraction for me. I've grown to quite like Wellington. It's like a worn pair of tennis shoes I once had. The toes are a bit tight and the shoe is pretty frayed

> around the back but it's comfortable. It's got the warm feeling of 'home' I guess. It is, however, a hard place to live. Like pauas on a rock we cling to our hills and dales.[47]

In July 1977, McCahon wrote to tell Peter of a 'lovely phone call' from a Miss Gilmour, who had commissioned a screen painting from him in the previous year.[48] 'She is shifting to "very cramped" quarters (a "rest" home or pensioner flat), is taking the small works she has & giving away the large ones … She is keeping the screen, she loves it & it keeps out the draughts.'[49]

Peter replied, 'Miss Gilmour? … She sounds real good. As you say "an enthusiast from years back". We need them today, as then. Particularly now for I fear that there is not much "enthusiasm" around in this land at this time. Muldoon is a bully and I sense a mood of fear and frustration in New Zealand … Perhaps it's me but there isn't much love around. We Kiwis hold back too much. We don't give ourselves … We fear passion; its consuming flames may overwhelm.'[50]

Peter was awaiting the birth of his third child, and was in a pensive mood. Dominic was born several days later, and Peter sent McCahon a telegram, following up with a letter: 'Yes; a boy. An eight and a half pounder. A big boy. We are very happy and our two girls are thrilled to bits. Insist on taking him into bed with them. Not yet. The delivery went beautifully; no complications.'[51] He had taken time off to look after his daughters: 'And that is work for they are like a couple of jumping jacks and one's life is keeping one jump ahead of them.'[52]

Returning to the gallery, Peter wrote again. 'I got the shock of my life a few minutes ago when I went downstairs to buy a paper and read the billboard "EXIT ELVIS". On reading it I find that the King is dead. That's sad for I've always had a great love of Elvis and his music.' In the same letter he reported that the Art Gallery of New South Wales had decided not to buy *Through the Wall of Death: A Banner*. 'However they are keen to see other works so once the "Wall" returns I will send over slides of other works by you here. As you know, we must plug away; slowly but surely. Little disappointments like this must not worry us, but in fact will become a spur for better and more purposeful efforts … Yes, I'm working towards Australia.'

Peter was quietly optimistic about McCahon's prospects in Australia, but even he would be surprised by the events of the following year.

VERONICA.
NO 3

THIRTEEN

The whole of New Zealand and Australia must have heard of you.

In the winter of 1977, Peter wrote to Gordon Walters: 'You will be interested to know that I have the Northland Panels back in stock. They are not $3000.00 any more. Multiply it by 8 and you will be close.'[1] McCahon had agreed to sell the work for $25,000, but only to a public gallery: '[T]hat price was set quite some years back and is really obsolete. I'm mean enough to hate the thought that a citizen could get the panels for that and flog them for 25+ to a gallery in a few years' time. So $25,000 to "reputable" galleries only. The painting does belong here.'[2]

Two weeks later, Peter informed McCahon that the National Art Gallery had taken an option on the work. 'I am not counting my chickens before they are hatched,' he wrote, 'but I feel they could buy it. It's just a feeling.'[3] But as the weeks dragged by with no update from the gallery, McCahon became increasingly testy. 'I think the Nat. Gal. has had a bloody good go. I have a great dislike for that institution & hope they don't get them – this is spite: Christchurch I like & also the sound of the new Hamilton Gallery. But what does it really matter. If all my paintings were gathered together & laid on me I'd be flat and thin as a sheet of paper – how I feel. Not to worry. I'll get over it.'[4]

In September, Peter showed McCahon's 'magnum opus', *The Second Gate Series* of 1962.[5] 'What a fine work it is too, a pleasure to have it here,' he told Walters. 'It fills up the whole gallery. And, surprisingly a lot of people have come in to see it. And that without one advertisement. Yes, the good old word of mouth advertising does work and this show really does seem to be bringing a lot of the McCahon fans in out of the woodwork. They're out there; no doubt about it.'[6]

Colin McCahon, *The Five Wounds of Christ no. 3: Veronica*, 1977–78
Acrylic on unstretched canvas
Dunedin Public Art Gallery, purchased 1981 with funds from the Dunedin Public Art Gallery Society

During the exhibition Peter heard that the National Art Gallery had decided against purchasing the *Northland panels*. '[T]o me it's all grist to the mill,' he informed McCahon. 'One thing; I gather Janet Paul did a heroic job behind the scenes but, regretfully, to no avail.'[7] Ormond Wilson, the chairman of the board of trustees, wrote in conciliatory fashion to McCahon: 'The impecunious situation of the National Art Gallery is of course none of your affair, and I report it only to let you understand our difficulties ... the present Council is deeply concerned that the gallery lacks a representative collection of your works and is prepared to stretch its resources to the utmost to remedy this deficiency.'[8]

In the final months of the year, McCahon was occupied with a commission for Peter and Hilary. Peter had first planted the idea in 1974, when he evoked what he had in mind: 'The land at five o'clock on a Sunday afternoon; the hermitage snuggled in the hills; St Jerome's place. Perhaps the lion is in his whare. A candle; a few books; plenty of blue, green, some grey, plenty of black; a heightening white.'[9] But it was only now he felt confident of being able to pay off the large painting he envisaged. He sent McCahon a map of the living room at Hill Street with dimensions of the main walls, and the artist conceived the idea of a suite of paintings relating to the Crucifixion – specifically Christ's hours on the cross when, according to the Gospels, 'there was darkness over all the land'.[10]

McCahon wrote to Peter in December: 'There are 3 of these "Five Wounds of Christ". One is OK the biggest one. I spent about 10 minutes with it last weekend & locked the door. Today – I think I got it right when I locked the door. I'm going to see it again tomorrow & sign it if I still feel happy'.[11] McCahon continued to work on the series in the new year, but by now he was concerned that it was too austere for 'home use': '[T]hese are not paintings to bring up children on. I am scared. O there is a beauty – I see it – and so can kids but I am scared. I paint you some real joy – eh! I want a few weeks more work – you don't get this lot till I'm happy ... I must know I don't send rubbish. Peter, you keep me on a thing I call honest – and my honesty demands I equal yours.'[12]

Just as McCahon was completing the paintings, he was swept into what Peter described as a 'local hoolah'.[13] The fuss began at a Lower Hutt City Council meeting in February, when Councillor Chen Werry criticised the art at the Dowse, declaring that he wanted 'to smash everything up' when he went to the gallery.[14] His remark caught the attention of the media, and he was interviewed in front of one of the most bracingly austere works in the collection – the recently acquired

Jim Barr and Councillor Chen Werry, 1978, in front of McCahon's *Through the Wall of Death: A Banner*, 1972

Through the Wall of Death: A Banner.[15] Predictably, Werry was dismissive, claiming that he could 'knock up a Colin McCahon-type painting' in his lunch break.[16] Sensing a good story, national television challenged him to do just that on its *Good day* programme, while the *Evening Post* featured the story on the front page and published an editorial expressing some sympathy for Werry's views.

Peter told McCahon that the incident was a reminder of how much Wellington remained a 'frontier culture'.[17] In the 1950s, the critic Eric Ramsden had lambasted modern art in the *Evening Post* and even now, twenty years later, McCahon's art was still subject to ridicule. 'We are the hot bed of the Academy,' Peter proclaimed, 'and its influence pervades so many parts of this city and province. I'm a fighter; and [have] never lost sight of the fact that it is pretty rampant in these parts; amateurism and the ordinary and everyman can make his own paintings. Art making is not democratic.'

The next day, Peter sent McCahon a batch of press clippings. 'Councillor Werry is an old man,' he wrote. 'His ideas on art are ignorant and he has just sort of stumbled into a media trap... I don't feel we should over-react. It is a bad business, I agree, but we must not let it overpower us. It is just silly. The thing that saddens me is that it may upset you. Please don't let it. It is just not worth it. We have the future.'[18]

He also wrote to the director-general of television, declaring his disgust at the plan for Werry to paint a 'McCahon' in the name of public entertainment. 'It is difficult enough in our land to develop and grow artistically. Colin McCahon has done that. He is one of the very few authentic creative persons to come out of this frontier culture. To find him and his work manipulated by the Good Day programme in this manner saddens me.'[19]

McCahon thanked Peter for his efforts:

> The Werry bit is stupid – I'm not saying he is but he *has* got caught in a net alright... But you know – if this sort of thing didn't happen I would know I was dead. It all started back in the late 1930s times & has been with me since. Don't worry about me – I get furious for an hour or so but realise I'm getting just what I ask for – a reaction and those who have eyes do see. Mr Werry has learnt more about painting than he might know now. Painting is aimed at the guts & heart – it depends on very great honesty (which I spend a lot of time trying to achieve). Seeing is not only eyesight. The Lazarus story is to me one of the really great stories about seeing – all those people saw as never before.
>
> Never mind, I was out in the garden at 7 a.m. this morning (N.Z. Standard Time) digging, clearing up the ruins of the dry summer, being gently rained on. Coffee at 9 & back to work till 11. Have stretched 2 canvases as best I could & after lunch & more garden work gave them a first coat of paint...
>
> Thanks for all you have done.
>
> Greetings. A most happy fella.
>
> Colin.[20]

Within days, however, another rumpus was brewing. On 8 March, Peter had been notified of a major sale: thanks to the efforts of Hamish Keith, the chairman of the arts council, and Frank Corner, the secretary for Foreign Affairs, the New Zealand Government had confirmed the purchase of one of McCahon's largest works, *Victory over death 2*, as a gift to the Australian Government. The painting was to be presented by Deputy Prime Minister Brian Talboys on his first official visit to Australia, and would be housed in the new state-of-the-art Australian National Gallery in Canberra.

Peter was elated by the news. 'This is, for me, a most important event, *symbolically*,' he declared. 'For the first time a New Zealand Government has gifted an object that represents the best. The excellence that is found in the imagination and in the human heart. A work of the spirit. It is a brave thing, I feel.'[21] He told McCahon that James Mollison, the gallery's director, was delighted to be receiving the painting. 'Frankly,' Mollison admitted to Peter a little later, 'I would not like to see a painting of this consequence by an Australian artist leave this country. A great many people here are flattered that Australia should have received such a fine gift.'[22]

Peter's pleasure in the $9000 sale was soon dampened by the media storm that followed. On both sides of the Tasman the painting was lampooned: Senator George Georges dubbed it 'Muldoon's revenge', while Muldoon implied that the gift was a publicity stunt.[23] The opinion of James Mollison – one of the few experts to be consulted – was all but overlooked in the fracas. To him, *Victory over death 2* was 'a work of great power … one of the most important paintings to have been made in this hemisphere in recent times'.[24]

At Muriwai, McCahon was inundated with queries from the media. 'I was rung by some creep from the Herald last night,' he told Peter, 'with a jolly line about the Australian politicians breaking up with laughter when they saw the painting – & so on … I was on and off the phone all morning … And now in about 10 minutes Werry takes the air. I'm not looking. It's all too difficult to get to a TV set'.[25]

Amid all the fuss, Peter had not yet had a chance to open a package McCahon had sent, containing the three 'Five Wounds of Christ' paintings. 'They are at home, safe and sound,' he noted on 8 March, 'but I've just not had the opportunity to look at them. I'll hopefully have that pleasure in store tonight. Goodie.'[26]

Nine days later he wrote again:

> Looking back over all the material I have sent you over the last couple of weeks it is really amazing. Councillor Werry, and Mr Talboys, and Mr Muldoon and you; all together on page one. You have to smile. Yes, and in a way it is all probably beneficial. I'm not sure how, but I just feel it is. The whole of New Zealand and Australia must have heard of you and your works, by now.
>
> All the energy and press material that you have engendered. All the conversations. The mind truly boggles …

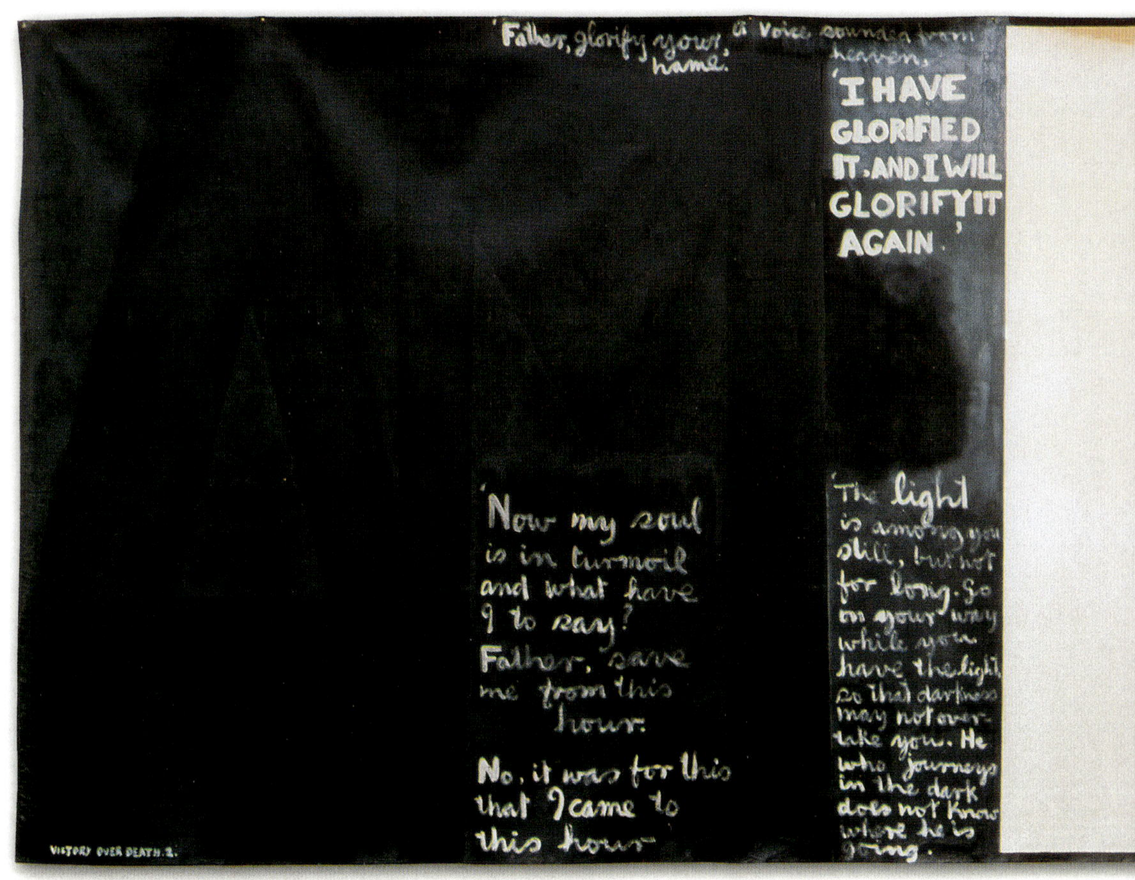

Colin McCahon, *Victory over death 2*, 1970
Acrylic on unstretched canvas
National Gallery of Australia, Canberra,
gift of the New Zealand Government, 1978

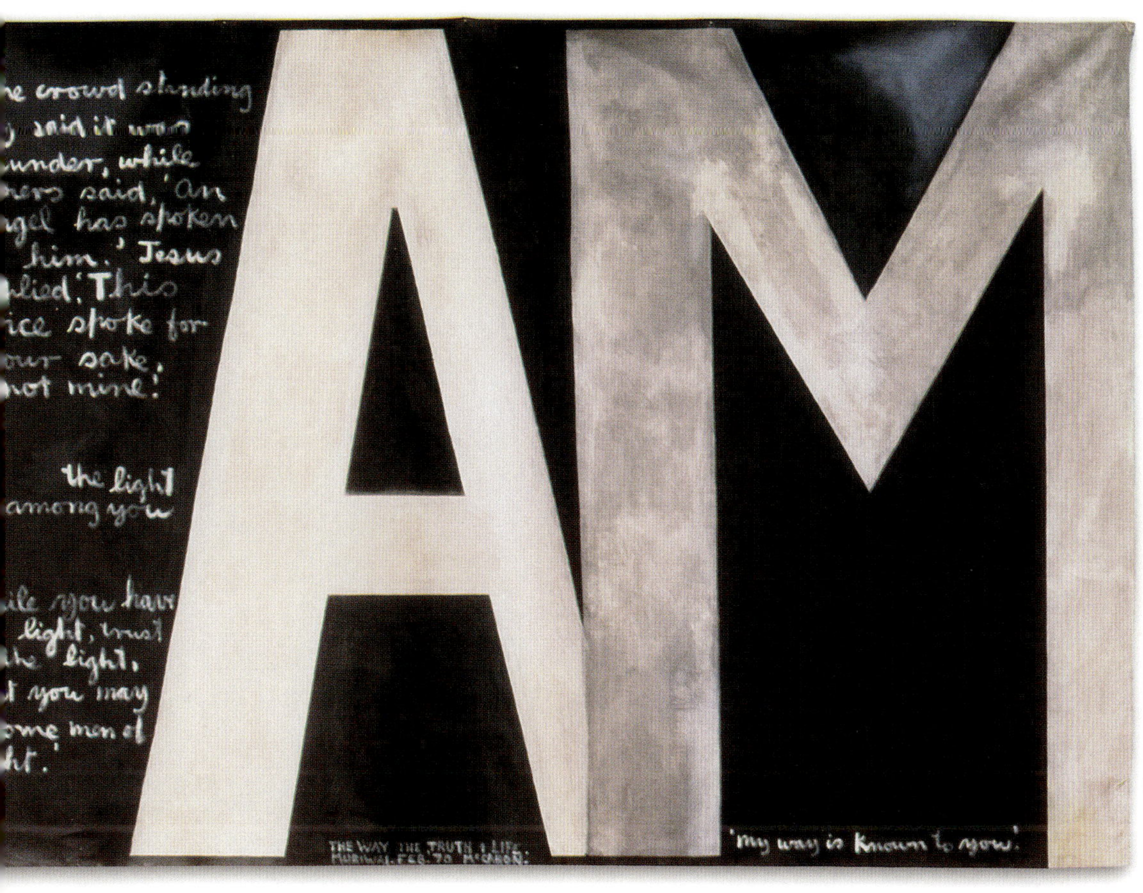
AM
crowd standing
said it was
under, while
said, 'An
has spoken
him.' Jesus
'This
spoke for
sake,
not mine.'
the light
among you
you have
light, trust
light,
you may
men of
THE WAY THE TRUTH & LIFE.
MURIWAI FEB.'70 McCAHON.
'my way is known to you'.

And now. Well, we will settle back to things and the next sensation will come to fill the papers and the media. It's like a great bear, or lion, that has to be continually fed. One day parsley; the next, sausages; next week, rice pudding; on it goes continually feeding on 'things'...

Anyway, I better get back on an even keel for it's been a very exciting week. Firstly hanging the 'Five Wounds of Christ' (the big one is a cracker) and then all the hoohah about '*Victory*', well, it's been a real 'roller-coaster'...

This is a disjointed letter isn't it? And I look out the window down on Cuba Street and everyone is walking around during their lunch hour. A Maori chap walks down the street carrying a gun in a sheath; going pig shooting, I suppose. And the boys in the butcher shop (opposite) are flat out with the lunch time crowds...

We are proceeding with our kitchen renovations and that's good. At present the place looks as if the IRA have just let off one of those devices. It smells of soil; of the earth. A good smell. The cat likes it too, for he goes in and sits down on the earth. And at night, he sleeps in that deserted kitchen.

Well, Colin, I must go. Thank you for everything;
Love to you both
Peter.[27]

McCahon reported 'a great heap of letters from all sorts of people' about the gift of *Victory over death 2*. 'All good & kind. These people do see what I'm on about. I've answered a few – a lot have no addresses. But that's good too. Luit Bieringa has been standing up for me too'.[28] But all the negative publicity had taken a toll. 'I've been going through a black hole and no stars to guide me,' he told Peter a month later. 'I just feel swamped and useless... My soul is black & I must light it up.'[29] McCahon had begun two new canvases, but was struggling to find a way forward. 'Without the bones where does the meat hang. The bones do imply a knowledge of the whole being & it's this lack of understanding is making me kick shit in my own face. Someday I will be told the truth of what is wanted – and will rebel, naturally. If God and I gave up our arguments I wouldn't paint again. I like the old man's persistence.'

For Peter, the commission from *Victory over death 2* had been a godsend. '[It has] really helped us with the kitchen, I must say... I expect that we may not now need to borrow monies from my father.'[30] Hilary, in particular, was looking forward to its completion. 'It will make a great difference to her, I know. Yes, I'm blind, you know, I did not sort of click until the other day, how important the kitchen is to

Peter and Hilary in the new kitchen at Hill Street, 1980

one's wife. Those blinkers I wear.'[31] But for McCahon the sale prompted mixed feelings. He told Peter, 'The big money rolled in – these things throw me a bit. I feel kind of helpless – even in my work pants I get a small bow from my bank manager.'[32]

The gift had been crucial, however, in securing McCahon's reputation in Australia. In the following years other leading Australian galleries made it a priority to acquire his paintings, so that today there are seventeen McCahons in public collections. At the Australian National Gallery, meanwhile, *Victory over death 2* took its place as a key work in the finest art collection in the southern hemisphere, often displayed beside Jackson Pollock's celebrated *Blue poles*.[33] Reflecting on it in 2012, James Mollison commented, 'The only problem is the painting's never on the walls, because it's forever being borrowed. Everyone seems to want it!'[34]

On 18 March, in the midst of the *Victory over death* furore, Peter had received a visit from Ormond Wilson on behalf of the National Art

Gallery Council. 'Don't laugh,' he cautioned McCahon afterwards, 'but he wants the National Gallery to purchase the painting [the *Northland panels*]. The operative word is "Wants". You see, he has to (or rather is going to) call on the Minister of Internal Affairs (Mr Highet) to see if he can raise some funds via that gentleman.'[35]

McCahon was incensed. 'Bung the prices up as high as you can for the Nat. Gal. It is really a great dishonour for me to be bought there & they should pay for my suffering in the past at their hands ... God spare me, I think we are too tolerant. I see this as a battle. I love fights. The meaner & nastier the more I like them – that arsehole palace of flopped painting.'[36]

It was all Peter could do to calm him:

> I know your feelings about the National Art Gallery for they are mine. I look forward to the time when that place will be the best gallery we have – I know it will be. Its time will come. That, I believe.
>
> I hear rumours that the present director is being shoehorned out ... And Government is, I gather, starting to move its loins and will more heavily finance the place. With a new director (a non painter, perhaps) the place has great potential. I look to the future. And I see the panels hanging in a lovely gallery being seen by lots of our countrymen and overseas visitors. The panels should be in a major public collection.
>
> Love to you and Anne
>
> Peter.
>
> P.S. If the sale of the Northland Panels proceeds I will be glad. If it does not proceed I will also be glad. I go on to the future; my job is my life. These ups and downs add spice but ultimately I view them all with a philosophical eye.

Peter wrote that letter on 4 May. The very next day he received a visit from James Mollison and Warwick Reader from the Australian National Gallery who had made an appointment to view McCahon's works.[37] 'What a time we had,' Peter told the artist.

> Let me tell you about Mr Mollison. He came in. He spent about half an hour looking through what I had by yourself. At the end he stood up. He said I want that; and that; and those two leaning against the wall; and that; and those three. No talk about referring to his selection committee. In fact, with most of the works he did not even ask the price. I was staggered. Excited. You could have knocked me over.

I keep my feet on the ground, however. One has the ups and the downs. It is a lifetime, for me. Me, in my two white rooms; an actor on a stage. People come in and go out. An hour goes by. Someone coughs on the stairs; a loose board creaks and in comes someone else. I wait; alone with my thoughts, and go home to my wife and children. It is a most particular type of job and in the final analysis it is the spiritual 'loneliness' that I find hardest. Not the financial strain, no; the loneliness of a man out front selling dreams. Sometimes falling on my face but always picking myself up and going on.[38]

Mollison had purchased eleven McCahons for the gallery, including works from the 'Angels and bed', 'Clouds' and 'Noughts and crosses' series. He had also acquired an oil painting by Toss Woollaston and two works by A Lois White.[39]

After nearly a decade at Cuba Street, this was a landmark day for Peter and a high point in his career. Looking back more than thirty years later, he recalled, 'That day when James Mollison came in and bought all those works – that just turned the tide. I knew that something had changed.'[40]

But something had changed closer to home as well. On the very day that Mollison bought an astonishing eleven works, Peter had word from the National Art Gallery to confirm the purchase of *two* paintings: the *Northland panels* and a key canvas of 1970, *A grain of wheat*.[41] Peter was jubilant, writing to McCahon, 'Yes, the 5th of May 1978 will be stamped on my head for a long time. The day I sold to the National Gallery of New Zealand and the Australian National Gallery.'[42]

The purchase of the *Northland panels* was a watershed for the National Art Gallery, a moment when it signalled its seriousness about collecting the best of New Zealand art. It was the most substantial single acquisition the gallery had ever made, and Neil Rowe predicted in the *Evening Post* that it would 'prove to be the cornerstone in the development of a truly representative national collection'.[43] His words were prescient. In the following years, moreover, the National Art Gallery and its successor the Museum of New Zealand Te Papa Tongarewa would go on to build what is arguably the finest collection of McCahon's work. Today there are seventy-one works by the artist in the collection.

In Auckland, meanwhile, McCahon seemed to have recovered his equilibrium after the trying autumn months. 'I got stuck into the garden for the afternoon ... and now today I've cleaned up another hunk of

Colin McCahon, *Truth from the King Country: Load bearing structures (Large) 5*, 1978
Acrylic on canvas board
Museum of New Zealand Te Papa Tongarewa, gift of Hans and Martha Lachmann, 1995

garden, been out paying bills, redesigned a few windows for St Ignatius, gone walking with Anne & have beginnings of 10 paintings... And so am I quite happy & pleasant than since the fame & fortune bit started. That rocked me. I lost my innocence and couldn't see any way back. I felt like Scrooge Macduck swimming in a money bin.'[44]

When McCahon announced the title of his new series, 'Truth from the King Country', Peter replied, 'I would love to show them.'[45] But he was feeling lucky to have a gallery at all after an explosion in Cuba Street had gutted a restaurant 'as clean as a shark's tooth' and blown out virtually every ground-floor window in the block. Peter suspected that gambling debts were behind the attack, and told McCahon he was sorry to see the demise of the restaurant – 'one of those one star places'.

Its clientele was mainly the broken down men and women that sit out and live out. The alkies from Glover Park (around the corner) and from Ma Hallam's hotel where you can get a room for 5 dollars and nobody asks any questions and there is a large sign in the foyer telling you not to smoke in bed. I had the odd meal there. I like those sort of places. It had atmosphere; the sort that money can't buy but which accumulates over the years like the dust and grime that coated the painting of a Greek port.

Steak, egg and chips; snapper and chips and plenty of sauce and then three slabs of extremely thinly buttered bread and a cup of tea. The old TV set would be on the blink. There was always something wrong with the sound and ears would strain to pick up what Dougal Stevenson [the newsreader] was saying. It had atmosphere, that place.

Peter had become attached to his pocket of Cuba Street, with his view over the road to Crazy Rick's Discount Warehouse and 'Cyril and his merry men' from the Manawatu Meat Company. ('Cyril is an "identity" around here... He is bald, with the most beautifully fine skin; a boyish 58 year old with a red whiskey nose. Mrs Cyril runs the office and peers down from her mezzanine aerie (where eagles live) way up the ladder. A fastidious woman with a lovely head of hair; and wears sensible shoes.')[46] But there were plans for the Ghuznee Street intersection to be widened, as he told McCahon – 'so it is only a matter of time when this building will be right on the four lane super highway. The noise? Still, there is no hurry, but a move will be ultimately inevitable.'[47]

Early the following year Peter visited McCahon and was concerned to find him rather despondent. The painter's new prosperity had 'taken the edge off his life,' Peter told his friends Tim and Sherrah Francis. 'He likes having his back to the wall and I suspect it is that that has given his work its strength. You have to be single minded; a loner, he has often said to me.'[48]

Peter was going through a difficult time himself, reporting 'a very unhappy few days' to McCahon in mid-February.[49] 'The usual depression that I sometimes get. Everything goes out the window. I don't know but I just get swept by so many feelings of loneliness and apartness. I look at my job and what I do and feel such a failure in it. The society of which I am a part does not feed me. Well, all of these feelings eddy and move around me.'

McCahon wrote back, troubled:

> Your letter worries me … You were born & bred to the Catholic faith – for that you were exceedingly lucky. You have been given ways of escape from and reconciliation to both yourself & to God. Some work in this part of your life could help.
>
> There is another solution. I was a 'follower' at Quaker meetings for a long time in Dunedin … The meetings are open to anybody the form of worship is silence … You don't *join* you *attend*. But with your inbuilt Catholicism – which if used well is close in meditation to the Quakers – seems your direct step. You are given so many ways to make the unbearable bearable. If you read the Gospels start to finish & note the promises made by Jesus – all of which I believe – try a few. I get depressed often. I even watch the depression deepen & so feel sorry for myself it's only work that shakes it off and walking.[50]

McCahon also recommended writing poetry: 'Nothing like it – your solutions come when walking the streets or digging the garden.'

By March, Peter was able to report he was feeling better: 'the show is back on the road, again'.[51] He told McCahon about an exhibition of his work – at the National Art Gallery, of all places. 'It looks great,' he commented, listing the paintings on display.[52] McCahon wrote to thank gallery staff for sending photographs of the installation: 'never knew I could thank the National Art Gallery for anything – ever. I'll grow fat and lazy on "recognition". It's a change.'[53] Peter remarked on a visit by McCahon's friend, the art historian Gordon H Brown: 'He had a lovely pair of pants on; black, and made from a slightly shiny material.'[54] McCahon, not usually an authority on fashion, noted that there was 'a fair sprinkling' of such 'disco' pants in Auckland: 'They suit Gordon but you won't see me in them'.[55]

Back in the studio, McCahon was preoccupied with his new 'Kumara god' paintings, inspired by a Māori stone carving of a fertility figure in Cornwall Park. In July he reported, 'Two of them are *really great* (I think) I hope they really are.'[56] Two months later he announced, 'I've finished No 2 of the "Kumara Gods" jobs & it glows like a Tintoretto. Its older brother is probably better but not so beautiful.'[57]

McCahon was also planning to revisit A Letter to Hebrews from the New Testament, with its meditation on the nature of faith.[58] His friend and supporter Ian Prior had suggested the text as a basis for a new painting seven years earlier, but McCahon felt ready to meet the challenge only now.[59] In September he wrote to Peter, 'I'm really *on*

Hebrews II – it's beautiful stuff'.[60] A few days later he sent an update: 'You won't get them for your immediate exhibition but for later – & then comes another much later – an elephant size job – it's one third done but the size you can't use – too big. Another is coming on – smaller – all on Hebrews. I've always been fond of Hebrews'.[61]

Meanwhile, Peter and Hilary had celebrated their ten-year wedding anniversary. 'Doesn't time fly,' Peter wrote to McCahon. 'It seems just the other day that we saw each other for the first time. And now, 10 years. Just like that. And another thing, which I am so aware of is that without Hilary I don't think (in fact I know) I would have carried on. She has given me so much support and encouragement. I don't think I could have sustained the long years without her.'[62] In September, Hilary organised a party for Peter's forty-third birthday, his first since turning twenty-one. 'I really enjoyed myself. The children stayed up. Mind you, they insisted on looking at "The 6 Million Dollar Man" at 7.30. That is sacrosanct with Catherine and Olivia … They came through later; very sleepy, heads full of Colonel Steve Austin and his deeds against the crooks.'[63]

In October, Peter opened an exhibition of McCahon's works: seven small paintings from the 'Truth from the King Country' series, two of the 'Five Wounds of Christ' series, and *St Matthew: lightning*.[64] He wrote to the artist next day, 'Everything is well hung. Plenty of space; no clutter on the floor. It looks just great. And the weather is kind; sunny days with a lovely light flooding the rooms.'[65] The smaller works, priced at $250, sold quickly.

By now, Peter had been representing McCahon for eleven years. In that time the artist had been extraordinarily productive, painting many of his finest works; he had held eleven solo exhibitions at the gallery, and established a reputation in Australia. But at sixty, McCahon was no longer in good health, undermined by years of heavy drinking. Peter was not yet aware of his friend's problems. 'When I went to see Colin he would always be drinking. But that wasn't so unusual – we weren't so aware of the dangers of alcohol in those days. I didn't realise that he was deteriorating – not for years. It was very much a gradual thing.'[66]

McCahon would continue to exhibit with Peter in the early 1980s, but his productivity was on the wane and there would be far fewer paintings in the last years of his life.

Peter
McLEAVEY
GALLERY
Peter
McLEAVEY
GALLERY
CONTEMPORARY NEW ZEALAND PAINTING
1st Floor.
bett-duncan studio gallery
HOURS
MON-THURS 11-00 5-00
FRIDAY 11-00 8-00
ELVA BETT
EXHIBITING CONTEMPORARY PAINTINGS PRINTS AND SCULPTURE

FOURTEEN

It is a very sensitive thing, selling art. A lack of faith or trust can really bugger things up.

In 1979, Toss Woollaston was awarded a knighthood – the first to be granted to a New Zealand painter.[1] Days before the announcement, Peter, who had long rued the lack of official recognition for local artists, wrote to him: 'We will all be thinking of you both on the weekend … It may be a bit of a trying time with the media and all the hoohah but you will cope and after a day or so things will settle down. It is a great thing. For all of us in the contemporary art movement to know that you have been recognised.'[2]

Peter was staying with the McCahons when the news came out. 'We were on our way to Muriwai,' he told some friends, 'and stopped at Huapai for the Herald. Toss greeted us from Page 3; a photo. Colin was tickled pink; delighted. He said "What a good thing". Later, that morning, we sat outside and talked about Toss and Edith. We drank some of that "Sherry" (plus water) that Colin favours. It was good. The sun was warm and Colin talked about those times, way back in Mapua and the Moutere, where he first got to know Toss. The boy from McKee's Lime Works had done us all proud.'[3]

Later in the year, Peter had news for Woollaston: 'I have heard on the grapevine that Luit has got the National Art Gallery job.'[4] Like many in the local art world, Woollaston was pleased to hear that Bieringa was to be the new director. In his nine years at the Manawatu Art Gallery, Bieringa had developed an ambitious exhibitions programme, and he was known for his commitment to current practice. In the next decade he acquired key works of contemporary art and raised the profile of the gallery nationwide.

One of Bieringa's first initiatives on taking up his new position was to visit Woollaston to discuss potential purchases. He raised the possibility of a concession price for a set of drawings, but Woollaston, who knew

Entrance to the Peter McLeavey Gallery, photographed by Richard Killeen, 1978 his dealer well, offered a word of warning. 'I fear you may find him adamant about concession rates,' he wrote, and quoted from one of Peter's letters on the subject:

> Not many people in today. Very quiet. I sit here and sometimes wonder if I'm a bit too prickly a customer for some people. I can be rude sometimes, you know, and I do rub people up the wrong way. I'm an elistist; an unbending one, to boot.
>
> Art is something very special in my world and I do not compromise when it comes to the handling or selling of it. I do not treat the works I sell as so much merchandise, like a car dealer.
>
> People can come into these rooms and look. But I'm not going to bend over backwards to make a sale. No discounts; no deals; no specials; no mates' rates; no arts council subsidies; no arse licking. Just the best art in New Zealand. At a price which those that want it can pay.[5]

Woollaston continued, 'It's a pretty formidable statement, eh? ... I feel the outlook for a concession rate on groups of drawings to the National Gallery may be a bit bleak.'

Peter's 'prickliness' was an essential part of his character, but it was fuelled by the challenges of his vocation. He saw himself as a flag-bearer for professional standards, and was swift to react if he sensed that he or his artists were being unfairly treated. In 1978, for example, he had a skirmish with arts council officials, who felt a hefty $200 reproduction fee for McCahon was too high. 'I don't want to be thought of as hard-nosed,' he told the artist, 'but ... we have to run things in a businesslike way. I am not an amateur muddling along on Arts Council grants; whistling in the dark. I'm a pro ... Doing things right for the artists whom I represent. Negotiating on their behalf. Doing it fairly and squarely.'[6]

But sometimes it was the artists, too, who had to be trained in the new professional system. As Peter informed Jeffrey Harris in 1979, 'The important thing about McLeavey's NATIONWIDE concept is that the PRICE BE NATIONWIDE ... The client must always know that the pricing is uniform. No Dunedin, Cromwell, or special price which is in variance with the rest of your outlets.'[7]

Jeffrey Harris grew up in a fairly isolated environment on his parents' farm on Banks Peninsula, and began painting in his teens. He held his first exhibition in Dunedin in 1969 and moved there in the following year, receiving encouragement from Michael Smither, Ralph Hotere and others. Peter regarded him as an unusually gifted artist, and saw something of his own temperament in the young man's vulnerability

Jeffrey Harris, *Deposition*, 1971
Oil on board
Auckland Art Gallery Toi o Tāmaki, purchased 1985

and occasional outbursts. 'We are both sensitive souls,' he remarked, 'both a little cranky, driven.'[8] Peter could be quick to dismiss an artist who failed to live up to his own code of conduct, but he was unusually patient and forgiving with Harris.[9]

Harris was just twenty-three when he held his first exhibition at the Peter McLeavey Gallery in 1972. Most of the six paintings showed scenes from the New Testament, transposed to a South Island landscape: they included *Deposition*, a stark and visionary work with its staring faces, awkward figures and unearthly chalky colours.[10] *Deposition* was priced at just $160, yet neither it nor any other paintings from the exhibition sold.

At Harris's next show in 1974, there were problems when Peter – who admitted to being 'a little disappointed' by some of the work –

Jeffrey Harris, *Relations at Okains*, 1976
Oil on board
Private collection

hung only half of those intended for the exhibition.[11] Harris took offence, which led to a cooling in the relationship. Two years later, Harris wrote to enquire about the state of play: was Peter still interested in representing him? 'I feel you may still be unsure or that you are not happy showing it in your gallery. That the work or that I are too difficult.'[12]

Peter was quick to set the record straight. 'No, that is not so for to me you are one of the best painters we have.'[13] But he admitted some concerns: in particular, he felt that Harris was not fully committed to the dealer-gallery system. Some of his visitors had commented on how much more expensive Peter's Harris paintings were than works they had acquired direct from the artist. In one case, a client wanted Peter to take a work he had bought in Dunedin and sell it at his market price.

> The fact that people have made these queries about the price difference has worried me. For it, like nothing else, destroys the dealer's credibility and erodes the confidence of his market...

> Perhaps I'm over reacting; shades of megalomania. No, I don't think so for I know how difficult it is to sell art. How critical it is that the market be national. And how the heart can be damaged and eroded just as the market by the lack of credibility. By that belief and trust between artist/client/dealer. It's a delicate balance.
>
> I now recap. I hope I've spoken clearly. What is past is past. And these administrative problems do not in any way effect my regard for you or your art.
>
> You are a good artist. I believe in you. And always will regardless of my comments for only art lives.

By the time Harris exhibited again with Peter in 1977, he had completed a series of exceptional small oils, painted in glowing primary colours with meticulous, obsessive detail. 'By working on a smaller scale,' he explained, 'I'm trying to pinpoint everything down to make a more powerful, charged statement.'[14] The twenty-four paintings in the exhibition included a number, like *Relations at Okains*, based on old family photographs – in this case Harris's paternal relatives, 'the outgoing hard-living direct Okains Bay crowd'.[15] The curiously wooden figures, all dressed up, are posed before a seething, superabundant landscape; the image is at once strange, mesmerising and unforgettable. As Peter Ireland observed in *Art New Zealand*, 'Harris's almost obsessional intensity at once attracts and repels, because, in his raw particulars of nature and monstrous figures, there is the recognisably familiar.'[16] Peter had great confidence in these works, but even he was astonished by the rapidity at which they sold; by the end of the exhibition, only two remained.

In the following year, Harris exhibited again, this time showing early works, and the artist–dealer relationship now seemed to be on a more secure footing.[17] The two spent entire days in conversation on Peter's trips to Dunedin, and maintained a frequent correspondence. 'I am glad that you have entered a period of calm,' Peter wrote in October. 'I know that feeling. I think it comes with the growth of confidence and belief that creative people have when they discover that they have a (unique) gift. It is a good feeling; enjoy it.'[18] Peter often revealed something of his own life in his letters, describing on one occasion a trip to see two artists:

> I set off on Saturday morning, flying to Wanganui. As usual I prepared myself by having about six or eight double brandies… It was a very good flight. On arrival at Wanganui, Allen (Maddox) met me and into his (brakeless) Kombi I climbed. We went out into

Jeffrey Harris in his studio, with (in background) *Ring her name with roses*, 1977–78, photographed by Marti Friedlander, 1977

the countryside to a small hamlet where he lives. He had a great flagon of sherry. We drank and talked. He is a lovely chap who lives life to the hilt…

Well back into Wanganui to get the New Plymouth bus and just as we head into Taupo Quay I sight the bus turning right; moving; heading north. We tracked the bus through Wanganui and (luckily) caught it on the edge of town.

I threw my bags and coat out the window of the Kombi. The 12 eggs inside the bag (a generous gift from Allen) hit the ground. 6 were saved. Rather drunk I did something I'd never done before. I ate 2 raw eggs. Shells and all. I can still feel the grit in between my teeth. I was hungry. I slept all the way to New Plymouth.

> Michael [Smither] met me and off to the hotel we went. More beer and talk. Then home to a feed and wine and more beer. The next morning I felt fine.
>
> I caught the Wellington bus at 2.30 and got home about 10.00. I felt thrashed. And it is now (Friday) that I feel back on deck.

Although Peter enjoyed some success in selling Harris's work during the late 1970s, it was not enough to keep the artist afloat. Anxious about his prospects and susceptible to art-world gossip, Harris suggested that gallery directors such as Bill Milbank, Jim Barr and Luit Bieringa were reluctant to buy from him: '[They] prefer a more open approach to what someone called your "antique dealer" approach.'[19] In September 1979, Harris told Peter that he had decided to appoint Patricia Bosshard, his Dunedin agent, as his sole dealer.

Peter responded immediately:

> [Regarding] Patricia Bosshard. Here, I must say I think that she is doing an outstanding job. And, yes, if she is moving things and has Barr, Bieringa and Milbank lined up she must be given (by you) carte blanche. You need the money now and must give to Patricia whatever she wants. That is the fact.
>
> Thirdly re criticisms of my style. Well, I have nothing to say on that. I note your comments on what Barr, Bieringa and Milbank think of me. I hope I'm big enough to just go forward with what I'm doing.
>
> Finally, I do appreciate your frankness.[20]

Peter may have seemed unperturbed in his letter to Harris, but the young artist's comments had troubled him, as he admitted to McCahon:

> It looks as if Jeffrey [and I] have come to a parting of the ways. Not my wish, but Jeffrey's ... [He] wrote to me a letter listing my failings and that really took the wind out of my sails and put me in a curious, twilight zone. And then the uncertainty and self-doubt came. Happily, those two didn't stick around and I've bounced back feeling positive and open.
>
> It is a very sensitive thing, selling art. A lack of faith or trust can really bugger things up. Still, we may get back together again. Only time will tell ...[21]

Indeed, less than a year later Harris had changed his mind. He wrote to Peter, 'If you want to give some consideration to re-handling my work in the Wgtn area, I'd be thrilled. O.K. some people spilled the beans against you. They don't really know you. And I put too much pressure on you. Wanting attention. I hope I'm learning to be more self-contained. To not push the crisis button everytime there's a little fire.'[22]

Harris had a show with Peter in 1981, and was planning to exhibit with him again following a study trip to the United States. He wrote to Peter after visiting Auckland and Wellington. 'I had the feeling as I walked into your gallery that this was the place. The best God-damn gallery in New Zealand... It was a good feeling. It was good to get away... To get an overview of things. The dealers, the collectors, the artists, the gallery directors, their staff. How small it all is. How few people there are. How important it is, that those few people keep going. They are working/making our art history. I guess you and I are among them.'[23]

In March 1983, however, Harris decided once again that Bosshard should be his sole dealer, bringing his on-again, off-again relationship with Peter to an end. Peter was not entirely surprised and took the news in good spirit, even sending a congratulatory letter to Bosshard. 'It seems very natural and proper,' he wrote, 'for you have done an outstanding job in showing and promoting his work.'[24]

Although they were rivals, he felt a bond with the Dunedin dealer. 'I regard her highly,' he told Richard Killeen. 'And I like that hard nosed, competitive streak she has. Which I have, too. It helps us both work better. This is why I welcome the competition and why any dealer should. It makes the whole damned business tick. It gives it muscle.'[25]

Peter waged another battle during the 1970s – against the public galleries that had begun to have selling exhibitions, thus eroding his business. For those institutions it was a phase of transition, as they moved from the control of art society volunteers to a new professional era. 'We were novices in the whole game – we didn't know the protocols,' Luit Bieringa recalled. 'Dealers like Peter were ahead of us in that sense, they had a very clear idea of where their patch was.'[26]

By the early 1980s the problem had resolved itself: the public galleries understood they should not compete with dealers. But in the interim it was a real problem for Peter, and one that caused him some bitterness. In 1976, for example, he was excited about his new Philip Trusttum show. 'I'm thrilled to bits with it,' he told the artist. 'In fact, it's almost a holiday just looking at them for they are so full of life, colour, and confidence... Thank you for a stunning exhibition.'[27]

Peach tree, c.1974, awaiting installation in the exhibition: *Philip Trusttum: 8 recent oil paintings*, March 1975

The fifteen works in the show were modestly priced: '$250 buys you a fine painting,' Peter informed Walters.[28] But there were no sales: a recent selling exhibition at the Dowse Art Gallery had pre-empted it.[29] 'Several of my clients bought from the Dowse,' Peter told Walters. 'It's a darn shame and also a bit of an irritant. More and more of the public galleries and institutions are getting into the act and mounting shows by contemporary artists and selling the stuff. It's a bit like the library hiring out the latest bestseller and selling it as well. I guess the city fathers approve. I mean it's a good way to raise additional monies.'

Six months later, Peter was still fuming over the Trusttum show: 'It was so good and yet not one sale.'[30] He continued:

> I don't think people realise how fragile it is, here in this country... how 'thin' the market is. The audience is just so small. The actual buyers are a fraction of that.
>
> It is hard to be a painter. But to be a dealer, and survive, it is harder. The financial loading to keep a place open is almost unbearable at times. Or rather, it has been with me...
>
> To do it properly, professionally, every day is hard. To take the knock backs, time and time again. And to keep climbing back through the ropes time and time again makes this job the loneliest in the world. Particularly in this country where the cult of the amateur pervades all attitudes towards my profession.

Peter held eight shows by Trusttum between 1972 and 1986, but the artist's habit of selling works outside the dealer-gallery system strained the relationship to breaking point. In 1977, Trusttum held an exhibition at his home in Christchurch; three years later, he organised a private auction in the city, selling 105 works for $17,500.[31] Peter was dismayed by these events, reporting to Walters, 'If the artist is not committed to the dealer (and the dealing system) it just has to end. Least, that is the case with me. It is just not worth the hassle.'[32] But the situation was complicated by Peter's high regard for Trusttum's art. In his case, as with Jeffrey Harris, he was prepared to let his instinct overrule his business principles. He continued to visit the artist on a regular basis, and in 1986 noted in his diary, 'Trusttum recent work is very good. Should I persevere??'[33]

Trusttum held his last show at the Peter McLeavey Gallery in August that year: fifteen works inspired by his domestic life, including a series of painted 'seed packets', complete with 'seeds' – cut-up fragments of old pictures. Shortly afterwards, Trusttum sold eight works at auction in Auckland. Peter wrote to terminate their professional association, emphasising that his decision had nothing to do with his personal feelings for Trusttum – 'I like and respect you' – or his opinion of his work: 'As I have told you, and others... you are simply the finest colourist; the most gifted painter, of your generation. Unqualified; total; complete. But, for some reason, you and I are unable to work together. Perhaps it is "temperament" (mine?). Perhaps it's something else... Who knows?'[34]

Trusttum replied in concilatory fashion. 'Yes it does seem our "temperament" gets in the way... But no problem, I respect everything you stand for and certainly you're top Gallery in N.Z.'[35]

Philip and Lee Trusttum, photographed by Marti Friedlander, c.1979

For Peter, 'temperament' was crucial in deciding who to represent. He had a high regard for the work of Philip Clairmont, for example, and had even raised the possibility of an exhibition in 1972. But, as he later explained to McCahon, something went wrong:

> Here it was partly my fault for I'm such a stickler for details and particulars. To cut a long story short he was going to send up a lovely 'Fireplace' painting. And he did, eventually. But it was about 3 months late. I sensed then that he was contrary and perhaps unreliable when it came to the business of dealing and selling paintings. Perhaps he was young. Anyway that irritated me. And in the way of these things I sort of lost interest. Decided to put my energies in other directions.

> Perhaps I made a mistake. We all do … I just did not feel happy with the 'vibes' that I got from Philip … His painting has remained, however, always the same, in its quality … He is a rare painter, and a fine one.[36]

Peter had similar reservations about Tony Fomison. He admired his paintings of lone figures in eerie, primordial landscapes, but doubted his reliability and never represented him. Aware of his own need for order and control, he instinctively knew that Clairmont and Fomison would be too difficult for him to work with. In the 1980s, however, when he came to establish an art collection for the Bank of New Zealand, he bought an exceptional suite of works by both artists.

Perhaps the most notable omission in Peter's stable was the Dunedin artist Ralph Hotere. 'I already represented McCahon, the other great New Zealand artist who combined painting and poetry,' Peter recalled. 'I liked Ralph and respected his work, but I just didn't think there was room for both artists in the gallery.'[37] Years later, when Hotere's retrospective opened in Auckland in 2000, Peter wrote to him, 'I'm sorry I will be away for the opening … I will toast *your health*; and *your art*, with the best *Rum* money can buy … I'll lift that glass heavenwards at about 6.30, Auckland time.'[38]

—

In the 1970s, Peter began to take photographs of artists in their studios, assembling multiple images in collages that recall the contemporaneous work of David Hockney. His interest in taking photographs was not new: he had owned a camera from his late teens, and even in the early 1960s Ivan Bootham felt his involvement was 'more than that of someone who took snapshots … His taking a photo was a conscious, thought-aware act.'[39] As a young dealer, Peter's interest in documenting his artists was influenced by the collector and gallery director Ron O'Reilly. 'He was always taking photos: he had a sense of history, and the importance of recording the present. And by then I was representing an older generation of artists.'[40]

Early in his career, Peter had bought a complete set of both *Art in New Zealand*, a quarterly journal of the 1930s and 1940s, and the *Year book of the arts* that followed. 'I combed through them,' he recalled. 'I was on a voyage of discovery. There were all these islands out there waiting to be discovered – the islands of Charles and John Tole, the republic of Adele Younghusband, and the United States of Lois White.'

Charles Tole, *Dredge, Paritutu, New Plymouth*, c.1949
Oil on board
Private collection

Peter paid his first visit to Charles Tole, a bachelor and a devout Catholic, at his small flat in Kohimarama in Auckland in 1977.[41] Back home, he wrote to thank the artist for agreeing to exhibit with him: 'Art is a lifetime and while I do expect sales things may be a little slow. This, as the economic climate these days is uncertain. However, have no fears about the work. You are a good painter and your work will live long after you and I have gone to meet our Maker.'[42]

He felt an affinity with Tole's art: images of suburban landscapes, often with industrial buildings, painted in a crisp, geometric style. Modest in scale and jewel-like, the pictures reminded him of icons in their clarity and precision; they also evoked the small-town New Zealand of Frank Sargeson, one of his personal heroes.[43] For Tole, then in his mid-seventies and still fully engaged in his work, Peter took on the role of critic. 'I find your visits very helpful,' he wrote, 'as I can get a "first, fresh view" of any works I may be currently painting whereas my own judgment I feel is tending to become stale through seeing too much of

Charles Tole in his studio at Piccadilly Place, Kohimarama, Auckland, photographed by Peter McLeavey, 1984

A Lois White, *Winter's approach*, c.1938
Oil on canvas
Museum of New Zealand Te Papa Tongarewa, purchased 1984 with New Zealand Lottery Board funds

them.'[44] He quoted the advice of his mentor, the artist John Weeks: 'turn the work face to the wall for three to six months'.

At Tole's first solo show in August 1977, Peter sold ten of the twelve paintings, including the outstanding *Dredge, Paritutu, New Plymouth*.[45] Writing in the *Listener*, critic and academic John Roberts commented on the singularity of Tole's vision: 'Nothing moves; the ships are still; no trains rush through the country station. There is no place for untidy humans in the careful sub-cubist constructions.'[46] It was an excellent start for Tole in the capital, and he would go on to have five more shows with Peter, including one with his brother John and a posthumous retrospective in 1989. He also exhibited in group shows.

A Lois White made her debut at the gallery in a group exhibition with Olivia Spencer Bower and Robin White in August 1975 – three regionalists of different generations.[47] In the 1940s, critics had praised her work for its rhythmic composition and imaginative qualities, but in the following decade, as art fashions changed, it fell from favour.

After twenty-eight years as a tutor at Elam School of Fine Arts, which she regarded as her second home, White was forced into retirement in 1963. It was a blow from which she never recovered.

In the late 1970s, Peter became a regular visitor at the house White shared with her sister Gwen in Blockhouse Bay in Auckland. 'Your interest has made me want to work,' she told him, 'but I admit that passing years have slowed my energies, and watching over Gwen tends to make me procrastinate.'[48] Biblical themes continued to attract her, and she and Peter often discussed religion and literature. In May 1976 he wrote to her:

> One of my favourite pleasures is reading the Lives of the Saints… I like to read them to my two small children; Catherine (aged four) and Olivia (aged two). A lot of the doings are above their heads, but not their hearts which seem to intuitively respond to the ideals and holiness of those brave men and women.
>
> Another pleasure is French symbolist poetry. People like Rimbaud, Baudelaire, Mallarmé, Valéry…I find it a vale of quiet and mystery in my world; a world which is so often demanding and exhausting.
>
> I hope I don't seem to be moaning for I don't mean to. I love my job. But to do it well (in fact to do *anything* well) you have to be committed. As you know. And sometimes I do get tired.[49]

White replied, 'You sound the kind of family man that my father was. He was an architect, but all his spare time was spent with his children.'[50] In fact, although Peter took delight in his children, he often struggled to cope with family life. 'I find fatherhood a pressure at times,' he admitted. 'I'm a solitary man who married late and I'd much sooner go off to my room and read at night and at weekends… The family don't see it that way (why should they, anyway) and calls for "Daddy do this", "Daddy do that" fill the air…At night, it is usually 8.30 before my wife and I can put our feet up and by then we are just "bushed". Invariably one hand moves towards the TV "ON" switch where packaged entertainment fills the air.'[51]

In October 1977, Peter held a retrospective of White's works on paper, including studies for some of her major oils. He also showed a painting from his own collection – *Winter's approach*, exhibited 'not for sale'. 'Lois came down for the show,' he told McCahon, 'and stayed with us for two days. I invited 20 people in to a small opening function at the gallery. It was a touching affair for it was Lois's first one man (or, person) show. And that at 74. She loved it and drank about three glasses of Spanish sherry (which she is partial to). I have sold to the Hocken Library, the McDougall Art Gallery, the Alexander Turnbull Library and several private clients.'[52] Neil Rowe described the exhibition

A Lois White, *Design*, c.1944
Gouache on pasteboard
Bank of New Zealand Art Collection

as an historic occasion. 'What is most striking about seeing for the first time a large group of her works is the recognition that Lois White has been much under-rated as a painter … Peter McLeavey is to be commended both for his acumen in recognising this quality and the work's historical status and for mounting this exhibition.'[53]

White's sister Gwen died in 1979, and she had a mild stroke late in the year. Peter sent flowers and continued to write encouraging letters, telling her about developments in the McLeavey household: Catherine and Olivia were at school, Dominic was attending play group and Hilary had enrolled in Women's Studies at Victoria University. White replied, commenting on Hilary's success with her studies:

> To run a home and at the same time care for three offspring is a feat in itself, let alone to have the urge and determination to carry university studies as well, is fantastic, I wish her every success in all her efforts.
>
> By contrast, your aged friend at Taunton Terrace lives the life of a drone, with dreams of painting which inhabit her mind – but she does not fulfil these dreams, alas. My doctor gave me an encouraging prod the other day and indicated that I was travelling on a long and slow journey back to health and strength … bless him!
>
> I am the last of my family now; Mother, Father, 2 brothers and a sister keep knocking on the door of my memories. This is when I sweep up my little dog and talk nonsense to him, and then cuddle my cat. They are comforting company to a solitary, sometimes lonely soul.[54]

Peter was moved by White's letter and replied immediately.

> I hope that I can always live with the courage and grace which you have. They are good, those two handmaidens. Courage and grace.
>
> It is a lovely word, grace. In the Catholic church we say, 'Hail Mary, full of Grace', and it evokes an angelic light burning within each heart. A light of Grace which illuminates and casts out darkness; it enables us to live.
>
> Your letter had that quality; it was full of grace.[55]

White suffered a second massive stroke in 1981 that left her incapacitated, and she died in hospital three years later. In 1979, Peter had suggested: 'One day you will have articles written about you (perhaps a book) but all that will be in the future. The critics and art followers are so often far behind the artist.'[56] Ten years after White's death, a major retrospective of her work opened at the Auckland City Art Gallery, accompanied by a substantial catalogue.

Richard Killeen wrote to Peter about the exhibition, and reflected on the way White had been a victim of fashion:

> Lois White was forced out of the Art School around 1962, 2 years before I arrived there … The new boys, Allen, Beadle and Ellis were in control. McCahon came in 1964 or 5. The funny thing to me is that the new guard that White was having trouble with was already the old guard to me and others in terms of their attitudes.
>
> In a larger country there would have been a place for Lois White regardless of the changes that went on about her. On television last night, Jane Campion and Don Clarke said they left New Zealand because they sensed that the country never valued a person for what they had achieved. This is what happened to Lois White.[57]

FIFTEEN

It's still about 1890 here as far as photography and the public is concerned.

The 1970s have been described as a 'missionary decade' for photography as an art form in New Zealand.[1] Impetus came from the new photography department at Elam School of Fine Arts, established in 1965, as well as from influential touring shows like *The photographer's eye* and *New photography U.S.A.*, curated by the Museum of Modern Art in New York,[2] which reflected a growing international interest in photography and its increasing representation in major art museums.

In Auckland in 1973, a group of photographers, including John B Turner and Max Oettli, founded PhotoForum to promote the medium in New Zealand. PhotoForum organised workshops, published a magazine of the same name and played a key role in inspiring a new generation to take up a camera.[3] In the following years, photographers opened galleries to show their work, among them Snaps Gallery in Auckland and PhotoForum Gallery in Wellington, and public museums began to exhibit the medium.[4] In 1975, in partnership with PhotoForum, the Manawatu Art Gallery toured *The active eye* – the largest survey of contemporary New Zealand photography to date.

Until the late 1970s, however, photography had little presence in the dealer-gallery scene. In 1972, photographer John Fields organised a group show including the work of Gary Baigent, Turner, Ans Westra and others at the Barry Lett Galleries, but the exhibition received a mixed response. '[I]t was not an impressive opening,' Walters reported to Peter, 'too many freeloaders and hangers on taking advantage of the affair for a get together. No sales so far – to the disappointment of the exhibitors, but I think that prices at around $30–$35 per print are too high. Barry and Rodney looked rather disenchanted with the whole

Peter Peryer, *Self-portrait*, 1977
Gelatin silver print
Te Manawa Museums Trust

affair.'[5] As the photographer Paul Hewson observed, the medium presented a challenge for art dealers: 'Even with running costs pared to the minimum ... the revenue in the form of sales commission is minimal. This is for two reasons: sales are low, and sale prices are low, too. Photographs must be today's greatest art bargain.'[6]

Peter had grown up with photography. As a child, curious about the outside world, he pored over popular magazines like *Life* and *Picture Post*, which transmitted images of current events around the globe. As a teenager, he admired the work of the famous Magnum photojournalists: Robert Capa, Henri Cartier-Bresson and others. In his short stint as an art critic he reviewed *The photographer's eye*, commenting on the exceptional nature of many of the images: 'In the hands of a great photographer the time and place become "real", the eye and mind are engaged at an artistic level.'[7]

During the 1970s, his interest in photography deepened – encouraged by friends such as Peter Ireland and Turner, and honed by extensive reading. In March 1977, he wrote to Wilson Buchanan, 'I am very interested in photography and would like to extend my business in the direction of a small photographic gallery. The only problem is the costing and the length of time I would have to carry it before it came on stream as a profitable unit. My guess is that it would take three to five years.'[8] Travelling to Australia several weeks later, he made a point of visiting galleries that specialised in the medium, such as the Australian Centre for Photography in Sydney. Back home, he wrote to Laurence Aberhart, 'I would be grateful if you would send to me a selection of your photographs. No; not to buy, but to look at ... I feel that I wish to study it more deeply.'[9]

Peter had met Aberhart in 1968, when the teenager was working for the Woollastons at Riwaka.[10] Later, when Aberhart had completed his teacher training and was posted to Paihia, he met up with Woollaston in Wellington on his way north. 'Toss took me to Peter McLeavey's Hataitai flat and Peter said, "Oh you're interested in photography, you must meet John Turner." So he got on the phone, and John was over in a flash. And John said, "When you're in Auckland you must look up Gary Baigent and Richard Collins and John Fields." Through them I was plunged into the whole Auckland art world which seemed to revolve around the Kiwi Tavern.'[11]

Turner's northern cohorts were quick to appreciate Aberhart's natural ability. From the start, the young photographer was drawn to the vernacular architecture and monuments of New Zealand: the modest churches, halls, war memorials and cemeteries that provided

Laurence Aberhart, *Lodge Clinton, Clinton 1979*, 1979
Gold and selenium-toned gelatin silver print
Auckland Art Gallery Toi o Tāmaki, purchased 1981

a map of human habitation across the land. To this archeological project of revealing the overlooked or the neglected, he brought a rigorously geometricising eye, framing his subjects with clarity and precision. Aberhart exhibited his work for the first time in *The active eye* in 1975, and when Peter contacted him two years later he was teaching at Ilam School of Fine Arts in Christchurch.

Peter's request took Aberhart by surprise: he was not accustomed to hearing from art dealers. In July, he dispatched a selection of images, and Peter responded unequivocally: 'I would like to handle your photographs.' He noted the works he liked best: 'the 1940s style bungalows; the OFCA building; the Judo Club ... the Donald Duck playthings at the motel and the shots around the motel'.[12] Aberhart was

Peter Peryer, *Erika, winter*, 1979
Gelatin silver print
Museum of New Zealand Te Papa Tongarewa, purchased 1981 with Harold Beauchamp Collection funds

delighted: 'I am grateful that you have made a committal to photography. I have the belief that you more than anyone probably will be able to bring about a greater acceptance of photography in this country. And if I can start to sell some work it will justify and make things much easier for me to get more deeply involved in the work I want to do.'[13]

Peter was also in contact with Peter Peryer, who had taken up photography in his early thirties. He, too, was mainly self-taught, applying himself to the study of photography with energy, discipline and focus. Peryer once remarked, 'My subject matter is certain emotions', and his early photographs, especially his portraits of his wife Erika Parkinson, are charged, edgy images.[14] In 1976, he held a solo show at the Peter Webb Gallery; in the following year, Jim Barr, the director at the Dowse, organised Peryer's first exhibition in a public gallery.

Peryer had made an impact on the local art world in just a few years but, like Aberhart, he had little chance of earning even a token income from his work. Interviewed in 1979, he commented on the challenge of being an artist, let alone a photographer, in a small country with a limited market. 'Sometimes I have to give myself a lot of reassurance that working as an artist is a worthwhile way to spend one's life. And as a photographer I have at times found it painful to know that many people don't look upon photography as having a legitimate place in the art world.'[15]

Peter certainly did. In 1977, he had purchased Peryer's 'Mars Hotel' portfolio as a gift for Colin McCahon. 'I did that from time to time,' he commented, 'if I felt an artist would appreciate it. I thought Colin would like Peter's photographs and so he did.'[16] The following year Peter began to represent Peryer, and in April he made his first sale of work held in stock. 'Just a hurried note to advise that after eight weeks we have hit paydirt,' he announced. 'Yes, two photographs sold at $50.00 each. A great thrill to me, as it is my first sale in the medium.'[17] The works – *Self-portrait* and *Christine Mathieson* – had been purchased by the Manawatu Art Gallery.[18]

Laurence Aberhart's first solo show, opened in July 1978, was also Peter's first photographic exhibition; it included works from 1974 to 1978, priced at $40 for an unframed print. He advised Aberhart that he had sold three works, all to private collectors.[19]

> The exhibition was, for me, a great success. Not, obviously, financially, but in a more important way. That is, it attracted large crowds who came in and looked, discussed and generally were involved with the photographs.
>
> Some did not like it. Many did. I was thrilled with the quality of the show and, while sales may seem to you to be slow, they are not really. Not when you consider that it takes many years to make much impact. And with your first show, here, you have taken the first steps out on a *real* career, that of a photographer.[20]

Aberhart replied, 'I didn't expect a lot of sales – even three impresses me! I think you may now have an understanding of how photography is regarded by the (art) world at large.'[21]

This was an issue that Peter Ireland addressed in his review of the exhibition in *PhotoForum*. He began with an observation: 'Notions of art and photography have never been easy bedfellows.'[22] He went on to suggest that photographs were too often assessed in terms of technical skill rather than aesthetic quality; moreover, because they could be produced in multiples, they posed a challenge to an art world traditionally concerned with unique objects. But for Ireland all these questions became irrelevant in the presence of certain images – 'work so unquestionably in the tradition we recognise stretching back through art-as-we-know-it to the Delos lions and the Harappa torso. The Is-It-Art debate has been decided; not by the philosophers but by the photographs themselves.'

Ireland also commented on the circumstances of the exhibition:

> This is the first photographic show in what has good claim to be New Zealand's leading dealer gallery, and as such is not an unhistoric event. It is the first visible sign of a commitment which likely will in the future be seen to have been a turning point for photography in this country.
>
> There is some extraordinarily fine work being done here – it could be said without exaggeration that photography is New Zealand's most vital contemporary art form – yet, oddly, the quality of work by some photographers seems in inverse proportion to the notice being taken of it.
>
> There are no longer excuses for galleries failing to exhibit and collect; no excuse for people failing to look and buy. Laurence Aberhart's nineteen photographs at Peter McLeavey's Gallery verify that.

Keen to increase the presence of photography in the gallery, Peter now invited Ireland to curate a group exhibition. After eleven years at Cuba Street, this was a first: Peter liked to keep a tight rein on what was shown, and it was unusual for him to cede control to anyone else. He was aware, however, that Ireland was one of New Zealand's leading photography critics with close links to contemporary practitioners.

Ireland's exhibition, entitled *The new image*, opened in August 1979, with works by twelve artists including Aberhart, Peryer, Gillian Chaplin, Megan Jenkinson, Rhondda Bosworth, Bruce Foster and Christine Lloyd-Fitt.[23] Two days later, Peter wrote to Jeffrey Harris,

‘[T]he more I look at it the more the feeling grows that it is probably a very important show. There is a wonderful sense of unity about it and, most interesting, each photographer’s work stands up and is not dominated by the others … And a lot of young people are coming through looking and “spreading the word”. A few oldies (post 30 years) can be sighted, too. And the odd arts council pops in. All very much “Day in the Life of Joe Egg” stuff.’[24] Writing to Walters, Peter commented on the number of talented young women in the exhibition ‘their stuff is often the most innovative and exciting’.[25]

Peter sold thirteen works, including six by Megan Jenkinson. A further three sales of Gillian Chaplin’s work were cancelled after Neil Rowe published a lukewarm review, suggesting that ‘Photography is fast becoming a fad.’[26] After reading that, Peter told Chaplin, ‘the prospective client requested that the sale be aborted. As in this business, the client is always right I agreed to do this. This, I hasten to add, has never happened to me before.’[27] In the *Listener*, Heather Curnow offered a much more positive assessment: ‘The prices for the photographs range from $30 to $60 – bargains for the collector who is informed enough to take advantage of the astonishing neglect of this creative and exciting art form.’[28]

As Peter told Peryer, he was well satisfied with the exhibition: ‘it was another step towards getting photography (more publicly) recognised, and accepted’.[29] He was hoping to follow up with a show of Peryer’s work, but the artist, although happy to provide images for stock, was unable to commit to a solo exhibition.[30] Peryer had been going through a difficult time, as he confided to Peter. ‘I have just come out of a big black hole the likes of which I do not want to experience again. Ever. It is called learning to cope with success or, learning to cope with the fear of being without it … My rhythms have been all wrong – overcommitted, out of balance, spinning wildly. Fulltime work, too many exhibitions rashly agreed to. Now I need to be more private, but strong.’[31]

Peter replied sympathetically:

> I’m sorry to read of the sadness that overcame you. I, too, know that dark prince …
>
> Yes, and I can understand your confusion over your success. I don’t know how you handle that one. I know how I handle it (or try to).
>
> It is a lifetime; the path you are on will have its ups and downs. Don’t rush into too many commitments. We can always have a show next year … The quality is the only thing. Stick at the book packing job and bide your time. Don’t wreck that talent, that gift, by rushing hither and yon with shows here, there, and everywhere.

Here, I'm probably telling my mother to suck eggs for, I feel that you know it all anyway. You will call the shots.[32]

By the early 1980s, the art market in New Zealand was beginning to mature, but photography was much slower to catch on. 'I think it's still about 1890 here as far as photography and the public is concerned,' Peter Ireland rued.[33] The situation was scarcely any better in Australia. Reporting back to Aberhart after his trip to Sydney in 1982 (when he sold three of his works to the Power Institute of Contemporary Art), Peter noted, 'The dealing scene regarding photography was virtually non existent. Most dealers in contemporary art just don't appear interested.'[34]

Locally, the National Art Gallery under director Luit Bieringa led the way in collecting contemporary photography, and in 1982, Peter Ireland curated *Views/Exposures*, an ambitious take on current New Zealand practice. Aberhart and Peryer were two of the ten featured artists, but even the sanction of the National Art Gallery had little impact on the market for their work. Peryer's comment of the previous year still held true: 'I now face the constant humiliation of extravagant praise on one hand & no sales on the other.'[35]

In 1981, Aberhart had written to Peter about a project that had been simmering in his imagination for a decade. On his first trip to Northland in 1970, he recalled, '[M]y mind, and my heart were opened by the Maori churches. I also knew that my photographic "technique" was neither adequate or sympathetic enough to reveal the simple beauty of these places of worship. I moved south again and waited 10 years'.[36] In 1982, he was awarded an arts council grant, and his project suddenly became a reality. With his partner Greta North, he spent three months on the road in Northland, seeking out the churches he remembered – 'looking, stopping, asking, talking, and just quietly "being" in these places of tranquillity and strength'. In May, he reported to Peter from Kaitaia:

> I'm getting a lot of work done; finding a lot of material, some of it humdrum (but worthy of recording) and some of it quite fantastic! Of course, some of the best experiences, which are meetings with people, cannot in any way be photographed as such, except in the mind's/heart's eye. There have been a number of Maori people (notably several older ladies) who have been quite remarkable …
>
> The norm of the trip is to find something – albeit a church or a marae – and then go and find someone to ask permission if it's

> o.k. to look and take pictures. This is often treated with a degree of, if not hostility at least a fair tempering of 'reserve'. But after 10 minutes or so, after the person has told me of all various wrong-doings committed by various persons (Pakeha-implied) in the past then I've been given the go-ahead. But, God, the terrible things that people (especially photographers) have done in the past!
>
> So, it is all going quite well... by persevering, and perhaps channelling my vision only into a couple of areas (ie churches etc) there comes along, every now and again, a situation that makes up for a whole lot of miles and dust covered.[37]

In December 1983, Aberhart exhibited sixty-two photographs from this journey, both interior and exterior views of the churches, at the Peter McLeavey Gallery. Reviewing the show for *PhotoForum*, fellow artist Janet Bayly commented on Aberhart's 'feeling for space, atmosphere, silence and stillness', and described his photographs as 'some of the most rare and beautiful images I have ever seen of this country'.[38]

Peter sold just three works from this show. '[P]eople seem very cagey to spend $250.00 per image on a photograph,' he had admitted to Walters in July. 'It needs a long term education plan, I feel, to get the public really interested in photography.'[39]

He was increasingly aware that he needed to focus on a smaller number of photographers, and in the following year he returned some work to Peter Hannken with an apologetic note: 'I have come to the conclusion that I need to examine the way I have been handling photography. For some reason it is just not possible (in this space) to do full justice to both.'[40]

For Aberhart, meanwhile, financial pressure was mounting. 'I have been feeling for a while now that something has to happen,' he told Peter in March 1984, 'that is, something "more" has to happen soon, or I will be forced out of the gallery, exhibiting side of photography for good. I wouldn't stop photographing, but at the moment I can't see how I can afford to be a "public" photographer for much longer.'[41] Weeks later, he was much relieved by a cheque from Peter. 'That put us on a real high – we were sitting, moping over morning coffee and you have no idea how a day is lifted by money in the mail!'[42]

Even in 1990, Aberhart was still considering that he might have to abandon photography. He wrote to Peter:

> It did get to the point whereby about a month ago, I had put a definite date down and when I reached that point and nothing had changed (economically) I had resolved to set in train a series of

events. The first of which was to sit down and write to yourself and Kerry [Aberhart, his brother and Auckland dealer], without any bitterness, only resignation, and ask that you both return all work as I was going to pull right out of *all* of the art world; this being the first step before going on the dole, finishing this house, selling it, shifting and getting a job in the 'real' world.[43]

But when it came to the time, Aberhart couldn't do it: 'To do so would have been a negation of too much'. He assured Peter he had recovered his sense of purpose – 'As soon as the money situation is on the improve I'm out and doing it' – and thanked him for his encouragement. 'I feel as though I'm on track again and at such moments it's necessary to look back a little and reflect – especially on the support.'

Peryer had his last show at the Peter McLeavey Gallery in December 1984. It was his decision to leave the gallery. 'I liked Peter. I respected him. But it's hard to sell photographs and the dealer model just wasn't working for me. It didn't work in Auckland either. I decided I had to go out and market the work myself – it was a matter of survival. I was very friendly with Jim and Mary Barr and I would go down to Wellington and set up in their front room, showing the photographs, and they'd invite people round. I sold quite a bit of work that way.'[44] Peryer had a small but dedicated group of collectors in Wellington. 'Les and Milly Paris, for example. They'd buy a work and then I would get a lovely letter: how they'd framed it, where they'd displayed it, and how they were responding to it. They were amazing.'

Peter often reflected on the position of the art dealer, located at a cusp between two very different worlds – that of the artist and the studio, on the one hand, and the collector on the other. '[E]ssentially as a dealer I feel that I am standing alone, in the middle. And spiritually, it's a very unusual point. I feel like a character out of a Graham Greene novel. You're dealing with passions and wishes, with yearnings and ideals, with people's drives and desire to possess the object. It's a curiously isolating and rather lonesome position, selling dreams. And it is that loneliness and a singular view of the world which has always made me identify with the occupants of Greeneland.'[45]

Laurence Aberhart, *Anglican church, Pawarenga Peninsula, Whangape Harbour, Northland, 10 May 1982*, (top) and *Interior, Anglican church, Pawarenga Peninsula, Whangape Harbour, Northland, 10 May 1982*, both 1982
Gelatin silver prints
Museum of New Zealand Te Papa Tongarewa, purchased 1984 with New Zealand Lottery Board funds

As a dealer, Peter had ample opportunity to observe his clients and study the psychology of collecting. 'There are a lot of people who buy art from time to time,' he commented. 'Very few become collectors.'[46] He was making a distinction between a casual interest in art and something much more consuming – a lifelong quest for the next acquisition. He often remarked that it was a handful of serious collectors who kept his business alive, but regardless of the level of commitment, he was careful to safeguard their privacy. 'Peter doesn't gossip,' family friend Margreta Chance noted. 'And that's most unusual in the art world.'[47]

Peter's key clients came from diverse backgrounds: from academics, lawyers and doctors to students and artists with little income to spare. Les and Milly Paris were not the only collectors who preferred to drive an old car if it meant they could afford a new painting. Hans and Martha Lachmann, a generation older than the Parises, were similarly focused and committed, using their modest funds to build a fine collection of contemporary painting, sculpture and ceramics.

Like many of the European migrants who helped to revitalise New Zealand culture in the post-war years, the Lachmanns left Vienna in 1938 to escape Nazi persecution. Hans, originally from Berlin, worked as an economist in Wellington, and he and his wife soon became a regular presence at local exhibitions and concerts. They began collecting art in the 1950s and by the mid-1970s, according to their son Stephen, 'the house was virtually a gallery. The pictures covered every inch of wall and many more were stored in a portfolio under the couch.'[48] The Lachmanns bought their first painting from Peter in 1971 – Mrkusich's *Four circles blue*, a work on paper, for $80. Over the next decade they acquired at least twenty more, by Killeen, Illingworth, Walters, Trusttum, Harris, Woollaston, McCahon, Smither, A Lois White, Charles Tole and Robin White. When Peter commissioned McCahon to make a series of fifteen drawings – 'Hear me O south wind' – to mark his first decade at Cuba Street, the Lachmanns, like the Parises, were among the recipients.

The Lachmanns bought art because they loved it and wanted to live with it; they were typical of an earlier generation of collectors in that they had no expectation of financial gain. Many years later, in 1995, they gifted fifty-three works to Te Papa. As their son recalled, 'They felt that many of the paintings were so significant in the progression of New Zealand art that they really belonged in a public museum.'[49]

Much has been written about the psychology of collecting: the desire to possess, the thrill of the chase and the ultimate gratification of attainment. The German-Jewish cultural critic Walter Benjamin described the mysterious and often obsessive relationship between

Interior of the Hans and Martha Lachmann home, 1991, showing works by Michael Illingworth, Robin White and Milan Mrkusich, all purchased from the Peter McLeavey Gallery

collector and object in a famous essay on book collecting. Unpacking his much-cherished library, he reflected on the way his books had become almost a part of him, a reflection of his identity: he remarked on the 'spring tide of memories which surges towards any collector as he contemplates his possessions'. Benjamin concluded, 'Ownership is the most intimate relationship that one can have to objects. Not that they come alive in him; it is he who lives in them.'[50] Peter copied a quotation from Benjamin into his journal: 'Every passion borders on the chaotic, but the collector's passion borders on the chaos of memories.'[51]

Peter described the longing of the collector in terms of a love affair. 'It's almost a psychic wound to possess the object... The object gazes at me. We're in a room alone. The object and I. The object consumes my heart. I possess it. It's a form of love. It's a form of hunger. It's a spiritual yearning.'[52] Peter was not merely observing his clients, for he had first-hand experience of the powerful emotional desire to possess an artwork. '[Hilary and I] are in our way collectors,' he told McCahon. 'We both love the paintings we have and while we don't possess a car

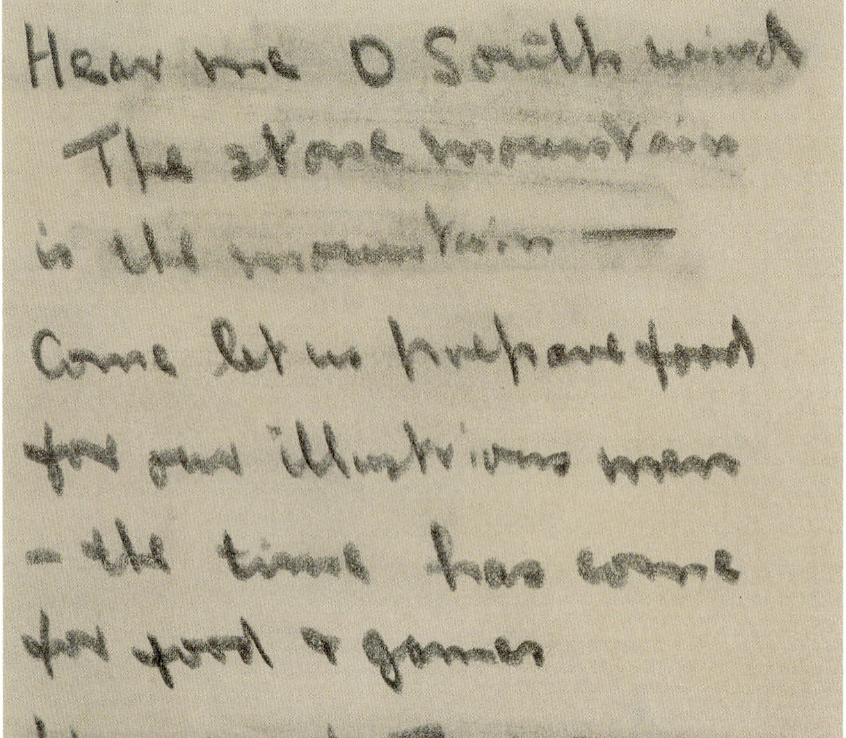

Hear me O South wind
The stone mountain
is the mountain —
Come let us prepare food
for our illustrious men
– the time has come
for food & games
Hear me! TUHOE and
the people and RUA
is their prophet.

See the stirring of the lake

14 C. McC 77

Colin McCahon, *Hear me O south wind 14*, 1977
Pencil on paper
Museum of New Zealand Te Papa Tongarewa,
gift of Hans and Martha Lachmann, 1995

and in a sense live close to the bone we do get so much from the art we have. In my case the works are central to my leisure and working… I bathe in their waters. I rest.'[53] And he shared with many of his clients a feeling of the responsibility that came with owning important works. Reflecting on Woollaston's portrait of his parents, he commented, 'One never owns paintings but has them on loan, on trust. Yes, we paid for it but somehow when you own a thing of that beauty you know in your bones that generations in the future must see it. And will'. Many years later, he and Hilary gifted this portrait to Te Papa.[54]

Like any true collector, Peter was willing to make sacrifices in his quest for a new treasure, even if Hilary was not always in agreement. In 1976, for example, when they were about to install a new kitchen, Peter fell for a carving he had seen in an international art catalogue – a northern Italian carving of a Christ figure. 'We ended up with the carving,' Hilary recalled, 'and the kitchen had to wait. Our old kitchen had been condemned – it was unsafe! – but Peter was determined to have the carving. I was not happy.'[55]

In his first decade in business, when his ability to buy art was limited, Peter's need to collect found other outlets. In the mid-1970s, he began to acquire first editions of New Zealand writing from the early modern period. 'It's in fact become an insatiable interest and I get great pleasure out of it,' he informed a friend. 'I've got complete sets of Eileen Duggan and (almost) Frank Sargeson as well as building up my collection of Charles Brasch, Ursula Bethell, R.A.K. Mason. It's something that keeps me "sane".'[56] On his travels around the country, with time to spare before the next bus, Peter frequented second-hand bookstores in pursuit of an elusive volume. 'It is important for me to have and collect these books,' he told McCahon, 'for they are sort of ikons of our land. They are points of reference for my heart. I guess that must say something about me and perhaps indicates some insecurity that I may have. I don't know.'[57] Occasionally he shared his finds: in 1979, for example, he sent McCahon a book of photographs of Timaru taken by the artist's grandfather, William Ferrier. He was delighted with the response: a long letter, recounting a childhood trip McCahon had made to the Mackenzie Country with Ferrier.

When his collection of first editions was complete, Peter moved on to a new pursuit – Crown Lynn ceramics of the more classical type. He also became interested in New Zealand domestic pottery, eventually focusing on the studio potters of the 1930s, such as Olive Jones and Briar Gardner. He recalled bringing home his first piece by Gardner: 'Hilary said it was as ugly as sin. But then she became hooked too, and

started collecting.'[58] Peter and Hilary enjoyed discovering an unfashionable art form, learning whatever they could glean by research, and testing their eye by constant comparison. It was an adventure and an education – 'All grist to the McLeavey mill.'[59]

Sometimes Peter brought his private world of collecting into the public space of the gallery. When Frank Sargeson died in 1982, for example, he gathered up his first editions and made a special display in the midst of his Robin White exhibition. He told McCahon, 'I have had a lot of people in on Friday and Saturday looking at the books and magazines and it is really fun; a sort of "last hurrah" to Frank Sargeson.'[60] In the following year he organised an exhibition in his series *Aspects of New Zealand regionalism* that combined linocuts by Adele Younghusband with a selection of Crown Lynn pieces of the same vintage displayed 'not for sale'. It was 'a considerable success', he reported. 'A lot of interested people coming in and looking at it and re-thinking their thoughts.'[61] Peter often described his role as an art dealer in just these terms: his task was to 'take something unappreciated, neglected, unloved – and make it loved'.[62] It was a role that he found deeply satisfying. It fulfilled his missionary spirit.

Aspects of New Zealand regionalism: Adele Younghusband and the Crown Lynn Potteries,
August–September 1983

How Billy Apple came to be selling pieces of the Peter McLeavey Gallery.

On November 19, 1979, Billy Apple's exhibition, CENSURE The Given as an Art-Political Statement, opened at the Peter McLeavey Gallery, Wellington. The artist had found certain features of the exhibition space objectionable; that is, they violated his sense of what constituted a proper environment in which to view works of art. For his show he painted those features red.

On November 30, the date the show was due to close, nothing was done about those red-painted features. They remained untouched throughout three subsequent exhibitions.
Finally, over Easter weekend, 1980, they were painted out – with white paint. CENSURE closed, 143 days after it had opened.

On May 30, 1980, Peter McLeavey met with the artist and Wystan Curnow, to discuss his response to CENSURE. It was suggested to him that CENSURE had left him with the following three options:

(1) To leave the red-painted features as they were, as a permanent censure.
(2) To repaint the features white, and so reject the censure by reinstating the status quo.
(3) To correct (by removal and/or repair) what the artist found at fault and so accept the censure.

For 143 days Peter McLeavey took option (1), after which he took option (2). He said he had not considered option (3). He had stayed with option (1) as long as he had because of the pleasure he took in the work. The artist concluded, therefore, that his censure had not been taken seriously. Unless option (3) was adopted he would have to sever his professional association with the gallery. Discussions as to a proposed drawing show came to a halt.

On December 29, 1981, following discussions between the artist and the gallery, Peter McLeavey agreed to correct eight of the ten features.
Billy Apple agreed to prepare five 'relics', with appropriate documentation, for sale in an exhibition set down to open on July 20, 1982.

– Wystan Curnow.

SIXTEEN

If you get too hung up on comparing this (frontier) culture to New York culture, well, you are just chasing rainbows.

By 1980, Peter's artists were travelling more frequently, and that year both Ian Scott and Gordon Walters visited New York – the hub of the international art world. They came back invigorated and enthusiastic about the experience, and by December, Peter was planning his own trip. '[I]f I am to be good at my job, I must see what is happening over there,' he told Woollaston. 'And it can be written off against the business.'[1] But as his departure loomed he became increasingly anxious about the long flight, and mulled over his options – tranquillisers or brandy? 'I am not sure which I'll take,' he reported to Jeffrey Harris. 'The good thing about Brandy is that the actual bottle, which I clutch as we hurtle through the sky, is also a sort of comfort object. Rather like a favoured blanket of a child.'[2]

Peter and Hilary arrived in New York in early February 1981, and began their survey of the art scene. Peter wanted to see the best dealer galleries in action – how they displayed, promoted and sold art – and he examined nearly sixty over the following month, often making multiple visits. 'By lunchtime I would be flagging,' Hilary recalled. 'But Peter would keep going all day, every day.'[3] He found that some dealers were more helpful than others: 'Many were not interested in me, or New Zealand. The impression I got was that most were hard nosed and only interested in selling... However the BEST dealers (and by using best, I mean the quality of their stock plus their human and warm personalities) loved art and handled it with the love and humility that we all must have towards it.'[4]

Billy Apple, *Censure: The given as an art-political statement*, 1979/82
Mixed media
Museum of New Zealand Te Papa Tongarewa,
purchased 1989 with Ellen Eames Collection funds

Peter was constantly evaluating what he found and considering the opportunities for his artists. He came to the conclusion that the only way to sell New Zealand art in Manhattan would be to establish a permanent gallery, open for the eight-month season. 'By having a visible presence, the very best New Zealand work I could get, plus time, I came to the conclusion that one could establish a foothold in that highly sophisticated and informed market. I would add, however, that whether I have the wish to do that I am unsure.'

As well as the dealer galleries, Peter and Hilary visited the great public art collections in Manhattan: the Metropolitan, the Modern, the Frick, the Guggenheim and the Whitney, where he was able to see the Whitney Biennial. 'This was a stroke of luck,' he noted, 'for the Whitney is probably the most important exhibition of emerging talent and trends mounted in the United States.' That year, the Biennial accorded greater prominence than ever before to film and video, but it also included painting, sculpture, installation and photography – represented for the first time by William Wegman, Robert Mapplethorpe, Richard Misrach and others.

Another highlight was a visit to Washington, where Peter saw a groundbreaking show at the Hirshhorn Museum and Sculpture Garden – *The avant-garde in Russia 1910–1930: New perspectives*.[5] He spent three days at the exhibition, which encompassed some 464 works, studying one of the great art movements of the twentieth century, rich in experimentation and artistic cross-fertilisation. The installation had been designed in witty, off-kilter fashion by the then little-known postmodern architect Frank Gehry, and its inventiveness was a revelation: 'I learnt a great amount from the installation and hanging.' Henceforth, Peter would be much more adventurous in displaying art in his own gallery.

Peter and Hilary also made excursions with Tim Francis (who was now New Zealand's permanent representative at the United Nations) and his wife Sherrah. Together, the two couples went to Philadelphia to see the Barnes Foundation and the Philadelphia Museum of Art, where Peter was especially impressed with the Arensberg collection of Brancusi sculpture.[6] 'This was another marvellous essay in how to mount artworks and I spent some time sketching the way the gallery space had been orchestrated to present each piece of art in its most sympathetic light.'

Peter was well pleased with his trip. After years of working in relative isolation, he had visited the most influential dealer galleries in the world and gained first-hand experience of new trends in contemporary art. He felt he had learnt much from such an intensive period of study. Writing to Killeen, he reflected on the challenge of being an artist – or a dealer – in the antipodes: 'One has to build on the good things about living in New Zealand... If you get too hung up on comparing this (frontier) culture to New York culture, well, you are just chasing rainbows. It is just counter productive and wasteful and, in my opinion, finally destructive. I can see this syndrome at work in the last generation who got caught up and lost their base (or ignored, belittled it)... With family, tribe, roots, and place you must come to accept it, and, hopefully, love. Otherwise you just never really develop yourself.'[7]

—

Peter's trip to New York could not have been a more timely affirmation of the changes he had made at the gallery in recent years. From July 1979 to May 1980, he had introduced four new artists whose work was sculptural or conceptual in nature: Jacqueline Fraser, Warren Viscoe, Christine Hellyar and Billy Apple. In July 1981, he showed a fifth, Neil Dawson.[8] All five would go on to have significant careers, but only Fraser, Viscoe and Apple would become long-term members of the McLeavey stable.[9]

Sculpture – defined in its broadest sense to include conceptual art, installation and performance – had flourished in New Zealand during the 1970s, thanks in part to the lively sculpture departments at Elam and Ilam art schools, which attracted many gifted young students. They looked to avant-garde artists overseas – Allan Kaprow, Joseph Beuys, Robert Smithson and others – who had been creating 'happenings', environments and installations from the late 1950s. Sculpture was also the focus of a growing trans-Tasman dialogue, nurtured by one of Australia's leading art events, the Mildura Sculpture Triennial in Victoria. New Zealanders had participated since the first triennial in 1967, and in 1978 seventeen artists were included in the seventh and largest exhibition to date. With the support of the arts council, work by the New Zealand contingent was packaged into a national touring exhibition the following year – the first such show to tour in over a decade and, in Neil Rowe's assessment, 'probably the most important event in the history of sculpture in this country'.[10]

Peter saw Jacqueline Fraser's work in *NZ sculptors at Mildura* at the National Art Gallery, and was immediately impressed by her delicate, ethereal assemblages made from wire and cloth.[11] Fraser was still a student at Elam when she was selected for Mildura – the only woman among the New Zealanders. She worked mainly with temporary installations, developed on-site in improvisatory fashion as she responded to the architectural qualities of a particular space. 'Ideally I would ignore art galleries,' she wrote in 1978, 'and build magnificent fiestas in a city park... or find an empty warehouse with windows and girders just waiting to be aired.'[12] She favoured the humble, pliable materials of traditional craft, often sourced from junk shops – raffia, cord, gauze, coloured ribbon and fabric – as well as natural materials like twigs and flax.

In February 1979, Peter travelled to Dunedin to meet Fraser and discuss her forthcoming show. Weeks later he wrote to confirm the details:

> Dear Jacqueline,
>
> Howdy?
>
> I enclose a plan of the gallery.
>
> Remember one thing: it has a beautiful light. Yes; limpid, soft, creamy, all-embracing (good old fashioned) natural. It's good. It's really good, I can tell you, about 3.00 in the afternoon when it floods and lifts everything up a key with it.
>
> The walls are white. The floor a grey brussella with just a dusting of red. The ceiling is cream.
>
> Yes, it's not such a bad place. It is smallish; but you get a great view from one gallery through to the other. I think you would like it and I know your work would...
>
> I'm pretty excited about the prospect of your show. I can see it now and I feel good. No; please don't misunderstand me. I ain't raving. I have a strong, intuitive, positive reaction to what you are doing. In short; I like it.
>
> Best Wishes
>
> Peter.[13]

Fraser's exhibition, which opened on 17 July, included sculptures made with twine, twigs, grasses and feathers, and fragile hanging forms constructed of wire bound in coloured cloth. Peter shared his enthusiasm with Killeen: 'I like the "primitivism" of it. Very gutsy.'[14]

When Fraser exhibited again in the following year, she spent two days transforming the main room of the gallery. Beginning with an armature of string suspended from the ceiling, she conjured a linear 'drawing' in space – a lively forest of sticks, wire, cloth and flax. Peter used a quote from Ralph Waldo Emerson to allude to the ceremonial, ritualistic nature of the work: 'In the woods is perpetual youth. Within these plantations of God, a decorum and sanctity reign, a perennial festival is dressed, and the guest sees not how he should tire of them in a thousand years.'[15]

Jacqueline Fraser, *Te ara a Hine*, 1997
Plastic-coated florist and electrical wire
Museum of New Zealand Te Papa Tongarewa,
gift of the Friends of Te Papa, 1997

Peter was enchanted with this installation, which he had priced at $600. He knew he had no real hope of selling it, given its fragile nature, but he could not bear to think of it being dismantled and lost. When the exhibition closed, he informed Fraser that he and Hilary had decided to buy it. 'I don't know what I will do with it yet,' he wrote. 'I can't see us putting it up at home (because of the children) however, we may find a public gallery who would like to have it on long term loan.'[16] Fraser was thrilled and surprised: 'It's actually taken a few days for the news to sink in. Thank you very much. I've always joked about selling a piece like that but never taken it seriously.'[17] In December, the piece was installed at the National Art Gallery. 'It looks really beaut,' Peter told Fraser. 'And it has been put up without any hitches.'[18] Six months later, he reported that he and Hilary had gifted the work to the gallery – 'They are delighted with it.'[19]

Fraser's third solo exhibition with Peter, in 1981, referenced her Māori heritage: a series of black and red wrapped stick constructions, suspended in the air, which seemed to dance across the gallery. Peter described his pleasure in the work in a letter to Peter Ireland: 'It is a lovely piece ... Very strong. I really respond to her "stuff" and have learnt a lot from it. The main thing (or one of the main things) is that I must follow my intuition, always. Not do anything because of what people say to me but, rather, follow my feelings. They always turn up trumps.'[20] Months later, he sold his first work by Fraser, a collage priced at $100, but sales remained infrequent even years later.[21] 'You must not worry about this,' he wrote. 'Rest assured you are a greatly gifted person. It is just that people have not "caught up" with your art, yet. They will.'[22]

Fraser went on to exhibit nearly every year at the Peter McLeavey Gallery and increasingly showed her work internationally. In the mid-1990s, Peter helped to secure a major commission for the new Museum of New Zealand Te Papa Tongarewa that enabled her to work on an unprecedented scale. In one of the museum's most charged spaces, the internal entrance to the marae, Fraser created a six-part work entitled *Te ara a Hine* (the pathway of women), which honours the goddesses of Māori legend and the spiritual realms they oversee, as well as the madonnas of European tradition. Made of humble materials – wire and metal rods – *Te ara a Hine* is a ceremonial environment of great beauty and subtlety, rich in narrative complexity and allusion.

Twenty years older than Fraser, Warren Viscoe had given up a career as a building apprentice to study art, graduating from Elam in 1965.

Warren Viscoe at the gallery, photographed by Peter McLeavey, 1986

Warren Viscoe, *Fifteen bird calls*, 1981
Wood and mixed media
Sarjeant Gallery Te Whare o Rehua, gift of the artist, 1997

By the time Peter met him in 1979, he recalled, 'I was beginning to find my feet as an artist.'[23] Viscoe's early work was ephemeral, consisting of short-term installations or interventions in the landscape. 'I was interested in disciplines like archeology and geology; I was working with ideas about space, gravity, weight, the dynamics of load and balance. It was an exciting time.'

Peter saw Viscoe's work in *NZ sculptors at Mildura* in 1978, and responded to its physicality and heft, as well as its wit and imagination. Two years later, the artist held his first exhibition at the Peter McLeavey Gallery: an installation of wood, fencing wire, volcanic stone, shells and mirrors. The National Art Gallery showed some interest, but eventually decided against acquiring it owing to problems of assemblage and storage. Viscoe wrote to Peter, 'I thought the Mildura show... might have changed some opinions on installations. I'm a little disappointed & not the least because of the low risk taking policy towards this type of work.'[24] Peter responded sympathetically: 'A problem with [the National Art Gallery] is that they do lack the room etc to show and conserve works... Still, as far as I am concerned the show was very important and I learnt a lot from living with it. And, I am very keen for us to have another show say next year or in 1982. I am concerned about the future and I am very excited with my contact with you.'[25] For Peter, showing Viscoe's work was a long-term commitment. 'We can't change people's attitude quickly. However, I am convinced of the quality of your works and I look forward, with high optimism to the future.'

In 1982, Viscoe exhibited a major new installation, *Fifteen bird calls*, inspired by his childhood memories of aviaries. Five mysterious wooden towers stood in a rough circle in the gallery, host to a clutter of objects perched on their shelves. Visitors were left to puzzle over the nature of this quirky enclosure – shelter and protection, entrapment, or both? The ambiguity was reinforced by the feathered objects that stood in for the absent birds: plastic shuttlecocks enclosed in jam-jars covered with paper lids pierced with breathing holes. Enigmatic and intriguing, *Fifteen bird calls* offered a meditation on one of the artist's key themes: the often precarious relationship between humankind and the natural environment.

Peter was unable to find a buyer for *Fifteen bird calls*, and he would not sell a major Viscoe installation until 1986, when the Sarjeant Gallery purchased *The quarryman's dream*.[26] But if sales were infrequent, artist and dealer went on to have a long and productive association. 'One thing I noticed,' Viscoe recalled, 'was that Peter would welcome all comers. One flight of stairs up. The grubbiest stairs I've ever seen. But they led to a good place, a very welcoming place. It didn't matter who you were – you could be a bum. And there were a lot of bums around in those days.' Viscoe was impressed with his dealer's discipline and patience, but he also noticed a more important quality: 'Peter had a dedication, a passion. He had an uncanny kind of intuition, a gut feeling, and that was the fire in his belly.'

For Viscoe, the Peter McLeavey Gallery was a refuge, a safe place for his art – somewhere that it would be protected, understood and appreciated. 'Because when you make art, you expose yourself. I was always conscious of my tradesman's background, and the feeling that I was going to be found out as an imposter. But Peter never ever made me feel that way. He never said anything, but I always knew that I was accepted. There was a great comfort in that.'

When Peter was just starting out as an art dealer in 1968, he had first written to the expatriate conceptual artist Billy Apple. Apple – born Barrie Bates in Auckland in 1935 – occupied an unusual position in the local art world. After leaving New Zealand in 1959, he studied at the Royal College of Art in London, where he met David Hockney, Derek Boshier and others, and became involved in the pop-art movement. In 1962, he changed his name to Billy Apple; two years later, he settled in New York, where he exhibited pop-art canvases and neon works before moving into conceptual art later in the decade.

Peter met Apple in 1975, when the artist returned to New Zealand for the first time in sixteen years. 'I found him a very likeable and charming person,' he told Gordon Walters. 'He was able to tell me a lot about the "scene" over there.'[27] Apple exhibited at the Settlement Gallery in Wellington as part of a national tour in which he made subtle architectural interventions at each venue – painting out tiles, raising carpet, removing all extraneous detail. Such austere conceptual art was not unusual in New York, but in New Zealand it was novel – and baffling. All over the country, Apple met with a barrage of publicity, much of it hostile and dismissive.

Returning in 1979, Apple embarked on a nine-venue project entitled *The given as an art-political statement*.[28] For *Censure*, at the Peter McLeavey Gallery in November, he identified ten features that detracted from the ideal modernist gallery space: cast-iron grilles, patched-up plaster work, protruding boltheads and so on. He then 'censured' these flaws by painting them a strident red. The empty white

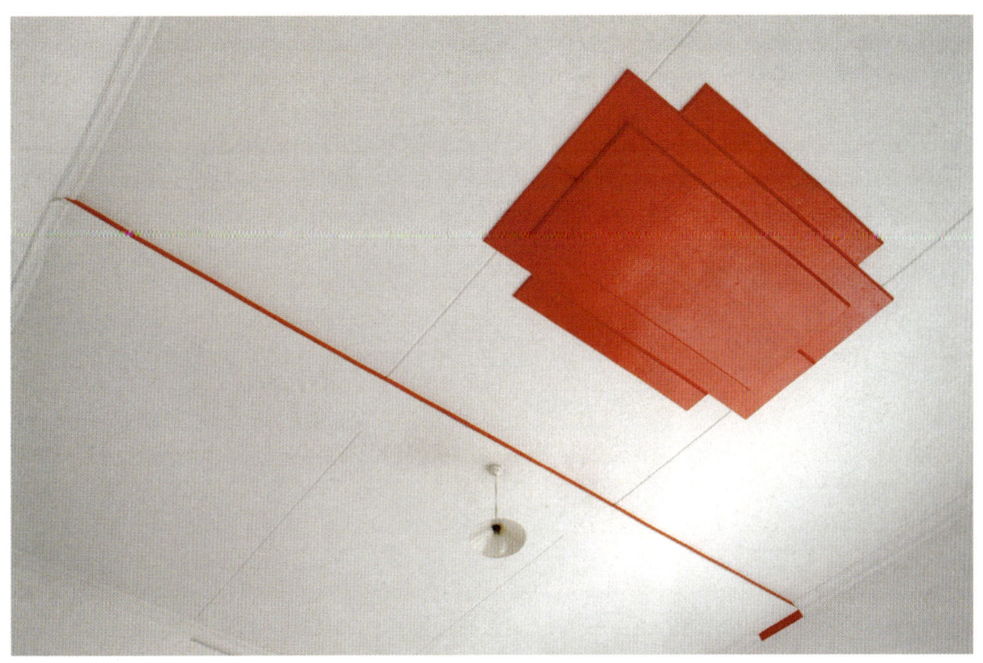

Billy Apple: Censure: The given as an art-political statement, November 1979

gallery, accented with red, offered a rather unusual art experience for Wellingtonians, but Neil Rowe was complimentary in the *Evening Post*, describing Apple's installation as 'a surprisingly tight aesthetic and formal statement'.[29] Rowe commented on the provocative nature of the piece: '[It] raises all kinds of questions about the nature of art – not least for Peter McLeavey who has to decide whether or not to leave the red paint in his gallery.' In fact, Apple had presented Peter with three options: to leave the red features, paint them out, or remove the distracting details.

Peter chose to whitewash Apple's 'intervention', and when the artist returned for another project in 1982 he picked up where he had left off.[30] Now he removed the offending features and framed them, with photographs and explanatory text by critic Wystan Curnow (see page 268). Apple had negotiated the removal of these 'relics', and Peter had initially requested that one detail remain – a grille on the wall. 'The reasons for this are spiritual,' he told the artist. 'I need a bit of my past retained here, in this gallery ... I know you will understand this. As a dealer I sell history and I do need something here that links me with my past as a dealer.'[31] He eventually gave way on this point, however, and the grille became part of the show.

Writing to Walters, Peter conveyed his delight in the installation: 'Prices are $1000.00. No sales to date. It looks very handsome.'[32] Avenal McKinnon and Elva Bett wrote positive reviews but, as always, there were dissenters. 'A lot of our local schoolmasters, academicians and cracker barrel art critics rubbished it,' Peter told Jeffrey Harris. 'Mind you most of them wouldn't know a work of art unless it bit them on the arse. Temper; temper; temper; I mustn't throw a McLeavey which is my wont at times when things get on my back.'[33]

In March 1982, Peter told Billy Apple, 'I've decided to go over to Sydney for the Biennale.'[34] The Biennale of Sydney was first established in 1973 as an international showcase for contemporary art; within a decade it had quadrupled in size and become the major art event in the southern hemisphere. For New Zealanders, who had virtually no presence on the international biennale circuit, it offered an especially important opportunity to exhibit with their overseas counterparts.[35] Local artists had participated, by invitation, since the first biennale – when McCahon and Bill Sutton were included – but it was only later in the decade that their presence began to make an impact. In part, this was due to a new professionalism in art administration: increasingly,

New Zealand curators, dealers and officials were making contact with their Australian colleagues.[36]

As the New Zealand commissioner for the sixth Biennale in 1982, Wystan Curnow selected eight artists – by far the largest New Zealand contingent to date – including five from Peter's stable: Richard Killeen, Peter Peryer, Billy Apple, Christine Hellyar and Philip Trusttum.[37] Visiting the exhibition, Peter was struck by Killeen's thirty-three-piece cut-out, *Island mentality no. 1*, which he had shown at the gallery in the previous year: it was hung on a key wall in the main hall and attracting much favourable attention. 'The New Zealand contribution was positive and strong,' he told a client. 'A lot of good feed back.'[38] Of the overseas artists, he singled out the Italian expressionists, Enzo Cucchi, Sandro Chia and Francesco Clemente, who had helped to spearhead an international revival in painting: '[T]he Cucchi took the cake for me... While there may not have been any masterpieces... I was very glad to see so much good art. Not great but good. That is something we see so little of and just to be exposed to so much was exciting to me. They even had a Brian Eno piece which I responded to.'[39]

Visiting the dealer galleries in Sydney, Peter felt that his artists stood up very well by comparison. '[T]he quality level of art there, was, if anything, lower than what we make here. Also the dealing scene was very corrupt with many people getting into handling art who had no commitment to it than making a (fast) buck. One or two galleries (dealers) impressed me but it was just that number: one or two.'[40]

On his arrival, Peter had put a notice in the *Sydney Morning Herald*, inviting collectors to view works by his artists. In the following days he visited curators and clients, but he also spent many hours alone in his hotel room, waiting for the phone to ring: 'On 17th of April [I] stayed inside all day, by the phone... No calls.'[41]

Returning home with sales of just over $2000, Peter was in a pensive mood. He wrote to Gordon Walters:

> It was a most stimulating show; the Biennale.
>
> It was interesting (my trip) in other ways, too. Mainly it gave me time to reflect on my business, and what Hilary and I have done here, in Wellington. All those years of struggle and striving which we have put in; the 50/60 hours a week; the stretches of 20/30 days of work in a row, without a break.
>
> And doing it from nothing. No silversmithing husband; no wealthy husband; no pottery shop, auction room, real estate investments. No doctor wife. We have done it alone.

We have grafted it on to this city. Not the art centre of New Zealand but here, in Wellington, a raw, Klondike sort of place.

All these thoughts came to me in Sydney …

And I thought of the price Hilary and I and our three children have paid. The 'never at home' father. The wife trying to make a go of it on a pittance. No big wage to fall back on. Just hoping for work that you could believe in and for the next commission; the next sale.

Richard Killeen, *Island mentality no. 1*, 1981
Alkyd on aluminium
Bank of New Zealand Art Collection

Yes, it gave me time to think of what we have done. What Hilary has done. What she has done for New Zealand art. Unsung.

It really hit me. For the first time I saw myself, the positive and the negative.

It will be good to see you sometime soon.

Warmest regards to you

Peter.[42]

20/40 This is me at Kaitangata
Robin White 6/77

SEVENTEEN

Art, as you know, is essentially a spiritual quest.

In 1981, Robin White wrote to Peter with important news: the National Spiritual Assembly of Bahá'ís in New Zealand had invited her and her husband to move to the Republic of Kiribati, the former Gilbert Islands, to assist the local community. 'We aren't planning to come back – not that you can necessarily "plan" the future. But that's our attitude. We're there for good. Sounds incredible, I know. But it's exciting – and very challenging.'[1]

White intended to carry on with her art as usual, although she expected there would be a period of adjustment in the equatorial heat. 'I haven't thought much beyond just getting there... but I am hopeful that you will continue to exhibit and sell my work. I consider myself very fortunate to have my work in your gallery, Peter, and I am loath to neglect such a good relationship. However, my circumstances are going to be quite different. New work, a new country. What do you think so far?'

Peter was enthusiastic. 'Your plan certainly has great attraction to me as I have always been drawn to the idea of being a missionary. I like to think that that idea has received some measure of fulfilment in my occupation of art dealer.'[2] Weeks later he wrote again. 'You are going into a completely new world that will change you in its own way; just as you will change it. It is a world as far away from these islands as Mars, or New York. And that is what I would find so exciting. I look forward to seeing what changes will be wrought in your art.'[3]

By now, Peter had been representing White for more than a decade. He had met her in 1969, when she was living at Bottle Creek in Paremata and working as an art teacher. 'I walked up those stairs to the gallery, and Peter was standing on a chair, putting up a painting. He got down

Robin White, *This is me at Kaitangata*, 1979
Screenprint
Museum of New Zealand Te Papa Tongarewa, purchased 1979

and said, "Hello, who are you?" I said, "I'm Robin White." And he said, "Oh, Colin McCahon has told me about you, I'd like to come and see your work."'[4]

White participated in a group show in December 1970, exhibiting prints of the Porirua landscape – examples of her practice of 'distilling the images from my environment' – priced at $5 to $7.[5] In 1971, she moved to Dunedin to work as a full-time artist and bought a cottage beside the harbour near Portobello; two years later, she married Mike Fudakowski, who shared her Bahá'í faith.

From the start, Peter was impressed with the strength and refinement of White's work, but he also appreciated her integrity and quiet dedication. Announcing the news of her first pregnancy in 1973, she told him, 'I am absolutely determined to continue working. Naturally there are going to be situations which will require much thought & organisation. But – the work must go on – there is so much to do, & my present ideas already stretch well into next year.'[6] The day after bringing her son Michael home from the hospital, she was back in the studio. 'If being both an artist and a mother was going to work, it was going to have to work right from the start.'[7]

The period that followed was challenging. 'For four years I'd lived on my own, and then suddenly I had this little person encroaching so much on my time. I remember Peter came down to Dunedin to see me, and I must have conveyed quite a depth of anxiety about it all. And he said to me, "Don't worry Robin. You've got forty years ahead of you at least. It will be all right." Just that little statement was incredibly empowering. That's what I needed to hear. It was very powerful.'[8]

By the time of her second solo show with Peter in 1978, White had completed an ambitious series of portraits of friends and family members. They included *Glenda at Tahakopa* and *Sam Hunt at the Portobello Pub*, both of which were bought by private collectors;[9] Victoria University acquired the watercolour *Glenda at Portobello*. Reviewing the exhibition, Neil Rowe described her as 'perhaps the most accomplished painter currently working within the regionalist tradition of New Zealand painting'.[10] Three years later, Alister Taylor published a substantial book on her work – a rare accolade for an artist in her mid-thirties.[11]

Early in May 1982, White and her family arrived on Tarawa, the largest island in the Kiribati group. Her initial reaction was one of shock. She had packed months of essential supplies – brushes, oils and canvas – but it was immediately obvious that she would need to radically

Robin White, *Sam Hunt at the Portobello Pub*, 1978
Acrylic on hardboard
Dunedin Public Art Gallery, purchased with funds from the Dunedin Public Art Gallery Society

change her art practice. Oil paint 'didn't fit with the surroundings, with the ambience of the place'; nor did the landscape, saturated with light and colour, seem a promising subject.[12] 'There would be no sense in being a landscape artist in Kiribati,' she commented later, 'because the land as a visual element is so minimal. What strikes you immediately is the human occupation of that land and all that it entails.'[13]

In June, White wrote to Peter about her new life.

> You were right when you said that coming here would be like going to Mars. Everything here is so different. The climate, the land, the people & their culture... One expatriate I spoke to who has been here for 30 years & is fluent in Gilbertese (& married to a Gilbertese lady) says that, in his experience, this is a land of exceptions. For every human habit or practice, or value that you may be familiar with elsewhere – Kiribati proves to be the exception. He was probably exaggerating – but there's an element of truth in what he says.

> Anyway, to date our experience of life here has been everything from exciting & uplifting to exhausting & bewildering. There are times when I am utterly struck down by homesickness & other times when I am completely absorbed by the unfolding magic & mystery of this little group of islands…
>
> [T]here are no words to describe the profound sense of isolation that comes to you when you stand on this thin strip of coral, the surf thundering on one side & the vast expanse of the lagoon on the other. And everywhere, infinity. The endless sky & the endless sea. It truly is a strange experience. To face such vastness & such emptiness for hundreds of years – one can begin to imagine what that does to a people's vision…
>
> It is very over-crowded on our part of the island – & the hygiene facilities are poor if not nil. The well-water is very dodgy. They had a cholera epidemic not long ago. No paradise, this.
>
> Still, there's an edge to it. And I wouldn't like to live in Paradise – that's strictly for the dead![14]

Peter was fascinated by White's account of her new home:

> It reminds me of the places that the early Desert Fathers searched out. A good place for spiritual growth. And a place to share with someone you love; God or man… And here? What is happening here? Well, we live out our lives and instead of measuring it with the rise and fall of tide and moon we measure it with possessions and pay days. I am at work; it is 4.40 on a mid winter Saturday afternoon. The T.A.B. over the road is full; the Evening Post is out; the Imperial Hotel is full and Cuba Street is empty; as are the hills; and our sky is your sky.[15]

Peter asked White if she had begun any new prints, and reiterated his commitment to her work: 'I greatly value our contact and hope that we can maintain it while being so separated by the waters of the Pacific.'[16]

While she waited for her printing press to arrive by ship, White made sketches of the interior of her house, and of her husband. 'Mike was struck down for several days with sunstroke not long after arrival here. So I drew him while he lay asleep on the bed.'[17] As she began to learn the Gilbertese language, White continued to make 'rough notes' of her new environment, sketching buildings, canoes, people, and the insects that made their way into her house. Soon this practice became a way of learning about the local culture and adapting to her new home: 'A young Gilbertese girl called Florence came and worked in our house

Robin White in Tarawa, photographed by Claudia Pond Eyley, 1984

every day and kept me company. I would draw something, ask Florence its name and then write it down.'[18] These sketches were the impetus for a series of five woodcuts that combined text and image, her first work in the Pacific: 'Beginners' guide to Gilbertese'.

White had never made woodcuts before: 'I'm working in a sort of vacuum,' she admitted to Peter.[19] In part, she was driven by necessity: her printing press had still not arrived, and with woodcuts, unlike

Robin White, *Michael is sleeping on the bed* (top)and *I am doing the washing in the bathroom* from the 'Beginners' guide to Gilbertese' series, 1983
Woodcuts
Museum of New Zealand Te Papa Tongarewa, purchased 1983 with Ellen Eames Collection funds

etchings, she was at least able to make 'proof' copies by hand. But she was also influenced by the memory of medieval woodcuts: simple, rough-hewn images in which there was a direct link between image and narrative. Such images seemed in tune with her new environment – a place where people lived an 'utterly simple' way of life:

> A way of life so bereft of trimmings that you wonder how people can still be people. And yet perhaps they have discovered a dimension of human existence that we will never know.

There is a house that I pass on my way to work every morning. It is smaller than the size of a single garage. The four corners are marked by branches sunk in the ground. These branches support a thatched roof. There are no walls at all... The entire earthly possessions of the inhabitants of that house are in one suitcase. I have no idea how many people live there. You can never tell. People come and go, but one thing I have never seen here – someone living on their own. For the Gilbertese, that would be unthinkable.

I think of NZ, our preoccupation with earthly possessions, and realise that we are no happier really. But these people are happy. Most of them. The children, naked, sitting in the sand. No toys. Nothing to eat but fish and coconut and rice. And they sing and sing. It makes me weep to hear them. Weep for the beauty and the sadness of it. I have learnt so much since I have been here, Peter. It is almost too much. Too much to put in words. One thing I know, being here has changed me. Probably for good, and, I hope, for the better.[20]

Early in 1983, White made a brief trip to Auckland to print 'Beginners' guide to Gilbertese'; four months later her second son, Conrad, was born in Tarawa. As well as tending the new baby, she spent the winter months hand-colouring prints and preparing for an upcoming group show at the Women's Gallery in Wellington.[21] In November, she sent Peter a photograph of her soon-to-be completed studio – 'It's going to be a beaut working space' – and recommended a book of feminist essays on art by Lucy Lippard, *From the centre*.[22] 'It's very interesting because she is verbalising many of the feelings, experiences and intuitively-arrived-at images of my own.' She ended her letter with a thank you: 'It's very encouraging to know that there is someone out there, beyond this great, lazy lagoon, who is being caring and helpful.'

In 1984, Peter exhibited three sets of 'Beginners' guide' in different states – brown and white, black and white, and hand-coloured – priced from $750 to $900. The *Evening Post*'s new art critic, the poet Ian Wedde, was impressed: 'The wood surface retains a striation, the cutting avoids intricacy without courting primitivism, and the accommodation of purpose (language-instruction manual) to artistic vision is unforced and harmonious.'[23] But in spite of such praise the works – for sale only as sets of five images – were slow to sell. White wrote to Peter, 'Do you think it would be a good idea to split up some of the sets? I'm reluctant to – but if some would sell better that way – I'll leave it up to you.

I wouldn't break up any of the hand-coloured sets though. I think that would be a shame.'[24]

White's financial situation was already vulnerable, but in June 1984 it was exacerbated by political and economic developments, as she reported to Peter:

> The BBC, in its thin and scratchy voice, informed us of the election of a new Prime Misery in NZ, with a 17-seat majority to Labour. And that's all the BBC had to say about it. Our interest in NZ political goings-on would have shrivelled up and died had it not been for an item a few days later informing us that NZ had devalued its dollar. This jolted us back into a state of consciousness. I've no doubt that devaluation was unavoidable, necessary, and probably beneficial. But for us it's a bit of a disaster. The NZ dollar is now worth under 60 Aussie cents, and we are wondering how long we can survive here.
>
> Our situation seems so precarious that I've even been contemplating the possibility of selling some of my work in Australia, a move which I've never really considered seriously before. I'm prompted to seek your advice and comment on this because I feel we have a close and honest relationship. I'm sure you'll appreciate this and I'm sure you'll be honest in reply. I hope you understand that in contemplating sending work to Australia I'm not considering sending less to you. I'm just trying to think of a way of compensating for a loss in income resulting from devaluation.
>
> There is a curious angle to this. If we are to keep in mind your analogy of the dealer/artist relationship then what I'm doing is a bit like asking one's spouse for advice on who to take on as a lover![25]

Peter was positive about White's suggestion: 'Yes, I think it is very good; that your work is available in Australia. And, further, I would recommend that you press on and try to arrange outlets there.' He suggested that White contact Ray Hughes, a long-established dealer in Brisbane.[26]

At the same time, Peter was pondering the slow buyer response to White's new Pacific prints:

> [I]t may be that as you are no longer living here that the culture feels you are no longer part of it. This does seem strange, I know, but art is a funny business and much of it is sold to people who are really looking for *ikons of place*. This seems particularly so when a culture is emerging from the 'frontier' stage and people are

> yearning for their own (very own) art. It may be that works based on Pacific Island culture do not necessarily relate to many of the people here. That said, it is my opinion that your 'island' prints are among your very best work. Perhaps your best...
>
> Another consideration is that in the art public's mind you are totally identified with your 'classic period' silkscreen prints. I must get one enquiry every two weeks for works of that Dunedin/Paremata time... And, interestingly, they are, in my opinion of less quality than the Tarawa works. They are, however, very rich and potent *ikons of place*. So the demand and interest...
>
> Just keep at it for it is my belief that, ultimately, the quality of your Tarawa work will be seen. And the demand will be stronger. I think all we can do is keep on plugging on; having faith in the knowledge of the work's great quality. Soon, the tide will turn, I know...
>
> Art, as you know, is essentially a spiritual quest. It is often financially unrewarding and cruel. All we can do is plug away knowing that we are on the right track. Follow our intuition; the murmur of the heart. Keep the Faith.[27]

White replied, 'I found your comments interesting – the idea of "ikons of place". Well, I'm working away on ikons of place – this place. Making some progress, I think. It's a long, slow process with me, getting an image to come together in the right way. And even then the "right way" is very subjective. These images I'm doing now have been born in isolation and I feel towards them as a mother might feel about her children. They are what they are and I like them. But how they will fit in to the big wide world is another story.'[28]

In fact, as Peter suspected, White's 'ikons of place' were ahead of their time; today they hold a unique place in the country's art history.[29] The 1980s was a period when many Pākehā New Zealanders were reassessing their relationship to the outside world. No longer yoked to Britain, and increasingly wary of pressure from the United States – especially over the issue of nuclear-powered vessels – they would, in the following years, begin to come to terms with themselves as belonging to a Pacific nation.

In the winter of 1982, Peter received an interesting offer: would he consider a role as the Bank of New Zealand's art adviser? 'It is a very big job,' he told Toss Woollaston, 'and I have had to give it a lot of thought. Well, to cut a long story short I've decided to have a crack at it. I feel almost a social responsibility to take it…They will pay me a retainer'.[30]

Peter had a sense of returning to his roots, as he had known two of the senior staff on the art committee when he was a young bank clerk in the late 1950s. But, most importantly, it was an irresistible opportunity. At the gallery, he was limited by the number of artists he could represent; at the bank, he could throw his net much wider, developing an expanded vision of New Zealand art. '[I]t was as if we set out one morning, saddled up the horses and sped off across the paddocks, up the rise and onto the high country on a voyage of discovery'.[31]

His first task was to establish some objectives for the collection: it would focus on contemporary art, maintain a high standard and reflect a national identity. 'It should be a growing and evolving thing,' he noted. 'The collection should not be concerned with investment. I do not see that as its purpose nor is it the image I would like to see it have in the eyes of the community.'[32] He was also concerned about how the bank's employees would view the project. 'It is essential that the staff relate to, and feel positive about the collection. It must not seem to be something forced on them. They should feel pride for it.'[33]

Peter was given a generous budget of $100,000 per year (the equivalent of $316,000 today), plus a further $20,000 to develop a sculpture commission for the bank's plaza at its Wellington headquarters. Over the following years he acquired paintings, prints, photographs, sculpture and ceramics, and the collection eventually grew to encompass nearly 500 items. As well as key works by his own artists (including Walters, Mrkusich, McCahon, Scott and Killeen), he bought from his dealer colleagues around the country, purchasing suites of work by those he particularly admired, such as Philip Clairmont and Tony Fomison.[34] He also acquired a small but significant group of paintings by an earlier generation – Helen Stewart, Leo Bensemann, Evelyn Page, Rita Angus and others.[35]

The work that gave Peter the greatest satisfaction, however, was a nineteenth-century tekoteko by an unknown Māori artist, purchased at auction in New York. In his recommendation in February 1984, he noted, 'I have long felt that, if one could draw up a list of 10 masterpieces made by the human hand in these islands, 7 or 8 of those works would be Maori wood carving…This opinion is still not generally accepted. But it will be, in time.'[36] Peter's words were prescient. Just months later, the watershed *Te Maori* exhibition opened at New York's Metropolitan Museum of Art to widespread acclaim; two years later, it returned home to tour the country.[37]

Billy Apple, *From the BNZ Art Collection*, 1988
Acrylic on canvas
Bank of New Zealand Art Collection

In 1984, Peter's reporting officer commented on his work to date. 'I consider Mr McLeavey is providing a first-class service for the Bank and is assembling a collection of which we can be truly proud... His strong will and high ideals occasionally lead to heated discussion and differences of opinion but this is healthy and encouraged in the achievement of our goal.'[38] Peter's idealism is evident in a press release he wrote that year when Neil Dawson's *The rock* was unveiled on the bank's forecourt:

> The aim of the Collection is to clothe the walls of BNZ Centre with artworks. It is also a commitment by the BNZ of a concern for a fuller quality of life; an extra dimension to the normal business day by providing a stimulating and humanising environment for staff, customers and visitors.

We are all aware of a growing feeling we have of our country's own special qualities and uniqueness. Much of our success as a civilised society will be judged by the creative activities of our artists. The visual arts are playing an important part in the development of this awareness. The aim of the BNZ Art Collection is to assist and encourage this vital growth.[39]

Peter's new role at the bank boosted his income, but it also intensified his travel and workload at a time when his marriage was under an increasing strain. He was aware that the problem lay in part with his temperament – in particular, his tendency to be self-absorbed, even narcissistic, and his constant need for love and reassurance. Back in 1976, he had made a note to himself in his diary:

STOP COMPLAINING
THINK OF HILARY
and OTHERS.[40]

Three years later, he confided in Woollaston:

I must look after Hilary for she has been feeling a bit down to it lately. I think a fair bit of it has to do with me as I am pretty impossible to live with. I am so self conscious and seem only concerned with the Gallery. It rules my life and most of my conversation seems to be about it. Not a good thing for a harmonious marriage. I must be more considerate or else I may lose out.

As with all the other things in life, we can't take our marriages for granted. You or I or anyone else.[41]

Peter had special reason to value his marriage. Growing up emotionally wary and withdrawn, he felt he had been lucky to find an understanding partner who could break through his reserve, and cope with his recurrent doubts and anxiety. He believed that marriage had softened him. 'For the first time I came close to another,' he admitted to McCahon. 'I had to try hard to persevere. I wanted to run away sometimes for I'd not been in that position. I learnt to give myself and to be open to receive. To receive with grace. That's the word; Grace.'[42] Now in his forties, Peter was grateful for the warmth, security and ballast that his wife and children provided. 'As I get a little older the times spent with Hilary and my family is increasingly precious,' he told Jeffrey Harris. 'We have lots of good times together and their love keeps me "on the road".'[43]

The gallery had always dominated Peter's life. 'These days I hardly see my family; hardly know my wife,' he told Woollaston back in 1978. 'I come home and sit down and mull over things. Then up to bed and a good sleep until the alarm at 6 or 6.30. Packing, calling, racing hither and yon.'[44] From the mid-1970s he had occasionally employed part-time assistants, and he was once again thinking of getting some help: 'One day a week sort of thing as I am just so busy … The correspondence and things pile up and I then get rattled. Hilary also wants me to spend more time with the children and wants me to not be so obsessed with the gallery. I am, in fact, a very boring mate.'[45]

Hilary had initially been attracted to Peter because he was 'different': he seemed to promise an unconventional life and a more equal form of partnership. Ten years later, she found herself at home with three small children, running the household almost single-handedly while he directed all his emotional energy into the gallery. 'I always felt that the gallery was Peter's real home, the place where he flourished and belonged. When he came home from work he would creep in, and he'd hope no one would notice so he could go upstairs and read. And I wanted him to engage with the children – to ask them how their day went, how did you get on at swimming sports, and he just didn't.'[46] He also avoided family holidays if he could: 'The whole idea of camping scares me as I just do not like smoke, sand, heat, sandflies, the sun, and greenery.'[47] Hilary felt isolated and taken for granted, and her concerns were reinforced by the debate that flourished in Women's Studies at Victoria University. 'The feminist movement was in full swing, and a key question of that time was, Who cleans the toilet? That was a biggie. Well! In our house there was no question.'[48]

By the winter of 1982, Peter and Hilary were seeing a marriage guidance counsellor – a painful experience from which Peter emerged with a sense of failure as a husband and father. '[I]t's been a bad year for me,' he admitted to Laurence Aberhart in October. 'A year during which I have often felt that I've lost the faith. Not the Faith in capitals. No, but the faith in a creative sense. A belief in oneself and the confidence in its rightness.'[49] He was now making a determined effort at home, trying to be more sensitive and communicative, and less emotionally demanding of Hilary. He was even taking his turn in the kitchen. 'I have been doing a bit of baking,' he informed Richard Killeen. 'I usually buy a Betty Crocker cake mix and find I can handle that. Still, ambition is nagging at my breast and I am about to plunge in and try scones. Possibly will do that over the weekend.'[50]

'My room where I lived upstairs at 147 Cuba Street after the breakup of my marriage, 10 November 1983', photographed by Peter McLeavey

A year later, after much deliberation, Peter and Hilary decided on a trial separation. 'This has been coming for a long time,' Peter told Robin White. 'No; nothing awful, or destructive, or hurtful. Just two people growing apart. There is no other man or woman; booze; violence; gambling; or any other factor involved. We just need time apart. We both want each other to be fully realised and happy in this life. Nothing more.'[51] Having moved out of the family home, Peter was camping in the attic in the gallery building – the 'Cuba Street penthouse' – as he related to Killeen: 'It reminds me so much of my early days and evokes memories of times spent in convents and monasteries. The sparseness and the simplicity strongly appeals to a side of me that many probably do not know. I think of Saint Ignatius Loyola; Saint Francis Xavier… Saint Teresa of Avila and Saint John of the Cross. All this probably sounds pretty barmy but memory is a potent thing in my imagination.'[52]

Later in the month, he wrote again:

> Hilary and the children are well, by the way. We see each other often and everything is working out. Naturally, I feel sad at times and in these rooms I've cried when, at night, I've thought about it all and about myself and why it went the way it did. Much of the problem lay with me and my creative drive.
>
> In a funny way this whole business has made me realise that I am, in fact, a sort of artist and that this gallery is something like a painting to me. Every show is like a painting. So much of my dreams, drives and ideals have been channelled into my job as an art dealer. I've not been a conventional Dad. I can never be that. I hate gardens. I don't swim. It's not my nature. I can't go against that. I'm a bit of a loner. A man who still looks at the world as an 11 year old with a head full of dreams of all those early Saints and Martyrs which so profoundly affected, and shaped, my subsequent life.
>
> I'm impossible to live with. I now realise my limitations and I must not pretend that I'm something I cannot be; something my nature will not allow me to be.[53]

Back in 1969, Mario Fleischl had warned Peter, 'I strongly urge you not to marry. You love women, but marriage is not for you.'[54] More than twenty years later, Peter felt that Fleischl had been proved correct.

Peter's son Dominic, who later trained as a counsellor, had some sympathy for his father. 'He was a workaholic, but even as a kid I could see what the gallery meant to him. I always had a sense of pride in my dad, he was so excited in his work. For me, that was a powerful model.' Dominic felt the gallery fulfilled an essential psychological need in his father. 'When Dad was at work he often seemed to be in a state of elation. He was totally focused, non-stop, on his game. But when he walked out the door there was a sea change, and all the old grievances and doubts and anxiety would come flooding in. The wolf was on his back. I think the gallery kept the world at bay for Dad. He needed it. It kept him balanced.'[55]

In January 1984, Peter wrote to Peter Ireland, 'I spent most of Christmas and New Year in Wellington. I went away for about 4 days; to Coroglen to see Michael Illingworth and lick my wound.'[56] By now the reality of his new life had set in:

> I feel like a cat or a dog that has been hit by a car or truck. I've managed, somehow, to drag myself off the road and all I want to do now is to crawl under the house and to snuggle up on the dirt against the piles. And to stay very quiet; and not to see anyone. I need time to lick myself better. Well, that process has started. It is hard... I am now looking at houses and flats as I start out on my quest; my new life. Like the young Parsifal, or good Tristan, I buckle on my belt and set off into the future.

In March, Peter purchased a flat in Brooklyn – a spartan, run-down apartment in an art deco block, but with three bedrooms to accommodate his children. 'The room in which I live is like the set for *Waiting for Godot*,' he told Mrkusich. 'It is bare, consisting as it does of just a bed and a suitcase with my clothes in it. The kitchen is where I live. No furniture; I sit on a case filled with newspapers. It is not too uncomfortable.'[57]

Peter reassured his artists that he was absolutely committed to them and the gallery, but privately he struggled to retain a sense of purpose. 'Everything seems so pointless,' he admitted to Peter Ireland. 'I have to go back 20 years when I lost the Faith to find a similar time in my life. Business is going well, certainly, and, yes, I suppose to some I am a success. But, not to my own heart. When I see the havoc I've wrought in my own life and Hilary's and the children I don't know about anything.'[58]

In an attempt to regain his momentum, Peter was working long hours and devoting all his emotional energy to the gallery: 'It is a haven; the only fixed point in my tumbling and unresolved life.'[59] He told Ireland about his recent Illingworth show: 'Michael came down for the opening and seemed to enjoy himself. We also had a visit from Sir Toss and he stayed with me, in my flat, for a night. We slept in the double bed together after consuming almost a bottle of Whiskey. All very proper, I can assure you; I have no plans, at this stage, to reassess my sexual preferences.'[60]

Peter was planning a trip to Dunedin to see Jeffrey Harris – when he could manage it.

> Much depends on all the bits and pieces I have crashing around my neck. The family; the legal nuts and bolts of dissolution; the gallery; the Bank; the Bank sculpture; the Flat – oh, well, we seem to be getting things sorted out, slowly.
>
> I pick up what I can on the side; a bit of skirt steak I call it. I haven't had a good feed in ages; and I'm not talking about food.
>
> I'll write the McLeavey memoirs, one day. They just won't believe it. I can hardly believe it. I'll call it 'How to live out of a paper bag'.
>
> Love from 'Ward 10'.
>
> Peter.[61]

Amid all the turmoil, however, Peter had begun to find some solace in religion.[62] After nearly two decades as a non-practising Catholic, he had returned to prayer and attending church, and he found the Mass especially sustaining. 'There's something about being in the presence of people who are believers. The priest, and his intensity... It's an incredibly powerful thing. It gave me a sense of being connected, part of a community – linked in to the tribal cultures, to the history of the world.'[63]

Twelve months after moving into his flat, Peter was able to report he was back on track and even regaining some semblance of a social life, attending openings and parties. 'At 48 years of age I recently have noted that I am more composed and relaxed. The pressure of all manner of things has lifted. Oh, don't worry, the McLeavey striving for God only knows what is still there but I am more resigned and, now, just want to get on with living.'[64] He and Hilary were now planning to divorce, and in November 1985, he remarked on the two-year anniversary of their separation. 'I want to be alone,' he told Ireland. 'No women; cats; gardens; lawns to mow. No more going to beaches; sandflies; peanut butter sandwiches. No more homilies about "setting boundaries", "being judgmental", "setting limits", "negotiating", and "one's own space". Horror of horror; no, no, one thousand times no. No more litanies of my failings; no more recitations about where I got it wrong. Amen. Sorry, sorry, for that little outburst. It's just that, well, soon I'll be free (sort of).'[65]

EIGHTEEN

This place is a bit like a dance hall.

During the 1980s, contemporary art became increasingly big business internationally. In the auction rooms of London and New York, the cost of works by living artists spiralled as a new breed of collector – celebrities, property developers and merchant bankers – pushed prices ever higher. By mid-decade, art auctions at Sotheby's and Christie's were breaking records on a regular basis.[1]

New Zealand followed the international trend, albeit at a more sedate level. As journalist Rosemary McLeod noted in 1986, 'You could get a decent car for what it takes these days to buy a painting by Gordon Walters... But a lot of people nowadays choose the art instead. At a time of gloomy economic forecasts, art here is a flourishing industry. Contemporary New Zealand art has come of age – and it may be the biggest growth industry we have.'[2]

Buyer confidence in the primary market – the dealer galleries – was reinforced by the prices fetched at auction. As McLeod observed, 'Art auctions surprised some people by proving that the prices dealers had created were realistic. The successful have never looked back.'[3] Once again, Peter Webb was a pioneer, entering the auction business in the 1960s, establishing his own company in 1976 and leading the way in producing illustrated catalogues in the following decade.[4] In 1985, Peter McLeavey described an auction in Auckland as 'a cross between a Fellini movie and the Cuba Mall on a Friday night. Everything that was awful, and good, and embarrassing, and right off the wall met, mingled, and then evaporated (for about 10 minutes). Prices were high when the real oil came on. Smither stood up well going for about $14,000/$16,000. And much more which I can't even remember'.[5]

Julian Dashper (left) and John Reynolds with their first exhibition at the Peter McLeavey Gallery, October–November 1984

The Smither that sold in 1985 would have cost less than $1000 ten years earlier; a Walters, originally sold for $1000 to $1500, could now fetch up to $25,000.[6] The gain compared favourably with more traditional investments, and suddenly contemporary art – or rather its value – became topical. In newspapers and popular magazines, articles appeared regularly on the subject of 'art-as-investment'. Peter remained sceptical. 'Approaching art with investment in mind is a perilous exercise,' he maintained. 'If people say something's a great investment, I'd grab my cheque book and leave.'[7]

It was McCahon, more than any other New Zealand artist, whose prices showed the most dramatic increase. In 1972, his large *Gate III* sold for $4000; six years later, a work of comparable scale, the *Northland panels*, was acquired by the National Art Gallery for $25,000. In 1985, the gallery paid $130,000, the highest price publicly recorded in New Zealand, for *Practical religion*.[8] From the late 1970s, in consultation with McCahon and his family, Peter limited the number of works that could be sold every year so the artist avoided a huge tax bill. In any case, their value was increasing so swiftly it was prudent to retain them. 'A lot of people didn't like that,' Peter recalled. 'They thought I was being too controlling. But my concern was really to protect Colin's interests.'[9]

In the corporate world of the 1980s, contemporary art became a symbol of success and sophistication. As Peter Webb put it, 'If you go out and see that business rivals have some good New Zealand paintings on their walls and you have only some tatty old reproductions then you have to do something about it.'[10] In the auction room, collecting became a competitive sport as buyers jostled to outdo each other. Many artists scorned the one-upmanship of the auction room and the 'diarrhoea of the chequebook' it encouraged. 'It's bizarre,' Pat Hanly declared in March 1987. 'People have gone crackers over painting.'[11]

Amid all the hype about the market, however, many people continued to buy art simply because they wanted to live with it, with no expectation of short-term gain. And some of those who began with an eye to investment became hooked at a deeper level, so that art became a passion in their lives. Many new collectors became involved with contemporary art through buying groups, which had their heyday in the 1980s. The Prospect collection, formed in Auckland in July 1976, was a precursor, developing out of discussions between merchant banker Grahame Reeves, lawyer Warwick Brown and adviser Peter Webb.[12] It spawned a number of similar groups in the following decade and encouraged many members to become collectors in their own right.

By the mid-1980s, Peter had a small but committed group of Auckland clients. Some would come down regularly for shows by the artists they were interested in; others would inspect reproductions or have works sent up to them. Some bought paintings by McCahon and Walters on resale – works that Peter had originally sold in the 1970s[13] – and the commission from these sales (generally 10 percent) became a crucial part of his business. Jenny and Alan Gibbs, who went on to become important patrons and promoters of New Zealand art, acquired three paintings by McCahon on resale in the late 1980s, as well as other significant works.[14]

Writing to Walters in 1985, Peter reflected on the Wellington art market:

> I seem to have more and more people coming through. Particularly young people. As always I spend virtually all the time we are open (11.00 to 5.00) talking to them all. It's always been my 'motto', *if it moves I talk to it.* That, irrespective of age, gender, economic or class status...
>
> Business is all go and sales are good. It's an interesting observation, however, that the Wellington market is not the [same] 'profile' as Auckland. We don't have any 'sell outs' here. Everything proceeds on a 52 week basis. I personally feel that 'sell-outs' are very counter productive and create in the market's mind a *destabilised and false* state. A '*flavour of the month*' mentality is formed with the market racing hither and yon. Not really productive for the medium or long term interests of the artist or dealer. It does seem to me that mentality is increasingly abroad in Auckland.
>
> But then, perhaps I'm out of touch. Perhaps we should encourage investment trusts; groupings of well heeled lawyers (i.e. Prospect collection) and people who look upon your works as commodities to buy up.[15]

As the art market matured, a new crop of dealer galleries opened across the country. Peter inspected the new venues in Auckland in May 1985 – Artis, the Sue Crockford and Red Metro[16] – and reported back to Walters: 'The 3 new galleries in Auckland will make us all work harder. I'm sure there is enough art to go around.'[17] Other galleries followed, including the Aberhart North and the Gow Langsford. In Wellington, Peter was now one of a group of art dealers: Louise Beale had taken over from Elva Bett in 1980, while Janne Land ran the Galerie Legard (later the Brooker Gallery) for a legal firm before establishing her own gallery in 1981.[18] Jenny Neligan's Bowen Galleries opened in the same year, followed by others later in the decade.[19]

It was a time of growing confidence and expansion in the local art world, with more artists and administrators, and new residencies, funding opportunities and venues.[20] There were more international touring exhibitions, notably *The British show*, *Wild visionary spectral* and *Cindy Sherman*, and more visiting artists: Marina Abramović, Barbara Kruger, Daniel Buren and Jörg Immendorff, to name a few. In 1982, Wystan Curnow had characterised a key problem in New Zealand art: not only did local artists have no presence overseas, but 'almost no recent art from elsewhere is seen here. No in-put, no out-put.'[21] During the decade, that situation began to change; as Luit Bieringa noted, 'There was a sense that New Zealand was starting to catch up.'[22]

To Peter, it seemed that local artists were finally beginning to attract the support they deserved – not just in the market place, but also at a curatorial level. He was especially pleased by efforts to show their work overseas, for example in *ANZART-in-Edinburgh* at the Edinburgh International Festival in 1984.[23] '[T]his is all part of that push, that is not only going to do art well, but will bleed back into the culture by giving all of us who live in these islands a feeling of self worth, of confidence, that we too can stand tall in the world asserting our own identity and sense of nationhood.'[24]

—

In 1984, Peter began to show John Reynolds and Julian Dashper, two young Aucklanders who had met at art school in 1978. Peter had first contacted Reynolds in 1981 but, from the artist's point of view, his timing was terrible. Aware that he needed an income to support his art practice, Reynolds was about to open 'John's Diner' – a café in Albert Street.

> Peter rang and said, 'I'm coming to Auckland, and I'd like to talk about us possibly having a show.' And I was virtually melting on the end of the phone. I mean Peter was at the apex, at that stage he had demi-god status to me … and of course he showed all those artists that I absolutely admired …
>
> So I had to say, 'Well, Peter, I'm opening this business soon, come and meet me there.' He called in just before I opened. He sat down and we had a great conversation about art and he said, 'Well, this looks very interesting, it's fantastic you're doing this, I was going to offer you a show, but look, you'll be very busy, I'll come back in two years' time. So good luck with things – and bye!'
>
> Well – I waved him goodbye, and I just about broke down. I couldn't believe it. I thought, Here's the pre-eminent dealer and art

impresario in New Zealand, he's just come and said, Love your work, but I'll come and see you in two years' time. I was crushed.

But the remarkable thing was that Peter was true to his word. In two years exactly to the day – and by then I'd sold the café – Peter came back. He said, 'Right, are you ready for that show?'[25]

For Reynolds, then in his early twenties, it was an important lesson: 'It showed me that time in the art world was different. Peter wasn't interested in fashion, what's hot just now – bronze animals, right, that's what we're doing. Julian and I were sharing a studio in High Street, and just knowing that Peter was down there in Wellington beaming up that regard, that interest, was sufficient for us to think it was do-able.' For his part, Peter was impressed by the energy and verve of the two young artists. 'It was very pleasant seeing you and your "works in progress",' he wrote to Reynolds in November 1983. 'I liked the scale of some of them and the "Look Ma, no hands" feel. It was exciting.'[26]

For their first exhibition with Peter, and their first dealer-gallery show, in October 1984, Dashper and Reynolds packed the gallery wall to wall with twenty-two exuberant abstract paintings, all titled for the landscapes or buildings that had provided an imaginative departure point.[27] Reynolds' style was gestural and calligraphic, with flurries and eddies of lines; Dashper's was more colourful, structured and painterly. Critic Ian Wedde noted the influence of contemporary American artists such as David Salle and Julian Schnabel, and a similarly irrepressible attitude – what he dubbed the 'heck-with-it' trend in painting.[28] As Wedde intimated, Dashper and Reynolds represented a new generation in New Zealand art. They rejected the earnestness of high modernism – as evidenced by McCahon and others – and made a virtue of wit, humour, the tumult of popular culture, and the provisional over the grand statement.

Peter sold only three works on paper (one by Reynolds and two by Dashper), but he was delighted with the show, and the artists were upbeat. Early the following year, he wrote to Dashper about a large painting from the exhibition – *Rural Sheraton*, priced at $1000. 'So far I've not sold it. But, I am fond of it so we might hit "pay dirt" soon.'[29] Peter found it interesting that many of the local 'experts' resisted Dashper's work. 'I always feel that it is a good sign. Those who work for our art institutions or consider themselves as being "in the know" are always about 3 to 5 years behind good art. Most of them are only now starting to "catch on" to Killeen and Harris. You have a talent. It is going to be really exciting for you (and for me) to follow it. And to have the courage to follow it wherever it may lead.'

Peter installing *Julian Dashper and John Reynolds: Recent works*, October–November 1984

In September 1985, Peter advised Dashper that he had sold *Rural Sheraton* to the influential Wellington collectors, Jim and Mary Barr. The couple had acquired their first work from Peter – a Robin White print – in 1971, and gone on to become key clients, purchasing work by young artists when they were fresh on the scene and following their careers show by show. They had been early buyers of Killeen and

Peryer, and their support of Dashper would be crucial in the following years. Dashper met the Barrs soon afterwards and reported back to Peter: 'They live and breathe art, and seem to be having no trouble doing what they believe should be done in the art world. I am impressed by them both and so glad they have a work of mine. Thank-you for this.'[30]

Some twenty years older than Dashper and Reynolds, Peter felt a rapport with them personally and professionally. 'It was a thrill, for me, to visit you in the studio,' he told Reynolds.

> These visits are so important for me. From them I seem to receive all manner of insights ... Last Sunday, for example, I saw (and felt) those two strains which are central to your work.
>
> One is your interest in *recording*, *depicting*, *reproducing*, and *rendering* the (real) world. The world of what we see; what's there.
>
> The other is that contemplative aspect of your 'self'. An interest in that which is 'abstract' (perhaps even '*utopian*') ...
>
> Plans, schemes, proposals; yes, even 'Propositions'.
> A striving towards some 'Ideal'; something not *seen* but felt.
>
> A lifetime, for you, John.
> A lifetime of squaring these two opposites –
> All power to you on that, most enduring, quest.[31]

Peter also felt protective of the two young painters. After twenty years in business, he was aware of the perils of early success, and the pressures and demands it could bring. In January 1986, he wrote to Reynolds, 'I've been thinking about you lately. I know that there are many demands on you and your talent. Always husband and protect it; always do what you want to do and not what others may expect or demand of you and your gift. It is a gift. Protect it ... Develop, extend, and take risks in it. Have fun with it; kick it around a bit. And, always, keep the faith.'[32] Reynolds, who developed a strong bond with Peter, saw his relationship with his dealer as more than representation in the conventional sense. 'It was a personal engagement, an adventure, and we would go on together. Neither of us knew where it would go, what would happen, how it would play out, but that commitment was total from the beginning.'

Both Reynolds and Dashper held their first solo shows with Peter in the winter of 1986. Dashper challenged conventional good taste with four paintings on velvet – 'that staple support of luminous kitsch', as the critic Rob Taylor put it.[33] In *Purple rain at Glorit*, the lurid oils – orange, gold and green – are squeezed straight from the tube, and smeared and scraped across the rich indigo surface of the painting.[34]

John Reynolds, *Lever*, 1986
Oil on canvas
Museum of New Zealand Te Papa Tongarewa,
purchased 1986 with New Zealand Lottery Board funds

The title reflects the work's origins: Dashper had made the preliminary drawings at Glorit on the Kaipara coast while listening to Prince's album.

This exhibition was a hit with the local art fraternity. Luit Bieringa purchased *Purple rain at Glorit* for the National Art Gallery collection; Jim and Mary Barr bought a large painting, *Auction at the Regent*, as well as a work for Foreign Affairs, for which they were acting as advisers. Reynolds' show, which followed on from Dashper's, was similarly well received, with the sale of *Lever* to the National Art Gallery, and purchases by Foreign Affairs and influential private collectors.

In 1985, Peter received a letter from Richard Killeen. 'Congratulations on making your 20 years as a dealer in this country. It is a really major achievement to be able to survive that long and still be doubting and questioning the position that you are in. It is probably the reason that you have been as successful as you have. That is, you don't sit on your laurels. This is probably what it is all about, a constant questioning and changing of attitudes. I feel that in myself'.[35]

Julian Dashper, *Purple rain at Glorit*, 1986
Oil and conté on velvet
Museum of New Zealand Te Papa Tongarewa,
purchased 1986 with Ellen Eames Collection funds

Peter had a special project in mind to mark his anniversary – a collaborative painting by Dashper and Reynolds and a third painter from his stable, Allen Maddox. 'I was talking to these young artists,' he told reporter Merill Coke, 'and I said, "Look, I've just got this great idea ... We'll get a canvas cut as big as this wall [the main wall of the gallery]. I want you to come in here on Saturday afternoon at one o'clock and start painting it. You'll be here all day Sunday, Monday, Tuesday and the show hits the road ... at 5.30 pm on Tuesday".'[36] He dubbed the project 'Omaha Beach', as a metaphor for his life in contemporary art: 'you just get out there and do your damndest, as soldiers did at the World War II D Day landings'.

Dashper and Reynolds were enthusiastic. 'I wrote to Allen today, explaining the idea about the Omaha Beach project,' Dashper wrote. 'I hope he is keen ... John and I are champing at the bit about it. It sounds and feels correct. The vibes are just right.'[37] But by the spring of 1986 the project had become a two-artist affair, as Dashper and

Reynolds had grown weary of Maddox's constant drinking and aggressive behaviour. 'Maddox and Clairmont and Fomison were very visible when we were emerging,' Reynolds recalled. 'We saw them as successful, articulate artists, but under the table. We were ambitious and we wanted to make art: we did not want to be self-destructive like them. We saw it in generational terms.'

After driving down from Auckland for the Omaha Beach project on a Saturday, the two artists worked right through the night, Dashper starting from the left, Reynolds from the right of the canvas. 'We'd done drawings around it beforehand,' recalled Reynolds, 'but we'd worked together for so many years that we had a lot of faith in each other's ability.' In the early hours of Sunday morning, when they were starting to tire, they had a surprise visit: Peter, on his way home from a fancy-dress party, called to check in on progress. He was wearing his favourite costume – a nun's outfit. 'They got a helluva fright,' he reported.[38]

As well as the large collaborative painting, which Peter was thrilled with, the exhibition included a number of smaller preparatory sketches, many of which sold to private collectors.[39] Writing about the large painting, Ian Wedde remarked on the artists' disparate styles, Dashper's exuberant, open brushstrokes, and Reynolds' spidery, angular marks: 'The convergence of their different signatures toward the centre of this invasion has produced one of the best events of the silly season.'[40]

In the following year, Dashper was awarded an arts council grant, enabling him to make his first trip beyond Australia. He wrote to Peter, 'I can tell you the thought of it makes me very scared but at the same time it leaves me very excited about what I shall see and the ideas I shall bring back. I am looking forward to my future shows at Peter McLeavey Gallery I can tell you!'[41] From London he sent a postcard of Velázquez' *The toilet of Venus* of 1647–51. '[E]veryday I sit in front of it for 2 hours. I think I know how beautiful it is, and then something comes into it which I never saw before... It is the force.'[42]

By November, Dashper was in Texas and his thoughts were turning towards home. 'The whole trip has left me full of new ideas and ways of looking at things... I'm very keen to show with you in 1988... I think a lot about being an artist in New Zealand and how good that is. You realise how exciting and vital the art being produced there is... you get hit by that as soon as you see any breadth of overseas work – it is good to be coming home.'[43]

Although they remained sensitive to their relative isolation as artists in New Zealand, Dashper and Reynolds had a different relationship to

Peter (left) and party-goers in fancy dress with *The Omaha panels* by John Reynolds and Julian Dashper, 1986

'overseas' than the preceding generation. Emerging in the early 1980s, they recognised that the local art world was still very limited. 'At that stage there were only two or three dealer galleries in Auckland,' Reynolds remarked. 'The audience for art was tiny. It just wasn't enough. We had to look further afield.' Both painters had travelled extensively by the time they were thirty, and they saw themselves as part of a global network of artists. In 1989, Dashper wrote to Peter about his friend Hamish Kilgour, whose band The Clean was finding an overseas audience. '[T]hey've done it their way. They've taken New Zealand away rather than expatriate. I'm impressed. They've been an inspiration to me. It's so great to see people feeling good about their own culture and knowing other people will be interested in it as it's so different. Ours is a time now when we can achieve things in this country. It is amazing how much change has happened in just the last 4–5 years.'[44]

For Reynolds, there was even something galvanising in New Zealand's relative isolation. 'Distance gives us, by default, an incubator process: our giant wetas can live in some protection from giant rats. But it also makes us intensely anxious: "How are we doing? How do we look? What are they doing over there?" and that anxiousness can be very productive.'[45] Both Dashper and Reynolds would interrogate the concept of distance, using it to fuel their work and articulate their position in the world as New Zealand artists.

Internationally, the art world of the 1980s was influenced by a new wave of postmodern theory. Sceptical and highly politicised, the new theorists 'deconstructed' the certainties of modernism, challenging long-held hierarchies such as the importance of originality as the ultimate measure of value, the superiority of high culture over popular culture, and the value of 'civilised' society over the so-called 'primitive'. Art critics analysed the nature of representation and the complicity of images in the history of power: in America, for example, Benjamin Buchloh linked neo-expressionist painting with authoritarian politics.[46] At the same time, there emerged a new group of artists – Barbara Kruger, Jenny Holzer, Hans Haacke and others – who used the tropes of the mass media to scrutinise representations of power.[47]

Locally, postmodernism had an invigorating effect on the art scene. Artists brought a more theoretical approach to their work, and critics adopted a more analytical and intellectual style of writing. But in some cases the new criticism could be very prescriptive and judgemental. Writing for the *National Business Review*, the feminist critic Lita Barrie favoured art that offered a social critique and dismissed work that did not advance her agenda. Following American critics, she became increasingly censorious of her key target: contemporary expressionist painting. 'Neo-expressionism,' she wrote in 1987, 'is a prime example of what art critic Harold Rosenberg calls devajunk art which plays upon an audience's desire to be won over by what has already been assimilated dressed up as the new.'[48] Barrie reserved particular scorn for Julian Schnabel, the young American art star with a knack for self-promotion, and often typecast Reynolds and Dashper as 'Schnabel clones'.[49] Her inference was that they, like the American, were pandering to an avid and gullible art market with a mindlessly macho brand of painting.

Even in 1987, however, Dashper's work was becoming more pared back and conceptual. Like Reynolds, he had a keen interest in New

Zealand art history and an awareness of his own place in the tradition, exhibiting in the same rooms as McCahon, Walters and other key figures. A collector himself, he had purchased a small landscape painting by Charles Tole from Peter – 'Something incredibly New Zealand about it, a very powerful and consistent vision.'[50] Dashper had also remarked on Woollaston's largest painting to date, *Above Wellington* of 1986, which Peter later sold to the National Art Gallery. 'It is a classic, a real beauty,' he told Peter. 'John had gone on and on about it and I can see why.'[51] For Dashper, the history of New Zealand art would form a ready source of material for his own practice.

Exhibiting with Peter in 1987, he sampled Michael Smither's rock paintings, using an enlarged rock pattern as the ground for an abstract work entitled, in typical Dashper fashion, after an iconic New Zealand landscape – *Young Nick's Head*. In the following year he drew on Gordon Walters' gouaches of the 1950s in works that toyed with the notion of corporate branding: *Proposed mural for the Koru club*, *Design for a pyjamas manufacturers logo*, and others.[52] Such work was postmodern in its strategies of quotation and appropriation – and in the way it drew attention to the production, reception and marketing of art.

In the last days of Dashper's show in 1988, some recent works by Walters happened to arrive and Peter, struck by the link between the two artists, promptly hung them in the exhibition. Dashper was delighted to have his work displayed next to that of the modern painter he so admired. He and Reynolds had befriended Walters, and found stimulus and encouragement in the association. 'It is great to have someone like Gordon to look at,' Dashper wrote to Peter in 1989. 'He is a true master I feel, very much in control. I find that we can talk very easily about art. Our concerns are surprisingly similar. I find his 1955 work extremely interesting as I find his 1989 work also. I find the support from Gordon and Richard [Killeen] to be so valuable. I only hope I can offer another artist the same one day.'[53]

Dashper's work may have shifted in focus, but he could not escape the ire of Lita Barrie. His exhibition in October 1989 prompted a particularly hostile review under the title, 'Just take a look at all that "devajunk" piling up': '[T]he market adulation is out of proportion for a still-developing artist,' she claimed.[54] Barrie also mentioned a new book on Walters, on sale in the gallery during the show, and made much of the connection, suggesting that Peter was opportunistically trying to boost the young artist's reputation by 'ensuring Dashper's pedigree line to an aristocratic ancestor'.[55] Peter wrote immediately to the artist:

> I try not to allow these bad press reviews to get me down. And you must not. When you're good (and trying to be good) everyman and his mother has a pot shot at you. That is the nature of things. And it's not just a particular of this place (as some would have us believe). Envy is universal.
>
> You're good. We are both good. Don't waste time worrying about mean minded people. They're not worth it. Just keep at it. Head up; roll your shoulders; and go for it. They will all be left in the exhaust tail; way back; way way back, on the other side of town.[56]

Dashper replied, 'Many thanks for your letter today. I didn't know about the Lita Barrie review so I went and got a copy of N.B.R. I must say I'm glad I got your letter first ... Anyway with your letter under my belt I don't have to worry about it. Thank you for all your support Peter.'[57]

On the final day of Dashper's exhibition, Peter wrote to Reynolds to thank him for his hospitality on a recent visit to Auckland:

> I had a good trip back and now, at 11.00 am on a Saturday morning, I'm sitting in Cuba Street with the Dashper show.
>
> It has two hours to run.
>
> Then, at 1.00 pm, the blokes from Stan's carpet laying services will move in. They will rip up the existing brown and replace it with a grey. They say they will have it 'all cleaned up' by 4.00. Not bad; they are very fast workers I gather.
>
> My end of year show will be a real humdinger. I'll flesh it out for you later but expect it to not only include your chalks but works by W Hammond and a stunning Billy Apple.
>
> Yes, this place is a bit like a dance hall. It's the only joint where Billy can ask John, or W Hammond, for a dance. And they look great together. They're family (as in the Mob). It's real 'When Worlds Collide' stuff, and it will look great.
>
> Thank you, John, for all your enthusiasm and encouragement. It's appreciated; it buoys me up. And your loyalty.
>
> Warm Regards
>
> Peter.[58]

Julian Dashper, *Young Nick's Head*, 1987
Oil and mixed media
Auckland Art Gallery Toi o Tāmaki, on loan from the Dashper/Shannon Trust, 1997

is there anything of which one can say, Look,
this is New? NO it has already existed, long ago;
before our time.

ECCLESIASTES the emptiness of all endeavour.

I the speaker ruled as king over Israel;
in Jerusalem.

and in wisdom I applied
my mind to study and
explore all that is done
under heaven. It is a
sorry business that GOD
has given men to busy
themselves with.
I have seen all the deeds that
are done here under the Sun;
they are all emptiness and
chasing the wind.
What is crooked cannot
become straight;
what is not there
cannot be counted.

the sun rises and the sun goes down; back it
returns to its place and rises there again.
The wind blows south, the wind blows north
Round and round it goes and returns full
circle.
all streams run into the sea, yet the sea never
overflows, back to the place from which the
streams ran they return to run again.

So I applied my mind
to understand wisdom
and knowledge, madness
and folly, and I came to see
that this too is chasing
the wind. For in much
wisdom is much vexation,
and the more a man
knows, the more he has to
suffer.
I said to myself, 'Come, I will
plunge into pleasures and enjoy
myself' but this too was emptiness.
of laughter I said 'It is madness'
and of pleasure 'what is the good of that?'
So I sought to stimulate myself with wine, in
the hope of finding out what was good for
men to do under heaven throughout
the brief span of their lives.
But my mind was guided by wisdom
-not blinded by
folly.

NINETEEN

Good art is always hard to sell.

'I have had a busy time this week,' Peter wrote to Walters in March 1985. 'And, yesterday, I seemed to spend all day with just 4 people. Yes, they are all clients and we spent time just talking... Nothing much about art but, rather, they discussed their lives, aspirations and hopes. They talked about all manner of things.'[1] It was not unusual for Peter to spend hours with a single client, engaging their interest, drawing them out, and developing a relationship of trust and confidence.

Peter's days at work were a sharp contrast to his evenings in Brooklyn. '[A]t night, I get so much pleasure out of just going home on my own to an empty house. There, solitude and peace reign. No decisions have to be made. I cook a meal. I sit down on the floor and switch on the TV. And then, at 10.00, I go to bed. Up at 6.00. It is a somewhat monastic life and it does seem to appeal to my temperament, strange as that is.' His life was not entirely monastic, however. As he told Peter Ireland, 'Since I've been "doing a McLeavey" (i.e. living alone) I've had the odd fling; yes, I've been a bit of a scallywag and chased young women (à la Jimmy Carter); I've experienced good old-fashioned Lust. And it feels good.'[2]

After sixteen months with little more than a bed and a television, Peter was beginning to 'civilise' his apartment. With the purchase of a stereo, he announced, 'the flat has now moved from its BEIRUT period to more TOKYO or SANTA BARBARA'.[3] He was even threatening to do a little entertaining. 'My main bill of fare has been "Brooklyn Mince",' he informed a friend and client. 'The pleasures of that cuisine I hope to share with you'.[4] Woollaston was impressed with the flat when he visited in August 1985: 'What taste! What assurance! What an

Colin McCahon: 2 recent paintings, April–May 1983, showing *Is there anything of which one can say, look, this is new?*, 1980–82

atmosphere of quality – the same sort as you create in your gallery exhibitions. You are all of a piece. It is your greatest means of selling.'[5]

In 1986, fourteen-year-old Catherine McLeavey, who had always identified with her father, moved in with him at Brooklyn. 'Dad played a big part in my life when I was a kid,' she recalled, 'and when he left home I went through a rebellious stage. I was questioning authority and challenging the boundaries, and going to live with Dad was really good for me. He's always been sympathetic to the underdog, the rebel, and I felt he accepted me, he didn't judge.'[6] In fact, Peter took a certain pride in his wilful daughter. 'She has plenty of spirit,' he noted approvingly to Woollaston, 'and that should do her well.'[7] Writing to Peter Ireland, he remarked on the traits they shared: 'She is a very driven and dogmatic child. (Heaven only knows where she got those qualities from; "wink wink; nudge nudge").'[8]

Catherine found living with Peter rather like 'camping out': 'Dad did things a bit differently. All the washing was hung out to dry inside the flat, the towels on the chairs and Dad's shirts hanging everywhere. Dad did a cooking course at Wellington High and his cooking improved a bit, but we often got takeaways around the corner from the gallery – beef and black bean sauce was our favourite. I liked living with Dad, it was lots of fun.' Dominic, who stayed with his father every weekend, loved his stories. 'They were rather bizarre but quite magical, and fully realised. He had a cast of characters: Romulus and Remus, the Seven Founders of the Servite Order, and Cockabully and Eel. They were always going off on adventures together, and every night there was a new instalment. Dad was never the kind of father who would play ball in the park, but there were other things he gave us. There was always reading and conversation and constant learning.'[9]

To mark his fiftieth birthday in 1986, Peter commissioned the Wellington photographer Peter Black to make a portfolio of images of his flat. Black was initially rather apprehensive about the assignment: 'I didn't know Peter very well at that stage. I was concerned that he might want to edit the photographs, control the portfolio. But there was none of that. He gave me the key to his flat and said, "I'm just interested to see what you come up with."'[10] Black visited Brooklyn Terrace several times, mainly when Peter was out. 'It was a real bachelor pad, quite austere. But he's a cunning old dog and I think he may have set some things up for me. Some of the arrangements of objects were so good, I couldn't resist them. Perhaps it was simply the way he'd put things down, but it seemed so perfect, so well thought out. It was like a Peter McLeavey artwork. I've always thought that Peter is like an artist.'

Peter himself is mainly absent in the portfolio, '2 Brooklyn Terrace'. In one image he sits at a table, partly obscured by a carving of a saint; in another, he stands with his back to the photographer, trying to coax a television to life. The images suggest the provisional nature of his bachelor life, with its crumpled shirts, wonky appliances, untidy piles of magazines, and artworks stashed in wardrobes. Ian Wedde reviewed the portfolio when it was exhibited at Exposures Gallery in 1987: '[It] is wry, observant, affectionate, and unpretentious, and it has been able, with minimal manipulation, to adduce personality – even symbology – from very scant materials.'[11] Peter himself was pleased with it: 'A most interesting document of me, at this stage of my life.'[12]

—

In 1985, Peter wrote to the Brisbane art dealer Ray Hughes, who had recently opened a branch in Sydney.

> I have often wondered how you are. Occasionally I've thought of writing to you about trying to organise, together, a show by your artists. Something, I know not quite what, holds me back. I am just so aware that I must keep the place going with local (New Zealand) based painters and sculptors.
>
> However, I'm now thinking that the time is coming for me to do something. I'll get back to you on that, soon.
>
> Another thing that has crossed my mind (fuelled by my marriage break-up) is the thought of sometime shifting to Australia and exploring whatever openings there may be for me in any existing galleries.
>
> But, that said, I am still here and, happily, still find that I get a thrill whenever I make a sale. My greatest problem is to ensure that I combine an openness for the new with maintaining excellence in standards. It is easy to become infatuated by fashion.
>
> I know you; and yet we have only passed a couple of hours in conversation. Funny, that. I guess we are probably, deep down, creatures of the same 'tribe': art dealers, out there working both sides of the street and, always, hoping to hit 'pay dirt' with the next sale.[13]

Peter introduced a number of new artists to the gallery during this period, among them Maria Olsen, Derek Cowie, Barbara Tuck, Gavin Chilcott and Bill Hammond.[14] 'These, in turn, are bringing in a younger vital group of buyers and viewers,' he told Walters in August 1985. 'My current show is by Derek Cowie and it's a very interesting show.

will
no
be

Warren Viscoe

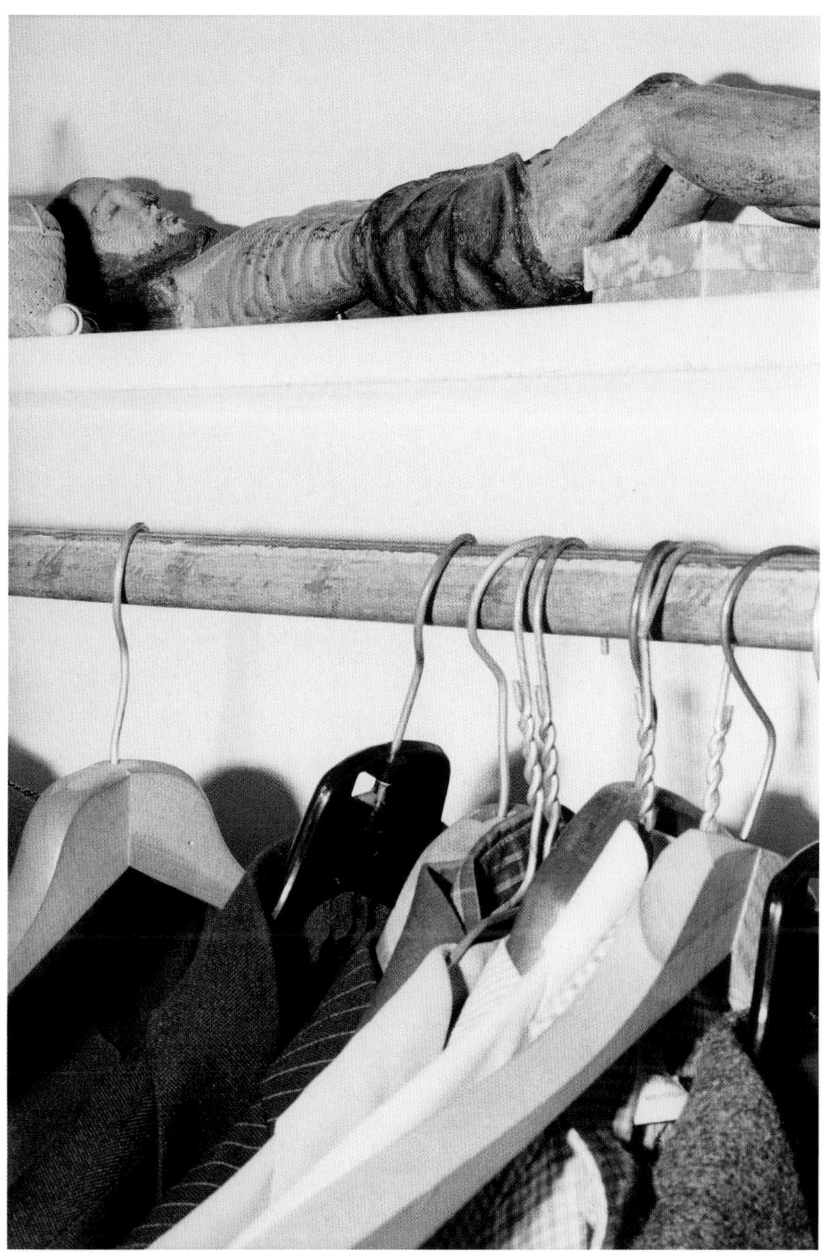

Peter Black, (clockwise from top left) *Untitled no. 13*, *Untitled no. 9* and *Untitled no. 14* from the '2 Brooklyn Terrace', portfolio, 1986
Gelatin silver prints
Museum of New Zealand Te Papa Tongarewa, purchased 1987 with Ellen Eames Collection funds

In a way it reminds me of the first Killeen shows I had. He is about 27; the work is singular, focused, and intelligent. He will be around for a while; all the markings of an authentic talent.'[15] Cowie soon became Peter's assistant, minding the gallery, liaising with artists and clients, packing and unpacking works, and helping with installation.

A number of established artists left the gallery during these years. As Peter so often remarked, a long-term relationship between an artist and a dealer was like a marriage, and inevitably there were break-ups: 'If you come home from work on Friday night and find them in bed with the butcher, the relationship is over. It's divorce.'[16] The annals of dealer galleries are full of tales of artists who leave a stable, mainly to move to a more prestigious venue that can offer better opportunities. Peter was unusual in that it was usually he who elected to end the relationship – or prompted an artist to move on.

Peter needed to believe wholeheartedly in the work he showed. Once he had doubts – about an artist's commitment, or the quality of their work – the relationship was inevitably affected, although it might take years to reach breaking point. Sometimes he found himself overcommitted: too many artists, all of them gifted, and he could not possibly continue to represent them all. Sometimes a relationship ended by mutual agreement, artist and dealer recognising that they were no longer in complete accord. Occasionally, he was caught between his loyalty to an artist and his conviction that the work no longer met his standards; at times, a long-held friendship came to an end. 'It can be difficult,' he noted. 'The artist identifies so closely with their work that any criticism of the art is taken very personally. It can be hard to maintain a friendship once the artist–dealer relationship is over. Although in most cases it comes right with time.'[17]

Don Binney had his last show with Peter in 1976. 'I got dumped by McLeavey,' he recalled. 'But then all the best people did. I'm in good company.'[18] His relationship with Peter had been under a strain for some time. In 1976, the two had a standoff when Binney sent fourteen works for an exhibition and Peter announced his intention to feature just four. Binney was incensed.

> I said, 'Peter, it's all or nothing.' There was a deadly silence. I said, 'Either you're showing that body of work or not… I am the author of this sequence.' He wanted to play the final editor. He wanted to pick bits out of it that he felt were equal to his own expectations… The whole show was shown, at my insistence, but Peter sulked, and Hilary made negative noises… I was made to feel that rather

Michael Smither at the gallery, photographed by Peter McLeavey, 1988

> than furnishing them with a show I had put up a demonstration of unacceptable wilfulness. And yet I was the artist.

Peter paid his last visit to Binney in 1980. 'He looked at several of my big new prints that were on litho stones at the time – they weren't bad prints either, thank you. He also saw a pretty nice painting I'd done and said, "Yes, I could exhibit that", but he did not… Shortly after, he simply shunted all the rest of the work of my authorship, out of the door of his suite in Cuba Street and pushed them along the corridor, around the stairwell to Elva Bett… the equivalent of leaving a baby in a basket on somebody's doorstep.'

Michael Smither had been one of Peter's stalwarts, but by 1980 he had effectively stopped painting to focus on his musical interests.[19] Three years later, he exhibited a series of drawings that explored the

Pat Hanly at Mount Eden, photographed by Peter McLeavey, 1984

analogies between art and music, and Peter described the show for a mutual friend: 'The exhibition does not consist of any "great works" but it is a very interesting show all the same. Interesting in the way that Smither, at 43, is trying to break patterns and explore and not get painted into a corner ... I personally found it a good show and it said lots of things to me. Things that have nothing to do with art but with living a life.'[20]

This was Smither's last show at the Peter McLeavey Gallery. The relationship was under pressure: Peter felt that Smither's commitment to painting had dwindled, and Smither recognised that his dealer had lost confidence in his work. In 1984, Smither wrote to him: 'This is a note to inform you officially that Janne [Land] is now my dealer in Wellington as for some time now I've felt our artist–dealer relationship to be unworkable. I hope your endeavours in the field continue to prosper & thank you for the better times we shared.'[21]

Peter's association with Pat Hanly ended a few years later. He felt that Hanly's *Golden age* exhibition in 1981 was a highlight of his programme, but by 1987 his confidence in the artist's paintings had waned, and he was unwilling to show them.[22] 'I seem to be unable to relate to the paintings,' he admitted. 'It's nobody's fault. It is just the way it is.'[23] He suggested a show of prints instead, but Hanly was determined to find a venue for his paintings in Wellington and arranged to have an exhibition with Janne Land. In December 1987, Peter sent a farewell note. 'I will shortly return the couple of graphics by you I have in stock. This concludes our business. It does not, however, erase my friendship for you. I will always regard, with great warmth, the advice, assistance and time you have given me since the time I started out on this curious and lonely quest... I will cherish those memories to the grave.'

In 2011, Binney speculated about Peter's longevity as a dealer. 'It's interesting how someone like McLeavey can bring about, almost become, incidentally, a factor of change, in historic epoch-turning terms. It might have to do with the way he felt it expedient to chuck so many people over the side. He was living through different sub-epochs of cultural history. In a way each one was incompatible sequentially with the last, and it was either him or his artists who had to go. Maybe that's why he's survived so long, when so many other dealers have fallen by the way.'[24]

Binney's observations are perceptive, and highlight a central issue for any art dealer. How to manage a stable of artists, so that a gallery remains topical in an art world eager for novelty and new talent? How to sustain a gallery over decades? Some dealers tend to be aligned with a certain generation, but Peter felt it was crucial to remain open to the new. It kept him interested. In periodically clearing the decks, he was able to 'refresh' his gallery by bringing on young artists. And he fed off their energy and ambition.

Richard Killeen, whose relationship with Peter spans more than forty years, made a pertinent comment:

> Peter's gallery is about him. He has a particular viewpoint, and that's his value – he stands or falls by his own opinions. That's a really important role for a person to have, that filtering role. That should be valued. But a lot of people got upset by it. Here was this dealer who was supposed to have a lot of status and he wouldn't show them. And it's the nature of our smallness as a country that you just don't have many Peter McLeaveys. There aren't enough like him, doing that job.[25]

Peter's long relationship with Colin McCahon was an anchor in his life, both personally and professionally, but by the early 1980s the artist's health was failing, and he was painting only with great difficulty. Aware that his career was coming to an end, McCahon was concerned with the fate of the works that remained in his studio, and had already begun the process of gifting significant paintings to public collections.[26] Having worked as a curator himself, he was aware of the importance of this process in ensuring his legacy.

In June 1980, Peter enquired on behalf of James Mollison, who hoped to buy several early works for the Australian National Gallery, scheduled to open in 1982. Peter believed it was crucial for McCahon to be well represented at the most important art museum in the southern hemisphere, but the artist had mixed feelings: '[S]omewhere along the line I want a few good works to mark my passing in New Zealand… I just don't want a sell out [to] the Australian Nat Gallery.'[27] McCahon had felt a 'traitor', he told Peter, when *Victory over death 2* was gifted to Canberra. 'Oh yes I was pleased – one way – and so bereft & lost – as me, one of us'. He wanted his early work in particular to remain in New Zealand: 'It's all much more personal & talks to N.Z. people more than the recent work which is more international.'[28]

> …I am always conscious of my death & nothing left for Anne – and for this lovely country. This is where my heart is all the time – could be Dunedin Christchurch Nelson Auckland & Muriwai – the whole place. It sits over me as a potent magic. Ahipara – I thank God for Ahipara – a beauty of a day up on the huge sandhill & only sea & sky and an old dog …I'm here perhaps saying a farewell to 'the land of my loving' – that from an old old Maori woman…
>
> Peter – I just don't know how it all goes – I need just as much as I need to live on (and paint). I'm not on the fame and fortune bit. I don't want too much fame & fortune.[29]

McCahon's late paintings reflect his preoccupation with two texts from the Bible: A Letter to Hebrews, with its meditation on the nature of faith, and the more pessimistic Book of Ecclesiastes. In September 1980, his old friend Ian Prior, who had suggested the former text as the basis for a painting, purchased *A Letter to Hebrews* and subsequently gifted it to the National Art Gallery.[30] 'I'm very happy he liked it,' McCahon told Peter. 'I'm not painting to sell but to state a message about the land & the people.'[31]

When the Australian National Gallery opened in 1982, Peter sent McCahon a colour supplement published to mark the occasion. 'There is

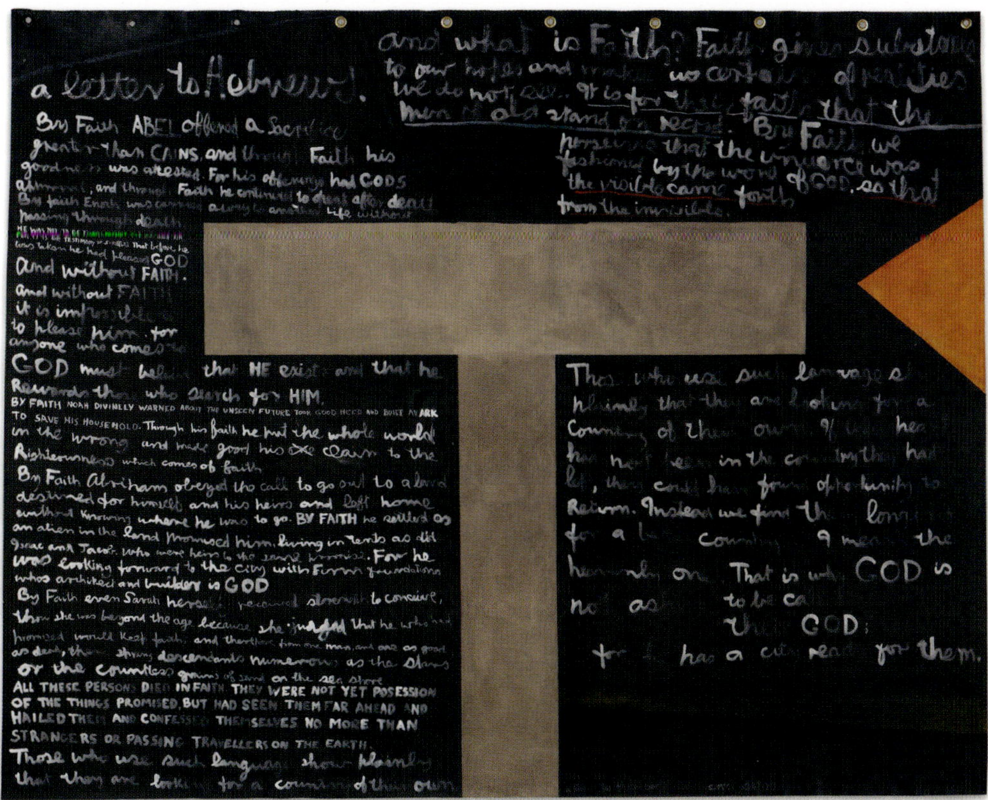

Colin McCahon, *A Letter to Hebrews*, 1979
Acrylic on unstretched canvas
Museum of New Zealand Te Papa Tongarewa, gift of anonymous donors with assistance from the Willi Fels Memorial Trust, 1981

a reference to your painting "*I am*" on page 10. They expect one million people a year will visit the gallery so it will be "all hands on deck" I would say. Congratulations, Colin, and thank you for all your art. This, I know, comes from all of us who love and affirm life. Both here, in these islands, and all those people overseas who will see and know your art.'[32]

In one of his last letters to Peter in February 1983, McCahon reported that he was working once more. 'For me it's been a kind of nothing period but I'm getting back into painting again, thank goodness. I have armed myself with paint and have a large canvas on the studio floor. It's a start at least and I think I know again what I am on about.'[33] But McCahon's life as an artist was over. In April that year, Peter showed two of his final paintings, based on Ecclesiastes and completed between

March and May 1982: *I applied my mind*, and *Is there anything of which one can say, look, this is new?* Peter purchased the latter, priced at $9000, for the Bank of New Zealand collection. This, exhibition number 163, was McCahon's last show of new work at the Peter McLeavey Gallery (see page 318).

In April 1984, McCahon was honoured with a major exhibition, *I will need words*, curated by Wystan Curnow for the Fifth Biennale of Sydney – the first time a survey of his work had been shown overseas.[34] It should have been a fine moment for McCahon, but by now he was seriously ill, suffering from dementia. The day before the opening, he was visiting the Royal Botanic Gardens in Sydney with his wife Anne and curator Alexa Johnston when he wandered off and went missing. By the time he was found the next day, he was thoroughly disoriented, and was admitted to hospital.

The opening of *I will need words* was a sombre occasion for McCahon's supporters, but the exhibition itself was a highlight of the Biennale. In a lengthy review in the *Sydney Morning Herald*, critic Terence Maloon discussed one of the key works, *Victory over death 2* – 'a noble addition to our public collections' – and declared, '[N]ow it is time for us to honour Colin McCahon.'[35] With support from the Scottish gallery director Richard Demarco, *I will need words* toured to the Edinburgh International Festival later in the year before returning home for a showing at the National Art Gallery.[36] The publication of Gordon H Brown's landmark book, *Colin McCahon: Artist*, helped to consolidate his reputation further.

McCahon spent his final years at home, cared for by his wife, until he was hospitalised in his last months. The news of his death on 27 May 1987 made national headlines, and Peter attended the funeral at St Joseph's Catholic Church in Grey Lynn.[37] Interviewed in the *Evening Post*, he remarked on McCahon's achievement: 'An artist like that has immortality. His work will survive long after this generation.'[38] Peter referred to the part McCahon had played in his own life by encouraging him to open his gallery: 'It was largely because of him, and one or two other artists, that I decided to stay in New Zealand.' He also mentioned McCahon's pioneering role as a curator in the 1950s, when he recognised the quality of early Pākehā painting. He concluded: 'It was a privilege to have known that civilised and cultured intelligence.'

While McCahon's death was not unexpected, the loss of Michael Illingworth in 1988 was a great shock to his family and friends.

Michael Illingworth at Coroglen, photographed by Peter McLeavey, 1986

Illingworth's farm had continued to dominate his life, but in 1984 he held a successful show with Peter, and in the following year he seemed to be making some headway. 'Michael has suddenly started to paint with more purpose,' Peter informed Killeen after a visit to Coroglen. 'While it is early days yet I must say I did like what I saw. The plan at present is for him to order six new large stretchers and to carry on working with the hope that we can have a show early 1987.'[39]

Peter was still planning an exhibition in 1988, but early in July, Illingworth suddenly weakened and collapsed. From Thames Hospital he wrote to reassure his dealer, 'Have not had the strength to frame the pictures but hope to as soon as I am put right.'[40] He died from cancer, with his family around him, two weeks later. He was just fifty-five.

Peter attended Illingworth's tangi at Coroglen, and reported back to Peter Ireland. 'The funeral was great with John Baxter's Maori rant the most totally Illingworth "thing" you, or me, or (yes) Mike, could ever wish for ... He really "wound us up" and then capped the whole thing with Jim's *High Country weather*. Mike would have been jumping up and down in the coffin, I'm sure. You could have heard a pin drop from Whitianga through to Coroglen when Johnny Baxter "did his thing".'[41]

Days later Peter wrote to Illingworth's widow, Dene:

> What a lovely send off we all gave Michael.
>
> Now, over a week later, his death is only just starting to sink in. I'll certainly miss him. His good humour, intelligence, and grace. And his friendship. And his sound business advice contributed, so much, to my 'enterprise' here, in Wellington.
>
> And didn't he enjoy those trips south, to the capital. It was such fun; the little Greek restaurant he loved, the Retsina, and the talk; yards and yards (and, yes) miles of it.
>
> Good times; goodnight, sweet prince.[42]

—

In 1986, Peter began a habit of travelling overseas in summer while the gallery was closed, and it soon became a crucial part of his year, an opportunity to recharge and consider the months ahead. His first trip was to Chicago, where he visited dealer galleries and art museums. He also purchased a work by the feminist artist Barbara Kruger: a photo-collage combining text and sign language – *Untitled (We will no longer be seen and not heard)* of 1985. The work seems to speak for all those who feel disenfranchised and overlooked, and for Peter it touched a nerve, recalling his childhood and early struggle for independence.

Back home, he reported on his trip to Peter Ireland:

> Chicago; well for me it was the essential American city. Very strong; straight; no holds barred. It was all I had expected; multiplied by 100.
>
> The architecture was visually stunning with key examples of the skyscraper from Louis Sullivan through Frank Lloyd Wright to Mies and the post modernists. They are all slammed down in one part of town, a square mile of commercial space known as 'The Loop'.
>
> It's a blue collar town with a no frills attitude to everything;

> including the 'pointy headed faggots' of New York. Yes, there seemed to be a strong inter city rivalry…
>
> And Cuba Street? Well, strangely enough I am happy with it all. I know I could get a job in Sydney or in the US. But, and because of my three children, I just can't shoot through. I need them, as much as they need me.
>
> And the gallery; I am lucky having that. It gives me a feeling that I'm propagating the 'Faith'.[43]

In January the following year Peter was off again, this time with Toss Woollaston, to Spain, London and New York. Just days before their departure, Peter wrote to Julian Dashper, 'This has all happened over the last week or so. In fact you could blame it all on "Riwaka Sundaes" [ice cream doused in red wine] for, it was consuming one (or was it three) of those excellent concoctions that the idea emerged.'[44] Peter described the trip as a 'pilgrimage' for himself and for Woollaston, who hoped to renew his art by an encounter with Goya. 'It's truly amazing (and inspiring) that at 77 he is still trying to "get it right" and make his art better and more meaningful.'[45]

Arriving in Madrid, the two men established separate routines: Woollaston visited the Prado nearly every day, while Peter attended ARCO, an international art fair, and divided his time between the dealer galleries and the great historical museums. He also spent several days at Santiago de Compostela, a Catholic pilgrimage site since the ninth century: '[N]othing in my experience prepared me for that ancient place; it was staggeringly beautiful'.[46]

In New York, Peter visited dealer galleries to pursue his idea of showing prints by American artists in Wellington. As a result, he exhibited four etchings by Julian Schnabel in association with the Pace Gallery later in the year.[47] '[T]he Schnabel show is of great interest to people,' he informed Barbara Tuck. 'While they are prints they are very very large; 8 feet by 5 and are most impressive. Many people (young ones, in particular) have called to see them.'[48] Lita Barrie wrote a dismissive review, getting in a jibe at Julian Dashper,[49] but Ian Wedde was impressed with the complexity and subtlety of the work: 'Despite some cavilling from the Fortress New Zealand garrison, the major event of the week is certainly American artist Julian Schnabel taking over the world at Peter McLeavey's.'[50] James Mollison wrote to Peter, 'Your intention to bring occasional exhibitions of international artists into New Zealand every year or so is to be congratulated.'[51]

In March 1987, critic Garth Cartwright wrote a feature article about the local art market in the *Listener*. 'New Zealand's art investment market is skyrocketing,' he observed, 'with prices for some painters' work increasing across the board by 80% per annum.'[52] The buoyancy of the local market reflected an international trend: as Cartwright put it, '[C]apitalism's trickle-down effect is reaching New Zealand.' But the boom was not to last, coming to a sudden end with the stockmarket crash in October 1987. Peter's Auckland counterparts were particularly hard hit; as John Gow commented nine months later, 'Corporates have other priorities and art seems to have been put on the back burner.'[53] Peter Webb estimated that auction prices were down by 40 percent on pre-crash figures.[54]

Peter's annual income had fluctuated considerably during the 1980s, peaking in the 1987–88 financial year, and initially, at least, the stockmarket crash made little impact. A year later he wrote to Gordon Walters, '[I]t is business as usual around here and I continue to sell albeit at a slower pace. It is, in fact, like it was up to say two years ago. And, it's more sensible, that way. The corporate buyer has all but vanished and it strikes me that a whole generation of investors (and investing) has been wiped out.'[55] It was not until 1990 that he noticed a slump in his sales. 'Early that year I went seventeen weeks without selling a single work on exhibition. I just held on, and then one day a buyer came down from Auckland and the dyke broke. We were back in business.'[56]

It would take several years for sales to return to a pre-crash level, but Peter remained positive and philosophical. 'Good art is always hard to sell,' he remarked in 1991. 'It's not any harder to sell now than it's ever been... For me, anyway, business continues, people are still interested in buying art.'[57] Peter conceded that he was possibly less vulnerable than some of his dealer colleagues: 'I've been on the road for 20-odd years. I've got a modest space and you could hardly call the lighting system hi-tech.'

Peter began to show the Lyttelton painter Bill Hammond in 1987, just months before the stockmarket crash. 'Laurence Aberhart told Peter to check me out,' recalled Hammond, 'and Peter rang up and said, "Can we meet?" That's the thing about Peter – he doesn't just rely on his own taste. He canvasses your opinion. He asks everyone, "What have you seen lately?"'[58] As the famous New York art dealer Leo Castelli remarked of his profession, 'You have to have a good eye but also a good ear.'[59]

The easy-going Hammond soon established a rapport with Peter. 'I provided the paintings, and he did his thing. He hung the shows. He used to say to me, "Bill, you really should realise, a gallery is not a drop-in centre for the artists. It's where I do business. So why don't you take this five dollars and go up the road to Silvio's second-hand records and find something by The Doors. How can I work with you sitting around here?"'

Initially, Hammond was sometimes surprised by his dealer. 'After my second show with him, he said, "Let's go to the pub." And I thought, Gee, Peter goes to the pub! So we went up Cuba Street to a pub, an old, old, old public bar. He had his big black hat on, his black coat and his briefcase, and I thought, Wow, this is not the pub for Peter. There were about twenty men leaning on the bar, drinking straight out of jugs, and pictures of racehorses round the walls. And Peter said, "Shall we sit there?" and pointed to the very middle of the room, and he went and got two jugs. But then when he came back he took my hand in his, and he started talking in a very loud voice about developing our relationship. Everyone was listening and I went, Oh hell, this is it! But we polished off those jugs without any trouble and he said, "Let's get another round," and the barmaid said to him, "So, how's the art biz goin', Pete?" And I realised, This is where he drinks! They all knew him there!'

When Peter began to represent him, Hammond had already exhibited for eleven years, mainly at the Brooke Gifford Gallery in Christchurch. He would eventually become one of the most commercially successful of Peter's artists, but it would take time for his paintings to find an audience. 'I'm on the bones of my arse again,' he wrote in the lead-up to his fourth show in 1990, 'and I'm wondering if you are able to give me a bit of an advance on our Nov. show to keep me going. Would be most grateful if you can manage it.'[60] Peter sent a cheque, but the sales from the show barely covered it, much to his surprise. He blamed the economic downturn: 'The market is flat and all over the place these days.'[61]

In fact, this had been a crucial show for Hammond, signalling a fertile new direction in his work. In the previous year he had travelled to the sub-Antarctic Auckland Islands with other artists including Laurence Aberhart. Their destination was windswept Enderby Island, a former whaling station, which Hammond described as a paradise for birds – a sanctuary free from predators. 'You feel like a time-traveller,' he remarked, 'as if you have just stumbled upon it – primeval forests, ratas like Walt Disney would make. It's a beautiful place, but it's also full of ghosts, shipwrecks, death'.[62] Everywhere on the island, birds congregated on the shoreline, gazing out to sea. 'You could walk past

Bill Hammond, his sons and their half-brother (left) at Webb Lane, Lyttelton, photographed by Peter McLeavey, 1989

As Supplied To
His Majesty

yellow-eyed penguins with their heads back, their eyes rolled up strangely, their wings raised, then come back three hours later and they would still be there, in exactly the same position, in a beautiful trance-like state.'

Returning home, Hammond began a new series inspired by the voyage, some of which were shown at the gallery in 1990. Peter was impressed with the paintings, especially the large *Death row, Auckland Islands*, and retained the unsold works in stock. Nine months later he wrote to the artist, 'I've held off writing for some time. I guess I've been

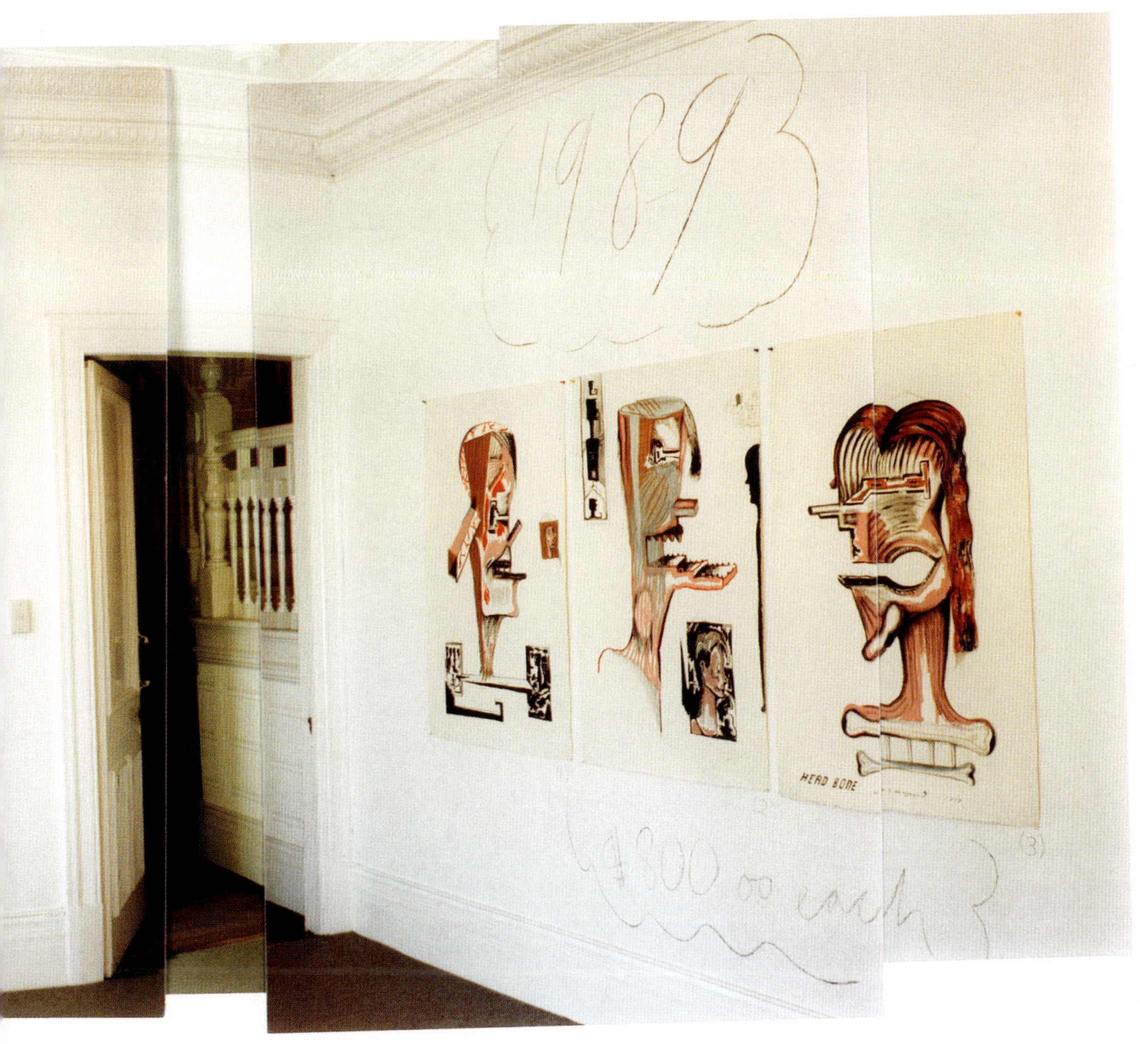

Bill Hammond unplugged: A selection of works from stock,
May–June 1995, photographed by Peter McLeavey

embarrassed by the lack of sales and have been waiting for some good news to give you. No such luck. Yes, it's been a slow year.'[63]

Hammond's exhibition late in 1991 was no more successful in terms of sales. 'I was thrilled with the show,' Peter wrote. '[I]t looked great. And the feedback was very positive ... You are an outstanding artist but, the market and people are just behind. Remember; it won't always be like that. As in the case of Toss (and Colin, to mention two locals), the tide will turn. One has to have courage and patience.'[64]

Bill Hammond, *Living large 6*, 1995
Acrylic on unstretched canvas
Christchurch Art Gallery Te Puna o Waiwhetu

In 1993, Hammond began a new suite of paintings, once again influenced by his experience on Enderby Island. He had been studying Walter Buller's book, *A history of the birds of New Zealand*, and reading about the nineteenth-century trade in native birds that had decimated many rare species and hastened the extinction of the huia. In his new 'Buller's birds' paintings, hybrid bird-figures would become a metaphor for all wronged and threatened creatures: actors on a stage, playing out scenes in an endless drama.

In a bid to promote Hammond, Peter held two exhibitions of his work in 1995. The first, *Bill Hammond unplugged*, showed pictures from stock; the second presented six recent paintings from the 'Living large' series, which revealed a new degree of subtlety and complexity in his work.[65] In *Living large 6*, the ghost-like birds, modelled on the huia, gather in expectation around a mysterious and poignant figure – a seated horse who holds a cello at arm's length. Painted in a monochromatic palette of inky blues, *Living large 6* – the biggest work in the exhibition – was purchased by Celia Dunlop, one of many Wellington collectors Peter had mentored over the years.[66]

Living large was Hammond's first sell-out show, and by the late 1990s the auction market for his work was booming. His 'bird' paintings, with their instantly recognisable imagery and local content, had become highly sought after. In December 1998, Peter sold a painting entitled *Containers* for $30,000; less than four years later, it fetched $200,000 at auction.[67] By then, Peter had a waiting list for Hammond's work. 'I wish I had met you four or five years ago,' he wrote to a young Auckland collector. 'Then I could have shown you a range of Bill's work. That is no longer the case.'[68] Instead, Peter offered works from an earlier series of 1991 entitled 'Self motivation' – six paintings that commented on contemporary life. 'In them,' he wrote, 'Hammond depicts what one has to do to "get on" in the world... You have to be lean. You have to work out. The days of lying around in bed, perhaps smoking a joint or drinking beers have to go... The hero dresses Armani. He is up early... He works the phone. Self motivation; it's hard to be a success.'

As Hammond's auction prices soared, Peter became increasingly concerned to find 'good homes' for his paintings – and ever more evasive with clients who seemed to be after a quick turnover. 'I heard last evening that I have sold the screen,' he wrote to the artist on one occasion. 'I have sold it to a private collector and I'm confident that it will be loved and that we will not see it sold off in the next 6 months.' He ended his letter on a reflective note: '[T]hank you for all your support and confidence in me. I often think of our earlier times and the first shows and the difficult times they were. Like a good farmer I've set the plough again and I'm off, driving across another paddock. Who knows what riches its fertile soil will furnish.'[69]

TWENTY

These walls have been good to me.

By 1988, Peter was preoccupied with the health of his elderly parents. Les and Betty were still living in the same home at Riverside Drive, but they were both increasingly frail and Betty was becoming forgetful. Aware that a move was imminent, Peter met with the family doctor to discuss the options. But early one morning in August his father phoned in panic: Betty had fallen by her favourite chair and was unable to move. By the time Peter caught a taxi to Lower Hutt, she was dead.

'I had, because of her age, prepared myself "intellectually",' Peter told a friend. '[H]owever when Death did call, that Sunday morning, nothing I knew had made me ready for the deep deep sense of loss'.[1] Betty's death was also a great shock to eighty-two-year-old Les, who spent seven weeks in hospital to recuperate. Peter had hoped he might move to a rest home, but his father was more than ever determined to remain at Riverside Drive.

In February the following year, Peter made his annual overseas trip – this time to Ireland to visit galleries and museums, and to look up his mother's family. At Keadue, a hamlet in County Roscommon, he met a relative, Paddy Tiernan, who showed him the ruined foundations of her birthplace. It was a poignant moment. 'I thought of Betty and [her sisters] Rosie, Doreen and Kathleen Tiernan. It was from this spot that they had started out on that long voyage that took them right around the World to Lower Hutt; to the arms of the men they married and, eventually, to four plots in a cemetery far away from Boyle.'[2] Kneeling to say a decade of the Rosary, Peter felt his mother's spirit had come full circle. 'Through me they had, all four, returned home.' He dug out two small rocks from the soil to bring back for his father.

Peter at the gallery window, 1989

From Ireland, it was back to business: Peter flew to New York, where he visited nearly fifty dealer galleries and saw a major retrospective exhibition by Andy Warhol. But by then he had developed a viral infection that affected his lungs, and he cancelled the rest of his trip and returned home. He would remain in poor health, on and off, for much of the year.

Back at work in March, the pressure of running the gallery was exacerbated by the departure for London of his assistant, Derek Cowie. Given the unpredictability of the art market, Peter had planned to 'muddle along' on his own for a while but, as he informed John Reynolds, Cowie's departure had interesting consequences:

> It has certainly increased the demands on me with the days of me ducking out for a cup of coffee with a client now a thing of the past. However, it has revealed to me the importance of me having to be here all the time.
>
> I mean it seems that people want to see me, and only me, when they come and need my involvement in the selling process. When I'm here we do business. Sometimes big business.
>
> I suppose it's got something to do with the cult of the personality. The dealer becomes an artist with his own stamp, or style. And that's what the buyers seem to like; down here, anyway.[3]

Writing from London, Cowie agreed with Peter's assessment: 'I always said to you that your clients wanted to be sold paintings by Peter McLeavey. The Duveen McLeavey personality aspect to my mind is sadly lacking in galleries here. They are spik and span or so uptight about their policies and exhibitions that upon entering them one feels as though it's just another wing of a National Institution.'[4] As Cowie appreciated, Peter had become a personality in the small New Zealand art world: 'I think many people came into the gallery for sustenance from the art but equally from Peter, some recognition and contact with living history.'[5]

For Kathlene Fogarty, then a young art dealer, 'Peter was the Holy Grail – one really couldn't aspire to any greater respect and standing. I was almost apoplectic when I handed him my first ever business card… it was only his gracious good manners – that gave me a lovely smile and asked me to sit down.' Just then a client dashed in, wanting something urgently as a christening present for his godchild. Peter located a print – 'beautiful colours giving a sense of hope to the future'; the client loved it and asked if Peter could wrap it for him:

Peter's business card, c.1995

> Peter slipped into that mysterious room off the gallery – closing the door firmly behind him. Moments later the door was opened and quickly and firmly closed – Peter walked slowly across the gallery – his outstretched hands – carrying – as if a precious sacrament – a roll of tattered and stained brown paper – held together by a used piece of string.
>
> It would be fair to say the client looked crestfallen – McLeavey handed over the package with the words, 'The first McCahon I ever had came wrapped in this'.
>
> The client walked out – as if carrying the child itself.[6]

Earlier in his career, Peter had fretted about the competition in Auckland. 'He was always freaking out about it,' recalled Richard Killeen. 'Always. It was like, all the artists are in Auckland, the dealers up there are getting all the best work and I'm stuck in Wellington. Should I move to Auckland, da-de-da-de-da? Should I do up this joint, da-de-da-de-da?'[7] But as he entered his third decade as a dealer, Peter began to cultivate his difference. As Derek Cowie observed, 'His humble rooms at 147 Cuba Street became part of the strategy. Eccentric, teetering.'[8]

He was now earning a comfortable living, but Peter maintained the frugal habits of his early days in business. Nothing was wasted. When he replaced the carpet at the gallery, the old one was installed at home.[9] He continued to send handwritten receipts in green ink ('Auditors always use green ink ... And, in a way, I'm still an auditor'); he continued to use a manual typewriter and file carbon copies of his correspondence.[10] His business card read simply 'Peter McLeavey, Art Dealer, Wellington,

Gallery entrance, 147 Cuba Street,
photographed by Peter McLeavey, 1988

JAM HAIR C
headbands
EL 344420
LOADING
ZONE
GOODS
VEHICLES
ONLY
AT ALL TIMES

Derek Cowie with *Concentrate's flattery*, 1989, in *Derek Cowie: Recent paintings*, March 1989, photographed by Peter McLeavey

New Zealand' – it did not include a telephone number, let alone an address. Deeply superstitious about his gallery – 'these walls have been good to me' – he was reluctant to bring in changes, as if that would affect the spirit of the entire enterprise.[11] In any case, he identified with the faded bohemian quality of the Cuba Street precinct. He had no inclination to tidy things up.

Peter's regulars appreciated his way of doing things. As Sir David Gascoigne commented, 'One of the things I've always liked is the fact that the entranceway to the gallery is not grand. It's covered in old posters and graffiti. It looks terrible. It's deeply unprepossessing. And it gives no hint of the untold treasures in store.'[12]

In May 1989, Peter sent Cowie news of his forthcoming show: 'Next up is "NEW WELLINGTON ART". This essay in McLeaveyese highlights the works of the two Anthony brothers [Ivan and Dale] plus your good self. Don't worry. It will be a humdinger. The opening promises to be a "Headbangers only" affair with the bus load of the Palmerston North Anthonys heading south, Tuesday week'.[13]

By the time the exhibition opened in late June, Peter was seriously ill, his viral infection exacerbated by a bout of his long-dormant asthma. He spent two months recuperating while a friend looked after the gallery. Cowie wrote, 'My immediate hasty response is to come home. Can this letter be personal? But can anything be personal with Peter McLeavey? Your difference to the rest is rare. You have a responsibility to us for what you are. You *must* delegate!...Delegate *anyone* to carry out your directions, your wishes!'[14]

By September, Peter was able to visit the gallery for a few hours each day. Worried that the damp in his flat was affecting his health, he spent a week in a hotel before going to stay with Hilary and the family at Hill Street. 'They are looking after me,' he told Jacqueline Fraser, 'good food and a pleasant environment.'[15] He reassured Cowie that he was on the mend: 'I am responding to the medicine and am back to what I used to be like. A healthy, balanced, caring human being. Remember?'[16] By December, he had returned to Brooklyn, rehanging the artwork to signal a fresh start.

To celebrate the end of his 'grey period', Peter purchased a photograph from an American gallery – Robert Frank's *View from hotel window – Butte, Montana*. 'It now joins my modest collection of bits and pieces,' he informed Cowie. 'I now, in addition, own the Oxford English Dictionary. Yes, I thought I'd lash out. It has 20 volumes so will be a bit of a storage problem. However, it will keep me entertained.'[17] He told Cowie about his next show, the 'end of year special', including Billy Apple, Bill Hammond, the Christchurch painter Helm Ruifrok and John Reynolds: 'And, if the goods arrive from the U.K. – you too.'

As he moved into the 1990s, Peter continued to experiment with his gallery; and Australia, with its much larger art market, was very much on his mind. 'I am convinced that the cultural and commercial contacts between our 2 countries will increase,' he wrote in September 1991. 'I see my role as very much involved in that process.'[18] He introduced two Australian artists – the painter Imants Tillers and the photographer Bill Henson – and toyed, yet again, with the idea of opening a branch in Sydney. For a brief period he considered relocating the gallery across the Tasman, and even went to Sydney to assess potential premises in the inner city. Peter found the idea of change challenging and invigorating, but as his son Dominic reflected, 'I think he knew deep down that he couldn't go anywhere else. He was nurtured by that whole milieu of Cuba Street. He was too attached to it.'[19]

In 1993, Peter investigated the possibility of recruiting one or two more Australian artists, but later in the year his relationship with Imants Tillers came to an end over a point of principle. The National Art Gallery purchased a major work through Tillers' Sydney dealer, and Peter felt that he, as the local agent who had represented the artist since 1990 and cultivated the ground for such a sale, should have been included in the commission. 'Regretfully Imants and I are no longer a couple,' he told the Sydney writer Murray Bail. 'I'll tell you about it one day. It was very sad; and very painful; and has made me rethink my position vis a vis introducing Australian art here. In the end it just does not seem worth all the emotional wear and tear.'[20] It was essential for Peter to feel a close working relationship with his artists, and that was difficult to maintain with those, such as Tillers, whom he saw infrequently.

There were also significant changes closer to hand, as Peter's long relationship with Milan Mrkusich had come to an end. The problem began back in 1985, when he sold two works to a young American couple. 'They were beautiful paintings, just beautiful. But the owners took them back to Seattle and they began to warp. I said, "Well look, go to your local art museum and see what they can do about it." So they went to the Seattle Art Museum and the staff said there was a flaw in the construction of the paintings. They could fix the problem, but the paintings were technically flawed. So, the owners wanted their money back.'[21]

It is not difficult to see Mrkusich's side of the story: as a consummate craftsman, he was deeply insulted by the suggestion that his works were technically unsound. Aware that the paintings could have been damaged by poor handling or environmental conditions, he refused to accept responsibility.[22] But Peter was caught in a spot: the owners threatened to sue, and he had no option but to buy back the two works. 'That destroyed the relationship,' Peter recalled. 'It went through my heart like a saw, and in the end, after about eighteen months, I couldn't carry on any more. So one day I rang Dave – he was transporting paintings for me at the time – and I said, "Will you come in tomorrow morning. I've got some paintings to return to Milan." I just wrapped them all up and sent them back to him. Milan had about nineteen shows with me at the gallery. He's a great man. But I just couldn't carry on with it.'

Peter wrote a short letter to the artist in March 1991:

> Dear Milan,
>
> This letter is written with a sad and heavy heart.
>
> There is something wrong with our relationship.
>
> Its roots lie in the Smith[23] transaction.
>
> As hard as I've tried I've not been able to put that wretched business out of my mind. It has tainted and eroded my ability to effectively represent you.
>
> It is no one's fault; it just is.
>
> I have thought long about what to do.
>
> I have decided that it is in both our interests to discontinue our business relationship; to go our separate ways.
>
> Dave will be returning your works, in two or three consignments, over the next six weeks.
>
> With respect.
>
> Peter.[24]

It was not unusual for Peter to brood on a matter for months and even years, but when he finally reached a decision he acted swiftly and conclusively. The matter was often personal: Peter felt that his relationship with an artist was somehow compromised or thrown out of balance. He needed to feel that his professionalism and integrity was respected, and, most importantly, he needed to retain control. Occasionally an artist was not even aware that there was a problem, and Peter's final letter – for it was nearly always a letter – came as a shock. In 1990, for example, Peter ended his association with Billy Apple abruptly, and the artist demanded an explanation. Peter's minimalist reply was hardly edifying.

Dear Billy,

I acknowledge receipt of your letter 7th instant received 21st.

I note your request for me to amplify my decision to discontinue handling your work.

All I can add to my earlier letter is that I'm tired.

Tired.

Sincerely

Peter McLeavey.[25]

Peter had represented Apple for more than a decade, and felt that the market was finally catching up with him. In the late 1980s, he had sold two works to private collectors, arranged a commission for the Bank of New Zealand, and sold the major installation *Censure* to the National Art Gallery. He was full of optimism for the artist's future. 'Now, as we enter a new decade,' he wrote, 'I predict that the market for your work will grow and expand and that you will be recognised for the greatly gifted artist you are.'[26]

But Peter had also been troubled by some of Apple's recent proposals. He jibbed at the idea that Apple might incorporate his chaise longue, a long-time fixture in the gallery, into an installation;[27] he was concerned at the suggestion that he show works that had already been exhibited in Auckland. But these incidents were merely contributing factors. Peter wrote to the artist and critic John Hurrell, 'Yes, it is with a real sense of loss and regret that I advise that I am no longer involved with Billy's work. He is a truly gifted and inspiring artist but, in the end, I could no longer take the pressures he placed on me … I had to withdraw.'[28]

Peter was aware that his heart ruled his head – and that in times of stress he sometimes acted rather hastily. Writing to John Reynolds, he reflected on this point. 'I sometimes think that my whole thing; my gallery, if you like, is too "emotion" driven. It is, I suppose its strength and its greatest weakness. I feel things too much. But then, that's me.'[29]

Both Mrkusich and Apple would later show at a new Wellington venue, the Hamish McKay Gallery, established in 1993. Meanwhile, changes were afoot at the National Art Gallery, now under the directorship of art historian Jenny Harper. In 1992, an Act of Parliament united the gallery with the National Museum as a single entity – the Museum of New Zealand Te Papa Tongarewa. Six years later, the new Te Papa building opened on the Wellington waterfront.

In 1990, Peter left his Brooklyn flat and took a lease on an apartment in Hawker Street in sunny Mount Victoria. By now his father's health

Catherine (left), Dominic and Olivia McLeavey at Hill Street, photographed by Peter McLeavey, 1994

was failing, and he decided to cancel his travel plans for the following summer. 'Three weeks ago,' he informed Julian Dashper in February 1991, 'I thought that there is no way in Hell that he would make it. Every day I'd get the unit out to the Hutt and visit him at the Hutt Hospital. On leaving I'd pray over him, kiss his head, and wonder if he would make it through to the next day. Well, he did. He had his op. And is now back on the mend. It's the greatest comeback since the Resurrection.'[30]

Peter was also distracted by the fate of his gallery building, which was soon to be auctioned. 'It will probably sell,' he told Dashper. 'I may be here for the next decade; or the next year; or the next month. Or I may have to relocate. Whatever happens I'll be in business somewhere. I could even end up selling Dashpers off the back of a truck like those

Hilary on a beach near Pirinoa, Palliser Bay, photographed by Peter McLeavey, 1993

Polynesians sell sea eggs on the Bombay Hill. The spirit of Cuba Street doesn't roll over and go belly up just because the building sells. Stay tuned.'

Despite these worries, Peter told Dashper that he was feeling great about 1991: 'I feel we could be at the bottom of a roll and that we are starting to barrel up.' In fact, his new optimism owed a good deal to an upturn in his private life. In April, he left his flat in Mount Victoria and moved back to Hill Street – permanently. 'Hilary and I have decided to "have another crack at it",' he announced. '[W]e hope that things will work out.'[31]

Catherine McLeavey was now twenty, and had already been on a working holiday in London; Olivia was sixteen and Dominic was at high school. 'The children were growing up,' Hilary recalled, 'they weren't so demanding, and things were quieter at home. Life was a bit easier. I was working, so I had my independence. Peter had been ill, and I was concerned about him – I had a continuing sense of responsibility. And when you've had three children and experienced so much together, you have a strong bond. Peter and I were older, and perhaps a bit wiser.'[32]

The McLeavey children were surprised by the reconciliation. Olivia had seen her father only infrequently in recent years: 'Dad seemed so obsessed with the gallery and I'd lost interest in spending time with him.'[33] Now, however, she found him changed. 'Maybe it was growing older, but he was gentler, more sensitive, and I think Poppa's decline had something to do with it. He had thought about what it meant to be a father and was very aware of his failings in the past. He was 100 percent committed to getting our relationship back on track.' Initially Peter and Olivia went to counselling together: 'We really had to start from scratch to build an adult relationship, but temperamentally we just clicked. It was the beginning of a really strong friendship. And Dad's been so generous to me since then, with his time and his love and his energy.'

At Cuba Street, meanwhile, Peter's building sold, but he was able to negotiate a reasonable rental with the new owner. 'That building has always attracted a landlord with a sense of responsibility to the community,' he remarked years later. 'Someone who wasn't in it just for the money.'[34] And he continued to spend time with his father, visiting him three times a week. 'Now, he wants to go,' he told Dashper in May 1992. 'To die and meet his wife (my Mother) and to show her his pet childhood dog "Creamy" do his tricks. And then to go off, together, to do some whitebaiting. He knows the best possey. It's out on the edge of town where the river meets the sea and where the whitebait run with the incoming tide. And where, if you're lucky, you can take a kerosene can home, full to the brim, for that breakfast.'[35]

On 2 October 1992, Les McLeavey died peacefully at Hutt Hospital. He was eighty-five. 'Now that the responsibility of looking after my Father is past I'm feeling happier,' Peter told Dashper, 'and can, for the first time in a while, look ahead. And what I see looks good.'[36] Dominic McLeavey felt that Peter was 'unshackled' by his father's death. 'There was always a tension between them, even when my grandfather was dying. They were never at peace with each other.'[37]

In the following month, Peter opened a major installation by Warren Viscoe entitled *Coral gardens, cultured pearls*, which was later purchased by the Sarjeant Gallery. He ended the year with a show by Barry Brickell, the artist, conservationist and railway enthusiast who had first exhibited at the gallery in 1969. Peter had written to invite

Brickell to have a fourth solo show: 'It would be something special. Something that you really wanted to do; to shake the bars on the cage.'[38] Brickell took the opportunity to install seven large ceramic pots under the title *Resurrection of the Goddess*; he also wrote a mystical statement directly on the gallery walls, celebrating the 'passion of women's love': '[O]ur children, their earth, and their children and *their* Earth, will live with such *Love* as never seen in 2000 years... [L]et us pay homage to this earthly Motherhood principle.'[39]

In 1991, Peter reached an agreement with the Auckland artist Merylyn Tweedie. 'I would like to show your work; and handle it, and sell it from my gallery... I'm very pleased (and excited) that we have made contact.'[40] Tweedie, whose work was informed by feminist theory, had been exhibiting since 1975, mainly as a photographer and film-maker. In May 1992, she discussed the arrangements for her first show with Peter, in which she planned to exhibit under a nom de plume, Merit Gröting.

On the morning of Saturday 20 June, Tweedie arrived in Wellington to install her exhibition over the weekend. Peter was out of town, so he left a key for her at the fruit-seller below; it was not until Monday that he returned to the gallery. When he unlocked the door he was stunned: Tweedie's installation incorporated his chaise longue, now covered in white paint and entitled, in a nod to McCahon, *Peter McLeavey sat here too.* It was priced at $2000.

Tweedie's exhibition followed a conceptual art tradition: like Billy Apple, she had used features of the gallery to make a work that commented on the fabrication and marketing of art. But, unlike Apple, she had not sought permission first. To Peter, this was vandalism and desecration of his personal property.[41] He was particularly upset about the chaise longue – a gift from a friend, and a deeply personal symbol that linked back to his origins as a dealer. Peter's first reaction was to ring Hilary and seek her opinion. Early the next morning, the day of the opening, he telephoned Tweedie and cancelled the show. By midday, the work – with the exception of the chaise longue, which was dispatched to the upholsterer – was on its way back to her.[42]

In March the following year, Richard Killeen sent Peter some photographs of a billboard that had recently been installed in Auckland. It showed an image of Tweedie, seated on the painted chaise longue, in the Peter McLeavey Gallery. But by now Peter was philosophical. He wrote to thank Killeen for the images. 'I presume that Jim (or Mary) [Barr] must have photographed Merylyn reclining on the painted chaise longue

Peter on the chaise longue, 2008

in the gallery ... I see both the works as loveletters. A curious thing, but feeding off some sort of passion, or attraction, or need, or hunger.'[43]

Years later, Killeen looked back on the Tweedie episode – one of the most talked-about incidents at the Peter McLeavey Gallery. 'That was a classic. Peter got so much out of that ... In the art world, it was one of those mafia type, horse-head-in-the-bed sort of situations you never forget. People still talk about it. And Peter told the story so well, you know: "I walked in there, I looked around, then I went and had a cup of coffee, and I came back and I said to Ivan, Get the truck, it's all going out. It's over."'[44]

Hilary added a postscript. 'Peter ran into Merylyn a few years later. He said to her, "Well, you hold the record for the shortest exhibition at the Peter McLeavey Gallery."'[45]

SORRY
SOLD
OUT
ART

TWENTY-ONE

We need you to 'make your stand', here.

Late in 1993, Peter wrote to the Australian author Murray Bail, 'I've introduced a very talented young (part Maori) painter this year. His name is Peter Robinson. You may see his work around, in the future.'[1]

Peter met Robinson in April 1991, when his work was included in a group show of young artists in Christchurch.[2] 'I wasn't really aware of his status,' Robinson recalled. 'I was still reasonably green at that stage, I was just cutting my teeth in the art world. I remember I found Peter's handshake very disconcerting – it was a very soft, gentle handshake. For a farmer's son from mid-Canterbury, well, it threw me a bit. I was struck by his hair and his glasses and his manner and somehow put him in the Andy Warhol category.'[3]

In the following year Peter kept in touch with Robinson, and wrote to congratulate him on his work in *Shadow of style* at the City Gallery in Wellington: 'Your ability to handle scale has impressed me from the start. This time I also liked the manner in which you had worked the surface of the painting.'[4] He added a cautionary note: 'To be an artist is a long, and often heart-breaking, thing. It's a sort of quest. A puzzle to give (when it is solved) a meaning to your existence (and your culture's, too). All power to your gift and the heart that feeds it.'

Peter saw Robinson as a raw talent, but he felt the young artist needed time to develop. 'I've wanted to allow you space to just get on with things,' he wrote in 1993.

> I sense that you have enough people calling on you and, in fact, while encouragement is (generally) good in the hot house environment of art, here, it can become very distracting.
>
> The '*flavour of the month*' syndrome is destructive when a gifted artist is still (as you are) forming.

Peter Robinson: 100%, November–December 1994, photographed by Peter McLeavey

And it is of no interest to me.

I'm in it for the long haul and operate outside the cosy (neo-academic) tea party which is *moderne* New Zealand art.

This self serving clique of back scratchers and cultural apparatchiks is so politically correct; and so dangerous to the emerging artist.

Not that you have anything to worry about. Your Maori blood; your race. That will defend and shield your darkening gift.[5]

Like his contemporaries, Shane Cotton and Michael Parekowhai, Robinson represented a new wave of Māori artists, whose work was playful, irreverent and often ironic. Māori art had gained increasing notice in the 1980s, when biculturalism – the partnership between Māori and Pākehā, founded on the Treaty of Waitangi – became a key issue. Public galleries struggled to compensate for their previous lack of interest, and suddenly Māori art was topical, even fashionable. Robinson had personal experience of this shift: it was not until 1990 that he began to identify as Māori and explore his cultural heritage in his work, but when he did, '[T]hings changed rapidly. Suddenly I was being invited into private and public gallery shows.'[6]

In his first show with Peter in August 1993, Robinson tackled his identity as a Māori artist head-on. 'I wanted to address the fact that I had become a comfortable commodity for the art world, in that I didn't look particularly Maori but identified as Maori…I was a non-threatening package.'[7] He exhibited nine works, based on the motif of a percentage of 3.125 – the quota of his own Māori blood. Another recurring image was the aeroplane, which figured as a double metaphor: 'for spirituality, and as a vehicle for careerism or bandwagons.' Robinson had described his new work as 'a cynical look at political correctness'[8] – 'biting the hand that feeds me in a way'[9] – but his exhibition was a near sell-out all the same. The two largest works, both entitled *Painting 1993*, were purchased by Auckland City Art Gallery and Te Papa.[10]

Several weeks before the opening, Peter had told Robinson that he would hang the show. 'He said, "Your job is in the studio, and when the work comes into the gallery then I become the artist. And my artwork is the hanging of the exhibition."' Robinson was a little taken aback, but he trusted his dealer and felt he might learn from the experience. He was not at all prepared for the shock he felt on arriving at the gallery: 'Peter had hung the show in what seemed a very eccentric fashion at the time, with works scattered all over the place. But after about an hour or so I accepted it and I started to find it very exciting.'[11]

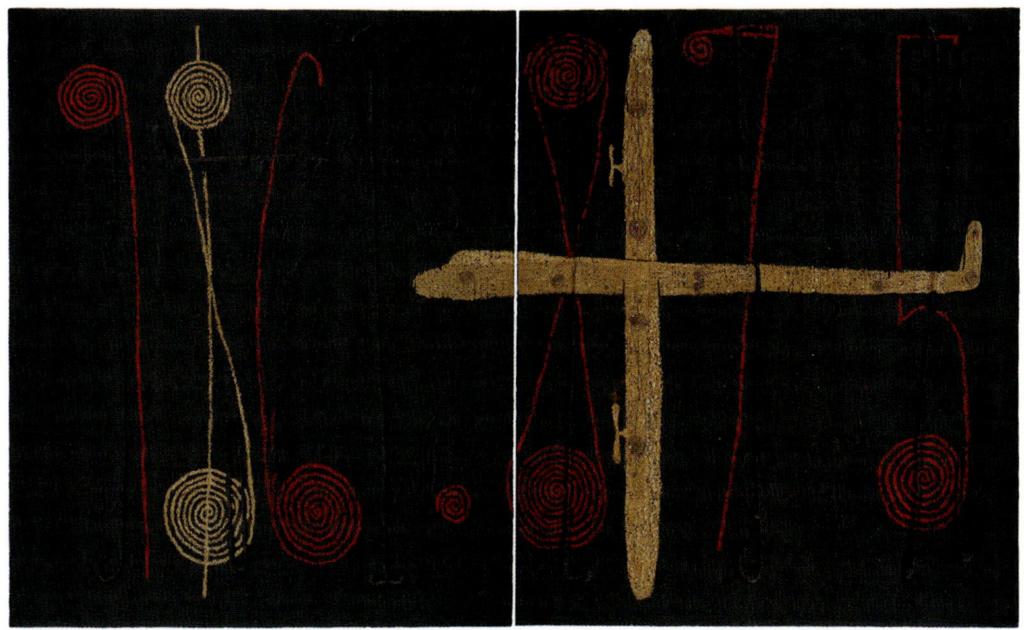

Peter Robinson, *Painting 1993*, 1993
Tar, wax and oil on canvas
Museum of New Zealand Te Papa Tongarewa, purchased 1993 with New Zealand Lottery Grants Board funds

Exhibiting with Peter a year later, Robinson followed up with a new series entitled '100%', which mocked the commodification of the art world in even more brazen fashion. Visitors entered the gallery to find an array of crates, panels and objects, all roughly painted with aggressive advertising slogans. Some echoed the racial subtext of Robinson's previous show with signs like 'Sorry Sold Out' and 'Lost Tribe Art: Cash in Today'. Critic Justin Paton saw these new works as 'a mock takeover, an ersatz sit-in, a tongue-in-cheek protest against a history of raw deals and hollow promises, both inside and outside the art world'.[12] They too sold swiftly.

In 1995, Robinson travelled overseas to take up an artist's residency in Aachen, Germany. Peter wrote to him, 'You will not have visited Europe until you have come back home. Once here the circle will be completed ... Everything will shake down. Gaps will appear and, somewhere, between the cracks the art will be ... And, Europe will still be there. And you will go back. And soon. And the dream would be to

Peter Robinson: 100%, November–December 1994

be there and be here. Two worlds. Two places where you and your great gift will live.'[13]

For Robinson, the trip sparked a period of reappraisal. He wrote to Peter, 'I can feel the work moving away from the specific identity issues of Maoriness towards one of being a New Zealander in the world but perhaps told in a Maori voice, in the same way as some of our Maori singers express themselves as Maori but through American and English songs… Whatever the case I think I'm trying to say that I have found myself again.'[14] Meanwhile, Peter sent a memento of home: an exhibition catalogue about the relationship between McCahon and James K Baxter.[15] 'The lives and example of both artists are so bound up with issues that we all face, living here,' he wrote. 'I remember Colin telling me that he stayed because this was where he was going to "*make his stand*". Not America ... but here; this place; this neck of the woods. And Jim Baxter, too. From rooms in South Brighton, Linwood, Ngaio, Grafton Gully, and Jerusalem came many songs. Wonderful poems that today, still make the hair prickle on the back of my neck.'[16] McCahon's paintings and Baxter's poems had provided Peter with a 'home' in which he could live, a way of identifying as a New Zealander. His younger artists, like Robinson, had a different set of questions to negotiate.

Apart from brief trips home, Robinson based himself in Germany in the late 1990s. His arrival coincided with a time of keen interest in 'post-colonial' identity art, and he soon found himself on the biennial circuit. In 1996, he told Peter he had been invited to exhibit in the São Paulo Biennial, curated by Jean-Hubert Martin. 'I'll be showing alongside Kabakov and the Japanese artist that makes the ant farm national flag works. When he told me this I felt like a boy in N.Z. who is about to be the ball boy for the All Blacks ... My cousin Andrew who is Tane Norton's son always got to do this and I was always very envious.'[17]

Robinson continued to show with Peter, and in November 1996 he tackled the touchy subject of race relations in Germany and New Zealand. *Home and away* featured poster-like works with provocative slogans and symbols: *Pakeha have rights too!*, with a wonky, inverted swastika, and *Maori have rights too!*, featuring a swastika adorned with koru-like fronds.[18] When Jenny Harper, now head of art history at Victoria University, purchased the former work and installed it in her office, it became the focus of national debate over questions of censorship and freedom of expression.[19]

By 1999, Robinson was well established in Germany, with a dealer in Berlin and growing interest in his work. He reflected on his position as a Māori artist in Europe in a letter prompted by a visit to Burg Frankenstein – the castle that had inspired the name of Mary Shelley's doctor, creator of the famous monster:

> I sometimes feel like him myself. Being a bit Maori, a bit Italian, and a bit anglo sax. Maybe that's what being a New Zealander is. Now the condition of living in these two worlds only complicates matters especially in terms of self identity. I sometimes feel it will either destroy my work or be the making of a new kind of monster. Who knows.

Some good news is that I've been invited into a show in the Ludwig Museum in Cologne. It's a millennium show. The show is a historical overview of Europe's and America's dialogue with the world and vice versa. It starts at Gauguin moving through to Picasso on to Pollock and then to the flipside of this with artists that have emerged from the 'world', e.g. Tracey Moffat, Gordon Bennett etc. I always see these 'world art' shows as a double edged sword, it's a great privilege to show in them and in such company but they always feel like a bit of a ghetto as well.[20]

Peter enjoyed Robinson's lively, thoughtful missives – letters, faxes, and the emails that arrived via his daughter Catherine's account. He even composed the odd email in reply. 'I miss you not being here,' he wrote in one of his first, in 1999. 'Come back. We need you to "make your stand", here. There are not a lot with your qualities.'[21] Although he was proud of Robinson's success in the European art world, Peter was concerned about losing him completely – as the artist was well aware. 'I was very conscious of the fact that Peter believed in New Zealand artists living and working in New Zealand, contributing to the culture. Or if they moved overseas, they had to essentially cut their ties and become part of that culture. Which was something I was ambivalent about. So I think there was a tension between us, an unspoken tension.'

In the winter of 1999, Peter noticed an article in the newspaper: fashion designer Karen Walker, addressing the National Party conference in Wellington, had urged delegates to stop the 'brain drain'. Peter wrote to endorse her comments.

Yes, many of our best and brightest leave. And, for those that stay it can sometimes be a lonely place…

To extract and fashion something from this place; to make it as good as the best anywhere; to address the wider world in a truly 'contemporary' manner; that is our quest.

And it can be done; has been done; is being done. But it is difficult. The mood, the nature, the reality, the aesthetic of New Zealand.

As an art dealer I 'know' these issues. And, like you, I fear the future of this place with so many of the best shipping out.

Conversely, I wonder if the 'loss' in some mad way further 'deepens the national wound' and, in turn, embellishes the Gothic, Puritan nature which is a hallmark of our best art, literature and (yes) fashion.

Many questions have circled my mind after reading your remarks and are knocking at its doors wanting answers.[22]

Peter regarded Gordon Walters as an exemplary figure in New Zealand art: a painter who had dedicated himself to abstraction in a culture that was for many years completely unresponsive.

But as Māori critics became more politicised, they also challenged Pākehā artists over their right to use Māori imagery, and Walters was accused of cultural appropriation for his adaptation of the koru motif. The controversy peaked in 1992 when the exhibition *Headlands: Thinking through New Zealand art* was shown in Sydney.[23] Peter was dismayed by the way Walters' work was discussed in the catalogue.[24] 'I suppose I should have gone over [to Sydney],' he told John Reynolds, 'but, in the end, I just could not face it... The art world can be a jungle.'[25]

In 1994, the Auckland City Art Gallery held an exhibition of Walters' work to mark his seventy-fifth birthday.[26] Peter, laid low with influenza, sent a letter to be read at the opening that looked back to the beginning of their long association: 'So many memories. And the strongest ones for me? Firstly, the work. Then, the life. Then your Mother, coming up the stairs to see your show in 1969. And, finally, Margaret: her love, her heart, her belief. That's what frames the art. Thank you for your art, Gordon. We can all walk taller, here, because of it and the way you have lived the life.[27] Reviewing the exhibition, Justin Paton remarked on the achievement of the 'Koru' paintings: 'the local cross-bred with the international, the stylised fern-bulb pulsing and dilating with the modernist grid. We have no more lucid metaphor for the constant back-and-forth between the indigenous and the imported in New Zealand culture.'[28]

In the same month, Peter showed Walters' new work, and sold four of the five paintings in the exhibition. 'Naturally I am keen to get one or two works to replenish my stock,' he reported to the artist. 'However, maybe it's time to "sit down and have a cup of tea" before doing anything. One thing I know. The market is firm and strong and will increase.'[29] Peter wrote to thank the critic Keith Stewart for a rave review: '[T]he Walters was my 12th one man show of his work and my 308th exhibition at 147 Cuba Street. Yep, a lot of Gordon has gone up and down these stairs. Long may that continue. Amen.'[30]

Walters was scheduled to exhibit in 1995, but in August he telephoned Peter with grave news: he had been diagnosed with terminal cancer. Peter immediately cancelled the show and took all his works off the market.

'This will remain,' he wrote, 'until you (and Margaret) have time to think about other, more important, issues. I do not know if it is of any sustenance but I'll say some prayers for you at Mass on Sunday. That may be of comfort to you. It will be to me.'[31]

In late September, Peter and Hilary flew to Christchurch to say farewell, and Peter reported back to Richard Killeen:

> Gordon looked a little frail but was in excellent spirits. We spent 90 minutes and covered our shared past. Sometimes we laughed some. Sometimes it was quiet. Sometimes it was silence. The 'predicament' (Gordon's word for his cancer) was a presence during this visitation.
>
> We had a cup of tea. We talked about the 12 one person shows we had had. He reminded me of the first time he had shown with me. This I had completely forgotten. It was a group show in the front room of my 270 The Terrace gallery...
>
> I joked about 'having your bags packed'. About meeting death. He laughed. And smiled. More quiet. The taxi had turned up. I hugged Margaret. Her face was warm. We left. From the taxi we waved. They smiled back; two figures in the blur of the window.[32]

When Walters died on 5 November, Peter wrote to tell Knight Landesman, the publisher of *Artforum*: 'His death was relatively painless and it ended a long productive career as one of our best artists.'[33] Peter had sold a Walters painting to Landesman in the mid-1990s; later, when he visited the *Artforum* offices in New York, '[T]here was the Gordon Walters, hanging behind his desk. I felt that Gordon, who so loved modern art, and spent his life painting on the edge of the world, had come home. His painting had found its place in the epicentre of the art world.'[34] It was one of the most satisfying moments of Peter's career.

Walters' death was felt keenly in the local art world. 'It knocked me around a bit,' Laurence Aberhart admitted. 'Gordon was the one person, on this side of the "business" that I unreservedly admired, respected.'[35] John Reynolds echoed those sentiments: 'I look forward, Peter, to raising a glass or two with you when you're next in Auckland. And I wonder can one be held to something, across a generation or two, with little declared and nothing asked? I sense this is the crux for those in my position.'[36]

By now, Peter was no longer representing Julian Dashper – he felt they had grown apart, and tensions had crept into their relationship[37] – but his association with Reynolds continued to flourish. Reynolds exhibited every year, working increasingly with text and experimenting with large-scale drawings. In 1992, he was included in the exhibition *Distance looks our way* at the Seville Expo, with Jacqueline Fraser, Bill Hammond and others; two years later he won New Zealand's richest art prize, the Visa Gold Art Award. By 1996, Reynolds was married and expecting his first child, and Peter wrote to him after a visit to Auckland.

> I need these things for my stock. PAINTINGS. Things you bang on the wall. You know the size. They often measure about 4 by 4 or 5 or six. Something in the 3, 4, 5, 6, 7, 8 thousand dollar range.
>
> I realise that you have a bit on your plate. Your A.S.A. [teaching] commitments. The house. And, most (most; most) important, Claire and the new life which, soon (sooner, soonest) will break out into the world of Auckland. Then even cooking a couple of chops will seem tire(some).
>
> And the fun of it all.
>
> Well, the good news is that there is plenty of time. There is no hurry. You don't have to prove anything to anyone. You have a whole rich life ahead. And art can wait. Love is the most important thing.
>
> Does this letter add up? Am I getting it down; getting it across? Yes, I am.
>
> Love
>
> Peter.[38]

After twelve years with Peter, Reynolds had developed a keen appreciation of his ethos. 'Commerce is part of what he does but it's not the overruling part, and that's a value that gives me great calm. Sometimes there's no income, no sales, and you're doing good work, and you're thinking I can't go on like this. And part of it is that you just accept that it will change. You know, as long as you stick to your knitting, and as long as you don't bow to some pressure, you don't lose your bearings, or get exasperated and walk away, you know, it will come.'[39]

By now, the young artists Peter had taken on in his early years had become the veterans of his gallery. At his twenty-fourth exhibition with Peter in 1996, Richard Killeen showed a work that explored the nature of collections as cultural repositories of knowledge and meaning. *Book of the Hook* presented anthropological fragments from The Hook Museum – a fictitious institution of Killeen's invention – accompanied by a pseudo-scientific journal purporting to document its collection. At 253 pieces, this was Killeen's largest cut-out to date, and Peter saw it as

Book of the Hook, 1996, in *Richard Killeen: Objects and images from the Cult of the Hook and other works*, October–November 1996

a highlight of his programme. 'It is, for me, a great feeling having this wonderful work hanging. I think back to other shows which have (now) in my memory, the same power. The great shows of Colin, Gordon (in particular the "Koru" exhibition of May 1969), Mrkusich (my reconstruction of Milan's first 1949 exhibition)... It's one of the best. I thank you.'[40] The work was later purchased by the Christchurch Art Gallery – one of its key acquisitions of the decade.

For another of Peter's stalwarts, 1996 was a tumultuous year. In August, Robin White lost her house, studio and all her belongings in Tarawa in a fire. Peter wrote at once, 'I do hope that you are managing and that the shock of it all is bearable. I wonder if anything was salvageable? How did the press get on? Was much work lost?'[41] White told Peter that she and her family would probably rebuild: 'It'll work out OK, but in the meantime I have been more than a little distracted as far as my work goes.'[42] She was philosophical, however, about losing

Robin White and Te Itoiningaina Catholic Women's Training Centre, *Instant sunshine* from the 'New angel' series, 1998
Woven pandanus, natural and commercial dyes
Museum of New Zealand Te Papa Tongarewa, purchased 2000

all her art materials. 'The fire has cleared the ground for a fresh start and, looking ahead, I feel very optimistic. I'll keep in touch and let you know how I'm getting along.'

Determined to work with the materials at hand, White began a dialogue and eventually a collaboration with her Kiribati friends, designing a series of pandanus mats that were woven by local women. Each series focused on an imported product available in Tarawa, such as New Angel tinned mackerel, Instant Sunshine milk powder and Hibiscus safety matches. Combining traditional weaving patterns with imagery from the outside world, and symbols of Christian tradition, the 'New angel' series reflected on the process of colonisation, and the way that identity and belief systems are subject to change.

On a personal level, the project demonstrated White's longstanding interest in 'the space between cultures ... where overlap and integration can happen'.[43] It also offered a new way of working: 'Every time you set out on a collaborative project, you have to relinquish the kind of control that you're used to.'[44] When the 'New angel' series was exhibited at the Peter McLeavey Gallery in 1999, it created great interest: both Te Papa and the Auckland City Art Gallery purchased a full set, as did art museums in Australia.

—

Peter introduced a number of young artists during the mid-1990s: Mark Braunias, Valerie Nielsen and William Dunning joined the gallery in 1994, followed by Simon Endres and Chris Heaphy. Peter was fascinated by the idiosyncratic, labour-intensive art of Dunning – works described by Justin Paton as 'among the oddest dishes on the current art-world menu'.[45] In 1997, Dunning showed a suite of fourteen large works on paper entitled *Antipodean pictorial*. 'It's a sort of History of New Zealand,' Peter told Chris Heaphy. 'Pakeha New Zealand. It's the flip side to [Shane] Cotton and Robinson and, maybe, yourself. It's about Pakeha roots. Pakeha whanau. Pakeha history here, in all its many mutations. Not everyone likes it. Some find its "strangeness" and its "obsessiveness" unsettling. Weird. And curious. And like good art it's all the above and, it's hugely ambitious.'[46] The entire set was purchased by Te Papa.

Like Dunning, Mark Braunias was a self-confessed 'relentless drawer' who had honed his own distinctive artistic territory. What Peter dubbed 'Brauniasland' was a teeming, tragic-comic world filled with goofy, down-and-out cartoon characters and blob-like forms. Peter enjoyed the artist's dark humour, tinged with irony, and his trenchant dissection of contemporary life. As the critic David Eggleton observed, 'His ensemble of characters combines his own memories of visits to the cartoonland of yesteryear with a stroll down to the town centre just yesterday.'[47]

—

As he entered his sixties, Peter felt it was more important than ever to refresh his spirit by travel and contact with other cultures. He always took a journal – a handsome volume made by Oamaru bookbinder Michael O'Brien – and his daily notes show the tireless thirst for knowledge that had fuelled him all his life. As well as souvenirs such as entry tickets, postcards, samples of local toilet paper and teabag wrappers, the journals are crammed with historical facts, diagrams and,

Pages from Peter's travel journal, 2003

21/10/03
a side elevation of a Moroccan mosque tower
the new Casablanca mosque stands 210 metres
NOTE: Iman calling the Faithful to Prayer from Tower

a section of the Fes medina "Fes el Bali".
500,000 people live here: 15000 streets
Mosque
Madressa
RIVER
FES
OUED
TOWER
Mosque
① Tanneries

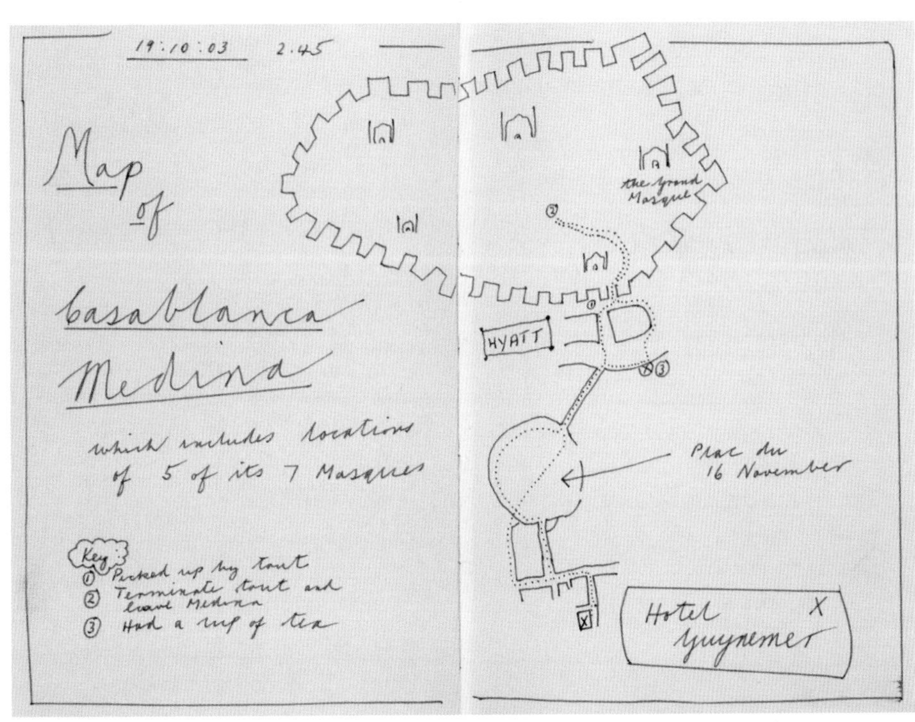
19:10:03
2.45
Map of Casablanca Medina
which includes locations of 5 of its 7 Mosques
Key:
① Picked up by tout
② Terminate tout and leave Medina
③ Had a cup of tea
the Grand Mosque
HYATT
Plac du 16 November
Hotel Guynemer

above all, maps of journeys. The sense of journeying – of exploration, in an intellectual and physical sense – was crucial, and in travelling to see great art and architecture he found a way of reflecting on his two small rooms in Cuba Street.

In April 1998, he and Hilary spent a month travelling in the Middle East, seeking out the landmarks of Islamic and classical Persian art in Iran and Jordan. As always, he was fascinated by the intersection of different cultures: the Saint Sarkis Cathedral in Tehran, for example, an Armenian church where an Islamic decorative style co-existed with the Catholic figurative tradition. Three years later, the McLeaveys flew to Uzbekistan to visit Tashkent, Samarkand, Khiva and Bukhara – places Peter found to be of immense interest. 'It fed into my profession of art dealer,' he commented, 'namely the growth of culture in small, or "remote" places. I kept thinking of New Zealand... And I saw links between Khiva and Wellington. How plants on the edge of the forest grow, or die.'[48]

In July, Peter opened exhibition number 361: five works by Toss Woollaston that spanned his sixty-year career. As he noted on the invitation, it marked the thirtieth anniversary of Woollaston's first show at Cuba Street; what he did not mention was that it was also three decades since the gallery had opened. Peter Ireland – who had met Peter at that first exhibition – wrote at once. 'Your understated few words carry a great deal, and I wanted to acknowledge that. It's a good opportunity to recognise the artist's importance to your commitment to 147... And a chance for me to express my inexpressively deep appreciation of what you have done and continue to do there: to make visible what makes us us.'[49]

The anniversary was actually in September, but Peter had brought the exhibition forward because Woollaston's health was failing. He died on 30 August, at the age of eighty-eight. In the following month, Peter wrote to Ian Brown in Melbourne, 'The recent passing of Toss was very much the end of an era for art, here... I had said my "goodbyes" several months ago. That said, it was still a shock. And, just to realise that he is not around any more seems strange and unsettling.'[50]

Indeed, Peter was feeling restless. 'I feel an itch to give this place a radical shake up,' he told Peter Ireland. 'I'm just a bit bored by it all. Signs of aging, maybe. Still, for all that, business still trucks along. I've just sold a $80,000.00 Fomison [on resale] so I shouldn't complain.'[51] Peter often used group exhibitions to give the gallery a 'shake up' during this period. Like other dealers, he relied on group shows at a practical level: to fill a gap, rehang old stock, give a snapshot of the gallery stable or introduce a new artist. 'It's a bit of a mixed grill today,' he liked to tell his visitors.

What we do here, group exhibition, April–May 1998, photographed by Peter McLeavey

But group shows were also a chance to experiment and be more provocative. As Ian Wedde observed, 'Mixed shows at McLeavey's are usually fun. You sense behind them the orchestrations of a man whose yearly calendar is a work of art which may be declaimed with attention to dramatic light and shade, before it gets seen in episodes which, like soap opera, feature confrontations of style and personality ... The group shows allow McLeavey to run pilots of these operas – to stage-manage mini dramas and confrontations.'[52]

The titles of Peter's group shows became increasingly playful: *The right stuff*, *Shiny things*, *The really really good exhibition* and *It will be OK*. In *What we do here* in 1998 he packed the gallery walls bargain-basement style, curating his own mini-history of New Zealand art. Reviewing the exhibition, Damian Skinner noted, 'A Gordon Walters *Koru* painting hung next to a cut-out by Richard Killeen, a drawing by John Reynolds, and a painting by Peter Robinson – all appropriators, and all implicated in various ways in the debate about the relationship between Pakeha and Maori art and culture.'[53] Peter had commissioned Killeen to produce number tags for the works – a play on the idea of the cut-outs – and Robinson to make name tags, which were attached to the skirting boards. As Skinner observed, these names offered 'a roll call of art history' and signalled Peter's part in establishing a canon of New Zealand art. Writing to Peter Robinson, Peter delivered his own verdict on the show: 'Was it a dog's breakfast????; was it an inspired piece of curatorial taste????; was it an essay in flim flam???? – only time will tell.'[54]

In *Blood brothers*, a group exhibition in 1998, Peter showed a photograph from his personal collection by the American Joel-Peter Witkin. Entitled *Glassman, Mexico City*, it shows a naked corpse, photographed in a morgue, clumsily stitched from neck to groin.[55] The image is startling, even shocking; and yet the anonymous subject, his face uplifted, also has a kind of grace. *Glassman* recalls the figures of Christ in medieval religious art, and Peter found it deeply affecting.

Olivia McLeavey was still a teenager when her father began to collect Witkin's controversial photographs, which often deal with death and disfigurement. 'I didn't know what to think at first. It was quite disconcerting. That's what it was like growing up with Dad: photographs would arrive and you'd think, "What's this?" But then after a while you'd become just as fascinated by the work as he was.'[56]

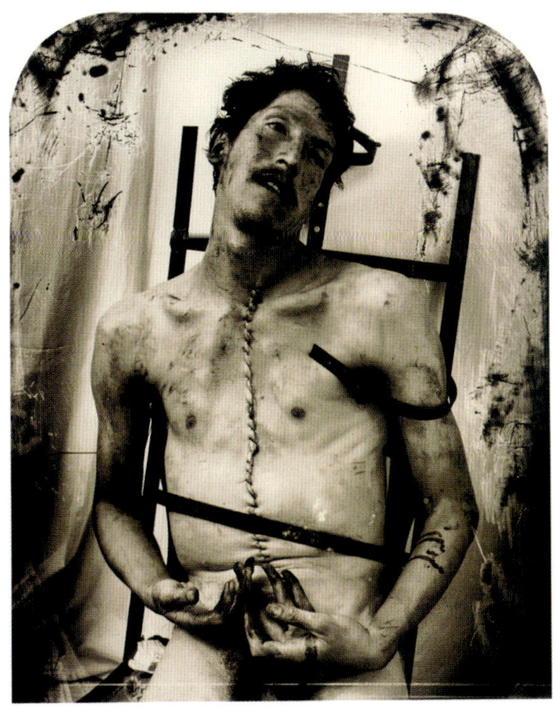

Joel-Peter Witkin, *Glassman, Mexico City*, 1994
Gelatin silver print
Peter and Hilary McLeavey collection

Peter had always been a collector, pursuing different interests – paintings, first editions and ceramics – as the years passed by. In the 1980s, living alone in Brooklyn, he began to buy international photographs, and by 2000 he had a superb collection of nearly sixty images: nineteenth-century views by Francis Frith, Eugène Atget, Charles Clifford and the Bisson Frères; twentieth-century works by Robert Frank, Dorothea Lange, Paul Strand, Berenice Abbott, Bill Brandt and Ralph Eugene Meatyard; and contemporary photographs by Sherrie Levine, Barbara Kruger and Witkin.

In these images he found a collecting focus of his own – one in which he would not be competing with his clients – but that was just part of the attraction. International photography represented a new field in which he could apply himself, developing his eye and his knowledge with constant study. He took pleasure in subscribing to specialist catalogues, from Christie's, Sotheby's and the Fraenkel Gallery in San Francisco, and underpinning his acquisitions with substantial research. Peter compared the emotional effect of certain photographs to that of the German art songs he loved by Schubert and Schumann:

'There's just the piano and the human voice, and the music takes me to another world. There's an austerity, an astringency, a purity – it's a very intimate and intense experience.'[57]

As his collection began to take shape, Peter noticed that a pattern was emerging. 'I'd had such a strange childhood, and I'd always felt displaced and alone. I was living on my own [in the 1980s], apart from my family. I began to put my life back together through the images I collected. The photographs became a map of my life.'[58] He eventually came to think of the collection as his very own work of art – 'a sort of self-portrait consisting of images which trigger memory. My past, and all its various times, places, people, and emotional/sexual states, gaze at me (from the walls) and I gaze back. I confront the self. I find sustenance.'[59] His account of collecting as a healing activity – putting the pieces of himself back together – echoes his description of psychoanalysis with Mario Fleischl.

At the gallery, meanwhile, Peter's passion for photography found an outlet in occasional exhibitions like *Masterworks of 19th century New Zealand photography* in 1997. A note in the catalogue reflected the source of his fascination with the medium. 'Look hard at these photographs. They are of a country none can return to. Our beginnings. They are vintage, and rare, and carry with them memories of that time and place.'[60] Peter also commissioned Peter Ireland, who had curated *The new image* in 1979, to produce two exhibitions, both of which explored issues central to photography. The first, *Looking back*, in 2001, focused on the human experience of being photographed – 'hedged about as it is by conventions, expectations and fears' – and the complex and shifting relationship between subject, photographer and viewer.[61] *Victory over death*, in 2002, explored photography's burden of 'literal realism', aligning it with a more transformative role: 'to forget reality, to promise the world miracles, to sing of victory, and to deny death'.[62] Like *Looking back*, it presented familiar and unfamiliar images spanning several decades, with recent work by young artists Ben Cauchi, Andrew Ross and Nikolai Kokx.[63]

Apart from these one-off photography projects, Peter continued to show new work by Laurence Aberhart, as well as earlier images by Les Cleveland and Gary Baigent. He admired the quiet poetry in Cleveland's photographs of everyday life – the workplaces, racing clubs and hotels that he had grown up with – and found that they, too, struck an emotional chord in him. A journalist, mountaineer, bushman, musicologist and academic, Cleveland had 'knocked about' in the small towns of Peter's childhood. 'I'd spent time in Otira driving a front-end loader in the

The living room at the McLeavey home, showing part of Peter's photography collection, 2012

riverbed, and I knew the railway people who regarded the place as a sort of penal colony. I'd listened to their grievances. So I understood a bit about Peter's background. I understood what an act of courage it had been, to break with a safe career at the bank and launch himself as an art dealer.'[64]

Cleveland often visited Peter at the gallery.

> We used to sit on that old green couch he had. I'd go across the road and get tea and sandwiches, and we'd sit there and eat and ruminate about things in general. Peter was interested in what I would call fundamental questions like Who am I?, What is life about?, and also notions of providence. I'd had some quite miraculous escapes during the war and I felt guilty about that. I'd thought a lot about fate and the mystery that shapes people's lives, that decides

EUROPE
HOTEL
M.G.SHELDON

180

whether a person lives or dies. Peter was fascinated by this too, about ideas of fate and mortality. He collected some interesting art around the subject of death and suffering.

In his first show at the gallery in 1990, Cleveland exhibited vintage photographs from the 1950s, mainly of Wellington. Peter quoted from the American poet John Berryman's *Dream songs* on the catalogue, alluding to the powerful interior life that sustains a creative project:

> During those years he met his seminars,
> went & lectured & read, talked with human beings,
> paid insurance & taxes;
> but his mind was not on it. His mind was elsewheres
> in an area where the soul not talks but sings
> & where foes are attacked with axes.[65]

Seventeen years later, at his fifth solo show at the gallery, Cleveland juxtaposed historical and contemporary images of Wellington alongside poems lamenting the loss of the city's architectural heritage. Writing to the critic Mark Amery, Peter described *The secret city* as one of his ten most important shows: 'and it was about Wellington. In fact, it was an anthem; a love song; a sermon; and maybe a rant, to or about our city. And in particular the issue with the inner city and Cuba Street… Yes, at 86 [Les] still has fire in his belly and can shake his fist at the powerful, the greedy, and the apathetic.'[66] There could have been no higher praise.

Les Cleveland, *The European Hotel, Charleston, Westland, proprietor Mick Sheldon in doorway 1956*, 1956 (top) and *Morning sun outside a pakapoo den in Taranaki St, Wellington 1957*, 1957
Gelatin silver prints
Museum of New Zealand Te Papa Tongarewa, purchased 1985 with New Zealand Lottery Board funds

TWENTY-TWO

The tectonic plates are shifting.

Ivan Anthony was still a student when he discovered the Peter McLeavey Gallery in 1983. 'I walked in and saw Mrkusich's "Segmented arcs" – the most sensational things I'd ever seen. And Peter chatted to me and I thought, Wow, what a strange world this is.'[1] In 1989, Ivan exhibited at the gallery with his brother Dale and Derek Cowie; soon afterwards he began to work for Peter.

In his nearly eight years at the gallery, Anthony saw another side to the normally courteous, softly spoken dealer. 'One day a museum director came in,' he recalled, 'someone who liked to buy at auction, on the secondary market. Of course Peter hated that, because the artist doesn't get a cent. He thought the museums should lead the way. So this guy told Peter he was in town for an auction, and Peter said, "Only hogs feed there. Are you a hog?" This guy just didn't know what to do.' Anthony also saw Peter lock himself in the bathroom rather than deal with a client. 'He hated it when people thought they could just walk in and flash their chequebook and buy anything. Art had to be treated with respect, with a degree of reverence.'

When Anthony left Wellington in 1997 to establish his own gallery in Auckland, Peter's initial response was one of concern: 'He was genuinely worried – he knew how difficult it would be.'[2] Anthony had an advantage, however, in his long apprenticeship. 'I learned so much from Peter. I saw that being an art dealer was all about potential: it wasn't mercantile, it was never about money. The art came first.' Anthony established his gallery on the Cuba Street model, renting cheap premises in Karangahape Road. 'Peter always kept his overheads low and that was a great lesson to me. I knew that you had to pay the artists promptly, pay your bills on time. People had great loyalty to Peter because he was

Peter McLeavey stand, Auckland Art Fair, 2007, showing William Dunning's *Antipodean altar 1840–1900*, 2007

meticulous about money, he was so reliable, he treated the artists as professionals.'

Like Peter before him, Anthony took a part-time job to support his fledgling gallery. In his first year he established an impressive stable of young artists, and in 2001 he began to represent Richard Killeen, Bill Hammond and Michael Harrison in Auckland. 'That's when I knew it was going to work. I felt I was really under way.'

Peter took a keen interest in Anthony's artists, and it was at his gallery in 1998 that he saw the work of Andrew McLeod, a recent Elam graduate. McLeod's 'Camowhaiwhai' paintings were witty, irreverent and frenetic, melding military camouflage with the curvilinear patterns of kowhaiwhai. 'As soon as I saw his work I knew that I loved it,' Peter recalled. 'His commitment, his drive ... he was for real.'[3]

McLeod, a relative newcomer to the art world, was already aware of Peter's reputation: 'I knew that if I showed at his gallery, all these new people would be looking at my work who'd never looked at me before.'[4] On a personal level, McLeod recognised Peter as a fellow eccentric. 'He's a very emotional man. He's made his weaknesses into his strengths; he's successful in managing his own personality. And that's a total inspiration.' Peter included McLeod's work in the November 1998 *Blood brothers* exhibition. 'I find that I am engaged by you and what you are making,' he wrote. 'You have a gift. I would like to think that I can help you in your exploration of it.'[5]

In the following year, McLeod had a joint show, *Cleaning up*, with his friend and contemporary Brendon Wilkinson. McLeod exhibited his 'Blue dot' paintings, which referenced high modernist abstraction as well as something more mundane – toilet-paper packaging. 'He paints Gordon Walters with an axe,' Peter told the artist Darryn George. 'Yes, they are "rough". And yes, they find, and hit, the mark.'[6] Wilkinson contributed assemblages made with empty food cans and other detritus. For critic Aaron Lister, the 'hallowed space' of the Peter McLeavey Gallery provided the perfect backdrop for the two young artists' ironic interrogation of art history and the market – 'with the customary knowing wink acknowledging their courting of these very processes'.[7]

As he had done so many times before, Peter wrote to caution McLeod about taking too much notice of critics. 'The "*knockbacks*" and "*rejections*" we all receive in life do make us strong. And more determined. You are a very gifted young artist. The current show is (in a way) an overture to a long and enriching creative life. Look upon it as the overture to a five-act opera. Or, maybe, it will end up "The Ring". That's what Killeen has done.'[8]

Brendon Wilkinson at *Cleaning up*, September–October 1999, photographed by Peter McLeavey

By 1999, Peter Robinson was moving into installation, and in his sixth show with Peter that year he exhibited a work entitled *The uncertainty principle – recent work*. Comprised of found and constructed items – photographs, placards and polystyrene chains – it was one of his most noisy and clamorous works to date and, at 5 metres in width, one of the largest. Peter did not expect it to sell, and especially not to a private owner, but Wellington collector Celia Dunlop fell for it, although she had nowhere to show it in her Hataitai home. 'Peter was particularly excited about that one,' Robinson recalled. 'But then again, he seemed to be excited about every sale.'[9]

Peter Robinson: The uncertainty principle – recent work, July–August 1999, showing the work of the same title, photographed by Peter McLeavey

In the following year, Peter commissioned a number of shows to mark the end of the millennium, including Robinson's *The end of the twentieth century*, which opened in December 2000. Following on from *The uncertainty principle*, Robinson transformed the gallery with gimcrack souvenirs and bric-a-brac, slogans and placards, all spilling out of cheap metal suitcases. Curator Robert Leonard, who purchased the work for the Auckland City Art Gallery, described it as 'a flea market wunderkammer, a demented cultural core-sample of world kitsch, a shambling tourist guide to bad globalism'.[10]

Internationally, the role of the dealer gallery changed dramatically during Peter's long career. In New York in the 1960s, Leo Castelli had formed collaborative relationships with other dealers, extending the market for his artists across Europe and the United States. Thirty years later, Castelli's one-time collaborator, Larry Gagosian, took the model a step further, developing a global empire of galleries to become the most powerful dealer in the world. By 2012, he had eleven galleries worldwide, with an estimated annual turnover of $1 billion.

The rise of the super-dealer was accompanied by a change in the way galleries did business. Art fairs, which brought dealer galleries together for a few days, were increasingly important, often accounting for a significant percentage of annual income. Meanwhile, auctions commandeered an even greater slice of the contemporary (and resale) market, and art stars like Damien Hirst, Jeff Koons and Takashi Murakami became highly adept at marketing themselves, sometimes bypassing their dealers to send work directly to auction. The market base was changing too, as China began to rival the United States and the United Kingdom in terms of money spent on art.[11]

Peter watched these developments with some fascination, and took every opportunity to visit art fairs on his overseas travels.[12] It was not until 2000, however, that he took the plunge himself, showing works by Hammond, Killeen and Fraser at the Melbourne Art Fair.[13] 'We are not dealing with a highly refined, aestheticised environment,' he told a reporter. 'We are looking at essentially a bazaar.'[14] Although he hoped to make sales, he was philosophical – 'this exhibition would be a success if I allowed more people to appreciate the quality of our art, the distinctiveness of our culture'. Peter's New Zealand-centric attitude differed from that of his younger colleagues at the fair, John Gow and Andrew Jensen. Both showed works by international artists as well as New Zealanders, and made it clear that they were not there to fly a flag for their country. They identified as art dealers – or 'gallerists' in the new parlance – rather than New Zealand dealers.

On a personal level, Peter found the fair exhausting yet exhilarating. '[T]here seemed to be thousands of people continually and perpetually moving through; intent expressions, all searching for something. Later, I had a cup of tea, and thought that an [art fair] was the closest I'll ever get to comprehending what it must be like going on a blind date with Jennifer Lopez'.[15] Peter didn't sell anything: 'I came home with my tail between my legs, really. But a strange thing happened. When I went to open the gallery next day, a well-dressed woman was there – just waiting for me on the stairs. She said, "I really liked what you had in Melbourne and I've flown over to see your gallery. What can you show me?"'[16] Peter's new client bought works by Fraser, Hammond and Killeen, and the commission paid for the entire trip to Melbourne: the cost of the airfares, accommodation and the stand itself.

In the following year, Peter and Hilary travelled to Italy to support Fraser and Robinson at one of the most prestigious events in the international art world, the Venice Biennale. 'You (and Jaccy) did New Zealand proud,' Peter wrote to Robinson afterwards. '[A]t one stage I almost burst into tears – I was moved, and proud, and happy.'[17] Back in 1968, he had urged local artists to take their place on an international stage; now, more than thirty years later, he was delighted to see the way Robinson and his contemporaries moved between New Zealand and the world, taking advantage of new residencies and exhibiting opportunities.[18]

Late in 2001, Peter's building was temporarily closed for earthquake strengthening, and he moved next door, holding three group shows at 151 Cuba Street before reopening in March with an exhibition by Andrew McLeod. Robin White, now returned to New Zealand, noticed how stressful this interval was for him. 'He was growing more and more anxious. By the end I think he was almost at breaking point, he seemed terrified that he wasn't going to be able to get back in to those rooms.'[19]

Peter was also considering the future of the gallery, and when he visited Olivia in London he asked if she would be interested in joining the business. 'It came out of left field for me,' she recalled. 'I had a great job in marketing and I was living the high life. The time wasn't right – I still had things I needed to do. But it lodged in my mind. Dad didn't mention it again.'[20]

Peter took a keen interest, however, in the exhibitions Olivia saw in London. 'There you experience the best,' he wrote in 2002:

> And that influences and shapes your taste. Hones it and refines it. It also, I feel, deepens one's spirit! Makes you aware of those values that transcend material things.
>
> Yes, it's wonderful (for me) to know that you have seen and experienced so many beautiful (and quality) things. They will always be with you, darling.
>
> Today it's sunny in Cuba Street. Tony and the Jam team are doing well. The Crazy Lounge is full and Midnight Espresso is about to launch its Ruffo retrospective. Yes it's all go down this end.[21]

Peter enclosed an obituary for Ruffo – a Cuba Street identity, always clad in an army surplus anorak, who had long been a regular at the gallery.[22] 'Ruffo lived rough on the streets,' Olivia recalled. 'And he could be cranky – he was quite opinionated about art and very critical of the contemporary art world. But he was always welcome at the gallery, and when I was a kid we often ran into him at Dad's hangouts

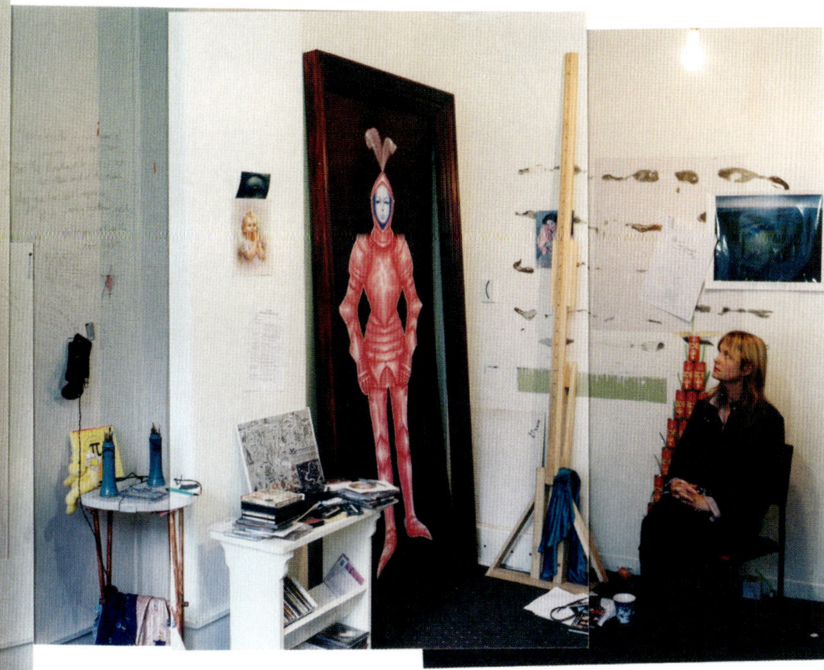

Liz Maw in her studio at Elam School of Fine Arts, photographed by Peter McLeavey, 2002

like the Masters Coffee Bar in Manners Street. I think Ruffo captured Dad's imagination – he always felt for the underdog, the outcast, and he identified with him at some level.'[23] Peter told Olivia about Ruffo's final visit. 'He had come in to the gallery a week or so ago to look at the Hammond show. He was a great admirer of Bill's work; however he could also be critical and did, in fact, pull Bill up sometimes (he felt his "composition" was weak!!!).'

In December 2002, Peter wrote to Knight Landesman about his recent travels in Iran. 'As I grow older the past beckons me. Fortunately, however, not in respect of my gallery. I have a number of artists (Yvonne [Todd] is one) and they totally absorb me. And they are so much fun. And yes, I'm still in the same two rooms and, in two weeks time I hold the 421st exhibition which has graced its walls.'[24]

Yvonne Todd at the Smith & Caughey tearooms, photographed by Peter McLeavey, 2002

Exhibition 421 was by Ava Seymour, one of a group of young artists – including Andrew McLeod, Brendon Wilkinson, Darryn George, Liz Maw and Yvonne Todd – who joined the gallery between 1998 and 2004. 'They are, if you like the Eminems and Ani DiFrancos of this civilisation,' Peter told media mogul Brent Hansen. 'Our art Datsuns... I do feel that the tectonic plates are shifting here and a younger (hungrier and gifted) group are now claiming their birthright. It is so exciting for me to have them in my gallery. I feel a new chapter is now being penned which takes me back to those heady days in 1966, when I first started my journey, as a dealer in New Zealand.'[25]

Peter first saw the work of Liz Maw at the Ivan Anthony Gallery in 2002. 'He walked in,' recalled Anthony. 'He looked at these in-your-face paintings, and he was stunned. He immediately said, "I want to meet this girl."'[26] When Maw met Peter later in the year, he reminded her of someone. 'I couldn't think who it was. Then eventually I realised, he reminded me of the Irish Catholic priests I knew as a kid. And I thought, Ah, that gallery is his church, and because the art world is so small he is the village priest of that community. He had the same way of delivering his belief system, and the same kind of conviction – it's a faith-based culture, you know, that art has meaning, that it's important.'[27]

It was at Fiat Lux, an artist-run space in Auckland, that Peter first saw the work of Yvonne Todd in the late 1990s. When Todd had her debut exhibition at the Ivan Anthony Gallery in 2000, Peter was impressed, and aquired a close-cropped photograph of a young woman's head, entitled *Kirsten*. Later in the year he wrote to Todd and arranged a visit.

The two met at the Smith & Caughey tearooms, with its apricot colour scheme and old-fashioned establishment air. 'That was my office in Auckland,' Peter noted. 'You, never ran into anyone from the art world there, and that was a good thing.'[28] Peter was now in his late sixties – nearly forty years older than Todd – but she felt there was something youthful about him. 'He had those steely blue eyes that fixed themselves on you,' she recalled, 'and he was very intense but also very calm. Everything was very carefully measured and I could see there was a degree of protocol in everything he did. At that first meeting he had lots of questions. It wasn't like a job interview, but he asked about my background – my parents, my brother – he wanted to get the overview. He wasn't asking what camera I shot on or anything like that. Nothing technical.'[29] Peter and Todd soon established a pattern to their meetings at the tearooms. 'We used to go and browse afterwards at the Lladró figurines, and just admire them for what they were. Expensive geegaws. And they were those weird pastel shades, quite chaste and pure, but the high gloss on them made them also slightly tawdry. So we had quite a ritual.'

Peter made up his mind about Todd very quickly. Six months after their first meeting, he scheduled an exhibition for her in August 2002. As it happened, his timing could not have been better: just a week before the show was due to open, Todd, the youngest and most inexperienced finalist, won New Zealand's premier art award, the $50,000 Walters Prize. Suddenly she was at the centre of a media whirl.

'I was quite frazzled by all that,' Todd recalled. 'And then I had to fly to Wellington. It was my first time in a plane for ten years because I was afraid of flying. But Peter was really good. He and Hilary were so composed and reassuring.'

Todd's show was entitled *Sea of tranquility*: five immaculate yet disconcerting photographs of pale, primped young women, dewy-lipped and bewigged, garbed in chaste, high-necked blouses. Peter was thrilled with it. 'These images are strong,' he told a client. 'They remind me of (what I call) New Zealand Gothic; Bensemann, Fomison and Hammond to cite 3 other examples…To me she is the first New Zealand photographer who understands the emotional and psychological "weight" of colour.'[30] The entire edition sold out quickly, with purchases by Te Papa and Auckland Art Gallery.

Yvonne Todd, *Susan Blunton* (left) and *Emerey Weschlette*, both 2002
Colour photograph, type C print
Museum of New Zealand Te Papa Tongarewa, purchased 2002

Wellington collectors Howard Greive and Gabrielle McKone began to buy Todd's work at her second show with Peter in the following year. 'Her whole body of work of women represents an unusual and powerful group of archetypes that you can easily recognise in New Zealand,' Greive commented. 'But by then she was photographing beauty consultants and they represent a fascinating subset of her work – the illusion of beauty. I see these particular women as the sales team. They sell beauty and desire. The pursuit of which can have its downside'.[31]

Peter had been a mentor for Greive since the late 1980s when, as creative adviser at Saatchi & Saatchi, he bought works for the corporate collection. 'I don't think Peter ever sold me a picture. All he would do was talk about the work and the artist and place it in a context.' To him, that was Peter's point of difference. 'If you went to one of the big galleries in Auckland, you knew you were being corralled – just subtly, but you knew you were being sold. Whereas with Peter you never felt that – you just ended up buying the thing! But in a way, that was part of the showmanship as well. You were drawn into this world of high culture.'

Greive admired the way Peter 'read' his clients. 'He was such a clever bugger – he could see what you were interested in and hone in on that.

And he could put an advertising spin on the art as well. Like any good Catholic, he understood branding, he really had the juice on brands. You could sit down with Peter and have a great talk about artists as brands. For a lot of people in his business it would be anathema, but he was really open to it.'

Like many collectors before him, Greive was intrigued by the mystique of the McLeavey storeroom. 'It was like a little magic box – completely off limits. He'd say, "I won't be a minute," and he'd disappear, shut the door. Then out he'd pop with something to show you – Ta da!' The element of theatre was not lost on Greive. 'There's a great saying in advertising,' he remarked. 'Where's there's mystery, there's margin.'

In March 2005, Peter reflected on the proposed Auckland Art Fair in a letter to Killeen. '[H]ow much has changed,' he wrote. '[T]he commodification of "art" is now so pervasive; and maybe total. And we are all affected by it; some swept along by it.'[32] Peter was in a pensive mood after two calls from the media, requesting interviews. 'Things like that "throw" me. My life and I become fodder (maybe) for the whole business of "art" and its industry.'

Peter had a love–hate relationship with the idea of personal publicity. He was – and remains – a marvellous interview subject, spinning yarns about his past and proffering droll comments on the nature of his business. Grant Smithies interviewed him in the gallery that year:

> [I]mmaculately dressed in a pinstriped brown suit, his fine white hair framing an unusually kind face… But facing him on the nearest wall is a huge panorama called *AK79* by photographic artist Ava Seymour. In it, various members of early New Zealand punk bands such as Toy Love and Suburban Reptiles – their familiar heads affixed to unknown bodies – are puking in the gutter, strangling each other, pashing, or being beaten and sexually assaulted outside Auckland's Central Police Station. It is gruesome, fantastic, repellent and exciting, and for $8000 it could be yours. It looks like something this kindly gentleman would hate, but McLeavey loves it.[33]

Smithies noted that Peter was 'far less conservative and reactionary than most 25-year-olds', a point that was not lost on his artists. Robin White, for example, was baffled by her son Conrad's contemporary music. 'But he'll bump into Peter on the street and they'll have a conversation about it. I wouldn't be able to have that conversation with my son.'[34]

There was one area, however, in which Peter lagged behind. He often quizzed his visitors. What did they think: should he buy a computer? Even get a website? Then he could 'send all sorts of things all over the Universe'. 'I'm unsure,' he admitted in 2004. 'I don't really want to change. The artists are all happy. But the clients???? Maybe I have to for them. Anyway, as they say, watch this space.'[35]

In the following year he reflected on his business in a letter to the Sydney dealer Darren Knight:

> I hope business is going well for you. Yes, it still seems to here, too.
>
> The main thing, with me, is that I come in to work most days, open up, put the lights on, and wait. Every day is a surprise for one never knows what is going to come through the door. And, usually, I do business.
>
> So far I've been able to get by without sending emails, or a computer, or a digital camera. Just me, and the phone, and the stock; it's a no-frills operation. And, happily, it still works.
>
> Couldn't do it in Sydney.[36]

Peter continued to maintain his trans-Tasman links and, in 2008, he and Hilary flew to Melbourne for a special occasion: Ian Brown, one of Peter's long-time clients, had decided to gift his entire collection to the National Gallery of Victoria. Brown had bought his first works by Australian and international artists in the late 1960s, and when he met Peter in 1971 he began to buy New Zealand art: first Woollaston, McCahon, Walters and Killeen, and later Billy Apple, Peter Robinson, Andrew McLeod and Ava Seymour. 'Peter mentored me,' Brown recalled. 'All the New Zealand art in my collection is really due to Peter saying "Come and look, trust your judgement." He made me confident in what I was doing.'[37]

———

With forty years as a dealer behind him, Peter continued to be amazed by his artists. For John Reynolds, 2006 was the year of *Cloud*: a shimmering installation of 7081 tiny canvases featuring words and phrases from Harry Orsman's *Dictionary of New Zealand English*. A highlight of the Sydney Biennale, *Cloud* was later purchased by Te Papa.

Towards the end of the year, Peter wrote to Reynolds about his upcoming exhibition at Cuba Street. 'As you know, John, I'm very open to ideas. And, with all the shows I see them as the venue where the artist conducts experiments on their gift. Rather in the manner of Doctor Viktor Frankenstein.'[38] He went on to offer some suggestions.

Peter Robinson: Soft rock baroque, March–April 2008, photographed by Peter McLeavey

'Maybe one big thing. Maybe something directly on the wall like we used to do. Something about New Zealand.'

For Reynolds, Peter's comments were like seeds – 'nano-seconds of possibility' that might germinate for months or even years. 'It's like the artist is in the soup, baffled, and with their own electricity, and he's the conduit, the live wire, from the culture, from all that listening he does, from people trudging up those stairs. He's coming back to you and saying, "You know, here's an avenue to pursue."'[39]

For his show with Peter in July 2007, Reynolds produced a companion piece to *Cloud*, a work he described as 'the black heart of the big work, the little dark sister'.[40] Entitled *Looking west, late afternoon, low water*

AKA AKE AKE AKI-RAHO AKE PIRO AKA-TEA AMO KURA ANGI ANGI ANGLO MAORI AOTEA-ROA AO-TEAR-OAN ARA-ARA TE ARIKI ARIKI-SHIP A-ROHA AROHA JOB AROH-ANUI ARU-HE ATA-ATA A-TUA AUA-AWA
HA-PUA HA-PUKA HARA-KEKE HARA-MAI HA-RORE HAU-AMA HAU-HAU HAU-MAKO-ROA HAU-MATA HAU-RANGI HAU-TURE HA-WAIKI HEI-TIKI HEKE HEKE-TARA HEKE WAR HEN-ARE HERU-HERU HIHI-IHI HI-KOI HIKU HINA-HINA
HORO-EKA HORO-KAKA HORO-PITO HOU-HERE HOUI HOUHI HOU-PARA HUA-HUA HUE HU-HU HUI HUI-WORKER HUIA HUIA FEATHER HU-NE HU-PEREI HU-PIRO HUTI-WAI HUTU IHE IN-ANGA IWI JACK NOHI KAEO KAIO KAHA-KAHA
KA-KA KAKA-BEAK KAK-AHA KA-KAHI KA-KAHO KA-KAHU KAK-APO KAKA-RIKI KAKI KA-MAHI KAMO-KAMO KA-NAE KAN-AKA KANA-KANA KANGA PIRAU KA-NONO KA-NUKA KA-PAI KAPE-TA KA-PIA KA-PUKA KA-RAKA KARAKA BERRY KARA-KAHIA KAR-AKIA
KAU-REHE KAURI KAURI FOREST KAURI-GUM KAURI SNAIL KA-URU KA-UTA KAWA KA-WAKA KAWA-KAWA KA-WANA KAWAN-ATANGA KA-WAU KAWAU-PAKA KAWE KAWE-KAWEA KEA KEA SMUG-GLER KEHE KE-HUA KEKE KE-KENO KEKE-RENGU KEKE-TEREHE KERE-RU
KIWI-LAND KO KO-AREA KO-ARO KO-AUAU KOE-KOEA KOHA KOHAN-GA REO KOHE-KOHE KOHE-PIRO KO-HERU KO-HIA KOHI-KOHI KOHO-PEROA KO-HUA KO-HUHU KOHU-KOHU KOHU-TUHUTU KO-INGA KOITA-REKE KOK-AKO KO-KIHI KO-KIRI KOKO KOKO-MUKA
KORO-I KORO-KIO KORO-KORO KORO-MIKO KORO-RA KORO-TANGI KORU KORO-WAI KO-RURU KOTAHI-TANGA KOTAR-ETARE KO-TERO KO-TIRO KO-TUKU KOTUKU FEATHER KOTUKU-NGUTU-PAPA KOTUK-UTUKU KOU-KOU KO-URA KO-WHAI KOWHAI NGUTU-KAKA KOWHAI-WHAI KO-WHARA-WHARA KU-AKA
KUTAI KUTU DE-KUTU MAE-ROERO MA-HOE MA-HUE MAI MAIHI MAI-KAIKA MAIKA-KA MAIRE MAIRE-RAUNUI MAIRE-HAU MAKO-MAKO MAIRE TAWAKE MA-KAKA MAKA-MAKA MAKO MA-KUTU MA-MAKU MAM-ANGI MA-NA MAN-AIA MAN-ATU
HALF-MAORI TOWN MAORI URBAN MAORI MAORI CHICKEN MAORI DEVIL MAORI FIRE MAORI GOOSE-BERRY MAORI LEMON MAORI MELON MAORI PEACH MAORI PONY MAORI RABBIT MAORI AFFAIRS MAORI ALL BLACK MAORI ASSES-SOR MAORI AXE MAORI BASKET MAORI BELLY WOOL MAORI BIBLE MAORI BOTTOM MAORI BREAD MAORI BURN MAORI CALENDAR MAORI CHAIN MAORI CHURCH
MAORI LANG-UAGE MAORI MAGNA CARTA MAORI MAT MAORI NUT MAORI PARLI-AMENT MAORI PATH MAORI PIONEER MAORI PROBLEM (QUESTION) MAORI RENAIS-SANCE MAORI RESERVE MAORI SANDAL MAORI SCARE MAORI SCENT MAORI SCONE MAORI SHOE MAORI SICK-NESS MAORI SKIRT MAORI SORE MAORI SPADE MAORI SPEAR MAORI STONE MAORI SUMMER MAORI SWING MAORI TEA MAORI TIME
MAORI OATS MAORI OVER-DRIVE MAORI PORRIDGE MAORI POT MAORI POX MAORI ROAST MAORI SEASON MAORI SIDE-STEP MAORI TACKLE MAORI WED-DING MAORI WEED MAORI WIFE MAORI-BRED MAORI-OWNED ANTI-MAORI HALF-MAORI NON-MAORI PAN-MAORI
MAORI LAND MAORI LAND-ERS MAORI LAND COURT MAORI MISSION MAORI MISSION-ARY MAORI-NESS MAORI OVEN MAORI PAKEHA MAORI-PHILE MAORI POTATO MAORI PT MAORI QUEEN MAORI SCHOOL MAORI-TANGA MAORI TITLE MAORI WAR MAORI WARS
MAURI MA-WHAI MENS WHARE MERE MERE-MERE MERE POU-NAMU MIHA MIHA-NERE MIHI MIKI-MIKI MI-KOIKOI MIMI MINGI-MINGI MIRO MIRO-MIRO MOA GIANT MOA MOA-GREY
MURU PARTY NA-HUI NA-MU NA-NUA NEI-NEI NGA-IO NGA-RARA NGATI NGATI D.B. NGATI-DRONGO NGATI-NAUGHTY NGATI-ONE NGATI-PAKEHA NGATI BLOW NGATI POROU MAFIA NGA-WHA NGERI
ORO-ORO O-TAGO THE OTAGOS OTAGO BLOCK OTAG-(O)AN OTAGO-ITE PA BACK TO THE PA PA MAORI PA LOT (MOB) PA-FUL PAE-PAE PA-HAU-TEA PAI MARIRE PAI MARIRE POLE PAI MARIRE-ISM PAKA-HA PA-KARU
PA-NOKO-NOKO PANUI PAPA PAPA ROCK PAPA COUNTRY PAPA-KAINGA PA-PANGO PAPA-NOKO PAPA-TANIWHA-NIWHA PAPA-UMA PARA PA-RAERAE PA-RAHA PARA-KI PA-RANI PA-RAOA PARAOA REWANA PARA-PARA
VIRGIN PAUA YELLOW FOOTED PAUA PAUA DIVER PAUA POACHER PAUA STEAK PAUA-SHELL PAUA SHELL ASHTRAY PAUA SLUG PEKA-PEKA PEREI PIA PIDGIN-MAORI PAI (ANA) PIHA-PIHA-RAU PI-HOIHOI PIKAU PIKI-ARERO PIKO-PIKO
POHO-WERA PO-HUE POHU-TAKA-ROA PO-HUTU-KAWA INLAND POHUT-UKAWA KERMADEC POHUT-UKAWA POHUT-UKAWA HONEY POI POI-BALL DOUBLE POI POI DANCE PO-KAKA PO-KEKA PONG-A PONGA TREE-FERN PUNG-A BLACK PONGA SILVER PONGA
PUK-AHU PUKA-PUKA PUKA-TEA PUKATEA WEED PU-KEKO STEWED PUKAKI PUKEKO SOUP PUKU A PAIN IN THE PUKU PUKU-NUI PUKU-RAU PUNGA PUNGA PU-NUI PUPU PUPU-HARA-KEKE PUPU-RANGI PU-RIRI PUROU-ROU
RATANA CHURCH RATANA-ISM RATANA-ITE RAU-HUIA RAU-KAWA RAU-PATU RAUPATU (LAND) CLAIM RAU-PEKA RAU-PO RAUPO CHURCH RAUPO COTTAGE RAUPO WHARE RAU-REKAU RAU-RAU RAU-RIKI RAU-RIMU SPIRAL RAU-TINI RA-WARU
RUNANGA HOUSE RURU PAKIHI RUSH MAORI SETTLE-MENT ROTO-RUA SMELT TAUPO SNOW-BERRY MOKI-KINUI SPUD MAORI SPURGE STIFF KUMARA SWAMP KAURI TAE-WA TAHA TA-HAE TAHA MAORI TAHA PAKEHA TAIA-HA TAI-EPA TAIERI PET
TANI-WHA TA-ONGA TAPA-NUI FLU TAPU TAPU-LIFTING TAPU-REMOVAL TAPU-ED TAPU-ING TARA TARA-HINA TA-RAIRE TARA-KIHI KING TARAKIHI TARA-MEA TARA-NAKI TARA-NAKI SALUTE TARA-NAKI VIOLIN TARA-NAKIAN
TA-WHIRI TEKO-TEKO TEN-AKOE TENA KOUTOU TENA KOUTOU KATOA TE REO TETE-AWAKA TE WAIPOU-NAMU TE-WHATE-WHA TE WHITI TE WHITI-ISM TI TITI-TREE TI-KAPU TI-KAUKA TI-EKE TI-HORE TIKA

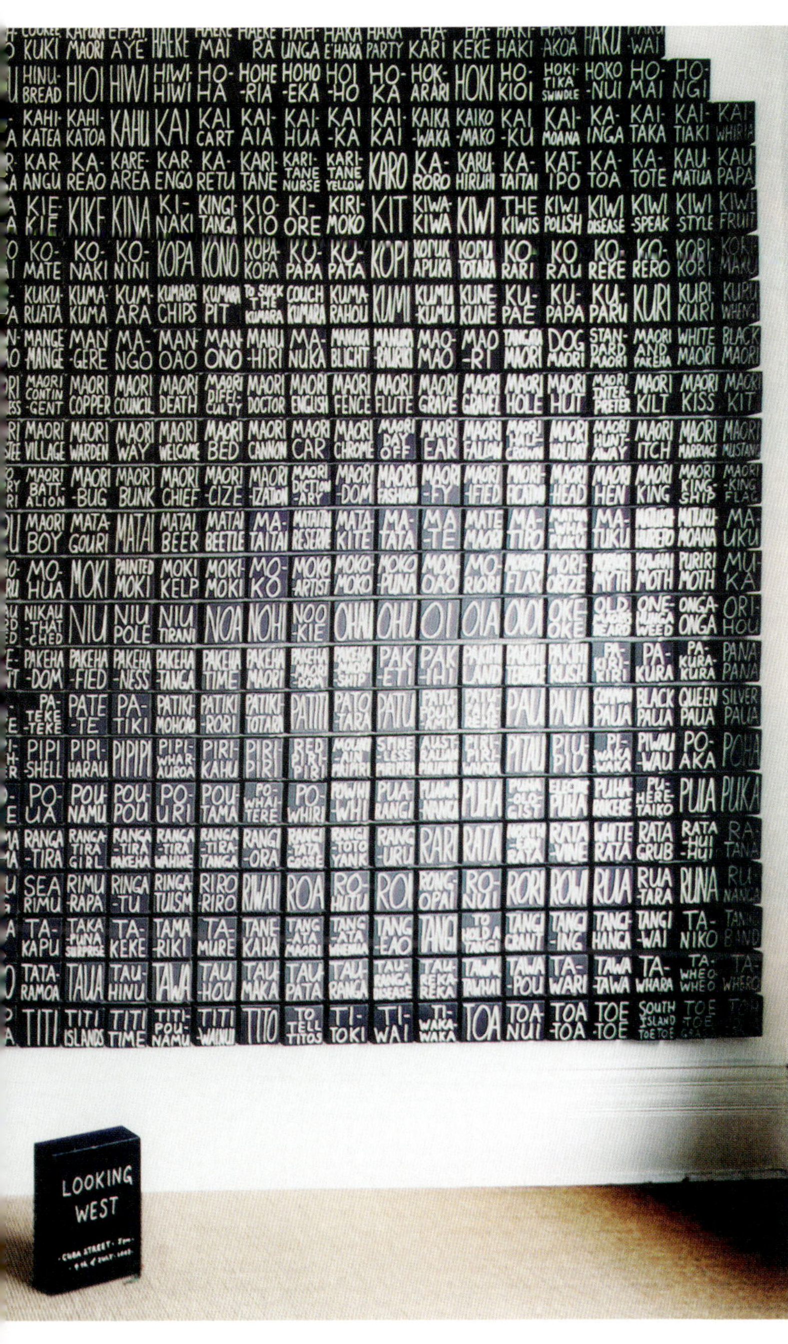

Peter with John Reynolds' *Looking west, late afternoon, low water*, July–August 2007

after a poem by Allen Curnow, the 1175-piece work contains every Māori colloquialism in Harry Orsman's dictionary, inscribed in silver marker on black canvas. Peter installed it like the façade of a wharenui, so that it filled the largest wall of his gallery. Fittingly, it was purchased by Victoria University, where Orsman had taught for twenty-eight years, and displayed on campus.

By now Peter's modest rooms posed a limitation for some of his artists – especially Peter Robinson, back in New Zealand and developing large-scale installations with expanded polystyrene foam. 'The gallery is difficult for some kinds of sculpture,' Robinson admitted, 'but at the same time it offers you a problem, and sometimes limitations offer you solutions.'[41] In 2008, he created *Soft rock baroque*, a teeming cascade of miniature polystyrene chains that was framed to dramatic effect in Peter's main room. Gorgeous, dazzling, yet reeking of the chemicals used in the foam's manufacture, the piece evoked stalagmites, frozen waterfalls and geological wonders (see page 393). 'The artist feels it is one of his best works,' Peter told a client. 'I concur.'[42]

That year, Robin White wrote to Peter about an unusual project. Soon after her return to New Zealand in 1999, she had been stunned by the murder of an infant girl, Hinewaoriki Karaitiana-Matiaha, in nearby Carterton. 'When the Lillybing story hit the local headlines I couldn't believe it. I thought, What? This is New Zealand! That would be unthinkable on Kiribati.' She began a file on the case, collecting newspaper cuttings. 'And then whammo, next minute it's the Aplin girls. Shit. So I started another file. And then there was Coral Burrows.'[43]

For years, White's files on the four children lay in a pile in her studio. 'They sat there in the back of my mind ... And it came to a point when I thought, It's time to pull all of this together, these three different stories that were really one story.' She began to talk to local women about collaborating on a series of works – and she began to talk to Peter. 'We had long talks about what it was about, the sensitivities around it and the fact that whoever committed these crimes, they're a victim as well. Everyone's a victim in that situation.'

White's exhibition *Sorry*, opened in October 2009, was a collaboration with Wairarapa artists Holly Jackson and Robyn McFarlane. It included a set of four piupiu, made with Jackson; a 'cloak' embroidered by McFarlane; and a set of monoprints by White herself. Meticulously handcrafted, layered with narrative, all of the works were imbued with the symbolism of birth and nurturing; each made reference to the lives of the murdered children. A letter from White to Peter, reproduced as a giant white page in the gallery, explained the motivation for the

Sorry, September–October 2009, showing Robin White's 'Let the light shine on' series, 2008-09

exhibition: 'I suppose, in my small way, I am attempting to restore some sense of order and beauty to the story of their lives.'[44] For the critic Hamish Clayton, the project went beyond social comment to take an active part in a community's attempt at reconciliation: 'These are, in a very real, very pure sense, pieces of folk art... works that show the importance of story-telling, of art, to a community.'[45]

Peter celebrated his seventieth birthday in 2007 with a party at the Matterhorn restaurant in Cuba Street, attended by artists and clients as well as business owners from the neighbourhood. Olivia, who was

Invitation to Peter's seventieth birthday party, 2007

back from London and working for ACP Media, designed an invitation that featured him on the cover of *Woman's Day* with Sharon Stone – 'Peter & Sharon tell all!' it promised. 'Peter's seventieth was fantastic,' Robin White recalled. 'The Hindu couple were there, the funky hairdresser, the local personalities from Cuba Street, and all his family. So I was chatting with cousin someone-or-other, and he was saying, "Oh, I don't know what Peter sees in Colin McCahon." And that's the reality, they're family. There's room for everyone.'[46]

In the same year, Peter and Hilary became grandparents with the birth of Dominic's son, Alexander Mitikulena-McLeavey; Catherine's son, Maximus Nicholls, was born in 2008. Instead of travelling to see great art and architecture, they now tended to spend the summer holidays at a bach at Pakawau in Golden Bay, with the family coming

The McLeavey family bach, showing paintings by Cedric Savage, photographed by Peter McLeavey, 2008

and going around them. The art displayed at the bach was rather different from that at Hill Street – realistic landscapes of Golden Bay, painted by Cedric Savage during the 1940s and 1950s. They were precisely the type of pictures the young McLeavey would have scorned, but by now he was more tolerant. He and Hilary enjoyed searching out the landmarks in Savage's paintings, and finding works to add to their small collection.

The summer holiday offered Peter a much-needed respite, a chance to unwind and catch up on reading before returning to the fray at Cuba Street. 'My business here goes on all the time,' he told the art historian Gordon H Brown. 'Sometimes I think it's my mistress; sometimes my prison. However, when it's all set and done I still have the same optimism and drive that I had when, in December 1965, I started out on this adventure.'[47]

In 2009, Peter and Hilary marked their fortieth wedding anniversary, and Peter commissioned a ring for the occasion by a young Auckland artist, Octavia Cook, who would later exhibit at the gallery. He was more than ever aware of how much he owed Hilary. 'Dad always said he'd be chicken tucker without Mum,' Olivia remarked. 'And to me

The McLeavey family at Peter's investiture (clockwise from left) Olivia, Dominic, Hilary, Catherine and Peter, 2012.

Mum has been the backbone of the gallery: she's always there in the background, steering the ship, the calm, sensible, practical one, with her feet on the ground. She's Dad's sounding board. And I think you really need two people to run a gallery. It's such a complex job and you need so many skills – practical, intellectual, social, financial.'[48]

The gallery had been a constant presence for most of Hilary's adult life. 'It was difficult in the early days,' she reflected. 'I often thought that the gallery was really Peter's first wife. He was so driven, and it completely absorbed him. But it was also our livelihood, and because there were slim pickings for many years, I did whatever had to be done.'[49] Over the decades, she had often tended the gallery and helped in the background with book-keeping and other tasks, but she was clear about her priorities: 'Because Peter's always been rather eccentric and even fragile at times, I thought my role was really to keep the home fires burning.' In later years, however, she had enjoyed working every Friday at the gallery. 'It's such a positive environment: people want to be there, they're always interested. And the world of art and artists is so inspiring.'[50]

Hilary noticed that Peter had become more contented and peaceful as he grew older. 'I think he was able to fulfill his dreams at the gallery, and as the years went by he became more secure in himself. He realised that what he'd done was appreciated and acknowledged.' Hilary encouraged Peter when Luit and Jan Bieringa raised the possibility of a documentary film on his life. Initially, he was hesitant. 'He took some convincing,' Luit Bieringa recalled. 'We talked about it, on and off, for years.'[51] Eventually, Peter agreed to participate, and the resulting film, *The man in the hat*, premiered in Wellington in 2009 to packed audiences. Peter declared himself delighted, if rather bemused. 'I don't think Brad Pitt's got anything to worry about at the moment,' he told a reporter, 'but it was very amusing to see myself on the big screen.'[52]

The years that followed were a time of increasing recognition. In 2010, Peter was granted an honorary doctorate by Victoria University; two years later, he was awarded the New Zealand Order of Merit for his services to art.

By 2013, the Peter McLeavey Gallery was one of more than fifty dealer galleries in New Zealand. Most of them were in Auckland, but in Wellington a hub of galleries clustered around the Cuba–Ghuznee Street intersection. Upstairs from Peter was David Alsop's Suite Gallery; next door, in the room formerly occupied by Elva Bett and later Louise Beale, was the artist-run non-profit space, Enjoy. Around the corner in Ghuznee Street were the Bowen Galleries and the Hamish McKay Gallery; on the other side of the intersection was Alison Bartley at Bartley and Company. The newest addition, a two-minute walk away in Cuba Street's Left Bank, was Robert Heald, who had trained with Ivan Anthony in Auckland.

These galleries are part of an ever-shifting landscape. Galleries open, close, relocate; artists and dealers develop new alliances. At a time when the art market is changing dramatically, dealers are more than ever alert to new ways of supporting their artists.

Today, the only certainty is that change will continue. Who knows what will happen tomorrow?

EPILOGUE

You are the future.

In June 2010, Peter sent a letter to his artists, clients and friends to announce that he had been diagnosed with Parkinson's disease. He would continue to run the gallery, he wrote, with the assistance of Hilary and his daughters.[1]

For Catherine and Olivia it was in many ways a natural development. They had grown up with the gallery, helping out at openings, and artists had always occupied a special place in their family life. 'The artists were like diamonds in our world,' Olivia commented. 'They brought all their energy and perspective and excitement. They were such fun.'[2]

In the late 2000s, both sisters studied art history and became more involved in the gallery world – Catherine assisting Peter, and Olivia working for Anna Bibby and Anna Miles in Auckland. 'They really mentored me,' she said. 'At that stage it seemed that Cath would take over Dad's gallery, and I started thinking about opening my own place in Auckland.'

But in the meantime Catherine had decided that fronting the gallery was not for her. 'I felt I wasn't really a salesperson – I'd rather be working more back-of-house.'[3] Moreover, she and her husband Alistair were expecting their second child – a daughter Lily was born in 2010. 'I hope I'll always be involved in the gallery,' Catherine commented, 'but it will be in a different capacity. More like Mum – she was always working behind the scenes.'

Late in 2010, Olivia returned to Wellington to work with her father and enable him to keep the gallery open. In the following year, she launched a website with Catherine's involvement and took over the day-to-day management of the gallery.

The first exhibition on Olivia's watch opened in March 2011: a series of works by John Reynolds based on Colin McCahon's

Olivia and Peter at the gallery, 2010

John Reynolds: McLeavey sat here – recent works on paper, March–April 2011

drawing *McLeavey sat here*, each referencing Peter's long life as a dealer. Reynolds hadn't discussed the work with Peter and felt a little anxious about his reaction. 'But in the end I wanted to do it. I felt if someone had one of those works in their home, wherever, it would absolutely declare "Peter McLeavey sat here", like one of the little blue plaques they put up in London. It was an attempt to show some thanks. And there's a continuity which I was also trying to applaud, the way that Peter was a bridge for me and McCahon and Walters and the other artists, and all the wonderful context of Cuba Street. That was really something to celebrate.'[14]

In 2009, the painter Matt Hunt had joined the Peter McLeavey Gallery; in the following year, two young Aucklanders, Andrew Barber and Nick Austin, began to exhibit. For Peter, it was yet another beginning. Forty-four years and some 500 exhibitions later, he was still focused on the next show – and still tapping out letters on the typewriter. 'It is lovely for me getting to know you,' he wrote to Barber.[5]

> Sitting here, thinking about your work, I keep coming back to its vigour; ambition; and drive. All essential qualities.
>
> And your enthusiasm; so life affirming.
>
> As your work changes and develops and grows the world will impact on you and sometimes you will become afraid.
>
> How do you protect your gift; how do you prevent it from becoming formulaic. The answer lies in the future.
>
> Suffice to say, it is enough for me to be in your corner, and to know, in my heart, that you are the future.
>
> And now. Well I box on, I live every day. I read Proust. The affliction which courses through me comes and goes.
>
> I run towards the Sun. I touch the face of God.

ACKNOWLEDGEMENTS

This book owes its existence to the extraordinary generosity and trust of so many people. First of all, Peter McLeavey, who handed me the keys to his archive and gave me free rein to develop the project. Peter and his wife Hilary have been endlessly helpful and encouraging, patiently answering my many questions. Their children, Catherine, Olivia and Dominic, contributed their stories, while Peter's siblings, Michael McLeavey and Marie Oliver, also provided essential information. Thank you all so much – it's truly been a privilege and a pleasure to work with you.

To those who agreed to be interviewed: your stories and impressions have hugely enriched this book. I'm grateful to Laurence Aberhart, Ivan Anthony, Tim Beaglehole, Luit Bieringa, the late Don Binney, Ivan Bootham, Reverend Ian Brown, Les Cleveland, Lyn and Frank Corner, Tim and Sherrah Francis, Sir David Gascoigne, Howard Greive and Gabrielle McCone, Bill Hammond, Peter Ireland, Hamish Keith, Richard Killeen and Margreta Chance, Janne Land, Neil McGrath, Andrew McLeod, Liz Maw, Milly Paris, Peter Peryer, John Reynolds, Peter Robinson, the late Ian Scott and Nan Corson, Sir John Todd, Yvonne Todd, Warren Viscoe, Dame Robin White and several collectors who wish to remain anonymous.

Many others provided information in conversations, emails and letters, and I'd like to thank Gretchen Albrecht, Billy Apple and Mary Morrison, Grant Banbury, Gerald Barnett, Jim Barr and Mary Barr, Jan Bieringa, Peter Black, Patricia Bosshard, the L Budd estate, Victoria Carr, John Casserley, Derek Cowie, Tim Curnow, Alison Disbrowe, Kathlene Fogarty, Marti Friedlander, Adam Gifford, John Gow, Jeffrey Harris, Mark Hutchins, Dene Illingworth, Stephen Lachman, Tony

Toss Woollaston painting *Above Wellington*, photographed by Peter McLeavey, 1985

Lane, the Len Lye Foundation, Hamish McKay, Malcolm McNeill, Robin Maconie, Bill Milbank, James Mollison, Milan Mrkusich, Jenny Neligan, Sam Neill, Gregory O'Brien, Neil Robertson, Lesleigh Salinger, Marie Shannon, Michael Smither, Daniel Thomas, Barbara Tuck, Linda Tyler, Don Wood and Philip Woollaston.

My special thanks to those who read the manuscript in draft form: your comments and criticisms were invaluable as the text neared completion. I'm indebted to Luit Bieringa, Wystan Curnow, Peter Ireland, Hamish Keith, Gregory O'Brien, Vincent O'Sullivan and Peter Simpson. And to the Ministry for Culture and Heritage, and Creative New Zealand, who supported this project with research and writing grants: thank you. There would have been no book without your assistance.

Once again, it has been a delight to work with the incredibly able, committed, and good-humoured team at Te Papa Press: Claire Murdoch, who provided crucial feedback as the manuscript developed; Odessa Owens, who saw the book through the press with such flair, patience and tireless attention to detail; and Sue Beaton, Barbara Graham, Elizabeth Heritage, Hannah Newport-Watson and Angela Radford. Jane Parkin edited the manuscript with sensitivity and insight, Alan Deare brought a fresh approach to the design, Rebecca Lal, Louise Belcher and Mike Wagg were meticulous proofreaders, and Robin Briggs created the substantial index. I'd also like to thank the skilled staff in Te Papa's Image Services Team – photographer Michael Hall, imaging technician Jeremy Glyde and image programming coordinator Julie Ann Larsen.

For advice and help with research enquiries, I'm grateful to the staff of museums, dealer galleries and libraries throughout the country, especially Victoria Boyack, Martin Lewis, Tony Mackle, Rebecca Rice, Megan Tamati-Quennell and Jennifer Twist (Te Papa); Ron Brownson (Auckland Art Gallery Toi o Tāmaki); Caroline McBride (EH McCormick Research Library, Auckland Art Gallery Toi o Tāmaki); Rebekah Clements (Te Manawa Museum of Art, Science and History); Bev Eng (Dowse Art Museum); Sian van Dyk (Sarjeant Gallery Te Whare o Rehua Whanganui); and Peter Vangioni (Christchurch Art Gallery Te Puna o Waiwhetu).

My thanks to everyone who granted copyright permissions, including many of those mentioned above. Considerable time and effort was expended in tracing copyright holders, and I would like to offer my sincere apologies for any omissions.

Finally, I owe a huge debt to my friends and family, who took a keen interest in the project, but also provided plenty of fun, silliness and diversion along the way. Thanks to all the Trevelyans, Canes,

Hansen-Canes (Tessa and Jack) and Williamses, especially my parents, Netty and Tony Trevelyan, and the next generation – Ben and Libby Trevelyan, and Frances and Louis Williams. Last, but most important of all, thanks to my partner Chris Cane, whose generosity, good humour and perceptiveness have sustained me throughout this project.

Peter McLeavey Gallery Contemporary New Zealand Painting

Laurence aberhart

Matt Hunt

Upcoming Exhibitions

W. D. Hammond

Brendon Wilkinson

auckland art fair 2009

andrew McLeod

147 Cuba Street Wellington New Zealand
P O Box 11052 Telephone 847 356 723 334

LIST OF EXHIBITIONS

1968–2013

This appendix is based on two sources in the Peter McLeavey Gallery archive. The exhibition register provides a summary list of exhibitions, but more detailed information (invitation, catalogue, correspondence, slides and photographs, and so on) is found in the exhibition files, numbered from 1 to 534.[1]

1968–1969

1 *MT Woollaston: Paintings, drawings and watercolours*, 4–21 Sept 1968
2 *Colin McCahon: The Northland panels: a series of 8 paintings*, 23 Oct–16 Nov 1968
3 *Juliet Peter, Roy Cowan, Peter Wilde: Pottery*, 27 Nov–7 Dec 1968
4 *Don Driver: Painted reliefs*, 19 Mar–5 Apr 1969
5 *Michael Smither: Paintings*, 16 Apr–3 May 1969
6 *Gordon Walters: Paintings*, 6–24 May 1969
7 *Michael Illingworth: Paintings*, 17 June–5 July 1969
8 *Colin McCahon: Paintings*, 22 July–9 Aug 1969
9 *Colin McCahon: A retrospective exhibition of paintings and watercolours from the collection of RN O'Reilly*, 18–29 Aug 1969
10 *Milan Mrkusich: Paintings*, 2–20 Sept 1969
11 *Suzanne Goldberg: Paintings*, 7–24 Oct 1969
12 *MT Woollaston: Watercolours and drawings*, 4–14 Nov 1969
13 *Barry Brickell: Pots*, 26 Nov–6 Dec 1969

1970–1974

14 *Ray Thorburn: Paintings*, 24 Mar–11 Apr 1970
15 *Toss Woollaston: Drawings and watercolours at Palmerston North Art Gallery*, Mar 1970[2]
16 *Carl Sydow: Sculpture*, 14 Apr–1 May 1970[3]
17 *Patrick Hanly: 15 prints*, 12–22 May 1970
18 *Robert Ellis: Paintings*, 26 May–10 June 1970
19 *Ian Scott: Paintings*, 16 June–3 July 1970
20 *Wong Sing Tai: 6 Yantras – paintings*, 7–24 July 1970
21 *Don Binney: Paintings and drawings*, 28 July–14 Aug 1970
22 *Michael Smither: Paintings (14 Stations of the Cross, in memory of Rita Angus)*, 29 Sept–16 Oct 1970
23 *MT Woollaston: A retrospective exhibition of portraits*, 19–30 Oct 1970
23b *Don Binney: Grackle, Veracruz – prints*, Nov 1970[4]
24 *Watercolours, prints and multiples* (Binney, Hanly, McCahon, Smither, Walters, Robin White), 1–24 Dec 1970
25 *Don Driver: Paintings*, 2–12 Mar 1971
26 *The Californian image: Watercolours, drawings and prints by Robert Bechtle, Philip Linhares, Arthur Okamura, Kenneth Price*, 23 Mar–2 Apr 1971[5]

27 *Colin McCahon: View from the top of the cliff – watercolours*, 6–23 Apr 1971
28 *Milan Mrkusich: Paintings*, 27 Apr–14 May 1971
29 *Carl Sydow: Sculpture*, 25 May–11 June 1971
30 *Wong Sing Tai: Suddenly it dawned on me – watercolours*, 13–30 July 1971[6]
31 *Gordon Walters: Paintings*, 17 Aug–1 Sept 1971
32 *MT Woollaston: Paintings*, 12 Sept–1 Oct 1971
33 *Sue [Suzanne] Goldberg: Paintings*, 18–29 Oct 1971
34 *Michael Smither: Paintings*, 30 Nov–17 Dec 1971[7]
35 *Jeffrey Harris: Paintings*, 14 Feb–3 Mar 1972
36 *Colin McCahon: Paintings*, 6–24 Mar 1972
37 *Milan Mrkusich: Paintings*, 27 Mar–14 Apr 1972
38 *Philip Trusttum: Recent work*, 17 Apr–5 May 1972
39 *Robin White: Prints*, 26 June–7 July 1972
40 *Barry Brickell: Pots*, 17 July–4 Aug 1972
41 *Michael Illingworth: 9 untitled paintings*, 28 Aug–14 Sept 1972
42 *Michael Smither: Land and sea – a suite of watercolours*, 9–27 Oct 1972
43 *MT Woollaston: 2 recent oils*, 30 Oct–17 Nov 1972
44 *Prints* (Hanly, Kinross Maidens, Smither, Thorburn, Robin White), 4–22 Dec 1972[8]
45 *Ray Thorburn: Paintings and drawings*, 20 Feb–2 Mar 1973
46 The exhibition register is annotated, 'I presume that I must have had one stock show during this period' (April 1973).
47 *Milan Mrkusich: Recent paintings*, 24 Apr–11 May 1973
48 *Philip Trusttum: Canterbury landscape*, 22 May–8 June 1973
49 *Michael Smither: Domestic paintings, 1966–1973*, 3–21 July 1973
50 *Pat Hanly: Recent paintings*, 30 July–17 Aug 1973
51 *Carl Sydow: Sculpture*, 15–29 Aug 1973[9]
52 *Colin McCahon: Recent works*, 11–28 Sept 1973[10]
53 *MT Woollaston: The Greymouth years*, 30 Oct–16 Nov 1973
54 *Don Binney: London 1972–1973 – paintings and drawings*, 27 Nov–7 Dec 1973
55 *Works on paper* (Hanly, Harris, McCahon, Smither, Robin White), 10–24 Dec 1973
56 *Jeffrey Harris: Paintings and works on paper*, 26 Mar–12 Apr 1974
57 *Pat Hanly: Loveplates – 20 oil paintings*, 14–31 May 1974
58 *Philip Trusttum: Recent paintings*, 25 June–2 July 1974
59 *Ian Scott: Paintings*, 9–26 July 1974
60 *New Zealand on paper* (Driver, Harris, Killeen,[11] McCahon, Mrkusich, Smither, Trusttum, Walters, Robin White, Woollaston), 6–23 Aug 1974
61 *Milan Mrkusich: Recent works*, 27 Aug–13 Sept 1974
62 *Michael Smither: Works on paper*, 17 Sept–4 Oct 1974
63 *Gordon Walters: Gouaches, 1951–1959*, 15 Oct–1 Nov 1974
64 *Colin McCahon: Recent paintings*, 5–22 Nov 1974
65 *New Zealand works on paper, 1935–1958* (Angus, McCahon, Spencer Bower, Woollaston), and *Michael Smither: 3 oil paintings*, 26 Nov–6 Dec 1974
66 *Watercolours, drawings and prints* [and ceramics] (Brickell, Hanly, Killeen, McCahon, Scott, Sydow, Smither, Robin White), 10–24 Dec 1974

1975–1979

67 *Philip Trusttum: 8 recent oil paintings*, 11–28 Mar 1975
68 *Richard Killeen: Recent paintings*, 1–19 Apr 1975
69 *Ian Scott: 12 recent oils on paper*, and *MT Woollaston: 12 watercolours and drawings from life, 1936–1971*, 22 Apr–9 May 1975
70 *Carl Sydow: Sculpture*, 22 May–6 June 1975
71 *Michael Smither: Portraits and silkscreen prints*, 15 July–1 Aug 1975
72 *3 regionalists: Olivia Spencer Bower, A Lois White, Robin White*, 19–31 Aug 1975
73 *3 painters: Tony Lane, Robert McLeod, Allen Maddox*, 2–19 Sept 1975

74 *Michael Illingworth: Paintings, 1962–1973*, 23 Sept–10 Oct 1975
75 *Milan Mrkusich: Corner works, 1968–1975*, 4–21 Nov 1975
76 *Philip Trusttum: 7 paintings, 1965–1972*, 1–5 Dec 1975
77 *Watercolours, drawings and prints* (Hanly, Illingworth, Killeen, McCahon, Scott, Smither, Trusttum, Walters, Robin White), 9–24 Dec 1975
78 *Don Binney: Paintings and drawings*, 16 Mar–2 Apr 1976
79 *Pat Hanly: Suburban gems – 9 watercolours, 1971–1975*, 6–23 Apr 1976
80 *Gordon Walters: Recent paintings*, 27 Apr–14 May 1976
81 *MT Woollaston: Recent paintings and works on paper*, 19 May–11 June 1976
82 *Milan Mrkusich: Collages and reliefs, 1959–1963*, 15 June–2 July 1976
83 *Helen FV [Flora] Scales: 43 paintings, 1939–1970*, 5–16 July 1976[12]
84 *Richard Killeen: Recent paintings and watercolours*, 20 July–6 Aug 1976
85 *Colin McCahon: Recent works*, 17 Aug–3 Sept 1976
86 *Michael Smither: Recent paintings*, 7–24 Sept 1976
87 *Philip Trusttum: Recent paintings*, 9–26 Nov 1976[13]
88 *Works on paper* (Hanly, McCahon, Mrkusich, Scott, Smither, Charles Tole, Trusttum, Walters, Robin White), 7–24 Dec 1976
89 *Pat Hanly: Paintings, 1975–1976*, 22 Feb–11 Mar 1977
90 *Allen Maddox: Recent paintings*, 15 Mar–1 Apr 1977[14]
91 *Jeffrey Harris: 24 paintings, 1976–1977*, 3–20 May 1977
92 *Ian Scott: 6 paintings, 1977*, 8–24 June 1977
93 *Colin McCahon: Angels and bed*, 5–22 July 1977
94 *Charles Tole: Paintings, 1945–1977*, 9–26 Aug 1977
94a *Colin McCahon: The Second Gate Series, 1962*, 30 Aug–16 Sept 1977[15]
95 *Milan Mrkusich: Recent paintings and works on paper*, 20 Sept–7 Oct 1977
96 *A Lois White: 22 works on paper, 1926–1945*, 18 Oct–4 Nov 1977
97 *Michael Smither: Recent paintings*, 15 Nov–2 Dec 1977
98 *Works on paper* (Binney, Hanly, Harris, McCahon, Maddox, Mrkusich, Smither, Trusttum, Walters, Robin White), 6–24 Dec 1977
99 *MT Woollaston: 6 oil paintings, 1974–1977*, 7–31 Mar 1978
100 *Michael Illingworth: Paintings, works on paper and constructions, 1959–1977*, 4–21 Apr 1978
101 *Jeffrey Harris: 12 paintings, December 1969–September 1970*, 9–26 May 1978
102 *Allen Maddox: Paintings*, 13–30 June 1978
103 *Laurence Aberhart: 19 photographs, 1974–1978*, 4–21 July 1978
104 *Gordon Walters: Paintings* [and a screenprint], 25 July–12 Aug 1978
105 *Robin White: Paintings, watercolours, drawings and prints*, 29 Aug–15 Sept 1978
106 *Richard Killeen: Recent paintings*, 26 Sept–13 Oct 1978
107 *Milan Mrkusich: 8 paintings of 1977 and 1978*, 17 Oct–10 Nov 1978
108 *Michael Smither: 7 paintings of 1977 and 1978*, 14 Nov–1 Dec 1978
109 *Prints, works on paper and photographs* (Hanly, Harris, Killeen, Maddox, Mrkusich, Peryer, Scott, Smither, Charles Tole, Gary Tricker, Walters, A Lois White, Robin White), 5–22 Dec 1978
110 *Philip Trusttum: 4 paintings of 1977–1978*, 27 Feb–16 Mar 1979
111 *Ian Scott: 12 recent paintings on paper and canvas*, 20 Mar–6 Apr 1979
112 *Jeffrey Harris: Judith – a suite of 10 conté drawings*, 10–27 Apr 1979
113 *John Tole and Charles Tole: A retrospective exhibition of paintings*, 1–18 May 1979
114 *MT Woollaston: 2 recent oils* [and related works], 22 May–8 June 1979
115 *Milan Mrkusich: The first one man exhibition*, 26 June–13 July 1979
116 *Jacqueline Fraser: Sculpture*, 17 July–3 Aug 1979
117 *The new image: 12 contemporary photographers, curated by Peter Ireland* (Aberhart, Terry Austin, Rhondda Bosworth, Dinah Bradley, Gillian Chaplin, Gavin Colthart, Bruce Foster, Paul Gilbert, Jenkinson, Christine Lloyd-Fitt, Jim Payne, Peryer), 7–24 Aug 1979
118 *Richard Killeen: Recent paintings*, 18 Sept–5 Oct 1979
119 *New Zealand on paper, part II* (Gary Tricker, Walters, Robin White), 9–19 Oct 1979
120 *Colin McCahon: Paintings*, 30 Oct–16 Nov 1979

121 *Billy Apple: Censure: The given as an art-political statement*, 19–30 Nov 1979
122 *Prints, photographs and works on paper* (Aberhart, Hanly, Jenkinson, Killeen, McCahon, Peryer, Scott, Smither, Charles Tole, Gary Tricker, Walters, Robin White), 4–24 Dec 1979

1980–1984

123 *Ian Scott: 5 paintings*, 26 Feb–14 Mar 1980
124 *Christine Hellyar: Folds and keeps – 10 sculptures*, 18 Mar–4 Apr 1980
125 *Milan Mrkusich: 5 paintings*, 8 Apr–2 May 1980
126 *Milan Mrkusich: A retrospective exhibition of works from stock*, 5–16 May 1980
127 *Warren Viscoe: An installation*, 20 May–6 June 1980
128 *Michael Illingworth: Paintings, 1972–1980*, 10–27 June 1980
129 *Gordon Walters: Recent paintings*, 1–18 July 1980
130 *Charles Tole: Paintings, 1945–1980*, 22 July–8 Aug 1980
131 *Colin McCahon: 2 recent oils*, 12–29 Aug 1980
132 *Jacqueline Fraser: An installation*, 2–19 Sept 1980
133 *Richard Killeen: 4 cut-outs of 1980*, 23 Sept–10 Oct 1980
[133a] Untitled group exhibition (Fraser, Illingworth, Maddox, Mrkusich, Walters), Oct 1980[16]
134 *Gary Tricker: 17 etchings, 1963–1980*, 28 Oct–14 Nov 1980
135 *Michael Smither: 5 pieces for Gordon Burt*, 18 Nov–5 Dec 1980
136 *Prints, sculpture, photographs and works on paper* (Aberhart, Fraser, Hanly, Harris, Hellyar, Illingworth, Killeen, Mrkusich, Smither, Gary Tricker, Viscoe, Walters, Robin White), 6–24 Dec 1980
137 *Pat Hanly: Golden age – paintings of 1978–1980*, 8–26 Mar 1981
138 *Aspects of New Zealand regionalism* (Russell Clark, Ida Eise, Rhona Haszard, Charles Tole, A Lois White, Hilda Wiseman, Younghusband), 7–24 Apr 1981
139 *Tony Lane: Recent paintings and works on paper*, 25 Apr–15 May 1981
140 *Ian Scott: Recent paintings*, 16 May–5 June 1981
141 *Milan Mrkusich: 5 recent paintings*, 6 June–3 July 1981
142 *Neil Dawson: Recent sculpture*, 12–31 July 1981
143 *Laurence Aberhart: 23 photographs*, 1–21 Aug 1981
144 *Jacqueline Fraser: Recent sculpture*, 29 Aug–18 Sept 1981
145 *Richard Killeen: Recent work*, 19 Sept–9 Oct 1981
146 *Jeffrey Harris: 15 paintings on paper, 1968–1980*, 10–30 Oct 1981
147 *Colin McCahon: An exhibition to mark the centenary of Parihaka*, 2–8 Nov 1981
148 *Gordon Walters: 7 paintings*, 10–27 Nov 1981
149 *Works on paper, photographs and sculpture* (Aberhart, Janet Bayly, Dinah Bradley, Fraser, Hanly, Peter Hannken, Harris, Hellyar, Killeen, Lane, McCahon, Mrkusich, Peebles, Peryer, Scott, Smither, Walters, Robin White), 5–24 Dec 1981
150 *Robin White: 10 monoprints and works on paper*, 2–19 Mar 1982
151 *Robert Jesson: Sculpture and constructions*, 23 Mar–9 Apr 1982
152 The exhibition register is annotated, 'To Sydney Biennale' (Apr 1982)
153 *Milan Mrkusich: 6 recent works*, 4–21 May 1982
154 *MT Woollaston: 40 years on paper*, 1–18 June 1982
155 *Tony Lane: Recent paintings*, 22 June–9 July 1982
156 *Billy Apple: Sculpture [How Billy Apple came to be selling pieces of the Peter McLeavey Gallery]*, 20 July–7 Aug 1982[17]
157 *Charles Tole: 8 paintings, 1974–1982*, 10–27 Aug 1982
158 *Jacqueline Fraser: Sculpture*, 31 Aug–18 Sept 1982
159 *Richard Killeen: 6 recent works*, 28 Sept–15 Oct 1982
160 *Warren Viscoe: Fifteen bird calls – an installation*, 19 Oct–5 Nov 1982
161 *Works on paper, prints, photographs and sculpture* (Aberhart, Janet Bayly, Dinah Bradley, Fraser, Hanly, Peter Hannken, Illingworth, Killeen, Lane, McCahon, Maddox, Mrkusich, Smither), 7–24 Dec 1982
162 *Richard Killeen: Chance and inevitability – a cut-out*, 9–27 Mar 1983
163 *Colin McCahon: 2 recent paintings*, 12 Apr–1 May 1983
164 *Ian Scott: Recent paintings*, 10–28 May 1983

165 *Michael Smither: Works on paper, 1976–1982*, 31 May–18 June 1983
166 *Milan Mrkusich: Paintings, 1982*, 28 June–16 July 1983
167 *Tony Lane: Recent paintings and pastels*, 26 July–13 Aug 1983
168 *Aspects of New Zealand regionalism: Adele Younghusband and the Crown Lynn Potteries*, 24 Aug–10 Sept 1983
169 *Richard Killeen: New work*, 14 Sept–8 Oct 1983
170 *Allen Maddox: Paintings*, 25 Oct–12 Nov 1983
171 *3 artists: Michael Armstrong, Ingrid Banwell and Megan Jenkinson*, 15 Nov–3 Dec 1983
172 *Laurence Aberhart: About 62 black and white photographs, 1982–1983*, 6–24 Dec 1983
173 *Jacqueline Fraser: Poi poi*, 28 Feb–17 Mar 1984
174 *Robin White: Beginners' guide to Gilbertese*, 20 Mar–7 Apr 1984
175 *Warren Viscoe: New works*, 10 Apr–4 May 1984
176 *Milan Mrkusich: Recent paintings*, 8–26 May 1984
177 *Michael Illingworth: Paintings, 1979–1984*, 5–23 June 1984
[178] The exhibition register is annotated 'stock'; there is no exhibition file (June–July 1984)
179 *Pat Hanly: 11 large watercolours*, 14 July–4 Aug 1984
180 *Richard Killeen: Recent works*, 7–25 Aug 1984
181 *Tony Lane: Recent paintings*, 4–22 Sept 1984
182 *Warren Viscoe, Colin McCahon, Milan Mrkusich: Works from stock*, 25 Sept–13 Oct 1984[18]
183 *Julian Dashper and John Reynolds: Recent works*, 22 Oct–10 Nov 1984
184 *Charles Tole: 10 paintings*, 13–31 Nov 1984
185 *Peter Peryer: Recent photographs*, 8–24 Dec 1984

1985–1989

186 *Ian Scott: 6 paintings of 1968–1970*, 26 Feb–16 Mar 1985
187 *Ian Scott: Recent paintings*, 19 Mar–6 Apr 1985
188 *MT Woollaston: 3 recent paintings*, 9–27 Apr 1985
189 *Warren Viscoe: New works, 1985*, 7–25 May 1985
190 *Janet Bayly: 24 photographs*, 28 May–15 June 1985
191 *Works on paper* (Killeen, Lane, Reynolds, Walters), 18 June–6 July 1985
192 *Maria Olsen: 5 recent sculptures*, 9–27 July 1985
193 *Robin White: From Kiribati – recent woodblock prints*, 30 July–17 Aug 1985
194 *Derek Cowie: Recent paintings*, 20 Aug–7 Sept 1985
195 *Tony Lane: 17 recent paintings*, 10–28 Sept 1985
196 *Richard Killeen: 4 recent cut-outs*, 1–19 Oct 1985
197 *Jacqueline Fraser: 3 recent sculptures*, 22 Oct–9 Nov 1985
198 *Allen Maddox: Recent paintings and works on paper*, 12 Nov–1 Dec 1985
199 *Works by MT Woollaston, Gordon Walters, Laurence Aberhart and Derek Cowie* [and Philip Trusttum], 2–7 Dec 1985
200 *Barry Brickell: Some stations on the Main Trunk – a series of 14 ceramic panels*, 10–24 Dec 1985
201 *Warren Viscoe: Long waters – 4 wood assemblages*, 5–22 Mar 1986
202 *Laurence Aberhart: Recent photographs*, 1–26 Apr 1986
203 *Julian Dashper: Paintings of 1986*, 6–24 May 1986
204 *Milan Mrkusich: 5 paintings*, 27 May–21 June 1986
205 *John Reynolds: 8 works of 1986*, 24 June–12 July 1986
206 *MT Woollaston: Above Wellington, 1986, with preliminary drawings and watercolours*, 15 July–2 Aug 1986
207 *Philip Trusttum: Recent paintings*, 5–23 Aug 1986
208 *Jacqueline Fraser: 6 recent sculptures*, 26 Aug–13 Sept 1986
209 *Derek Cowie: Recent paintings*, 16 Sept–4 Oct 1986
210 *Gordon Walters: 6 recent paintings*, 7–25 Oct 1986
211 *Richard Killeen: 4 new works*, 28 Oct–15 Nov 1986
212 *Billy Apple: Recent paintings*, 18 Nov–6 Dec 1986[19]
213 *Julian Dashper and John Reynolds: Omaha Beach – an exhibition to mark 21 years of Peter McLeavey Gallery*, 9–24 Dec 1986[20]

214 *Bill Hammond: 10 recent paintings*, 17 Mar–11 Apr 1987
215 *Barbara Tuck: 8 recent paintings*, 14 Apr–2 May 1987
216 *Jacqueline Fraser: 8 generations*, 5–23 May 1987
217 *Julian Dashper: 7 new works*, 26 May–13 June 1987
218 *Warren Viscoe: The smoke house – a sculpture*, 16 June–4 July 1987
219 *Milan Mrkusich: Paintings and works on paper, 1946–1984*, 7–25 July 1987
220 *Maria Olsen: 5 paintings*, 28 July–15 Aug 1987
221 *Gavin Chilcott: Recent paintings*, 18 Aug–5 Sept 1987
222 *Julian Schnabel: 4 etchings*, 8–26 Sept 1987
223 *Warren Viscoe: Entries-exits – an installation*, 12–26 Sept 1987[21]
224 *John Reynolds: Recent work*, 29 Sept–17 Oct 1987
225 *Derek Cowie: Recent paintings*, 20 Oct–7 Nov 1987
226 *Richard Killeen: Recent work*, 10–28 Nov 1987
227 *Robin White: Recent monoprints and woodblock prints including 28 days in Kiribati*, 1–24 Dec 1987
228 *Ian Scott: Recent paintings*, 8–26 Mar 1988
229 *Jacqueline Fraser: Avondale – 6 recent sculptures*, 29 Mar–16 Apr 1988
230 *WD Hammond: Recent paintings*, 19 Apr–7 May 1988
231 *John Reynolds: New works*, 10–28 May 1988
232 *MT Woollaston: 8 paintings of 1985–1987*, 31 May–25 June 1988
233 See *Derek Cowie: Recent paintings*, 7–25 March 1989 (below)[22]
234 *Billy Apple: Recent paintings*, 28 June–16 July 1988
235 *Warren Viscoe: Recent sculpture*, 19 July–6 Aug 1988
236 *Richard Killeen: New works*, 9–27 Aug 1988
237 *Julian Dashper: 13 recent paintings*, 30 Aug–24 Sept 1988
238 *Gordon Walters: Recent works*, 27 Sept–15 Oct 1988
239 *Maria Olsen: Recent paintings*, 25 Oct–12 Nov 1988
240 *Milan Mrkusich: Recent paintings*, 15 Nov–3 Dec 1988
241 *Works on paper* (Aberhart, Cowie, Fraser, Hammond, Peter Ransom, Robin White), 6–24 Dec 1988
242 Three works from stock exhibitions, Feb 1989:
   i. *Small New Zealand paintings* (Apple, Cowie, Dashper, Hammond, Illingworth, Mrkusich, Reynolds, Walters, Woollaston)
   ii. *5 sculptures* (Fraser, Viscoe)
   iii. Untitled exhibition (Apple, Cowie, Dashper, Illingworth, Killeen, Mrkusich, Reynolds, Viscoe)
233[23] *Derek Cowie: Recent paintings*, 7–25 Mar 1989
243 *MT Woollaston: 1 large recent painting and 10 works on paper, 1940–1979*, 28 Mar–15 Apr 1989
244 *John Reynolds: New work*, 18 Apr–13 May 1989
245 *Laurence Aberhart: Recent photographs taken in the American south, October 1988*, and *Ian Scott: 3 paintings, 1969*, 16–27 May 1989
246 *Charles Tole: 14 paintings*, 30 May–17 June 1989
247 *New Wellington art: Dale Anthony, Ivan Anthony and Derek Cowie*, 27 June–15 July 1989
248 *Helm Ruifrok: Recent paintings and works on paper*, 18 July–5 Aug 1989
249 *Aspects of New Zealand art, part III: Paintings and works on paper of the 1950s and 1960s* (Rudolf Gopas, McCahon, Mrkusich, John Pine Snadden, Walters, Woollaston), 15–26 Aug 1989
250 *W Hammond: 6 painted works on pre-pasted wallpaper*, 29 Aug–23 Sept 1989
251 *Julian Dashper: 10 paintings, works on paper and photographs*, 26 Sept–14 Oct 1989
252 *Richard Killeen: 6 fish paintings*, 17 Oct–4 Nov 1989
253 *Jacqueline Fraser: 6 sculptures*, 14 Nov–2 Dec 1989
254 *New works by Billy Apple, W Hammond, Peter Ransom, John Reynolds, Helm Ruifrok, Ian Scott, Warren Viscoe and Robin White*, 5–24 Dec 1989

1990–1994

255 *John Reynolds: Recent works*, 27 Feb–17 Mar 1990
256 *Laurence Aberhart: 15 recent photographs*, 20 Mar–7 Apr 1990
257 *Ian Scott: 6 recent paintings*, 10–28 Apr 1990

258 *Gail Wright: 4 acrylic paintings of 1990*, 8–26 May 1990
259 *11 works* (Aberhart, Apple, Hammond, McCahon, Mrkusich, Walters), 29 May–16 June 1990
260 *Imants Tillers: Recent paintings*, 19 June–14 July 1990
261 *Gordon Walters: Recent paintings*, 17 July–4 Aug 1990
262 *Barbara Tuck: Recent paintings*, 7–25 Aug 1990
263 *Julian Dashper: Recent work*, 4–22 Sept 1990
264 *Richard Killeen: Destruction of the circle – 8 recent works*, 25 Sept–13 Oct 1990
265 *Milan Mrkusich: Recent paintings*, 16 Oct–10 Nov 1990
266 *WD Hammond: 9 paintings based on a recent voyage to the Auckland Islands*, 13 Nov–1 Dec 1990
267 *Les Cleveland: 15 vintage photographs of the 1950s*, 4–24 Dec 1990
268 *Derek Cowie: Recent works*, 5–23 Mar 1991
269 *MT Woollaston: Recent paintings and works on paper*, 26 Mar–20 Apr 1991
270 *John Reynolds: Recent works*, 23 Apr–18 May 1991
271 *Jacqueline Fraser: Two garden sculptures*, 21 May–8 June 1991
272 *Bill Henson: Photographs*, 18 June–13 July 1991
273 *Helm Ruifrok: Recent paintings*, 16 July–3 Aug 1991
274 *Imants Tillers: Recent paintings*, 7–31 Aug 1991
275 *Julian Dashper: Recent works*, 3–28 Sept 1991
276 *Warren Viscoe: 3 sculptures*, 1–26 Oct 1991
277 *Richard Killeen: Letters from my father – 5 recent works*, 29 Oct–23 Nov 1991
278 *W Hammond: Recent paintings and lithographs*, 26 Nov–24 Dec 1991
279 *MT Woollaston: Paintings and works on paper*, 10 Mar–4 Apr 1992
280 *Les Cleveland: 17 vintage photographs of Westland*, 7–25 Apr 1992
281 *The selective eye* (Hammond, Illingworth, McCahon, Reynolds, Tillers, Charles Tole), 28 Apr–23 May 1992
282 *Gordon Walters: 6 recent works*, 26 May–20 June 1992
283 *Merit Gröting: Paintings and works on paper*[24] (scheduled for 23 June–18 July 1992; cancelled on 23 June and replaced by exhibition 284)
284 *Julian Dashper/Richard Killeen: Works on paper*, 23 June–18 July 1992
285 *Ian Scott: 13 recent paintings and a painting of 1966*, 21 July–15 Aug 1992
286 *Barbara Tuck: 4 recent paintings*, 18 Aug–12 Sept 1992
287 *Julian Dashper: Chain frame – a multiple*, 15 Sept–10 Oct 1992
288 *Richard Killeen: Recent works*, 13 Oct–7 Nov 1992
289 *Warren Viscoe: Coral gardens, cultured pearls – an installation*, 10 Nov–5 Dec 1992
290 *Barry Brickell: Resurrection of the Goddess – 7 recent pots*, 8–24 Dec 1992
291 *An exhibition for OEM*[25] (Dashper, Hammond, Henson, Reynolds, Tillers, Walters), 15–27 Feb 1993
292 *Jacqueline Fraser: New sculpture*, 2–27 Mar 1993
293 *W Hammond: 4 recent works*, 30 Mar–24 Apr 1993
294 *Ian Scott: 6 Lattice paintings*, 27 Apr–22 May 1993
295 *Steven Hemmings: 8 recent oil paintings*, 25 May–12 June 1993
296 *Laurence Aberhart: 64 photographs*, 15 June–10 July 1993
297 *Imants Tillers: 5 Pollock paintings*, 13 July–7 Aug 1993
298 *Peter Robinson: Recent paintings*, 10 Aug–4 Sept 1993
299 *The right stuff* (Dashper, Fraser, Hammond, Viscoe, Walters), 7 Sept–2 Oct 1993
300 *John Reynolds: 2 recent large paintings*, 5–30 Oct 1993
301 *Richard Killeen: Measuring tools – 9 recent works*, 2–27 Nov 1993
302 *Julian Dashper: 2 artworks of the 1980s*, 30 Nov–24 Dec 1993
303 *Warren Viscoe: Coral gardens, cultured pearls – an installation*, 3–27 Mar 1994[26]
304 *Richard Killeen: Dead woman, dead man – paintings and drawings, 1969*, 29 Mar–23 Apr 1994
305 *W Dunning: Time branching time: 13 recent works on paper*, 26 Apr–21 May 1994
306 *MT Woollaston: 6 recent paintings*, 24 May–18 June 1994
307 *WD Hammond: Recent paintings and drawings*, 21 June–16 July 1994
308 *Gordon Walters: 6 recent paintings*, 19 July–13 Aug 1994
309 *Barbara Tuck: 5 recent paintings*, 16 Aug–10 Sept 1994

310 *Colin McCahon: 7 paintings, 1940–1975*, 12–24 Sept 1994
311 *Artworks by Mark Braunias, W Dunning, Valerie Nielsen*, 27 Sept–15 Oct 1994
312 *Richard Killeen: 2 texts – paintings*, 18 Oct–12 Nov 1994
313 *Peter Robinson: 100%* [paintings and constructions], 15 Nov–3 Dec 1994
314 *Jacqueline Fraser and John Reynolds: Recent small works*, 6–24 Dec 1994

1995–1999

315 *Colin McCahon, Bill Henson, Michael Illingworth: 3 large works*, 9–25 Feb 1995
316 *John Reynolds: Recent works*, 28 Feb–25 May 1995
317 *Jacqueline Fraser: The deification of Mrs Walker* [sculpture], 28 Mar–22 Apr 1995
318 *Les Cleveland: 18 vintage photographs*, 25 Apr–13 May 1995
319 *Bill Hammond unplugged: A selection of works from stock*, 23 May–10 June 1995
320 *Simon Endres: Mass is best is mass by Plastikman (Tm.26) – recent sculpture*, 13 June–8 July 1995
321 *W Dunning: Timetables – eight drawings*, 11 July–5 Aug 1995
322 *Laurence Aberhart: 22 photographs*, 8 Aug–2 Sept 1995
323 *Shiny things* (Hammond, Henson, Illingworth, Nielsen, Reynolds, Walters, Woollaston), 5–23 Sept 1995
324 *Richard Killeen: Here sits Harold, king of the English – new works*, 26 Sept–21 Oct 1995
325 *WD Hammond: Living large – 6 recent works*, 24 Oct–11 Nov 1995
326 *Bill Henson: 8 recent photographs*, 14 Nov–2 Dec 1995
327 *Mark Braunias: 7 paintings*, 5–23 Dec 1995
328 *Peter Robinson, Ian Scott, MT Woollaston, Richard Killeen: Works from stock*, 20 Jan–2 Mar 1996
329 *MT Woollaston: 5 recent paintings*, 5–30 Mar 1996
330 *Warren Viscoe: Recent work*, 2–27 Apr 1996
331 *New Zealand views: 20 hand-tinted silver gelatin photographs made for the New Zealand Government Tourist Department, c.1910–1940*, 30 Apr–18 May 1996
332 *Chris Heaphy: 7 recent paintings*, 21 May–8 June 1996
333 *Barbara Tuck: 6 new paintings*, 11 June–6 July 1996
334 *Robin White: Recent prints*, 9–27 July 1996
335 *Jacqueline Fraser: Recent sculpture*, 30 July–24 Aug 1996
336 *Valerie Nielsen: 4 recent paintings*, 27 Aug–21 Sept 1996
337 *Several exceptionally good paintings and works on paper* (Fomison, McCahon, Walters, Woollaston), 24 Sept–12 Oct 1996
338 *Richard Killeen: Objects and images from the Cult of the Hook and other works*, 15 Oct–9 Nov 1996
339 *Peter Robinson: Home and away – 24 paintings on paper*, 12–30 Nov 1996
340 *WD Hammond: Gangland – 4 recent works*, 3–24 Dec 1996
341 *Sacred and profane: Works by Bill Henson and Tony Fomison*, 30 Dec 1996–9 Jan 1997
342 *Family values: An exhibition of 4 artworks* (Aberhart, Fraser, Robinson, Viscoe), 11 Jan–1 Mar 1997
343 *John Reynolds: Temptation of Saint Anthony – recent paintings*, 4–29 Mar 1997
344 *Masterworks of 19th century New Zealand photography* (James Bragge, FA Coxhead, Frank Denton, Herbert Deveril, Arthur James Iles, Josiah Martin, Muir and Moodie, Pulman studio, Edward Smallwood Richards, Charles Spencer, Tyree brothers), 5–19 Apr 1997
345 *Mark Braunias: Gank – recent paintings and works on paper*, 22 Apr–17 May 1997
346 *W Dunning: Antipodean pictorial – 14 paintings on paper*, 20 May–14 June 1997
347 *Peter Robinson: Canon fodder – an installation in 4 parts*, 18 June–12 July 1997
348 *McCahon to Robinson* (Fraser, Killeen, McCahon, Robinson, Walters), 15 July–9 Aug 1997
349 *Warren Viscoe: In the dead of night – recent sculpture*, 26 Aug–20 Sept 1997
350 *Chris Heaphy: Finding the gap – 2 paintings*, 23 Sept–11 Oct 1997
351 *Richard Killeen: Paths of seniority – recent works*, 14 Oct–8 Nov 1997
352 *Endres + Nielsen: Recent works*, 11–29 Nov 1997
353 *WD Hammond: Recent paintings*, 2–24 Dec 1997
354 *On travel: Paintings by MT Woollaston, Richard Killeen, Peter Robinson*, 28 Dec 1997–9 Jan 1998
355 *New Zealand on paper: Specially commissioned works by W Dunning, Simon Endres, WD Hammond, Valerie Nielsen, Richard Killeen, Chris Heaphy, John Reynolds, Peter Robinson, Mark Braunias, Barbara Tuck*, 10 Jan–5 Feb 1998

356 *The sixties: Vintage photographs by Gary Baigent and Les Cleveland*, 7–28 Feb 1998
357 *Richard Killeen: Interiors – paintings, 1968–1969*, 3–28 Mar 1998
358 *What we do here* (Aberhart, Baigent, Braunias, Cleveland, Dunning, Endres, Fraser, Hammond, Heaphy, Illingworth, Killeen, McCahon, Nielsen, Reynolds, Robinson, Smither, Tuck, Viscoe, Walters, Robin White, Woollaston), 7 Apr–30 May 1998
359 *Peter Robinson: Recent paintings and silkscreen prints*, 9–27 June 1998
360 *Jacqueline Fraser: A cultural guide for the elite – recent sculpture*, 30 June–25 July 1998
361 *MT Woollaston: Several classic works*, 28 July–15 Aug 1998
362 *W Dunning: Recent paintings and works on paper*, 18 Aug–12 Sept 1998
363 *Laurence Aberhart: The shadow has a dream – 21 photographs*, 15 Sept–3 Oct 1998
364 *Richard Killeen: 10 paintings in tins*, 6–31 Oct 1998
365 *Blood brothers* (Cowie, McCahon, McLeod, Robinson, Walters, Witkin), 5–28 Nov 1998
366 *Jacqueline Fraser and Gordon Walters* [works from stock], 30 Nov–8 Dec 1998
367 *Bill Hammond: Hokey pokey – recent paintings*, 10 Dec1998–6 Jan 1999
368 *What I photographed this summer* (Braunias, Dunning, Endres, Fraser, Hammond, Heaphy, Killeen, Nielsen, Reynolds, Robinson, Tuck, Viscoe), 9 Jan–6 Feb 1999
369 *Gary Baigent: Vintage photographs from The unseen city, 1967*, 6–27 Feb 1999
370 *Derek Cowie: 6 recent works and 1 dated 1992*, 2–27 Mar 1999
371 *Jacqueline Fraser: The flagellation of the true voice – recent work*, 30 Mar–24 Apr 1999
372 *Several exceptionally good paintings and works on paper from the collection of MT Woollaston, deceased; a private collector, Auckland; and an anonymous collector* (Fomison, Hammond, Hotere, McCahon, Helen FV Scales, Walters, Robin White), 5–22 May 1999
373 *William Dunning: Recent work*, 26 May–19 June 1999
374 *Mark Braunias: The Dibblos – 6 works, 1999*, 29 June–24 July 1999
375 *Peter Robinson: The uncertainty principle – recent work*, 27 July–21 Aug 1999
376 *Robin White: New angel – recent work*, 25 Aug–18 Sept 1999
377 *Andrew McLeod and Brendon Wilkinson: Cleaning up – recent work*, 21 Sept–16 Oct 1999
378 *Chris Heaphy: Five paintings of 1999*, 19 Oct–13 Nov 1999
379 *Richard Killeen: Song of Isis – recent paintings*, 16 Nov–11 Dec 1999
380 *WD Hammond: Zoomorphic lounge and other recent paintings*, 14 Dec 1999–15 Jan 2000

2000–2004

381 *The really really good exhibition* (Fraser, Hammond, Killeen, McLeod, Robinson, Viscoe, Robin White, Wilkinson), 22 Jan–19 Feb 2000
382 *Les Cleveland: Small towns – 22 vintage photographs*, 26 Feb–18 Mar 2000
383 *Jacqueline Fraser: The retrospective*, 23 Mar–15 Apr 2000
384 *Several exceptionally good paintings and works on paper* (Hammond, McCahon, Walters, Woollaston), 19 Apr–2 May 2000
385 *John Reynolds: Histrionics – recent oil paintings*, 9 May–3 June 2000
386 *Laurence Aberhart: 25 recent photographs*, 6 June–1 July 2000
387 *William Dunning: A picture show: a sense of time and place – recent paintings*, 4–29 July 2000
388 *Andrew McLeod: Recent paintings*, 1–26 Aug 2000
389 *MT Woollaston: Paintings and works on paper from the estate*, 30 Aug–23 Sept 2000
390 *A group show* (Fraser, Illingworth, McLeod, Walters), 27 Sept–14 Oct 2000
391 *Peter McLeavey at Melbourne Art Fair* (Fraser, Hammond, Killeen), 4–8 Oct 2000
392 *Richard Killeen: Codex: 2 recent paintings*, 17 Oct–11 Nov 2000
393 *Brendon Wilkinson: Cabin fever – recent works*, 14 Nov–9 Dec 2000
394 *Peter Robinson: The end of the 20th century – an installation*, 12 Dec 2000–13 Jan 2001
395 *Looking back, curated by Peter Ireland* (Aberhart, Terry Austin, Baigent, Janet Bayly, Peter Black, Rhondda Bosworth, Dinah Bradley, Glenn Busch, Fiona Clark, Cleveland, David Cook, Bruce Foster, Nicola Heath, Frank Hofmann, Jenkinson, Cecelia Kumeroa, John McDermott, Christopher Matthews, Robin Morrison, Peryer, Andrew Ross, Catherine Russ, Seymour, Ann Shelton, John B Turner, Jane Ussher, Julian Ward, Ans Westra, Richard Wotton, Stuart Young), 20 Jan–17 Feb 2001
396 *Warren Viscoe: New works including The portable stream*, 24 Feb–24 Mar 2001

397 *Jacqueline Fraser: The lone cowboy – recent works*, 27 Mar–21 Apr 2001
398 *It will be OK* (Binney, Dunning, Fraser, Hammond, Illingworth, Killeen, McCahon, McLeod, Reynolds, Robinson, Scott, Tuck, Walters, Robin White, Woollaston), 3 May–9 June 2001[27]
399 *WD Hammond: Singer, songwriter – recent work*, 19 June–14 July 2001
400 *Darryn George: The T.A.T. show! – eight paintings*, 17 July–11 Aug 2001
401 *Mark Braunias: Soft – recent work*, 14 Aug–8 Sept 2001
402 *Several exceptionally good paintings and works on paper, part III*[28] (Hammond, Killeen, McCahon, McLeod, Mrkusich, Peebles, Walters, Woollaston), 12–29 Sept 2001
403 *Richard Killeen: Jars and cases – 10 new works*, 2–20 Oct 2001
404 This exhibition file is labelled: 'The transition from 147 Cuba Street to 151 Cuba Street, 19 Oct–15 Nov 2001.'
405 *151 Cuba St: Exhibition no. 1* (Hammond, McLeod, Wilkinson, New Zealand views (Photochrom prints, *c.*1905)), 24 Nov–23 Dec 2001
406 *151 Cuba Street: Exhibition no. 2* (Dunning, Hammond, Robinson, Walters, Wilkinson, Woollaston), 3–27 Jan 2002
407 *151 Cuba St: Exhibition no. 3* (Dunning, Hammond, Killeen, Robinson, Walters, Woollaston), 29 Jan–23 Feb 2002
408 *Andrew McLeod: Interior monologues – recent works*, 6–30 Mar 2002
409 *William Dunning: Recent paintings*, 2–27 Apr 2002
410 *Several exceptionally good paintings and works on paper, part V* (Hammond, Hanly, Hotere, Killeen, Walters, Woollaston), 16–27 Apr 2002[29]
411 *Brendon Wilkinson: Somnambulant perimeter – 9 recent works*, 30 Apr–25 May 2002
412 *Laurence Aberhart: The photographic print in the year 2002*, 28 May–22 June 2002
413 *Robin White: Summer grass – a painting in 12 panels*, 25 June–20 July 2002
414 *Yvonne Todd: Sea of tranquility – 5 photographs*, 23 July–17 Aug 2002
415 *Peter Robinson: The return of the hand – 14 paintings*, 20 Aug–14 Sept 2002
416 *WD Hammond: Self motivation (6 paintings of 1991), and Threshing dog, the golden bough, 2002*, 17 Sept–12 Oct 2002
417 *Four New Zealand artists: Peter McLeavey at Melbourne Art Fair* (Hammond, Killeen, McLeod, Robinson), 2–6 Oct 2002[30]
418 *Richard Killeen: Containers various – 9 recent works*, 15 Oct–9 Nov 2002
418a *John Reynolds: It's fun to have fun, but you have to know how – 14 new paintings*, 12 Nov–7 Dec 2002
419 *Victory over death, curated by Peter Ireland* (Aberhart, Rick Alexander, Wayne Barrar, Janet Bayly, Gary Blackman, Rhondda Bosworth, Ben Cauchi, Fiona Clark, Margaret Dawson, Hayden Fritchley, Geoffrey Heath, Jenkinson, Paul Johns, Heyes Johnson, Nikolai Kokx, Virginia Lee, Christopher Matthews, Stephen Parkes, Peryer, Andrew Ross, Marsh Thompson, Richard Wotton, Scott Younger), 10 Dec 2002–18 Jan 2003
420 *Darryn George: Stairway to heaven – recent work*, 25 Jan–22 Feb 2003
421 *Several exceptionally good paintings, photographs and watercolours, part V* (Killeen, McCahon, McLeod, Seymour, Walters, Woollaston), 27 Feb–29 Mar 2003
422 *Ava Seymour: The seven deadly sins – photocollages*, 1–26 Apr 2003
423 *Les Cleveland: Vintage photographs*, and *MT Woollaston: Ink drawings*, 29 Apr–24 May 2003
424 *Andrew McLeod: New work*, 27 May–21 June 2003
425 *WD Hammond: Traffic Cop Bay – a recent painting*, 24 June–19 July 2003
426 *Mark Braunias: A day in my life – 9 recent works*, 23 July–16 Aug 2003
427 *Yvonne Todd: The Book of Martha – 8 recent colour photographs*, 19 Aug–13 Sept 2003
428 This exhibition number was not used
429 *Warren Viscoe: Pages from the book of birdsong – recent sculpture*, 16 Sept–8 Oct 2003
430 *What we do here II* (Dunning, Hammond, Killeen, McLeod, Robinson, Seymour, Wilkinson, Woollaston), 15 Oct–19 Nov 2003
431 *Richard Killeen: Ladybird – 5 recent digital paintings*, 22 Nov–13 Dec 2003
432 *William Dunning: 3 religious paintings – Colonial altars Nos. 1, 2 and 3*, 16 Dec 2003–17 Jan 2004
433 *Pauline Rhodes: Transience – an installation*, 24 Jan–21 Feb 2004
434 *Brendon Wilkinson: Trip over my lips – recent paintings and watercolours*, 24 Feb–20 Mar 2004

435 *MT Woollaston: Several paintings, watercolours and drawings from the estate*, 24 Mar–24 Apr 2004
436 *Peter Robinson: Club foot – 2 recent sculptures*, 29 Apr–22 May 2004
437 *Liz Maw: Julien and Deepa – 2 recent paintings*, 25 May–19 June 2004
438 *Peter Adsett: 4 for 4 walls – recent paintings*, 23 June–17 July 2004
439 *Laurence Aberhart: Ghosting – 23 photographs*, 20 July–14 Aug 2004
440 *WD Hammond: Last nightjar in congested sky – a new painting*, 18 Aug–11 Sept 2004
441 *Andrew McLeod: New work, 2004*, 15 Sept–9 Oct 2004
442 *Yvonne Todd: The bone of Jupiter – 10 photographs*, 19 Oct–13 Nov 2004
443 *Richard Killeen: Jars, tins and pots – 7 recent works*, 23 Nov–24 Dec 2004

2005–2009

444 *Gary Baigent: From the archive – 99 images, 1963–1971*, 9 Feb–5 Mar 2005
445 *Made in New Zealand* (Dunning, Hammond, Hanly, Killeen, McLeod, Robinson, Seymour, Todd, Wilkinson), 9 Mar–2 Apr 2005
446 *Ava Seymour: 3 panoramic photographs*, 6–30 Apr 2005
447 *John Reynolds: Painting is easy – recent work*, 4–28 May 2005
448 *William Dunning: New Zealand altar series – 7 drawings, 2004–2005*, 1–25 June 2005
449 *Mark Braunias and Peter Robinson: Works on paper*, 29 June–23 July 2005
450 *Robin White: Recent works*, 27 July–20 Aug 2005
451 *Andrew McLeod: Recent works*, 24 Aug–17 Sept 2005
452 *Peter Adsett: Game, set, match – 3 new paintings*, 21 Sept–15 Oct 2005
453 *I like this: 10 artworks from stock* (Aberhart, Baigent, McCahon, McLeod, Maw, Robinson, Todd, Wilkinson), 19–29 Oct 2005
454 *Richard Killeen: On paper at Peter's, 1975–2005 – 14 works*, 2–26 Nov 2005
455 *WD Hammond: 4 recent paintings and a limited edition book*, 3–24 Dec 2005
456 *Brendon Wilkinson: 4 new works*, 15 Feb–10 Mar 2006
457 *Yvonne Todd: Meat and liquor – 7 new photographs*, 15 Mar–8 Apr 2006
458 *Darryn George: Arawhata/Marama – 12 recent paintings*, 12 Apr–6 May 2006
459 *Laurence Aberhart: Museology – 22 photographs*, 10 May–3 June 2006
460 *Peter Robinson: 7 recent drawings*, 7 June–1 July 2006
461 *Liz Maw: Bill and Daughter of Cain, lover of Judas – recent paintings*, 5–29 July 2006
462 *Andrew McLeod: Artistic conscience – 19 new works*, 2–26 Aug 2006
463 *Ava Seymour: The White House years – 15 photographs*, 29 Aug–23 Sept 2006
464 *Mark Braunias: The shrink – recent works*, 27 Sept–21 Oct 2006
465 *WD Hammond: Great eagle – recent paintings and etchings*, 1–25 Nov 2006[31]
466 *Richard Killeen: Times – 7 new works*, 29 Nov–24 Dec 2006
467 *Les Cleveland: The secret city – 35 photographs*, 14 Mar–7 Apr 2007
468 *Andrew McLeod: 10 years – a survey*, 11–28 Apr 2007
469 *Several exceptionally good paintings, photographs and works on paper, part VI* (Aberhart, Hanly, Killeen, Maw, Smither, Todd), 2–26 May 2007
470 *Peter McLeavey at Auckland Art Fair (William Dunning: 5 works)*, 17–20 May 2007
471 *Yvonne Todd: The Lamb's Book of Life – 7 recent photographs*, 30 May–23 June 2007
472 *John Reynolds: Looking west, late afternoon, low water – a recent painting*, 4 July–4 Aug 2007
473 *Richard Killeen: 12 new graphics*, 8 Aug–1 Sept 2007
474 *Andrew McLeod: Recent work*, 5–29 Sept 2007
475 *Paint it black* (Dunning, Hammond, Killeen, McCahon, Walters, Woollaston), 3–27 Oct 2007
476 *Richard Killeen: Butterfly – 3 recent paintings*, 1–24 Nov 2007
477 *Brendon Wilkinson: Chillblade – recent work*, 5 Dec 2007–23 Feb 2008
478 *WD Hammond: Cave paintings – recent work*, 27 Feb–22 Mar 2008
479 *Peter Robinson: Soft rock baroque – an installation*, 29 Mar–15 Apr 2008
480 *Liz Maw: Cerebus, Solar messiah and The untitled – 3 new works*, 30 Apr–24 May 2008
481 *From the heroic period: Several exceptionally good paintings, drawings and photographs* (Cleveland, Hanly, Hotere, McCahon, Walters, Woollaston), 28 May–14 June 2008[32]
482 *Darryn George: Konae korero – 8 new paintings*, 18 June–12 July 2008

483 *WD Hammond and John Reynolds: The art of drawing – works on paper*, 16 July–9 Aug 2008
484 *Ava Seymour: Corinthos – 8 recent photographs*, 20 Aug–13 Sept 2008
485 A one-day exhibition mounted for Clemenger/Colenso, Auckland (Maw, Seymour, Todd), 9 Sept 2008
486 *Yvonne Todd: Mauve reaction – 4 recent photographs*, 1–25 Oct 2008
487 *Andrew McLeod: New works*, 29 Oct–22 Nov 2008
488 *Richard Killeen: Shadow – recent works on canvas and paper*, 26 Nov–20 Dec 2008
489 *Laurence Aberhart: A greater conceit – recent photographs*, 25 Feb–21 Mar 2009
490 *For Maxwell Fernie: 2 etchings by Gregory O'Brien, commissioned by the Maxwell Fernie Trust*, 29 Mar 2009
491 *Brendon Wilkinson: 4 recent works*, 1–25 Apr 2009
492 *Peter McLeavey at Auckland Art Fair* (Hammond, Ralph Eugene Meatyard, Todd, and an unknown photographer working for the New Zealand Tourist Board, *c.*1910), 30 Apr–3 May 2009[33]
493 *The sign of the 4* (McCahon, Charles Tole, Viscoe, Woollaston), 13 May–6 June 2009
494 *Matt Hunt: 5 recent paintings*, 10 June–4 July 2009
495 *WD Hammond: Farmers' market – recent paintings and etchings*, 8 July–1 Aug 2009
496 *What we do here, part III – a group show* (Braunias, Hammond, Hanly, Killeen, McCahon, Seymour, Todd, Charles Tole, Wilkinson), 19 Aug–19 Sept 2009
497 *Robin White, with Holly Jackson and Robyn McFarlane: Sorry*, 30 Sept–24 Oct 2009
498 *Andrew McLeod: New works*, 28 Oct–21 Nov 2009
499 *Mark Braunias: The periodic table – recent works*, 25 Nov–24 Dec 2009
500 *Art aristocracy: The launch of a book by Tao Wells*, 5 Dec 2009

2010–MAR 2013

501 *If: A group show* (Dunning, George, Killeen, McCahon, McLeod, Maw, Smither, Todd, Wilkinson), 20 Feb–13 Mar 2010
502 *Ava Seymour: Tree songs – 5 recent photographs*, 17 Mar–10 Apr 2010
503 *Toss Woollaston at 100: An exhibition to mark the centenary of the artist's birth*, 21 Apr–8 May 2010
504 *Liz Maw: Evil genius miscellaneous – new work*, 12 May–5 June 2010
505 *Nick Austin and Andrew Barber: Two man shoe – recent paintings*, 9 June–3 July 2010
506 *Me and Parkinson's: An exhibition by Peter McLeavey*, June 2010[34]
507 *Yvonne Todd: Sets and subsets – recent photographs*, 7–31 July 2010
508 *WD Hammond: Wishbone ash – 4 recent paintings*, 4–28 Aug 2010
509 *Darryn George: Rehita – recent paintings*, 1–25 Sept 2010
510 *Peter Robinson: Polymer monoliths – 3 sculptures*, 29 Sept–23 Oct 2010
511 *Andrew McLeod: Recent works*, 3–27 Nov 2010
512 *Richard Killeen: Objects from another planet – recent works*, 1–24 Dec 2010
513 *For Oscar: A group show*[35] (Austin, Barber, Illingworth, Killeen, McCahon, McLeod, Maw, Robinson, Seymour, Todd, Charles Tole), 6 Feb–5 Mar 2011
514 *John Reynolds: McLeavey sat here – recent works on paper*, 9 Mar–2 Apr 2011
515 *Matt Hunt: Supereality – 3 recent paintings*, 13 Apr–7 May 2011
516 *What I did last summer: A group exhibition* (Aberhart, Austin, Barber, Braunias, Cleveland, George, Hammond, Killeen, McLeod, Maw and Todd [a collaboration], Robinson, Seymour, Viscoe, Robin White), 11 May–4 June 2011
517 *Yvonne Todd: The sapphire aluminium corp – images made over the last decade*, 15 June–2 July 2011
518 *Laurence Aberhart: Monumental: Ice. America – recent photographs*, 6–30 July 2011
519 *Peter McLeavey at Auckland Art Fair* (Killeen, Seymour, Gilbert Melrose and Todd [a collaboration]), 3–7 Aug 2011
520 *Andrew Barber: Black and blue – recent paintings*, 17 Aug–17 Sept 2011
521 *Nick Austin: Interesting chewing gum – paintings*, 21 Sept–15 Oct 2011
522 *Brendon Wilkinson: Hexagony – recent works*, 19 Oct–12 Nov 2011
523 *WD Hammond: Cornwall Road cave – recent paintings*, 16 Nov–10 Dec 2011
524 *Andrew McLeod: The neo-aesthetics – recent works*, 7–31 Mar 2012
525 *Yvonne Todd: Seahorsel subset – recent photographs*, 4–28 Apr 2012
526 *Mark Braunias: Men on Mars – paintings 1995–2001*, 2–19 May 2012, and *Mark Braunias: Plan 9.5 from outer space – recent works*, 23 May–9 June 2012

527 *Liz Maw: The Montgomery twins' dead end – 5 recent paintings*, 13 June–7 July 2012
528 *Octavia Cook: Wanderjahr – new work*, 11–28 July 2012
529 *Darryn George: Waiata – 4 recent paintings*, 8 Aug–1 Sept 2012
530 *Ava Seymour: Slight matters – 9 recent works*, 5–29 Sept 2012
531 *Peter Robinson: Defunct mnemonics – new work*, 2–27 Oct 2012
532 *Richard Killeen: Reproductions from the image catalogue, 1–100*, 31 Oct–24 Nov 2012
533 *WD Hammond: Cave music – recent paintings*, 27 Nov–22 Dec 2012
534 *Andrew Barber: Earth, wind and fire, knock on wood – recent paintings*, 6–30 Mar 2013

NOTES

ABBREVIATIONS

AAG Auckland Art Gallery Toi o Tāmaki
ATL Alexander Turnbull Library
CAG Christchurch Art Gallery Te Puna o Waiwhetu
DPAG Dunedin Public Art Gallery
EP *Evening Post*
GBAG Govett-Brewster Art Gallery
HL Hocken Collections Uare Taoka o Hākena, University of Otago
NBR *National Business Review*
NZH *New Zealand Herald*
n.d. not dated
PM Peter McLeavey
PMG Peter McLeavey Gallery
SST *Sunday Star-Times*
TP Museum of New Zealand Te Papa Tongarewa

INTRODUCTION

1 Letter to Ralph von Kohorn, 6 May 1967.
2 PM used this phrase in letters to Ian Scott (14 Mar 1977), Michael Smither (17 June 1977), Charles Tole (13 July 1977), Michael Illingworth (3 Aug 1978), Warren Viscoe (24 May 1985), and John Reynolds (2 July 1990), as well as variations of it in correspondence with other artists.
3 Conversation with the author, 2 Mar 2012.
4 Lindsay Rabbitt, 'The dealer', *New Zealand Listener*, 17 Feb 2001, p. 50.
5 Letter to Richard Killeen, 22 Nov 1979.
6 Conversation with the author, 24 Nov 2012.
7 Letter to Peter Ireland, 11 Sept 1981.
8 'Not that everything one sells has to be a masterpiece. Far from it. But I like to think that the works I sell have a certain level of "quality".' Letter to Colin McCahon, 26 June 1975.
9 Laura de Coppet and Alan Jones, *The art dealers*, 2nd edn, Cooper Square Press, New York, 2002, p. 57. André Emmerich (1924–2007) was an influential German-born dealer who ran a gallery in Manhattan from 1954 to 1998. He was an early champion of colour-field painters such as Morris Louis, Kenneth Noland and Helen Frankenthaler.
10 Sally Blundell, 'I sell, therefore I am', *New Zealand Listener*, 28 Nov 2009, p. 36.
11 Diana Dekker, 'The art of buying art', *Dominion Post*, 10 Aug 2002, F3.
12 Letter to Helen Garner, 11 Nov 2006.
13 Interview with the author, 9 Aug 2012.
14 Letter to Megan Jenkinson, 27 Sept 1985.

15 Letter to McCahon, 2 Mar 1978.
16 Letter to Toss Woollaston, 16 Nov 1978.
17 Email to the author, 19 July 2012.
18 Grant Smithies, 'Art and soul', *SST*, 29 May 2005, *Sunday* supplement, p.25.

CHAPTER 1

1 Neil McGrath, who attended the funeral, remembered this phrase. Interview with the author, 13 July 2011.
2 Interview with the author, 21 Dec 2010.
3 *Ibid.*
4 Obituary, *EP*, 20 Oct 1945, p.8
5 Private James McLeavey arrived in Wellington with the 65th (2nd Yorkshire North Riding) Regiment in 1847, and served in Wellington and Whanganui. On his discharge in December 1853, he settled at Makara where he farmed 50 acres.
6 *The cyclopedia of New Zealand*, Vol.1: Wellington Provincial District, 1897, p.1107.
7 Letter to Michael Smither, 7 Sept 1977. The next quotation is also from this letter.
8 Interview with the author, 29 Mar 2012.
9 Letter to Colin McCahon, 16 Dec 1977.
10 The family adopted the name McTiernan when they moved to New Zealand. PM's mother told him that this was to signal their republican allegiances. Interview with the author, 10 Aug 2010.
11 Interview with the author, 10 Aug 2010.
12 It was at 120 Cuba Street – not far from the location of the PMG at 147 Cuba.
13 Interview with the author, 10 Aug 2010. The next quotation is also from this interview.
14 Letter to McCahon, 30 July 1977.
15 Pat White, *How the land lies: Of longing and belonging*, Victoria University Press, Wellington, 2010, p.16. The next two quotations are also from this page.
16 Interview with the author, 10 Aug 2010. The next quotation is also from this interview.
17 *View from hotel window – Butte, Montana*, 1955, was published in Robert Frank's famously melancholy book on his adopted country, *The Americans* (1958). Born in Switzerland in 1924, Frank migrated to the US in 1947.
18 Sally Blundell, 'I sell, therefore I am', *New Zealand Listener*, 28 Nov 2009, p.36.
19 Interview with the author, 10 Aug 2010. The next quotation is also from this interview.
20 Interview with the author, 20 Dec 2011. Unless otherwise noted, all the following quotations from Michael McLeavey are from this interview.
21 Interview with the author, 15 Mar 2012.
22 Interview with Marie Oliver, née McLeavey, 1 Aug 2011. All the following quotations from Marie Oliver are from this interview.
23 Interview with the author, 10 Aug 2010.
24 Interview with Dominic McLeavey, 28 Nov 2012.
25 Letter to McCahon, 1 Mar 1979.
26 [Beverley Simmons], 'Young man on way to the top', *NZH*, 24 June 1967, magazine section, p.2.
27 Lindsay Rabbitt, 'The dealer', *New Zealand Listener*, 17 Feb 2001, p.50.
28 Interview with Susan Fowke, 12 June 2007. PM amended this quotation slightly when he read the text for this chapter on 29 Mar 2012.
29 Diana Dekker, 'Portrait of a salesman', *Dominion Post Weekend*, 31 May 2008, p.5.
30 Interview with Susan Fowke, 12 June 2007. The next quotation is also from this interview.
31 Interview with the author, 10 Aug 2010.
32 Interview with Susan Fowke, 12 June 2007.
33 Letter to McCahon, 30 July 1977.
34 Letter to McCahon, 17 Mar 1982. The next quotation is also from this letter.
35 Letter to McCahon, 27 Aug 1976.
36 Interview with the author, 15 Mar 2012. Beginning in 1942 and dispensed through Catholic schools, *Topix* comics featured stories on Pope Pius XII, Catholic saints and biblical stories.
37 Published by Odhams Press, London, *c.*1920.

38 Interview with the author, 25 Aug 2011.
39 Interview with Susan Fowke, 12 June 2007.
40 Interview with the author, 25 Aug 2011.
41 Blundell, 'I sell, therefore I am', p. 34. PM told this same story in Luit and Jan Bieringa's film, *The man in the hat* (2009), and it was relayed to Mrs Palmer, by then in a retirement home in New Plymouth. 'That's the high point of my teaching career,' she declared.
42 Conversation with the author, 8 Nov 2012.
43 'I read every single book by Richard Halliburton in the library'. Interview with the author, 14 Mar 2012.
44 Interview with the author, 10 Aug 2010.
45 Letter to McCahon, 16 Dec 1977.
46 PM wrote these words in the front pages of his 1986 diary: they are from an anonymous short review of David Lynch's film *Blue velvet* in *New York Magazine*, 1 Dec 1986, p.165.
47 Interview with the author, 10 Aug 2010. The next quotation is also from this interview.
48 Interview with the author, 25 Aug 2010.
49 *Ibid.*
50 Letter to McCahon, 25 July 1980.
51 Conversation with the author, 3 Dec 2012.
52 Interview with the author, 25 Aug 2010.
53 Bryan Staff, 'Peter McLeavey interviewed for ChaCha', *ChaCha*, June 1984, p. 11. The next two quotations are also from this interview.
54 Art societies had made a vital contribution to New Zealand art in the late nineteenth century, but after the Second World War were increasingly seen as conservative cultural gatekeepers.
55 ARD Fairburn, 'Some reflections on New Zealand painting', *Landfall*, Vol. 1, No. 1, Mar 1947, p. 53.
56 ARD Fairburn, 'The Wertheim collection', *Year book of the arts in New Zealand*, No. 5, 1949, p. 2. The first full-time art gallery director in New Zealand was Stewart Maclennan, appointed at the National Art Gallery in 1948.
57 'Eric Lee-Johnson', *Year book of the arts in New Zealand*, No. 3, 1947, p. 74. In 1949, Charles Brasch posed a question: 'Why are our galleries so bad?' He laid the blame at the amateurism of those in charge, and the lack of policy. '[P]aintings are seldom bought except for their negative qualities: their chief merit must be not to offend any one on the council. That lets in almost anything that looks familiar, and keeps out almost anything that looks unfamiliar, irrespective of artistic merit.' See 'Art gallery policy', *Landfall*, Vol. 3, No. 2, June 1949, p. 181.
58 Allen Curnow and Ngaio Marsh, 'A dialogue by way of introduction', *First year book of the arts in New Zealand*, 1945, p. 2.
59 Douglas Lilburn, 'A search for tradition', 1946, in *A search for tradition & a search for a language*, Victoria University Press, Wellington, 2011, p. 24. Lilburn was referring to young composers, but his comments are just as relevant to artists.
60 None of them could afford to travel, but in any case the Second World War ruled out the prospect.
61 It was not until 1951 that *Pleasure garden* (1932) was accepted into the collection.
62 PM, 'When I first heard Colin McCahon's name', *Art New Zealand*, No. 8, Nov 1977–Jan 1978, p. 40. Unless otherwise noted, the following quotations in this paragraph are from this article.
63 See 'Rejection of art display defended', *Taranaki Herald*, 18 Nov 1954, p. 1. The exhibition, *New Zealand artists 1954: Harry Miller, Colin McCahon, Toss Woollaston*, had been toured by the Community Arts Service, a section of the adult education branch of the Department of Education.
64 Interview with the author, 25 Aug 2010.
65 See PM's diary, 30 July 1959: 'I was rather aggravated and also saddened to read what the "sub accountant" of the Bank had told Mother... Clearly it made an impression on her and, unfortunately it made all the bigger impression on Father, for in his letter Father wrote, "Your Mother was talking to the Sub Accountant and he said you would have gone a long way in the Bank and that the heads were pushing you as fast as they could."'
66 Both were relatively recent in origin: the National Orchestra was formed in 1946 and held its first performance in the following year; the Wellington Chamber Music Society was established in 1945.
67 Interview with Susan Fowke, 7 Aug 2007.
68 *Ibid.*

69 Interview with the author, 25 Aug 2010.
70 Staff, 'Peter McLeavey interviewed for ChaCha', p. 11.
71 Interview with Susan Fowke, 7 Aug 2007.

CHAPTER 2

1 Draft letter, 'Dear Sir', n.d. [Jan–Feb 1959].
2 Diary, 20 Apr 1959.
3 Letter to PM [?], 26 Apr 1959.
4 Letter to Les and Betty McLeavey, 19 May 1959.
5 Diary, 15 May 1959.
6 *Ibid.*
7 Letter to Les, Betty and Marie McLeavey, 10 May 1959. The next quotation is also from this letter.
8 Diary, 14 May 1959. The next quotation is also from this entry.
9 Letter to Les, Betty and Marie McLeavey, 26 Oct 1959.
10 Diary, 26 Sept 1959.
11 Letter to Les and Betty McLeavey, 1 Feb 1960.
12 *La belle Hollandaise* (1905) had been purchased in London for £55,000, setting a record for a work by a living artist. The purchase had been funded by grazier, art collector and philanthropist Harold de Vahl Rubin.
13 See, for example, 'Art row over Picasso nude', *Sun-Herald*, Sydney, 5 July 1959, p. 13.
14 Diary, 8 Feb 1960.
15 It was banned against the advice of the Customs literature committee in 1959; Diary, 20 Feb 1960.
16 Letter to Les and Betty McLeavey, 6 Mar 1960.
17 Letter to Les and Betty McLeavey, 16 Mar 1960. The next two quotations are also from this letter.
18 Sally Blundell, 'I sell, therefore I am', *New Zealand Listener*, 28 Nov 2009, p. 36. The next quotation is also from this article.
19 Letter to Les and Betty McLeavey, 23 Mar 1960.
20 Diary, 25 Mar 1960.
21 Diary, 6 Apr 1960. The next quotation is also from this entry.
22 Letter to Les and Betty McLeavey, n.d. [postmarked 9 May 1960]. The next three quotations are also from this letter.
23 Letter to Les and Betty McLeavey, n.d. [mid-May 1960]. The next two quotations are also from this letter.
24 Diary, 17 May 1960.
25 Letter to Les and Betty McLeavey, n.d. [early June 1960]. The quotations in the next two paragraphs are also from this letter.
26 Letter to Les and Betty McLeavey, 13 June 1960. The quotations in this and the next paragraph are also from this letter.
27 Letter to Les and Betty McLeavey, 24 Aug 1960.
28 Interview with the author, 10 Aug 2010. Published late in 1959, the book was highly praised by influential British critics, such as Muriel Spark, Stevie Smith and Alan Sillitoe, but in New Zealand the response was largely negative.
29 Letter to Les and Betty McLeavey, 3 Aug 1960.
30 Letter to Les and Betty McLeavey, 10 Oct 1960.
31 Letter to Les and Betty McLeavey, n.d. [postmarked 10 Nov 1960]. The next quotation is also from this letter.
32 Diary, 16 July 1960.
33 Diary, 20 July 1960.
34 Letter to Les and Betty McLeavey, n.d. [postmarked 10 Nov 1960].
35 Letter to Les and Betty McLeavey, 10 Oct 1960. The next quotation is also from this letter.
36 Letter to Michael McLeavey, 21 Dec 1960.
37 Letter to Les and Betty McLeavey, 20 Jan 1961. The next quotation is also from this letter.
38 Letter to Les and Betty McLeavey, 19 Feb 1961. The next quotation is also from this letter.
39 Letter to Les and Betty McLeavey, 5 May 1961.
40 Letter to Les and Betty McLeavey, n.d. [late May 1961].

41 Letter to Les and Betty McLeavey, 18 Apr 1961.
42 Interview with the author, 10 Aug 2010.

CHAPTER 3

1 Interview with the author, 16 Mar 2011.
2 Interview with the author, 1 Aug 2011.
3 Bryan Staff, 'Peter McLeavey interviewed for ChaCha', *ChaCha*, June 1984, p.11.
4 Merill Coke, 'Life is the next show', *New Zealand Listener*, 13 Dec 1986, p.62.
5 Interview with the author, 25 Aug 2010.
6 Letter to Ian Scott, 21 Oct 1976.
7 Interview with the author, 16 Mar 2011.
8 As remembered by Marie Oliver, née McLeavey; interview with the author, 1 Aug 2011.
9 Ivan Bootham recalled PM reading Read's *Art now* (1933) and Greene's essays. Interview with the author, 31 May 2011.
10 A ticketwriter used a paintbrush and poster paint to write the price and sometimes the name of a displayed item on card. On large cards, pictorial decoration and slogans were added. Evans's employed two ticketwriters in the early 1960s: Bootham and an assistant.
11 Interview with the author, 31 May 2011. All the quotations from Bootham in this chapter are from this interview.
12 Interview with the author, 16 Mar 2011.
13 Joe Bootham's pastel portrait, *Peter McLeavey* (1962), is in the ATL collection (G-405).
14 Interview with the author, 10 Aug 2010.
15 Although Ivan Bootham made the point that musically, at least, Wellington was well catered for. 'I found the musical activity here quite strong. I was really quite taken by the enthusiasm. It was really quite active. And being in the capital city we got the concert artists who didn't necessarily filter through past London in England.' Interview with the author, 31 May 2011.
16 The poem is entitled 'Way out Waiwhetu'.
17 Staff, 'Peter McLeavey interviewed for ChaCha', p.11.
18 *A retrospective exhibition: MT Woollaston, Colin McCahon* was organised by the Auckland City Art Gallery, opening in May 1963 and subsequently touring the country. In Wellington it could not be shown in its entirety at the Centre Gallery, so half the 96 works were shown one week and the other half the next.
19 Sally Blundell, 'I sell, therefore I am', *New Zealand Listener*, 28 Nov 2009, p.36.
20 PM, 'When I first heard Colin McCahon's name', *Art New Zealand*, No.8, Nov 1977–Jan 1978, p.40.
21 Letter to Colin McCahon, 31 Aug 1976.
22 Charles Brasch, *A private collection of New Zealand paintings: Thirty-seven New Zealand paintings from the collection of Charles Brasch and Rodney Kennedy*, Auckland City Art Gallery, Auckland, 1958, p.6. The next quotation is also from this catalogue.
23 PA Tomory, 'Unifying art – in New Zealand', *The Connoisseur*, Mar 1959, p.92. Tomory's predecessor, fellow Englishman Eric Westbrook, had begun the transformation from 1952 to 1955, acquiring contemporary New Zealand art and establishing the gallery as a lively cultural centre.
24 The series began in 1957 as *Eight New Zealand painters*, continuing as *Contemporary New Zealand painters* (and similar titles) from 1960 to 1966. The exhibitions provided artists with a rare opportunity to have their work shown nationally and, in a time of less frequent travel, did much to break down a sense of regional isolation.
25 Interview with the author, 31 Aug 2011.
26 Peter Tomory, 'Art can't be taught', *New Zealand Listener*, 20 Nov 1964, p.3.
27 'Gallery decision unanimous: Two grounds stated for refusing show', *EP*, 6 June 1958, p.7. Defending the decision, GGG Watson, chairman of the management committee, expressed a concern that 'the people should not be fooled by what is merely extravagant and grotesque in art'. Tomory had criticised the decision the previous day: see 'Dim view of other cities: Aucklanders "see the light" on modern art', *EP*, 5 June 1958, p.20. The exhibition was eventually shown in two parts at the Centre Gallery.
28 'Art's place in the capital', *EP*, 12 Feb 1966, p.20.
29 Its predecessor, the Arts Advisory Council, was established in 1960.

30 In 1969, Gil Docking, the director of the Auckland City Art Gallery, wrote an article listing the names of artists, curators, directors and academics concerned about the arts council's representation of the visual arts. See 'The Arts Council and the visual arts', *Arts & Community*, Vol. 5, No. 9, 1969, pp. 1–2.

31 Hamish Keith, 'Painting in the sixties', *New Zealand Listener*, 11 July 1969, p. 10.

32 'Art notes: Wellington: French Maid Coffee House art shows', *Art in New Zealand*, Vol. 14, No. 3, March 1942, p. 148.

33 Others included Mollers and Spooners in Auckland, the Willeston Gallery and JR Hamerton's in Wellington, and Fisher Galleries in Christchurch. In the capital in the 1960s, exhibitions were held in the Dunhill Foundation Room at the New Zealand Display Centre in Cuba Street, while Stocktons in Woodward Street occasionally showed paintings by arrangement with The Gallery (later Ikon Gallery) in Auckland.

34 Quoted in Damian Skinner, *Don Binney: Nga manu/nga motu – birds/islands*, Auckland University Press, Auckland, 2003, p. 5. One of the earliest full-time painters in New Zealand was Peter McIntyre, who painted realistic landscapes for a living from the late 1940s. Unless they had a private income, most artists depended on teaching, design work and other occupations to earn a living.

35 'Simple art for homely walls', *EP*, 18 Dec 1965, p. 20.

36 'Art appreciation as part of life', *EP*, 14 Dec 1965, p. 16. The next quotation is also from this article.

37 Hancock lobbied the city council ceaselessly during the mid- to late 1960s, linking the need for an art gallery to the broader issue of the city's development: 'Wellington is growing up, not only in the height of its buildings, but in civic feeling and aesthetic discernment … [T]he capital's first requirement is a city art gallery', Letter to Dr Morvyn Williams, 19 May 1966, Centre Gallery archive, ATL, 89–152, Box 1.

38 In 1944, the Thomas Report gave a new emphasis to the teaching of art and craft in schools; two years later, Director-General of Education Clarence Beeby established an Arts and Crafts Department within the Ministry of Education, and appointed Gordon Tovey the first superintendent. Tovey reorganised the administration of art education to transform teaching practices, encourage art appreciation, and develop community as well as primary school art education. He also appointed artists to work as advisers in schools, among them 13 young Māori who would go on to spearhead the modern Māori art movement: Ralph Hotere, Cliff Whiting, Cath Brown, Fred Graham, Arnold Wilson, Katerina Mataira and others.

39 The profession of the art dealer, selling pictures and works of art, goes back for centuries, but the concept of the dealer gallery – with a programme of constantly changing exhibitions of contemporary art – is an essentially modern one. In 1950, for example, New York had some 30 dealer galleries; within a decade, as the market for American art matured, that number climbed tenfold.

40 See Ann Calhoun's articles in *Art New Zealand*, 'Two Wellington entrepreneurs of the thirties: the Murray Fullers: Part I, Edwin Murray Fuller', No. 23, Autumn 1982, pp. 20–23; and 'Part II, Mary Murray Fuller', No. 24, Winter 1982, pp. 22–25.

41 When Webb's gallery closed, the Auckland City Art Gallery made an upstairs space available for selling exhibitions. As Hamish Keith notes, 'The only rule we had was that there were no solo shows. Colin McCahon's *Northland panels* were first exhibited there. We showed Louise Henderson, Kees Hos, people from Christchurch like Quentin Macfarlane … Because there was a gap. We felt there had to be a place for artists to sell their work.' Interview with the author, 31 Aug 2011.

42 See Anthony Green's 'Colin McCahon's paintings and drawings at the Ikon Gallery', *Bulletin of New Zealand Art History*, Vol. 2, 1974, pp. 28–43.

43 Letter from Don Wood to John Blackburn, 15 July 1963, Ikon Gallery archive, Auckland Art Gallery Research Library, Box 1, Folder 1. In an email to the author on 10 Oct 2012, Wood wrote: 'Around 1964, I was aware that having the Ikon tucked away from sight in the basement of Rationalist House was not smart marketing. So I moved it into the city to 31–33 Lorne Street immediately opposite Khartoum Place. These were ground floor premises with plate glass windows to the street. A sort of 1964 version of the Gow Langsford Gallery with a close connection to the Auckland City Gallery. I believed it brought in a lot of new customers and I had some good shows including one sell-out by Don Binney. But there still wasn't a viable art market. Time, money and energy were against me.'

44 Interview with the author, 12 Aug 2012.

45 *Was this the promised land* (1962), private collection.

46 PM has given various dates for his first meeting with McCahon (see, for example, Marja Bloem and Martin Browne, *Colin McCahon: A question of faith*, Stedelijk Museum, Amsterdam; Craig Potton Publishing, Nelson, 2002, p. 209), but according to my research this appears to be the first meeting.

47 *Koru, 1, 2, 3* (1965) is now in the TP collection; *Agnus Dei, Donna Nobis Pacem* (1966) is in the Victoria University collection (catalogued as *Landscape with waterfall*).

48 Hanly's *New order 28. Part 1* (1963) is now in the Fletcher Trust collection.

49 *On building bridges* (1952), AAG.

50 Interview with the author, 10 Aug 2012. The next quotation is also from this interview. Scott had attended McCahon's art classes at Auckland City Art Gallery in 1963, when he was in his sixth-form year at high school: '[H]e was giving lessons about the old masters, Giorgione, Titian, etc … & he was so good & kind to me. He was the only person up to that point I'd met who was deeply concerned with painting.' See letter to PM, 31 May 1987.

51 *Numerals* (1965) is now in the collection of the AAG, a gift of the McCahon family in 1988.

52 Hamish Keith, 'Painting in New Zealand', *Salient*, 5 Oct 1964, p. 3. The next two quotations are also from this article.

53 In the same year, Keith noted that Auckland's four dealer galleries – Ikon, Uptown, John Leech's and Hayah's – had presented nearly 60 shows during the year: 'At least a dozen of these exhibitions have come close to being sell-outs.' See 'Auckland is so "big-headed!"', *Auckland Star*, 16 Dec 1964, p. 24.

54 Interview with the author, 10 Aug 2010. Unless otherwise noted, the following quotations in this chapter are from this interview.

55 Quoted in Gerald Barnett, *Toss Woollaston: An illustrated biography*, Random Century, Auckland, in association with the National Art Gallery, Wellington, 1991, p. 85.

56 Letter from Woollaston to PM, 25 May 1964. 'Dad was so impressed,' Philip Woollaston recalled. 'First, that Peter had come to see his work and booked in at a hotel: he hadn't tried to beg a bed for the night. And second, that he bought a work and paid for it so quickly. After that Peter could do no wrong.' Conversation with the author, 8 Sept 2012.

57 Lindsay Rabbitt, 'The dealer', *New Zealand Listener*, 17 Feb 2001, p. 50.

58 Interview with the author, 25 Aug 2011. The next quotation is also from this interview.

59 Mario Fleischl (1905–71) settled in Wellington in 1943 and was a foundation member of the New Zealand branch of the British Psychological Society.

60 *Otago Peninsula* (1946) is now in the TP collection.

61 Among those who were most influential in the arts in Wellington were Fred Turnovsky, Ernst Plischke, Helmut and Ester Einhorn, Marie Vanderwart and Alfons Blaschke, and Hans and Martha Lachmann.

62 Interview with the author, 25 Aug 2010.

63 Letter to Jeffrey Harris, 1 Oct 1984.

CHAPTER 4

1 [Beverley Simmons], 'Young man on way to the top', *NZH*, 24 June 1967, magazine section, p. 2.

2 Interview with the author, 10 Aug 2010.

3 The gallery did, however, have a paid director from 1965 in John Stackhouse.

4 '"Shut" call to gallery', *Dominion*, 30 Oct 1965, p. 6. The discussion on 29 Oct, which followed the annual general meeting, was prompted by William Main's letter to Russell Hancock of 5 Oct, supporting Keith's view that amateurism was stifling the arts in New Zealand. Main suggested that the Centre Gallery was part of the problem: '[Its] policy of exhibitions and its public image needs a serious overhaul.' See the Centre Gallery archive, ATL, 89–152, Box 2.

5 *Ibid.*

6 [Beverley Simmons], 'Young man on way to the top', p. 2.

7 Interview with the author, 31 May 2011. Unless otherwise noted, all quotations from Ivan Bootham in this chapter are from this interview.

8 The artists who showed at the Uptown Gallery in its first year included John Perry, Paul Tangata, Paratene Matchitt, Ross Ritchie, Jeff Macklin and Teuane Tibbo.

9 PM, 'Auckland dealer has done much for visual arts', *Dominion*, 16 Sept 1967, p. 9.

10 Letter to Colin McCahon, 20 Oct 1971.

11 Email from Ivan Bootham to the author, 21 June 2012. Neither PM nor Bootham can recall the name of the artist.

12 Behrman's *Duveen* was first published as a set of six articles in the *New Yorker* in 1952, and issued in book form the following year.

13 Don Binney recalled a conversation with Barry Lett around this time: 'Barry said, "Peter's interested in getting into dealing." And I remember saying, "Well, you know him, don't you, why don't the two of you set up some kind of arrangement". Then Barry's face changed, and I immediately realised I'd said something wrong… And Barry said, "Ahhh, yes, well, Peter likes to do it his own way."' Interview with the author, 31 Aug 2011.

14 Letter to Michael Smither, 18 Mar 1966.

15 Interview with the author, 16 Mar 2011. Don Wood recalled his parents coming to his first opening at The Gallery in 1960: they thought he was 'completely mad and had "lost his marbles"'. See Lois R McIvor, *Memoir of the sixties*, Remuera Gallery, Auckland, 2008, p. 36.

16 Interview with Susan Fowke, 24 Oct 2007.

17 Conversation with the author, 20 Dec 2012.

18 Lindsay Rabbitt, 'The dealer', *New Zealand Listener*, 17 Feb 2001, p. 50.

19 The exact price of *Mount Alexander* (n.d.) was £94-10-0.

20 Another friend who became a client was Tim Curnow, who had recently moved from Auckland – where he knew people like McCahon, Tomory, Binney and Hanly – to work as AH & AW Reed's first educational editor. Like PM, he frequented the Western Park Hotel in Tinakori Road, a gathering point for a group of mutual friends interested in the arts. He recalled the Woollaston paintings stacked along the hallway at PM's flat, sharing space with boots and a bicycle, and the lingering smell of lamb chops and cabbage. Email to the author, 6 Aug 2012.

21 Interview with the author, 10 Aug 2010. Woollaston replied in a letter of 13 May 1966: '[T]hank you for offering to forgo any commission on sales, to help me to paint. I can't forget that offer, any more than I can accept it.'

22 Gallery staff selected the Auckland component. PM chose work by John Drawbridge, Don Driver, Joan Fanning, William Jenks, Jeff Macklin, Michael Smither and Gordon Walters.

23 *New Zealand painting 1966*, Auckland City Art Gallery, Auckland, 1966, unpaged.

24 In 1958, Victoria University's council made an annual grant of £100 for the purchase of pictures; that figure gradually increased to $1000 in 1971 (the year the staff club collection was formally amalgamated with the university collection). By 1984, it stood at $8000. See William McAloon (ed.), *Victoria's art: A university collection*, Adam Art Gallery Te Pātaka Toi, Wellington, 2005.

25 Many students had their first experience of New Zealand art at the Beaglehole home in Messines Road: works by John Weeks and TA McCormack during the 1930s and 1940s, and later by Woollaston and his contemporaries. Fred Page occasionally sold Woollaston's work from his home in Hobson Street, ringing up his friends and encouraging them to come and buy.

26 Interview with the author, 20 July 2011. All quotations from Tim Beaglehole in this chapter are from this interview.

27 Interview with the author, 14 July 2011. Sir David Gascoigne is a corporate lawyer and consultant, company director and arts administrator.

28 The Department of External Affairs became the Ministry of Foreign Affairs in 1970; in 1988 it was renamed the Ministry of External Relations and Trade, and since 1993 it has been known as the Ministry of Foreign Affairs and Trade.

29 The Woollastons were *Sunset at Bayly's Hill* (1966) and *Bayly's Hill* (*c.*1960). The latter was gifted to the DPAG in 2001 as part of the ministry's art repatriation project.

30 Bryan Staff, 'Peter McLeavey interviewed for ChaCha', *ChaCha*, June 1984, p. 11.

31 Interview with the author, 10 Aug 2010.

32 See letter from Toss Woollaston to Edith Woollaston, 15 Feb [1962], in Jill Trevelyan (ed.), *Toss Woollaston: A life in letters*, Te Papa Press, Wellington, 2004, p. 247. The work Corner purchased was *Blackball no 3* (1961), gifted to the Millennium Gallery, Blenheim, in 2001.

33 Interview with the author, 10 Aug 2010.

34 *Tasman Bay* had been purchased by the gallery's young director, James Mack, one of a new generation of administrators who would transform New Zealand's art museums in the following decade.

35 Letter to Milan Mrkusich, 23 Aug 1966.

36 Sally Blundell, 'I sell, therefore I am', *New Zealand Listener*, 28 Nov 2009, p. 34.

37 Rabbitt, 'The dealer', p. 50.
38 Interview with the author, 14 July 2011.
39 Letter to Pat Hanly, 27 Apr 1967.
40 The *Dominion* column was written by Russell Bond. It also had a weekly (Saturday) books column by Louis Johnson, which provided PM with a model for his own writing ambitions.
41 Interview with the author, 10 Aug 2010.
42 PM, 'Boost for visual arts in New Plymouth', *Dominion*, 5 Aug 1967, p. 6.
43 PM, 'Keen interest in Art Biennales', *Dominion*, 17 Feb 1968, p. 6. It was not until 2001 that New Zealand mounted an exhibition at the Venice Biennale, and then it was two of PM's artists – Peter Robinson and Jacqueline Fraser – who represented the country. See p. 386.
44 PM, 'New Zealand artist with rare distinction', *Dominion*, 10 Feb 1968, p. 8.
45 Letter to Hanly, 30 Sept 1967. The next quotation is also from this letter.
46 Interview with the author, 10 Aug 2010.
47 Letter to Ian Scott, 29 Nov 1976.
48 Letter to Ralph von Kohorn, 6 May 1967.
49 Letter from McCahon to PM, 17 Jan [1967].
50 Letter to Mrkusich, 30 Sept 1967.
51 [Beverley Simmons], 'Young man on way to the top'. All the quotations in this paragraph are from this article, which is interesting as many of the key themes in PM's later interviews are already present: the railway childhood ('we seemed never to be in one place for very long'), the early exposure to religious art, and the importance of his overseas trip in shaping his identity as a New Zealander.

CHAPTER 5

1 PM earned $1800 in sales for the financial year ending 31 March 1968. His commission (now 33.3%) was $570 and his expenses $762, leaving a loss of $192.
2 'While nothing came of my endeavours it was worth trying.' Letter to Len Lye, 13 Dec 1967; the next quotation is also from this letter.
3 PM, 'N.Z.-born artist has won renown in unusual idiom', *Dominion*, 18 Nov 1967, p. 8. Only a handful of people in New Zealand were aware of Lye's work at the time; they included Hamish Keith (who had recently paid him a visit), Gil Docking, Gordon Walters and Peter Tomory (who had recently left New Zealand to become an associate professor at Columbia University in New York).
4 Letter from Lye to PM, n.d. [early Dec 1967].
5 Letter to Lye, 13 Dec 1967.
6 Letter to Lye, 19 Nov 1967.
7 Letter to Lye, n.d. [*c.*Oct 1970].
8 Letter to Billy Apple, 3 Jan 1968. The quotations in this paragraph are all from this letter.
9 PM, 'Arts world indebted to Helen Hitchings', *Dominion*, 23 Mar 1968, p. 7. The next quotation is also from this article.
10 Interview with the author, 25 Aug 2010; see also letter to Pat Hanly, 2 Dec 1968. Hanly wrote to PM on 22 Mar 1968: '[H]earty congratulations on your very erudite and honest radio broadcast, it was quite the most firm and consistent appraisal of the National Gallery situation I have ever heard and very well received by those who heard it up here.'
11 Letter to Michael Smither, 11 Mar 1968.
12 Letter to Colin McCahon, 30 Mar 1977.
13 The papers delivered at the Australian Unesco Seminar on Criticism in the Arts were published in *Criticism in the arts: Australian UNESCO Seminar*, University of Sydney, May 1968, Australian National Advisory Committee for Unesco, Canberra, 1970. PM would have missed Greenberg's formal lecture, 'Avant-garde attitudes', which was delivered as the John Power Lecture in Contemporary Art at the University of Sydney on 17 May 1968.
14 AUD$35,000 (1968) would equal AUD$379,740 today. Stern, who had been buying art since he was a teenager, had bought the painting from fellow dealer Kym Bonython for $18,000, thus neatly upstaging him. Stern established his first gallery in 1959 to show his personal collection; three years later he opened the commercial Barry Stern Gallery in Paddington.
15 At the time, most commercial galleries in Sydney were in private houses or converted shop fronts, with traditional furniture and fittings.

16 Interview with Susan Fowke, 24 Oct 2007.

17 *Ayin* (1958) had been purchased in 1967.

18 PM, 'Exciting sculpture to grace building', *Dominion*, 8 June 1968, p. 12.

19 *Eight New Zealand artists*, including Binney, Robert Ellis, Tim Garrity, Hanly, McCahon, Mrkusich, Ross Ritchie and Greer Twiss, was exhibited in 1965 at the National Gallery of Victoria in Melbourne, the Bonython Art Gallery in Adelaide and the Rudy Komon Gallery in Sydney. This was the first time McCahon attracted significant attention in Australia, and led to his large solo exhibition at the Bonython Art Gallery in Sydney in July 1968, which was crucial in developing his trans-Tasman reputation. McCahon was also represented in *Five Auckland painters*, organised by the Barry Lett Galleries and shown at the Darlinghurst Galleries in Sydney in Feb–Mar 1966.

20 Gordon H Brown quoted in John McDonald, 'A star in our backyard', *Sydney Morning Herald*, 29 Jan 1994, p. 121. According to an editorial in the *Auckland City Art Gallery Quarterly* (No. 44, 1969, p. 2), Greenberg 'spoke well of McCahon's personal conviction as a painter that has enabled him to pursue an independent course without being overwhelmed by the winds of change that frequently storm through the realm of art'.

21 'Notable art not expected from NZ', *Press*, 1 July 1968, p. 10. In Wellington, where he spoke to some 300 people on 2 July, Greenberg made the point that in the last 400 years, 'major works of art had come almost entirely from centres of art'. He urged the importance of seeing art 'in the flesh': 'Reproductions in art magazines were of little value in judging the quality of the original, Mr Greenberg said.' See 'Art blossoms where art is nourished', *EP*, 3 July 1968, p. 10.

22 Letter to Lye, n.d. [early Aug 1968].

23 Letter from Toss Woollaston to PM, 2 July 1967 [1968].

24 Hanly wrote on 1 Sept 1968, 'Best wishes for success at your Gallery opening, everyone up here is behind you.'

25 Letter from Lye to PM, 27 Aug 1968.

26 Letter to Woollaston, 12 July 1968.

27 Initially the room that is now the 'office' was divided into two small rooms: it was converted in the early 1970s. The building, constructed in 1900, was designed by architect William Crichton as a photographic studio and workshop for William Berry.

28 See: www.fishhead.co.nz/articles/characters-of-cuba-street.aspx, 24 Sept 2012. Cuba Street does, however, have colonial associations: it was named after an immigrant ship, which arrived from England in Jan 1840.

29 Interview with the author, 25 Aug 2010.

30 Interview with the author, 21 Dec 2010.

31 Interview with the author, 25 Aug 2010.

32 Email from Tim Curnow to the author, 9 Aug 2012.

33 It was *Bayly's Hill, Taranaki* (*c.*1965); the first Woollaston purchased for the gallery was *View towards Mount Richmond, Nelson* (*c.*1938) in 1966.

34 Thanks to Tim Beaglehole for giving me this quotation, from a letter from JC Beaglehole to Janet Paul, 4 Sept 1968, ATL, MS-Papers-5738-24.

35 Letter from Woollaston to Edith Woollaston, 4 Sept 1968.

36 Interview with the author, 25 Aug 2011.

37 The professionals included physician Ian Prior, and George Laking from the Department of External Affairs; the artists and writers included Vera Jamieson, Louis Johnson and Walters.

38 Interview with the author, 14 July 2011.

39 '[It] gives relevance and a sense of proportion to works destined for private collections.' See 'Nearly sold out', *NZH*, 28 Sept 1968, magazine section, p. 5.

40 Letter from Milan Mrkusich to PM, 9 Oct 1968.

41 Letter to Lye, n.d. [late Sept 1968].

42 Melville delivered the Chancellor's Lectures at Victoria University in Sept 1968.

43 Letter to Lye, n.d. [late Sept 1968].

44 McCahon saw Pollock's *Autumn rhythm (number 30)* (1950), Picasso's *Guernica* (1937) and Rivera's murals on his trip.

45 Gordon H Brown, *Colin McCahon: Artist*, Reed, Wellington, 1993, p. 93.

46 *Ibid.*, p. 95.
47 See Hamish Keith's text for the exhibition, reproduced on the invitation.
48 As a comparison, the eight-part *Landscape theme and variations (series A)* (1963) was priced at $1600 when it was exhibited at the Bonython Art Gallery in Sydney in July 1968.
49 Letter from Hamish Keith to PM, n.d. [late Sept 1968]. Keith also recorded a 10-minute talk on the *Northland panels*, which was broadcast on 'Arts in Wellington', 2YC, on 27 Oct. 'It was bang on,' PM informed McCahon in a letter of 29 Oct 1968.
50 Letter to Keith, 11 Oct 1968.
51 Letter from McCahon to PM, 9 Oct [1968].
52 Letter to William Rubin, 11 Nov 1968. PM also mentioned that Clement Greenberg had been impressed by McCahon's work: 'He thought him one of the several good painters we have here.'
53 Letter from Rubin to PM, 4 Dec 1968.
54 Letter to McCahon, 24 Dec 1968. On 2 Nov, PM told McCahon that 147 visitors had seen the exhibition in the previous week. He was also pleased by Margaret Orbell's review in the *Dominion*: 'Like so much New Zealand art and literature, the "Northland Panels" conveys a sense of remoteness from a land still felt to be alien, and a strong, almost despairing desire to establish a spiritual relationship with it… In its successful expression of a vision which is highly personal yet of universal significance, it is a key work both in McCahon's development and in contemporary New Zealand painting.' See 'McCahon's panels', *Dominion*, 28 Oct 1968, p. 4.
55 Interview with Susan Fowke, 24 Oct 2007.
56 Interview with the author, 10 Aug 2010.
57 Grant Smithies, 'Art and soul', *SST*, 29 May 2005, *Sunday* supplement, p. 26.
58 Interview with Susan Fowke, 24 Oct 2007.
59 Brickell had four solo exhibitions (1969, 1972, 1985 and 1992) and also participated in a group show in 1975.
60 Interview with the author, 10 Aug 2010. A draft of this letter, dated 13 Sept 1968, is in the Rita Angus papers at the ATL, MS-Papers-1399-1/4.
61 Auckland dealer Rodney Kirk Smith, who entered the business in 1975, had a similar experience: the response from artists ranged from 'open-armed welcome' to 'sincere suspicion'. See William Dart, 'Rodney Kirk Smith: 25 years with art', *Art New Zealand*, No. 55, Winter 1990, p. 49.
62 Letter to Hanly, 2 Dec 1968.
63 Curated by Wellington painter and potter Roy Cowan, *Five guest artists* included work by Melvin Day, Ralph Hotere, John Drawbridge, Don Peebles and Hanly.
64 It was renamed the Elva Bett Gallery in 1976.
65 Interview with the author, 16 Mar 2011.
66 They included John Drawbridge, Tanya Ashken, Melvin Day, Helen Stewart, Joan Fanning, Paul Olds, Avis Higgs, Betty Clegg and Rita Angus.
67 Letter from Lye to PM, 23 Oct 1968.
68 Letter to Clyfford Still, 11 Feb 1969.
69 Roger Horrocks, *Len Lye: A biography*, Auckland University Press, Auckland, 2001, p. 343.
70 Letter to Still, 11 Feb 1969. On 18 Nov 1968, Still had sent PM two catalogues on his work in response to a fan letter: 'As for my being a recluse, that will usually depend upon the expressed purpose of the would-be visitor. And perhaps I am a bit crusty at times to those who would presume to indulge their insolence. However, to a gentleman of consideration and a will to understand, I herewith offer a sincere salute and my best wishes.'
71 Horrocks, *Len Lye*, p. 343.
72 Letter from Lye to PM, 27 Feb 1969.

CHAPTER 6

1 Interview with the author, 16 Mar 2011; unless otherwise noted, all quotations from Hilary McLeavey in this chapter are from this interview. Organist, teacher and conductor Maxwell Fernie was the director of music at St Mary of the Angels from 1958 until his death in 1999, and founded the Schola Polyphonica Choir in 1967. PM held him in great esteem, describing him as 'a McCahon-like figure' to poet and artist Gregory O'Brien. Conversation with the author, 18 Oct 2012.
2 Interview with the author, 19 Dec 2012.

3 Letter from Len Lye to PM, 8 Apr 1969.
4 He earned $1174 in commission during this financial year.
5 See 'Unfortunate reaction greets sculptor's creation', *Dominion*, 14 Oct 1967, p. 11.
6 *Zig zag-1* (1969). PM's recollection is that Driver decided to change the title during the show. Interview with the author, 21 Dec 2010.
7 Letter to Don Driver, 12 Nov 1968.
8 *Saracen* (1965–69).
9 Letter to Driver, 22 June 1969.
10 Letter to Driver, 24 Apr 1969. Driver had a second show with PM in 1971, but cancelled scheduled exhibitions in 1972 (because of a near sell-out show in Auckland) and in 1973 (because of an invitation to exhibit at the Dusseldorf Arts Fair).
11 *Dominion*, 18 Apr 1969, p. 18.
12 Walters' first solo exhibition since 1949 was at the New Vision Gallery in Auckland in 1966, and he exhibited there again in 1968.
13 Letter to Douglas Drury (producer, *Town and Around*), 1 May 1969.
14 PM, 'Gordon Walters: an interview', *Salient*, 7 May 1969, p. 8.
15 Melville began his article with the observation that New Zealand painting had been dominated by the landscape, and cited McCahon as the first 'real break' with an English topographical tradition. After praising traditional Māori art, and lamenting the fact that it seemed confined to museums, he went on to mention the work of three contemporary artists who attempted to engage with it: Paratene Matchitt, Robert Ellis and Walters. See 'A stranger in N.Z.', *Architectural Review*, Dec 1968, pp. 443–45.
16 For example, in the Walters' interview in *Salient*, in his advertisement in the *Dominion* (14 May 1969, p. 42), and in letters like the one to Douglas Drury.
17 Both works are dated 1968; *Tamatea* was also priced at $400.
18 Artists were often content to receive regular monthly payments instead of a lump sum, but in times of high inflation the system could work to their disadvantage. As Charles Tole pointed out in a letter of 23 May 1978, with the current level of depreciation in the dollar, the actual sale price was reduced by 10% for six months' credit, or by 20% over a year. PM would often pay out the artist's share and wait on his own commission. It was in his best interests to try to keep everyone happy, artists and collectors alike.
19 Letter from LR Gibbs, Egan Ogier, Gibbs & Co. to PM, 13 June 1969.
20 Letter to Michael Smither, 14 Aug 1969.
21 Letter to Richard Killeen, 10 Sept 1983. The quotations in the next paragraph are also from this letter.
22 Hilary recalled, 'Malcolm called in to the gallery in the morning and asked Peter if he'd like to have a drink that evening. And Peter said, "Well I'd like to, but I'm getting married." And when Malcolm heard who he was marrying he said, "I know her! I'm coming to your wedding."' Interview with the author, 16 Mar 2011.
23 PM paid Turner to photograph the exhibitions at the PMG until he moved to Auckland to take up a position at Elam School of Fine Arts in 1971.
24 Interview with the author, 20 July 2011.
25 Stephen Green, 'Karl Sidow [*sic*] – sculptor', *Arts & Community*, Vol. 6, No. 6, June 1970, p. 7.
26 'Contrasting art in two displays', *EP*, 18 Apr 1970, p. 3.
27 Letter to Carl Sydow, 16 May 1970.
28 PM sold two works on paper in Sept 1973 – one to John Malcolm and one to Elva Bett. In the same year, although he was not personally involved in the sale, he earned commission from a work purchased by the Robert McDougall Art Gallery from an exhibition in Christchurch: *Meander I*. In 1979, the National Art Gallery purchased two works from the Brooke Gifford Gallery, on behalf of Sydow's estate, both of which had been exhibited at the PMG: *Meander II* (1971) and *Construction II* (1973).
29 Interview with the author, 20 July 2011. The quotation from Beaglehole in the next paragraph is also from this interview.
30 An exception is *An introduction to New Zealand painting 1839–1967* (1969) by Gordon H Brown and Hamish Keith, with chapters on McCahon, Woollaston and Hanly. Earlier publications included Eric McCormick's *Letters and art in New Zealand* and AH McLintock's *National centennial exhibition of New Zealand art* catalogue (both 1940). Howard Wadman launched the quarterly *Art in New Zealand* in 1928, which continued (from 1944 as the bi-monthly *Arts in New Zealand*) until its demise in 1946; it was succeeded by the *Year book of the arts* from 1945 to 1951. A number of journals

published articles on visual art prior to the 1970s, notably *Landfall* and *Ascent: A journal of the arts*. The annual *Bulletin of New Zealand Art History* (now the *Journal of New Zealand Art History*) commenced in 1972; the quarterly *Art New Zealand* in 1975.

31 Email to the author, 25 July 2011.
32 Email to the author, 1 Nov 2012.
33 Hamish Keith, 'Capital neglects the NZ scene – why?', *Auckland Star*, 20 June 1970, p. 16.
34 JS Guiney, 'Swinging London has enlivened our art gallery', *EP*, 18 Feb 1969, p. 35. The exhibition included work by New Zealanders James Boswell and Douglas MacDiarmid, and Australians Sidney Nolan, Donald Friend and Brett Whiteley.
35 Letter to Lye, n.d. [Oct 1970].
36 Roger Horrocks, *Len Lye: A biography*, Auckland University Press, Auckland, 2001, p. 349.
37 WN (Bill) Sheat and John Malcolm were chairman and secretary (respectively) of the Queen Elizabeth II Arts Council; Dr Ian Prior was chairman of its visual arts panel; Melvin Day was a panel member.
38 Letter from Lye to PM, n.d. [early 1971].
39 Letter from Lye to PM, 5 Mar 1971.
40 Letter to Lye, 11 May 1971.
41 Letter to Lye, 22 June 1972.
42 Letter from Lye to PM, 5 July 1972.
43 A half-hour documentary made for the New Zealand Broadcasting Corporation in 1972, *Len Who?* was directed by Tony Rimmer and narrated by Hamish Keith.
44 Letter to Lye, 23 July 1973.
45 Letter from Lye to PM, 23 Aug 1973.
46 Letter to Gordon Walters, 31 Mar 1977.

CHAPTER 7

1 Letter from Colin McCahon to PM, n.d. [*c.*July 1972].
2 Like Rita Angus, James K Baxter and others who had lived through the turbulent years of the Depression and the Second World War, McCahon believed that art had a healing, redeeming role to play in society. He found sustenance in the Romantic conception of the artist as a moral force – an outsider with special insight. This ideal was especially compelling at a time when artists were such a tiny minority, struggling to find a voice in New Zealand society.
3 Letter to Peter Simpson, 3 Aug 1996. The next quotation is also from this letter.
4 'An awful lot of things went into it – basically milk & lots of cream & rose-buds then all the other little things – it was a vague pink-grey colour & most delicate & delicious.' Letter from McCahon to PM, 13 July [1971].
5 Letter from McCahon to PM, n.d. [postmarked 3 June 1970].
6 Letter from McCahon to PM, 19 Aug 1974.
7 Letter from McCahon to PM, n.d. [early to mid-Dec 1975].
8 Letter from McCahon to PM, 20 Oct 1972.
9 Letter from McCahon to PM, 17 Apr 1973.
10 Quoted in *Colin McCahon/A survey exhibition*, Auckland City Art Gallery, 1972, p. 19.
11 Letter from McCahon to PM, 26 [?] Sept 1972.
12 McCahon's interest in the book was also encouraged by his friendship with Sharon Dales, a student of Māori lore then married to the composer Robin Maconie (who had briefly flatted with PM at 270 The Terrace). Email from Maconie to the author, 11 July 2011.
13 Letter from McCahon to PM, n.d. [June–early July 1969].
14 Letter from McCahon to PM, n.d. [16 Apr 1969]. *The Canoe Tainui* (1969) remains in the same private collection in 2013.
15 Letter to McCahon, 19 Aug 1969.
16 The unsold works were *The Canoe Mamari* (1969), later purchased by the Rev. Ian Brown and now a promised gift to the National Gallery of Victoria; see p. 392; and *On going out with the tide* (1969), now in a private collection.
17 'McCahon works on show', *NZH*, 25 July 1969, section 1, p. 6.
18 Letter to McCahon, 7 Aug 1969.

19 *King of the Jews* (1947) is now in the TP collection, bequeathed by Ron O'Reilly in 1982; *Elias will he come to save him* (1959) is in a private collection.
20 O'Reilly had moved to Wellington in July 1968 to take up his job at the New Zealand Library School; he later became director of the Govett-Brewster from 1975 to 1979.
21 Conversation with the author, 8 Nov 2012.
22 Bill Emsley, 'Where was the gallery?', *Dominion*, 22 Aug 1969, p. 22.
23 The work was *North Otago landscape 2* (1967), one of McCahon's less challenging paintings of the period.
24 Letter to McCahon, 21 Apr 1970.
25 Letter from McCahon to PM, n.d. [late June–July 1970]. McCahon's 'giant summer painting spree' refers to the 'Victory over death' paintings, including *Practical religion: the resurrection of Lazarus showing Mount Martha* (1969–70; TP) and *Victory over death 2* (1970; National Gallery of Australia, Canberra).
26 Letter from McCahon to Maureen Hitchings, 18 May 1971, quoted in Gordon H Brown, *Colin McCahon: Artist*, Reed, Wellington, 1993, p. 109.
27 McCahon sent this work – identified in the catalogue as *Painting, dated 19th March 1963* – to give a sense of scale to the show. It is now in a private collection.
28 Letter to McCahon, 27 Apr 1971.
29 Letter from McCahon to PM, 13 July [1971]. The next quotation is also from this letter.
30 Letter to McCahon, 23 June 1971. The next quotation is also from this letter.
31 Letter to McCahon, n.d. [early Aug 1971]. The next quotation is also from this letter.
32 Letter from McCahon to PM, 5 Aug 1971.
33 Letter from McCahon to PM, n.d. [Aug 1971]. The next quotation is also from this letter.
34 The quotations from Tim Beaglehole in this chapter are from an interview with the author, 20 July 2011.
35 Letter from McCahon to PM, n.d. [postmarked 20 Mar 1972].
36 Earlier, when *Ten big paintings* was shown at the New Zealand Academy of Fine Arts in July 1971, *Gate III* had been priced at $10,000. See 'Breathtaking canvas – so is the price', *EP*, 29 July 1971, p. 8.
37 Letter to McCahon, 20 July 1972.
38 'Highest price for NZ painting?', *EP*, 19 Sept 1972, p. 7.
39 Letter from McCahon to PM, 4 Aug 1972. The negotiations for *Gate III* coincided with McCahon's fourth exhibition with PM in March 1972: four works, including *Are there not twelve hours of daylight* (1970), priced at $1200. There were no sales. The work is now in the Chartwell Collection, AAG.
40 Letter from McCahon to PM, 30 Mar 1973.
41 Letter from Barry Lett to PM, 2 Nov 1972.
42 Letter from McCahon to PM, 30 Mar 1973. Evidently it was business correspondence that troubled McCahon, as he continued to write lengthy and frequent letters to PM.
43 *Jim passes the northern beaches* (1972), private collection.
44 Letter from McCahon to PM, 2 July 1973.
45 Letter from McCahon to PM, 20 Oct 1972.
46 Letter from McCahon to PM, 16 Aug 1973.
47 The paintings were listed in the exhibition catalogue as *Series C* and *Series D*. PM's exhibition followed the showing of *Series A* and *Series B* at the Barry Lett Galleries in Aug 1973 under the title, *Colin McCahon: Jet out from Muriwai*. PM later took works from *Series A* into his stock, and sold panels *A11*, *A12* and *A13* to his Melbourne client, Rev. Ian Brown.
48 Letter to McCahon, 12 Sept 1973.
49 Letter from McCahon to PM, 16 Aug 1973.
50 Conversation with client, 29 Oct 2011.
51 Letter from McCahon to PM, 13 Oct 1974. The next quotation is also from this letter.
52 Letter from McCahon to PM, Labour Day [28 Oct 1974]. The next quotation is also from this letter.
53 Mason died in 1971, Baxter in 1972 and Brasch (one of McCahon's key early supporters) in 1973. McCahon gifted the work to the Hocken in 1977.
54 The two panels purchased by the Ministry of Foreign Affairs in 1980 were gifted to the GBAG in 2001 as part of the ministry's art repatriation project. The CAG owns panel V; I and II are in private collections. In 1996, Wystan Curnow reunited the work for the first time in the exhibition *Under Capricorn: Art in the age of globalisation* at the Stedelijk Museum in Amsterdam.

55 Letter from McCahon to PM, Labour Day [28 Oct 1974].

56 'The "Peter McLeavey sat here" drawing will be down to you soon', letter from McCahon to PM, July 1978. PM and Hilary McLeavey gifted the drawing to TP in 1986.

CHAPTER 8

1 Interview with the author, 25 Aug 2011.

2 Interview with the author, 31 Aug 2011.

3 In 1964, Woollaston had briefly contracted his son Philip to organise his exhibitions.

4 Postscript for *The Far-away hills*, July 1977, in Jill Trevelyan (ed.), *Toss Woollaston: A life in letters*, Te Papa Press, Wellington, 2004, p. 390.

5 Interview with the author, 19 Dec 2012.

6 Letter to Toss Woollaston, 27 July 1978.

7 Letter from Woollaston to Rodney Kirk Smith (copy), 19 Oct 1971.

8 Interview with the author, 1 Aug 2011.

9 Letter to Colin McCahon, 30 July 1977.

10 Interview with the author, 10 Aug 2010. PM mentioned the portrait in a letter to Woollaston on 26 Aug 1977: 'Thank you for doing it and creating such a splendid and living thing. As long as the painting will be around they, my parents, will live.'

11 The Auckland City Art Gallery loaned two works, including *Figures from life* (1936), while private lenders included Hamish Keith, the Nelson restaurateur Eelco Boswijk, and the artist's longtime friend and supporter Rodney Kennedy.

12 Letter from Woollaston to PM, 20 Aug 1971.

13 Interview with the author, 19 Aug 2011.

14 His standard large size was just over 1.2 metres wide, at 3 × 4 feet.

15 Letter from Woollaston to Faye Hill, 28 Jan 1971, ATL, MS-Group-1225.

16 Letter from Woollaston to Charles Brasch, 30 Jan 1971, Charles Brasch papers, HL, MS-0996-003.

17 The three, all dated 1971, are in private collections.

18 '$1000 painting on move in city', *Dominion*, 24 Sept 1971, p. 1.

19 Peter Cape, 'Art gallery round-up', *NBR*, 23 Sept 1971, p. 11.

20 Letter to Woollaston, 1 Oct 1971.

21 Letter to Woollaston, 8 Oct 1971.

22 Letter from Woollaston to PM, 12 Oct 1971.

23 Letter from Woollaston to Brasch, 5 Oct 1971.

24 This and the next quotation are from a conversation with John Casserley, 24 Feb 2012.

25 The post-war generation was highly educated compared to their parents. In 1944, the school leaving age was raised to 15 and a high school education became almost universal. The number of students enrolled at university soared from 8425 in 1945 to 42,436 in 1975. See GT Bloomfield, *New Zealand: A handbook of historical statistics*, GK Hall, Boston, 1984, p. 114. The next generation was even better informed, thanks to changes in the education system. In 1969, art became a University Entrance subject, and in 1974 a section on contemporary New Zealand art was introduced into the new School Certificate syllabus.

26 Letter from Tim Curnow to PM, 8 Oct 2006. Curnow moved to Sydney in 1970 to be the first managing editor for Reedkoala; a year later, he became the managing director of the literary agency Curtis Brown Australia.

27 Email to the author, 4 Oct 2012.

28 Letter from Tim Curnow to PM, 8 Oct 2006.

29 McCahon was one of many who were impressed, writing to PM: 'Now in praise of Luit Bieringa & Toss. A most beautiful job on Luit's part'. Letter from McCahon to PM, 16 Aug 1973.

30 One, *My house at Riwaka* (1971–72), was purchased by PM himself and is now in the TP collection. The other, *Wellington* (1972), acquired by the Ministry of Foreign Affairs and Trade, was gifted to the DPAG in 2001.

31 Letter to McCahon, 12 May 1976. Reviewing the exhibition in *Spleen*, Ian Wedde reserved his highest praise for *Tasman Bay, 1928*: 'The extraordinary accomplishment of this painting is that it says, with tenderness and some melancholy, that "landscapes" exist in time; they are real as what we remember and as what we see, "now".' See *Spleen*, No. 4, July 1976, unpaged.

32 This and the following quotation from Tim Beaglehole are from an interview with the author, 20 July 2011.

33 Letter from Woollaston to PM, 14 June 1976. In fact, although Woollaston knew the Beagleholes, he never availed himself of the opportunity of visiting *Tasman Bay, 1928*. 'He must have found he could live without it,' Tim Beaglehole commented in a conversation, 13 Jan 2013.

34 Letter to Michael Smither, 24 Dec 1969.

35 Letter to Smither, 19 Oct 1976. The next quotation is also from this letter.

36 AB, 'Happenings', *Thursday: The magazine for modern women*, 29 Oct 1970, p. 40.

37 Conversation with Neil Robertson, 1 Aug 2011. Robertson paid $180 for this painting – soon after he had paid $600, approximately one-fifth of his salary, for Don Binney's *Motukorea*. Robertson commented: 'In 1972, when I was on a posting in New Delhi, Peter wrote to us about a Smither landscape exhibition he was putting on – and said that he had reserved one of the paintings ("Tent After Storm") for us as he thought it was one we would like, at $300. Of course, we agreed to buy it – not because we wanted another Smither (and $300 seemed still a lot of money) but because Peter had chosen it for us, and we both appreciated his thoughtfulness and respected his judgement.' Email to the author, 10 Oct 2012.

38 Judith James, 'Smither: So stones make a mountain', *Dominion*, 4 Dec 1971, p. 18.

39 Transcript of a broadcast for *Arts in Wellington*, 2YC, July 1973, exhibition file no. 49.

40 Interview with the author, 21 Sept 2011. Unless otherwise noted, all quotations from Milly Paris in this chapter are from this interview.

41 Neil Rowe, 'Smither takes a new direction', *EP*, 18 Nov 1978, p. 19. Rowe was the *Evening Post*'s art critic from 1977 to 1982, and director of the Wairarapa Arts Centre (which later became Aratoi Wairarapa Museum of Art and History) from 1979 to 1984. *Gifts* (1978) was purchased by the National Art Gallery in 1980.

42 Letter to Smither, 2 Mar 1979.

43 Interview with the author, 31 Aug 2011.

44 Letter from Don Binney to PM, 15 June [1975].

45 Jim and Mary Barr, *Contemporary New Zealand painters*, Vol. 1, A–M, Alister Taylor, Martinborough, 1980, p. 26. The next quotation is also from this text.

46 BB, 'Year of controversy in art: City exhibitions broke record', *NZH*, 14 Jan 1964, p. 12.

47 Interview with the author, 31 Aug 2011.

48 Letter to Binney, 7 June 1966. PM had seen mention of Binney's waiting list in 'Exhibition sales have soared rapidly', *NZH*, 20 May 1966, section 1, p. 5.

49 Letter from Binney to PM, 24 Sept 1969.

50 Letter from Binney to PM, 8 Apr 1970. The ambassador and his wife, Kenneth and Barbara Franzheim, purchased several pictures from PM in 1970–71, including a large Binney in the lead-up to this exhibition. They gifted 10 items to the Dowse Art Gallery in 1972, including works by Don Driver, John Drawbridge, Walters and Robin White.

51 'Busy buyers hit record heights for Binney art', *EP*, 29 July 1970, p. 26. At the end of the financial year, PM discovered that of the five works he had sold for $500 or more, four were by Binney. (The other was by Woollaston.)

52 Stephen Green, 'Wellington – Don Binney', *Arts & Community*, Vol. 6, No. 9, Sept 1970, p. 11.

53 At Binney's third and final show with PM in 1976, Neil Rowe posed a question: 'Has the "visionary gleam" departed Don Binney? Will he join those of his contemporaries (particularly Illingworth) who seem to have painted themselves out in the sixties?' See 'Don Binney at the Peter McLeavey Gallery', *Salient*, 22 Mar 1976, p. 16.

54 This and the following quotation are from an interview with the author, 31 Aug 2011.

55 Like his near contemporary Peter McIntyre, Rei Hamon (1919–2008) was one of the most popular New Zealand artists of the 1970s and 1980s, renowned for his meticulously detailed drawings of native bush.

56 Letter to Binney, 2 July 1974.

57 This and the next quotations in this paragraph are from Alexa Johnston et al., *Dream collectors: One hundred years of art in New Zealand*, Te Papa Press, Wellington, 1998, p. 144.

58 *Old Wellington synagogue* (1976) was sold by the Gow Langsford Gallery in 2012 when Milly Paris moved to Melbourne. It is now in a private collection.

59 This and the following quotations from Milly Paris are from an interview with the author, 21 Sept 2011. Jim Barr was then the director of the Dowse Art Gallery.

CHAPTER 9

1 Letter to Richard Killeen, 31 Oct 1981.
2 Letter from Gordon Walters to PM, 31 Jan 1974.
3 Letter to Walters, 2 Apr 1975.
4 Interview with the author, 16 Mar 2011.
5 Letter to Ian Scott, 6 Nov 1976.
6 Letter to Colin McCahon, 11 Aug 1971.
7 Letter from Walters to PM, 2[6?] Aug 1971.
8 Letter to Brian [?], 13 Oct 1971.
9 Interview with the author, 10 Aug 2012. The painting is *Untitled* (1971), listed in the exhibition catalogue as *Waiata*, a title provided by PM.
10 Letter from Walters to PM, 17 Sept 1971. *Hautana* (1970), based on the Māori carving pattern rau-ponga, was exhibited under the title *Oriori*, bestowed by PM.
11 In an undated letter of 1973, Walters wrote to PM, 'I have decided to keep the canvas of the landscape you asked me to send down, sorry about this ... I am also having second thoughts about the large black koru, right now I can't bear to part with it.'
12 The New Vision Gallery (initially the New Vision Craft Centre) opened in 1965 and ran until 1986.
13 Vuletic opened his gallery in partnership with his brother James; later he moved to the Crown Chambers, 87 Customs Street East. His stable in the early 1970s included Stephen Bambury, Roy Good, Killeen, Ron Left, Mrkusich, Phillip O'Sullivan, Ian Scott, Geoff Thornley, Walters and Alan Wright. See Edward Hanfling and Alan Wright, *Vuletic and his circle*, Gus Fisher Gallery, Auckland, 2003.
14 Quoted in TJ McNamara, 'Avant-garde in their time', *NZH*, 29 May 2003, B5.
15 Letter to Don Binney, Aug 1972. This letter is annotated 'not delivered/returned Sept 1973'. Others to leave the Barry Lett Galleries for Vuletic included Ian Scott, Geoff Thornley and Roy Good.
16 Letter from Walters to PM, 26 May 1972.
17 This and the next quotation are from an interview with the author, 23 Dec 2011.
18 Harry M Miller (born in New Zealand in 1934) is a show business promoter and entrepreneur. Letter to Binney, Aug 1972. The quotations in this and the next paragraph are also from this letter.
19 The Rosalind Humphries Galleries in Armadale is best known for its rediscovery of the Australian painter Clarice Beckett. PM recalled, 'I knew Barry Humphries' former wife Ros – she was a Wellington girl – and she was keen for me to relocate from Wellington.' Interview with the author, 25 Aug 2011.
20 Michael Brett, 'Eyes opened in Sydney' (The Auckland Diary), *Auckland Star*, 11 July 1972, p. 8.
21 Letter to Walters, 11 Sept 1975.
22 Letter to Walters, 22 Dec 1975.
23 PM sold five works by Smither in this price bracket, and four each by Mrkusich, Binney and McCahon.
24 PM recalled, 'I sold a couple of paintings to George Fraser who was the driving force at Fletchers early on. The collection was established before I came along, and they bought mainly from Auckland dealers, but they were very encouraging to me, particularly Sir James and Lady Fletcher.' Interview with the author, 25 Aug 2011.
25 This and the following quotations from Sir John Todd are from an interview with the author, 17 Sept 2012.
26 Artworks featured in the Todd company magazine, *Network*, and PM helped John Todd establish some objectives for the collection, which were published in October 1973. As well as the obvious aims ('To provide attractive decorative elements for the interiors of Company buildings'), the company assumed more ambitious objectives, including 'To encourage the continuing development of New Zealand art and assist in its promotion'.
27 'Government support for the arts in general rose a staggering eightfold from $272,000 in 1970/71 to $2,179,000 by 1974/75.' See Athol McCredie, 'Going public: New Zealand art museums in the 1970s', MA thesis, Massey University, 1999, p. 88. The funds went to the Queen Elizabeth II Arts Council, the National Museum and National Art Gallery, the New Zealand Historic Places Trust, the New Zealand Literary Fund, the New Zealand Authors' Fund, and the Art Galleries and Museums Scheme.

28 David Millar, letter to the editor, *AGMANZ News* 3, No. 1, May 1972, p. 12.
29 Bieringa noted, 'I think Peter benefited from a new crop coming through who really wanted to push the contemporary art boundaries.' Interview with the author, 30 Aug 2012. The Manawatu Art Gallery had a professional director as early as 1966 in James Mack; he was followed by Brian Muir from 1967 to 1969.
30 The National Art Gallery, Museum and War Memorial Act 1972.
31 As chairman of the Queen Elizabeth II Arts Council, Keith was appointed to the National Art Gallery Council in 1976 – part of a move towards the arts council taking a more direct role in its management. As well as Ian Hunter, other young staff at the gallery in the 1970s included artists Andrew Drummond and Nicholas Spill.
32 The Brooke Gifford Gallery was established by Judith Gifford and Barbara Brooke in 1975, while Kobi and Patricia Bosshard, who opened the Bosshard Galleries in Akaroa late in 1970, relocated to Dunedin in 1976. Dunedin had been early on the dealer-gallery circuit: artist Hubert Struyk's Rosslyn Gallery in the 1960s had been succeeded by Dawson's Gallery (run by Maureen Hitchings) in the late 1960s and early 1970s.
33 Frank Lowe had sold his interest in the gallery to Kim Wright in 1966.
34 Webb had opened Auckland's first dealer gallery, the Argus Gallery in 1957. In 1963, he was the founding director of auction house John Cordy Limited; later he took up the post of exhibitions officer at the Auckland City Art Gallery from 1970 to 1974.
35 Letter to McCahon, 29 Aug 1974.
36 Letter to McCahon, 6 Mar 1975.
37 Letter to Walters, 6 Mar 1975.
38 Letter from Walters to PM, n.d. [early to mid-Mar 1975].
39 Letter to Walters, 18 Mar 1975.
40 Notably, Ian Scott exhibited his 'Lattice' paintings in Oct–Nov 1977 and July 1978. Vuletic's gallery continued in some form until 1987, showing young artists such as Julia Morison in the early 1980s.
41 Letter from Walters to PM, 10 Nov 1976. Data Gallery closed in 1978.
42 Artist's statement, 2 Oct 1974, on invitation and catalogue for *Gordon Walters: Gouaches 1951–59*.
43 Letter to John Casserley, 29 Oct 1974.
44 Conversation with the author, 27 July 2012. Ireland was copyright publications officer at the General Assembly Library at the time. In 1983, he gifted his gouache *Untitled* (1954) to the National Art Gallery on the occasion of the opening of the Gordon Walters retrospective.
45 Letter to Walters, 6 Nov 1974. The next quotation is also from this letter.
46 Walters sent PM a copy of his letter to Ron O'Reilly, 8 Sept 1975. The safety of his work was a constant concern for Walters, and in a letter of 6–7 Sept 1971 he had apologised for 'bombarding' PM with instructions about how to care for his paintings. 'The amount of work damaged in the Lett Galleries is amazing, I saw a collection at Auckland University the other day and half the paintings were damaged and unfit to be sold.'
47 Letter from Walters to PM, 29 Apr 1976. *Maho* (1973), was listed as *Painting C* in the catalogue and priced at $1200.
48 In 2004, nine years after Walters' death, TP purchased *Maho* from Margaret Orbell.
49 Letter from Walters to PM, 1 Sept 1976.
50 Letter from Walters to PM, 25 Mar 1977.
51 Letter from Walters to PM, 16 July 1977.
52 Letter from Walters to PM, 25 Aug 1977.
53 Letter from Walters to PM, 16 July 1977.
54 Letter to Walters, 23 Sept 1977.
55 Letter from Walters to PM, 24 Sept 1977.
56 Letter from Walters to PM, 17 Apr 1978.
57 Letter from Walters to PM, 23 May 1978.
58 Letter from Walters to PM, 8 July 1978.
59 The Ministry of Foreign Affairs and Trade gifted *Patere* (1977) to the AAG as part of its 2001 repatriation project. At the Dowse, director Jim Barr had approached PM about a commissioned 'Koru' painting in May 1978. There was just one hitch: given the conservatism of the gallery committee, he could not guarantee that the purchase would not be vetoed. Walters wrote to PM on 20 May 1978:

'I wd be delighted to do a work for Jim Barr. I quite appreciate his position vis-à-vis his committee, this is no problem. The work will sell anyway.' In the event, Barr bought *Waiata* (1977) from the July exhibition.

60 Neil Rowe, 'Where is the retrospective?', *EP*, 5 Aug 1978, p. 11.
61 Letter from Walters to PM, 10 Aug 1978.
62 Letter to Walters, 15 Aug 1978.

CHAPTER 10

1 Christine Moir, 'His art is strictly from the intellect', *New Zealand Woman's Weekly*, 10 Mar 1969, p. 16.
2 Letter to Jeffrey Harris, 11 July 1979.
3 Letter to Milan Mrkusich, 5 Sept 1977.
4 Letter to Mrkusich, 5 Sept 1969. The next quotation is also from this letter.
5 A month later PM sold another work, *Painting 62-10*, 1962, to a visiting diplomat; the price was $500.
6 Dr Gerda E Bell, 'The arts in Wellington', *Home & Building*, 1 Nov 1969, p. 59.
7 Letter to Colin McCahon, 4 May 1971. When PM sent out a press release about the sale, an article appeared in the *Dominion* under the headline, '$900 painting bamboozles passers-by'. See *Dominion*, 3 May 1971, p. 3.
8 'US collector pays well for NZ work', *EP*, 24 Mar 1972, p. 2.
9 Hamish Keith, 'A happy return to old style', *Auckland Star*, 1 Apr 1972, p. 11.
10 The retrospective was *Milan Mrkusich: Paintings 1946–1972*.
11 Victoria University bought *Chromatic meta-grey no. 2* (1970) for $900; the Govett-Brewster acquired *Chromatic suite I, number 1* and *Chromatic suite II, no. 3*; the Robert McDougall *Chromatic suite I, no. 2 1968* (all 1968).
12 Letter to Philip Trusttum, 10 July 1973.
13 It included the 11 works shown in 1949, dating from 1946 to 1949, and *Painting no. 7* (1950), completed shortly after the exhibition.
14 Letter to Richard Killeen, 27 June 1979.
15 Neil Rowe, 'McLeavey show important', *EP*, 7 July 1979, p. 13.
16 Letter to Jeffrey Harris, 11 July 1979.
17 Letter to Mrkusich, 17 July 1979.
18 Letter from Harris to PM, 26 July 1979.
19 Jim and Mary Barr, *Contemporary New Zealand painters*, Vol. 1, A–M, Alister Taylor, Martinborough, 1980, p. 160.
20 Letter to Smither, 21 Sept 1977.
21 Letter to Mrkusich, 21 Sept 1977.
22 Letter to Killeen, 10 Nov 1978.
23 Letter to Harris, 14 Mar 1979.
24 PM diary, 2006 (inserted in year planner page). The passage is from the play's requiem.
25 See, for example, letters to Killeen, 10 Nov 1978 and 11 Dec 1978.
26 Letter to John Casserley, 5 Sept 1978.
27 Letter to Trusttum, 26 May 1975.
28 Letter to Toss Woollaston, 10 Sept 1975.
29 Letter to Frank and Cathy Wheeler, 24 Dec 1975.
30 Quoted in 'Michael Illingworth: Alienation and search for innocence', *Craccum Art Supplement*, 2 Sept 1968, p. 10.
31 Letter from Michael Illingworth to PM, n.d. [*c.*May 1970].
32 Alex Veysey, 'Artist finds life has no rosy hue', *Dominion*, 1 Sept 1972, p. 1. Illingworth was the first Frances Hodgkins Fellow at the University of Otago in 1966.
33 Letter to WN (Bill) Sheat (copy), 7 June 1972.
34 *As Adam and Eve* (1965) is now in the TP collection, purchased from the Paris collection auction in 2012.
35 The buyer was Jock Ferrier, a pilot. Hamish Keith noted: 'Up until that moment [he] was not a collector at all ... He had come to the gallery by chance. His pockets were deep and having had his imagination seized by the paintings was determined to have them all.' See 'Illingworth: Tales of the outlaw artist', *SST*, 10 Feb 2002, F3.

36 Letter to Illingworth, 6 June 1967.
37 Illingworth had a special arrangement with Barry Lett in which he received a monthly stipend from the gallery.
38 Letter from Illingworth to PM, 1 Oct 1972.
39 Letter from Illingworth to PM, n.d. [late Mar–early Apr 1973]. The next quotation is also from this letter.
40 Letter from Illingworth to PM, n.d. [early July 1975].
41 Letter to Illingworth, 18 July 1974.
42 Letter from Illingworth to PM, n.d. [Nov–early Dec 1974].
43 Letter from Illingworth to PM, n.d. [*c.*15 Aug 1975].
44 Letter to Gordon Walters, 11 Sept 1975.
45 Letter to Walters, 24 Sept 1975. The next quotation is also from this letter.
46 'Adam and Eve', letter to the editor, *New Zealand Listener*, 10 Apr 1976, p. 6.
47 Letter from Illingworth to Ian Cross, editor, *New Zealand Listener*, 11 Apr 1976 (forwarded to Cross by PM, 15 Apr 1976).
48 Interview with the author, 21 Sept 2011.
49 Interview with the author, 16 Mar 2011.
50 Letter to Walters, 13 May 1977.
51 Letter from Illingworth to PM, n.d. [late Mar–Apr 1976].
52 Letter from Illingworth to PM, n.d. [Apr–May 1977]. The next quotation is also from this letter.
53 Letter to Illingworth, 13 July 1977.
54 Letter to Illingworth, 22 July 1977.
55 Letter from Illingworth to PM, n.d. [4–9 Aug 1977].
56 Entitled *Waiwawa* (1977) and priced at $600, it was purchased by the Robert McDougall Art Gallery. Other works in the show ranged from $400 to $2200.
57 Neil Rowe, 'Michael Illingworth: Looking for a subject', *EP*, 8 Apr 1978, p. 14. Rowe reversed his opinion at Illingworth's next show in 1980: 'On the strength of this exhibition... an efficiently running farm and a new studio has given his painting a new lease of life... This is vintage Illingworth.' See 'Illingworth comes back', *EP*, 12 June 1980, p. 11.
58 Letter from Illingworth to PM, 6 [Aug 1978].
59 Letter from Illingworth to PM, n.d. [early Oct 1978].
60 Letter from Illingworth to PM, n.d. [late Oct 1978].
61 Letter to Illingworth, 3 Nov 1978.

CHAPTER 11

1 Interview with the author, 10 Aug 2012. The quotation in the next paragraph is also from this interview.
2 *Jump over girl* (1969) is listed as *Fly-high girl* in the exhibition catalogue.
3 Letter from Colin McCahon to PM, n.d. [late June–July 1970]. PM had met Killeen at McCahon's house in 1967.
4 Interview with the author, 25 Aug 2010.
5 Grant Smithies, 'Art and soul', *SST*, 29 May 2005, *Sunday* supplement, p. 25.
6 Formal contracts are rare in the New Zealand dealer gallery world even today.
7 Interview with the author, 2 Sept 2011.
8 Letter to Richard Killeen, 15 Aug 1972.
9 Killeen had his last exhibition at Petar Vuletic's gallery in August 1974.
10 Letter to Killeen, 3 Apr 1974.
11 Letter to Killeen, 29 June 1974. As well as purchasing *Blue panel* (1974), John Todd also bought Robert Ellis's *Metropolitan landscape* (1973) from PM at this time.
12 The first in the series (not shown at the PMG) was entitled *Island influence* (1973).
13 The Parises purchased *Constructivist grid no. 3* (1974); *Tukutuku* (1974) was listed as *Tuku tuku* in the exhibition catalogue. When the Paris family collection was auctioned in 2012, the Chartwell Collection acquired *Constructivist grid no. 3*.
14 Letter from Killeen to PM, 14 Apr 1975.

15 By comparison, Ian Scott lived off the sales of his paintings from 1973, though 'it was pretty dicey at times'. Conversation with the author, 24 Oct 2012.
16 The quotations in this and the next paragraph are from an interview with the author, 2 Sept 2011.
17 Letter from Ian Scott to PM, 23 Oct 1974. Scott makes the point that for him the Morris Louis exhibition at Auckland City Art Gallery in 1971 was far more influential. Conversation with the author, 24 Oct 2012.
18 Interview with the author, 10 Aug 2012.
19 Conversation with the author, 24 Oct 2012.
20 Michael Dunn, 'Ian Scott talks about his Lattice series', *Art New Zealand*, No. 13, 1979, p. 34.
21 Letter to Scott, 31 July 1974. Apart from the Ministry of Foreign Affairs' purchase of *City of Auckland* (1974) in 1985, PM never had much success in selling the 'Sprayed stripe' paintings.
22 Letter to Scott, 26 May 1975.
23 Letter from Scott to PM, 11 June 1975.
24 Letter from Killeen to PM, 29 June 1975.
25 Letter from Killeen to PM, 23 Sept 1975.
26 Like Scott, Killeen had met Greenberg briefly in 1968; as he wrote to PM on 15 Apr 1976: '[H]e actually had one of my realist paintings hanging in his bedroom at the hotel (courtesy of B. Letts) and which he had actually noticed. (V good public relations).'
27 Letter to Greenberg, 5 May 1976.
28 *Frog shooter* (1976) is in the AAG collection.
29 *Some of his parts* (1976) was purchased by Tim and Helen Beaglehole.
30 Neil Rowe, 'Killeen's impeccable art: Enigmatic and witty', *The Week*, 6 Aug 1976, p. 15.
31 Letter from Scott to PM, 18 Oct 1976.
32 Letter from Scott to PM, 23 Nov 1976.
33 Letter to Killeen and Margreta Chance, 5 Nov 1975.
34 Letter to John Casserley, 9 Nov 1976.
35 Letter from Scott to PM, 13 June 1977.
36 Scott made the first drawings for the 'Lattice' works in 1975; the first paintings date from July 1976.
37 Letter from Scott to PM, 13 June 1977.
38 Neil Rowe, 'A whole lot of grids', *EP*, 18 June 1977, p. 10.
39 Letter from Gordon Walters to PM, 17 Apr 1978.
40 *Lattice no. 45* (1978) was purchased by the DPAG.
41 In 1981, for example, PM sold works to Todd Motors, Fletcher Challenge, the Ministry of Foreign Affairs and the National Art Gallery.
42 Letter to Scott, 31 Oct 1978.
43 Letter to Scott, 6 June 1978.
44 Letter to Jeffrey Harris, 10 July 1979.
45 Letter to Harris, 20 June 1979. Writing to Mrkusich on 18 May 1979, PM noted, 'I did not sell my first painting off the walls this year until the ninth week. Yes the 9th week. No sales from my Trusttum, Scott or Harris shows.'
46 Letter to Harris, 10 July 1979.
47 Letter to Toss Woollaston, 10 Nov 1978.
48 Postcard from Killeen to PM, n.d. [postmarked 30 Oct 1977].
49 Letter to Killeen, 15 Dec 1977.
50 Letter from Killeen to PM, 6 Aug 1978.
51 Letter from Killeen to PM, 2 Sept 1978.
52 Interview with the author, 19 Oct 2011.
53 *Collection from a Japanese garden 1937* (1978) was purchased by the GBAG in 1980.
54 Neil Rowe, 'A mature artist with a formidable talent', *EP*, 30 Sept 1978, p. 11. The following quotations in this paragraph are from this article.
55 The National Art Gallery purchased the watercolour *Collection Japanese garden, 1937* (1978).
56 Letter from Killeen to PM, 6 Nov 1978.
57 Letter from Killeen to PM, 27 Mar 1979.
58 Letter from Killeen to PM, 21 June 1979. Established in Ponsonby Road in 1975, Outreach operated under the aegis of the Auckland City Art Gallery.

59 Letter to Killeen, 27 June 1979. Killeen replied on 29 June: 'What you say about being yourself in regard to public relations in art is true. The problem is that one sees so many who have nothing to say in art terms practicing public relations to such good effect in terms of sales & interest in their work. Mrkusich is an example of a good artist who has hidden himself away possibly to his own detriment.'
60 Letter to Killeen, 14 Aug 1979.
61 Letter from Killeen to PM, 20 Nov 1979.
62 Letter to Killeen, 13 Dec 1979.

CHAPTER 12

1 Letter from Colin McCahon to PM, 23 Dec 1974.
2 Letter to McCahon, 22 Apr 1975.
3 Letter from McCahon to PM, 28 Apr 1975. All the quotations in this paragraph are from this letter.
4 Letter from McCahon to PM, 13 June 1975.
5 Letter to McCahon, 22 June 1975.
6 Letter from McCahon to PM, 16 July [1975].
7 Letter from McCahon to PM, n.d. [31 July 1975]: McCahon was, however, obliged to make some alterations to the text of the painting. The *Urewera mural* (1975) was taken from the visitor centre in 1997 but subsequently recovered, and is now on loan to the AAG.
8 Letter from McCahon to PM, 13 June 1975.
9 Letter to Robin White, 4 Dec 1975. One of these works, *A poster for the Urewera no. 2* (1975) was purchased by Dr Ian Prior, who subsequently gifted it to Aratoi Wairarapa Museum of Art and History.
10 *McCahon 'religious' works, 1946–1952* opened at the Manawatu Art Gallery and then toured to seven venues; *McCahon's 'Necessary protection'* opened at the GBAG and toured to nine venues.
11 New Zealand's most influential and long-lasting art magazine, *Art New Zealand* was edited first by Ross Fraser, and later by William Dart, who remains in the role today. The McCahon issue is No. 8, Nov 1977–Jan 1978.
12 Letter from McCahon to PM, n.d. [early Feb 1976]. The next quotation is also from this letter.
13 Letter from McCahon to PM, 28 Mar 1976.
14 Letter to Gordon Walters, 1 July 1976.
15 Letter to McCahon, 25 Aug 1976.
16 Letter from McCahon to PM, 5 Oct 1976. *Practical religion: the resurrection of Lazarus showing Mount Martha* (1969–70) was purchased by the National Art Gallery in 1985 and is now in the TP collection.
17 Letter to McCahon, 22 Nov 1976.
18 Letter from McCahon to PM, 23 Nov [1976].
19 Letter to McCahon, 2 Mar 1978.
20 Letter from McCahon to PM, 9 Aug 1977.
21 Letter from McCahon to PM, 12 Aug 1977.
22 Letter from McCahon to PM [annotated by McCahon 'No date possible but 76 & 77'; i.e. written over the new year period].
23 Letter to Wilson Buchanan, 29 Mar 1977. In particular, he wanted to see the exhibition *The heritage of American art: Paintings from the collection of the Metropolitan Museum of Art*, at the Art Gallery of New South Wales in Sydney.
24 McCahon's solo exhibitions were at the Bonython Art Gallery, Sydney (1968), and the Ray Hughes Gallery in Brisbane (1975). He had also represented New Zealand at the inaugural Sydney Biennale in 1973 with *Are there not twelve hours of daylight* (1970).
25 Letter from Daniel Thomas to PM, 5 Apr 1977. Thomas became aware of McCahon's work in the 1960s, viewing it in the exhibition *Eight New Zealand artists*, which toured Australia in 1965. He also saw McCahon's large solo exhibition at the Bonython Art Gallery in July 1968, buying a work for his personal collection (*North Otago landscape no. 14* (1967), now in the National Gallery of Australia in Canberra). Thomas remained a strong supporter of McCahon all his working life and in 1986, as director of the Art Gallery of South Australia in Adelaide, purchased *The Five Wounds of Christ no. 2* (1977–78) for the collection.
26 Letter from Ian North to PM, 13 Apr 1977.

27 Letter to McCahon, 30 Apr 1977.
28 *Art & Australia* had New Zealand editorial advisers from 1964 in Hamish Keith and Paul Beadle, and featured occasional articles on New Zealand art, notably Kurt von Meier, 'Contemporary painting in New Zealand', Vol. 2, No. 3, Dec 1964, pp. 190–202; Peter Tomory, 'New Zealand sculpture', Vol. 3, No. 2, Sept 1965, pp. 108–13; and Hamish Keith, 'Colin McCahon', Vol. 6, No. 1, June 1968, pp. 61–69.
29 Letter to McCahon, 30 Apr 1977. PM called Mollison 'Jim' in this letter, but corrected the name when he read the text for this chapter on 8 Nov 2012.
30 Letter to Daniel Thomas, 28 July 1977.
31 Letter to McCahon, 30 Apr 1977. The next quotation is also from this letter.
32 The works mentioned are *The Canoe Mamari* (1969), and the Muriwai panels on unstretched jute canvas listed on the Colin McCahon online catalogue (www.mccahon.co.nz) as *A11, A12, A13* (1973). PM sold Brown four works on paper on this trip, three by Woollaston and one by Allen Maddox.
33 Letter to Neil McGrath, 21 Aug 1977. Both quotations in this paragraph are from this letter.
34 Letter to McCahon, 30 Apr 1977. *Through the Wall of Death: A Banner* (1972) was purchased by the Dowse Art Museum late in 1977.
35 Letter to Gordon Walters, 13 May 1977.
36 Letter from McCahon to PM, 2 July 1976. In a letter of 11 Mar 1977, McCahon reported Kennedy's response: 'Rodney K wrote me a great letter over his "Angels" – he hated it & suddenly saw it. The image is from Peer Gynt. Peer's mother dying & Peer riding her chariot (bed) to heaven.' McCahon was referencing his and Kennedy's involvement in a production of Ibsen's *Peer Gynt* in 1953.
37 Letter from McCahon to PM, n.d. [early Mar 1977].
38 Letter from McCahon to PM, 10 Mar 1977.
39 Letter from McCahon to PM, 4 Apr 1977.
40 Letter from McCahon to PM, 4 May 1977.
41 Letter from McCahon to PM, 3 May 1977.
42 Letter to McCahon, 3 June 1977.
43 Letter to Walters, 7 July 1977.
44 Letter to Walters, 8 July 1977.
45 *Angels and bed no. 4: Hi-fi* (1976–77). As McCahon's primary dealer, PM shared in the commission.
46 Letter from McCahon to PM, 4 July 1977. (This section of the letter is dated 6 July.) The next quotation is also from this letter.
47 Letter to McCahon, 11 July 1977.
48 Letter from McCahon to PM, 19 July 1977. Both quotations in this paragraph are from this letter. The screen is *I talk of Goya* (1976; AAG, gift of Miss LD Gilmour, 1983).
49 Miss LD (Doreen) Gilmour was an Auckland librarian who met McCahon in the 1950s and purchased a number of works directly from him. She bequeathed seven to the Auckland City Art Gallery in 1990, including the important oil, *I and Thou* (1954–55), and also gifted two in 1977 and a further eight in 1983.
50 Letter to McCahon, 30 July 1977.
51 Letter to McCahon, 14 Aug 1977.
52 Letter to McCahon, 17 Aug 1977; the next two quotations are also from this letter. Peter Ireland manned the gallery while he was at home.

CHAPTER 13

1 Letter to Gordon Walters, 7 July 1977.
2 Letter from Colin McCahon to PM, 4 July 1977. This part of the letter is dated 6 July. Today's equivalent of $25,000 is $164,000.
3 Letter to McCahon, 25 July 1977.
4 Letter from McCahon to PM, 13 Sept 1977. The delay was due not to the council's indecision, but its administrative processes. Without substantial acquisition funds, it was in the tortuous and time-consuming position of needing to apply to the Minister of Internal Affairs for Lottery Board funds for major purchases.
5 The price, not noted on the catalogue, was $40,000. It did not sell.
6 Letter to Walters, 2 Sept 1977.

7 Letter to McCahon, 16 Sept 1977.

8 Letter from Ormond Wilson to McCahon, 19 Sept 1977. Wilson was chairman of the Board of Trustees of the National Art Gallery and Dominion Museum and National War Memorial from 1975 to 1979, and chaired the Council of the National Art Gallery from 1977 to 1979.

9 PM first mentioned the possibility of a commission in a letter of 3 May 1974. This quotation is from a letter to McCahon of 28 Aug 1974.

10 Matthew, 27:45.

11 Letter from McCahon to PM, 10 Dec 1977.

12 Letter from McCahon to PM, 28 Jan 1978.

13 Letter to Walters, 16 Mar 1978.

14 'Lower Hutt councillor elaborates on his urges', *EP*, 28 Feb 1978, p. 1. See also '"Way out" gallery exhibits attacked', p. 17.

15 *Through the Wall of Death: A Banner* (1972) was the work the Art Gallery of New South Wales had considered in the previous year. It had been purchased for the Dowse Art Gallery by director Jim Barr late in 1977.

16 'Lower Hutt councillor elaborates on his urges', p. 1.

17 Letter to McCahon, 2 Mar 1978. The next quotation is also from this letter.

18 Letter to McCahon, 3 Mar 1978.

19 Letter to the director-general, Television One, 3 Mar 1978.

20 Letter from McCahon to PM, 5 Mar 1978.

21 Letter to McCahon, 8 Mar 1978.

22 Letter from James Mollison to PM, 20 Mar 1978.

23 'New Zealand's gift "Muldoon's revenge?"', *Sydney Morning Herald*, 17 Mar 1978, p. 11. See also Dai Hayward, 'Muldoon confesses: Art gift a stunt', *The Australian*, 17 Mar 1978, p. 1.

24 'Painting is superb says expert', *Auckland Star*, 17 Mar 1978, p. 1.

25 Letter from McCahon to PM, 15 Mar 1978. On 12 Mar, McCahon told PM he had written to Chen Werry 'a friendly letter explaining where I stood on painting & suggesting he be careful for himself with the television people. I told him I was used to this business & it didn't worry me but that he was being caught up in a very sick joke.' On the 15th he informed PM, 'My letter to Werry bounced back by the next day, unopened & my address cancelled on the back & the Lower Hutt City Council cancelled & his home address written in on the side. So my necessary protection in his case didn't work. Too bad.'

26 Letter to McCahon, 8 Mar 1978.

27 Letter to McCahon, 17 Mar 1978.

28 Letter from McCahon to PM, 30 Mar 1978.

29 Letter from McCahon to PM, 28 Apr 1978. The next quotation is also from this letter.

30 Letter to McCahon, 4 Apr 1978.

31 Letter to Toss Woollaston, 22 Mar 1978.

32 Letter from McCahon to PM, 30 Mar 1978.

33 Mollison had purchased *Blue poles* (1952) in 1973, amid much controversy, for $1.3 million.

34 Conversation with the author, 10 Nov 2012.

35 Letter to McCahon, 18 Mar 1978.

36 Letter from McCahon to PM, 2 May 1978.

37 Mollison was in New Zealand to judge the Benson and Hedges Art Award.

38 Letter to McCahon, 12 May 1978.

39 Mollison acquired the following works on paper by McCahon: *Angels and bed Hi Fi no. 7: Watch* (1977); three works from the series 'Practical religion' (1969) (*Let us then stop discussing the rudiments of Christianity…*, *Shall we gather at the river*, and *Ecce Agnus Dei…*); *Clouds 1* and *Clouds 2* (both 1975); *Noughts and crosses 4* (1976); and 'Puketapu, Manukau', a set of four prints (1957). He also purchased Woollaston's oil painting *Edith Woollaston* (*c.*1948); and two works on paper by A Lois White, *Street mission* (*c.* 1935) and *Fire* (1943).

40 Interview with the author, 10 Aug 2010.

41 The *Northland panels* (1958) were $25,000; *A grain of wheat* (1970), $6000.

42 Letter to McCahon, 12 May 1978.

43 'McCahon panels go to gallery for $25,000', *EP*, 11 May 1978, p.4.
44 Letter from McCahon to PM, 13 June 1978.
45 Letter to McCahon, 10 July 1978. The quotations in this and the next two paragraphs are from this letter.
46 Letter to McCahon, 13 Oct 1978.
47 Letter to McCahon, 10 Nov 1978.
48 Letter to Tim and Sherrah Francis, 7 Feb 1979.
49 Letter to McCahon, 19 Feb 1979.
50 Letter from McCahon to PM, 22 Feb 1979. The next quotation is also from this letter.
51 Letter to McCahon, 1 Mar 1979.
52 Letter to McCahon, 10 Mar 1979. The exhibition, which included the *Northland panels* (1958), *A grain of wheat* (1970), *Through the Wall of Death: A Banner* (1972), the *Urewera triptych* (1975) and other works, was on display from 8 Mar to 8 Apr 1979.
53 Letter to Louise Upston [Pether], 29 May 1978 [1979], Colin McCahon object file (general), TP.
54 Letter to McCahon, 29 Mar 1979.
55 'I need something like "fun fur" all wafty to disguise my openended legs.' Letter from McCahon to PM, 3 Apr 1979.
56 Letter from McCahon to PM, 11 July 1979.
57 Letter from McCahon to PM, 17 Sept 1979. The works, both dated 1978–79, are *May His light shine (Cornwall Park)*, private collection, and *May His light shine (Tau Cross)*, Chartwell Collection, AAG.
58 McCahon had previously incorporated text from A Letter to Hebrews in some of his scroll paintings of 1969.
59 On 25 Sept 1979, McCahon wrote to PM: 'These were asked for – 1972 by Ian Prior & I couldn't manage them then. Now I'm sunk in Hebrews & Paul.'
60 Letter from McCahon to PM, 21 Sept 1979.
61 Letter from McCahon to PM, 25 Sept 1979.
62 Letter to McCahon, 22 Aug 1979.
63 Letter to McCahon, 28 Sept 1979.
64 The works from the 'Five Wounds of Christ' series were no. 2 (purchased by the Art Gallery of South Australia, Adelaide, in 1986) and no. 3 (purchased by the DPAG in 1981). *St Matthew: lightning* (1977–79) is in a private collection. Seven of the 25 works in the series 'Truth from the King Country' (1978–79) were in the show.
65 Letter to McCahon, 31 Oct 1979.
66 Interview with the author, 17 Mar 2012.

CHAPTER 14

1 The only other visual artist who had been awarded a knighthood was cartoonist Gordon Minhinnick in 1976.
2 Letter to Toss Woollaston, 30 May 1979. Woollaston's knighthood was largely due to the efforts of the businessman Sir Robert Jones, one of his key supporters in the 1970s. In 1979, Jones purchased *Mounts Owen, Arthur and Campbell from Motueka* (1978) from the PMG and gifted it to the Wellington Public Library.
3 Letter to Tim and Sherrah Francis, 14 Aug 1979.
4 Letter to Woollaston, 9 Aug 1979.
5 Woollaston's letter to Luit Bieringa is dated 16 Dec [1979]; the letter he quotes from is dated 16 Nov 1978. Woollaston made some small changes to PM's text.
6 Letter to McCahon, 4 Aug 1978.
7 Letter to Jeffrey Harris, 3 Apr 1979. Other dealers had similar problems; as Don Wood writes, 'I suppose it was to be expected. Painters previously had to grab sales wherever they may have come from. The idea of dealers in general or "having a dealer" was a strange concept to many artists. Galleries, whether dealer galleries or not, were places where you, the artist, had your exhibition. The dealer was a sod who took a commission off you if you sold a painting? Rita Angus demonstrated that attitude completely.' Email to the author, 11 Oct 2012.
8 Letter to Harris, 5 Nov 1980.
9 See, for example, his letter to Brent Wong, 7 July 1976.

10 *Deposition* (1971) is now in the AAG collection (purchased in 1985).

11 Letter to Harris, 25 Mar 1974.

12 Letter from Harris to PM, 4 Apr 1976.

13 Letter to Harris, 3 May 1976. PM had only just received Harris's letter dated 4 Apr 1976. The next quotation is also from this letter.

14 Quoted in Annette Seear, 'Artist paints about death', *Evening Star Saturday Magazine*, 12 Feb 1977, p. 9.

15 Quoted in Justin Paton, *Jeffrey Harris*, Victoria University Press, Wellington; Dunedin Public Art Gallery, Dunedin, 2005, p. 25.

16 Peter Ireland, 'The recent small paintings of Jeffrey Harris', *Art New Zealand*, No. 6, 1977, p. 12.

17 Harris exhibited 12 works painted between Dec 1969 and Sept 1970. He wrote to PM on 6 Feb 1978: '[They] were done at my parents' place at French Farm when I was twenty years old. My father had cleared a small space in the garden shed and I had a bench to stand up on and paint on.' The Ministry of Foreign Affairs, which had bought two works from the previous show, acquired a third Harris from this exhibition.

18 Letter to Harris, 13 Oct 1978. The next quotation is also from this letter.

19 Letter from Harris to PM, 21 Sept 1979. Luit Bieringa comments, 'There was no truth to that. Peter certainly had his own way of doing things, but he was the leading dealer at the time. There was no question of not buying from him.' Interview with the author, 30 Aug 2012. Jim Barr and Bill Milbank confirmed Bieringa's point.

20 Letter to Harris, 24 Sept 1979.

21 Letter to Colin McCahon, 12 Dec 1979.

22 Letter from Harris to PM, 16 May 1980. This section of the letter is dated 20 May.

23 Letter from Harris to PM, 14 July 1982.

24 Letter to Patricia Bosshard, 4 Mar 1983.

25 Letter to Richard Killeen, 1 Apr 1985. PM often remarked on his respect for his fellow dealers: see, for example, comments on Peter Webb (letters to Gordon Walters, 2 June 1978, and McCahon, 5 Sept 1977); Rodney Kirk Smith (letters to Walters, 11 June 1981, and Julian Dashper, 10 Sept 1983); and Elva Bett (letter to McCahon, 18 July 1980). See also chapter 18, note 16.

26 Interview with the author, 30 Aug 2012.

27 Letter to Philip Trusttum, 6 Nov 1976.

28 Letter to Walters, 15 Nov 1976. The next quotation is also from this letter. PM wrote to Ron O'Reilly, the director of the GBAG, on 12 Nov 1976: 'I feel that the artists that I'm involved with should not sell their works via public institutions. For me, the role of such civic bodies is, like public libraries, to educate, inform and mount non commercial (by this I mean non-selling) shows. I believe that the entrepreneurial function should be left to their dealer.'

29 Organised in association with the New Vision Gallery in Auckland, it included 16 works, priced $300–$950.

30 Letter to Trusttum, 1 Mar 1977. The next quotation is also from this letter.

31 See 'Paintings fetch $17,500', *Press*, 24 May 1980, p. 6.

32 Letter to Walters, 7 [17?] May 1980. This letter is a reply to Walters' of 11 May, which suggests it is misdated.

33 Note, diary, 23 Mar 1986.

34 Letter to Trusttum, 25 Aug 1986.

35 Letter from Trusttum to PM, 26 Aug 1986.

36 Letter to McCahon, 28 July 1978.

37 Conversation with the author, 8 Nov 2012.

38 Fax to Ralph Hotere, n.d. [*c.* 7 June 2000]. The exhibition was *Black light*, a collaboration between the DPAG and TP.

39 Email to the author, 12 Jan 2013.

40 Conversation with the author, 8 Nov 2012. The next quotation is also from this conversation. PM showed the work of A Lois White, Charles Tole, Olivia Spencer Bower, Hilda Wiseman, Ida Eise, Russell Clark and Rhona Haszard, and in 1975 hosted *Helen FV Scales*, an exhibition curated by the Auckland City Art Gallery. Woollaston purchased a painting from the Scales show, *Anemones* (*c.* 1969), which is now in TP.

41 Tole had first exhibited with PM in Dec 1976, contributing three conté drawings to a group show.
42 Letter to Charles Tole, 13 July 1977.
43 At Tole's first solo exhibition in Aug 1977, PM quoted from a Sargeson story, 'An affair of the heart', in the catalogue: 'I found that the place on the road where Mrs Crawley used to wait for a lift into town had been made into a bus terminus, and there was a little shelter shed and a store.' From Frank Sargeson, *Collected stories, 1935–1963*, Blackwood & Janet Paul, Auckland, 1964, p. 60.
44 Letter from Tole to PM, 8 Nov 1982. The next quotation is also from this letter.
45 PM sold works to the HL, the Robert McDougall Art Gallery and the Ministry of Foreign Affairs. In a letter to Tole on 2 Sept 1977, he remarked that many of his 'perceptive clients' were 'very impressed' by his paintings.
46 John Roberts, 'Theirs sincerely', *New Zealand Listener*, 10 Sept 1977, p. 29.
47 The show included three watercolours by Olivia Spencer Bower, three oils by A Lois White (two from PM's own collection and exhibited 'not for sale'), and four works on paper by Robin White. 'I should have had a "label" to hang the show on,' he told Killeen in a letter of 15 Aug 1975. '[S]omething like *three regionalists*... Also a quote from Emily Dickinson or Walt Whitman would have expressed the "ambience" that I'm trying to evoke.'
48 Letter from A Lois White to PM, 2 July 1977.
49 Letter to White, 31 May 1976.
50 Letter from White to PM, 9 July 1976.
51 Letter to White, 11 July 1977.
52 Letter to McCahon, 21 Oct 1977. The buyers included Helen Hitchings, Hans and Martha Lachmann, and the Ministry of Foreign Affairs, which purchased two works.
53 Neil Rowe, 'Late recognition for major painter', *EP*, 29 Oct 1977, p. 12.
54 Letter from White to PM, 14 July 1980.
55 Letter to White, 17 July 1980.
56 Letter to White, 9 May 1979.
57 Letter from Killeen to PM, 21 Mar 1994. Screenwriter, producer and director Jane Campion has lived overseas since 1976; All Black fullback Don Clarke – 'The Boot' – moved to South Africa in the same decade.

CHAPTER 15

1 'David Langman talks to Peter Ireland', 17 Feb 2001, see: www.nzcp.com/Features/tabid/122/articleType/ArticleView/articleId/24/David-Langman-talks-to-Peter-Ireland-Wanganui-based-painter-and-freelance-curator-of-photography.aspx, accessed 16 Feb 2013.
2 These exhibitions toured in 1967 and 1972 respectively. Other shows to come to New Zealand during this period included *Brassai* (1971), *Bill Brandt* (1972) and *Diane Arbus* (1978), all curated by John Szarkowski for MoMA.
3 *PhotoForum* magazine had a predecessor in John B Turner's *Photographic Art & History*, first published in 1970. After four issues it was renamed *New Zealand Photography*; 13 issues appeared before it became *PhotoForum* in 1974.
4 The first specialist photography gallery in New Zealand was Barry Hesson's Victoria Market Gallery in Wellington, opened in 1973. It lasted less than a year. Snaps – A Photographer's Gallery ran from 1975 to 1981; PhotoForum/Wellington from 1977 to 1981. Other galleries dedicated to photography included William Main's Exposures Gallery in Wellington (1977–late 1980s) and Real Pictures Gallery in Auckland (1979–90).
5 Letter from Gordon Walters to PM, n.d. [mid-July 1972].
6 Paul Hewson, 'Snaps Gallery and the exhibiting of photographs', *Art New Zealand*, No. 12, 1978, p. 14.
7 PM, 'Photographer's art over 100 years', *Dominion*, 26 Aug 1967, p. 7.
8 Letter to Wilson Buchanan, 29 Mar 1977.
9 Letter to Laurence Aberhart, 31 May 1977.
10 Aberhart, who had only recently discovered photography, had met the Woollastons through a schoolfriend, Alison du Fresne, whose father Viggo was a pioneering winemaker in Nelson (the Woollastons were partial to his red wine). For the young Aberhart, the Woollastons were different: 'They were the real bohemians, the New Zealand bohemians. And they took an interest in me, they saw something in me.' Conversation with the author, 2 Mar 2012.

11 *Ibid.*
12 Letter to Aberhart, 23 Aug 1977. The works mentioned include *Dunedin Warehouse façade*, 1975; *Christchurch (Continental Judo Club)*, 1975–76; and *Pines Beach, Island Motel, Kaiapoi*, 1977.
13 Letter from Aberhart to PM, 1 Sept 1977.
14 Gary Blackman, 'The photographic experience: A report from Dunedin', *PhotoForum Supplement*, No. 3, Spring 1979, p. 5.
15 Quoted in Ross Fraser 'Peter Peryer: The photograph as a portrait of the self', *Art New Zealand*, No. 8, 1978–79, p. 67.
16 Interview with the author, 17 Mar 2012.
17 Letter to Peter Peryer, 26 Apr 1978.
18 Both works, dated 1977, were purchased by director Luit Bieringa on behalf of the Manawatu Art Gallery Art Society.
19 The buyers were Marshall Seifert (who purchased *Kamala and Magdalena, Mornington, Dunedin*, 1978), photographer Paul Hewson, and the artist and critic Peter Ireland. Seifert, who had begun to collect New Zealand photography in 1968, established the Marshall Seifert Gallery in Dunedin in 1981 and often featured the medium.
20 Letter to Aberhart, 27 July 1978.
21 Letter from Aberhart to PM, 8 Aug 1978.
22 Peter Ireland, 'Laurence Aberhart: Nineteen photographs 1974–1978', *PhotoForum*, No. 43, Mar 1979, p. 43.
23 The exhibition included 34 works; the other photographers were Terry Austin, Gavin Colthart, Paul Gilbert, Jim Payne and Dinah Bradley. Ireland wrote to PM on 20 Jan 1979 about the selection: 'I think 10 or 12 would be a good number to work round, that would mean about two prints from each photographer ... My main criterion has been quality – but in excluding about six others I've depended on considerations of mix; to end up with a good mix of black-and-white with colour, colour print work with Polaroid, single images with groups, etc etc'. Ireland later curated two further shows for PM; see p. 376.
24 Letter to Jeffrey Harris, 9 Aug 1979.
25 Letter to Gordon Walters, 10 Aug 1979.
26 Neil Rowe, 'Everyone is going "click"', *EP*, 18 Aug 1979, p. 13.
27 Letter to Gillian Chaplin, 28 Sept 1979.
28 Heather Curnow, 'Developing art form', *New Zealand Listener*, 22 Sept 1979, p. 24.
29 Letter to Peryer, 7 Sept 1979. Peter Ireland recalled, '[N]ot long – within around a year – after the "New Image" show Peter raised the possibility of converting the "Cuba Street penthouse" into a small, separate photographic gallery which I would run for him. A very attractive prospect, but by then I was getting more seriously into my own work'. Shortly afterwards, at the invitation of Luit Bieringa, Ireland began to work as a part-time photography curator at the National Art Gallery. Letter to the author, 17 Nov 2012.
30 On 13 Oct 1978, PM wrote: 'Yes, I would give my back teeth for a show. But, as you have so wisely hinted, when and if you are ready. Your cache of images must first be unlocked before my (grubby?) fingers feel them. I'm excited; I'll say that. I'm excited to see what pops out.'
31 Letter from Peryer to PM, n.d. [early Aug 1979].
32 Letter to Peryer, 13 Aug 1979.
33 Letter from Peter Ireland to PM, 12 Aug 1981.
34 Letter to Aberhart, 19 May 1982.
35 Letter from Peryer to PM, 2 Mar 1981.
36 Laurence Aberhart, statement for Bosshard Gallery exhibition, 1982, Artist's file, Te Aka Matua Research Library, TP. The next quotation is also from this source.
37 Letter from Aberhart to PM, 13 May 1982.
38 Janet Bayly, 'Laurence Aberhart – Peter McLeavey Gallery', *PhotoForum* newsletter, No. 16, Mar 1984, p. 9.
39 Letter to Walters, 11 July 1983.
40 Letter to Peter Hannken, 17 Aug 1983.
41 Letter from Aberhart to PM, 25 Mar 1984.

42 Letter from Aberhart to PM, 9 Apr 1984.
43 Letter from Aberhart to PM, 9 Oct 1990. The quotations in the next paragraph are also from this letter.
44 This and the next quotation are from a conversation with the author, 7 Mar 2012.
45 Bryan Staff, 'Peter McLeavey interviewed for ChaCha', *ChaCha*, June 1984, p. 11.
46 Interview with the author, 16 Dec 2008.
47 Interview with the author, 2 Sept 2011.
48 Conversation with Stephen Lachman (who spells his name with only one 'n'), 24 Jan 2012. The next quotation is also from this conversation.
49 One of their paintings, Michael Illingworth's *Untitled* (1971), was later reproduced on the cover of the museum's landmark book, *Art at Te Papa* (ed. William McAloon), 2009. Stephen Lachman gifted a further seven works to the collection in 1996.
50 Walter Benjamin, 'Unpacking my library: A talk about book collecting', in Hannah Arendt (ed.), *Illuminations*, Harcourt, Brace & World, New York, 1955, p. 60.
51 This quotation is in a small marbled-cover journal of 1997.
52 Lindsay Rabbitt, 'The dealer', *New Zealand Listener*, 17 Feb 2001, p. 51.
53 Letter to Colin McCahon, 14 Mar 1977. The next quotation is also from this letter.
54 *Mr and Mrs L.F.M.* (1968–70) was gifted to TP in 2012.
55 Interview with the author, 16 Mar 2011.
56 Letter to Donald Cornes, 2 Sept 1977.
57 Letter to McCahon, 21 June 1977.
58 Conversation with the author, 24 Nov 2012.
59 Letter to Walters, 1 July 1976.
60 Letter to McCahon, 7 Mar 1982.
61 Letter to Ireland, 9 Sept 1983.
62 Interview with the author, 16 Mar 2011.

CHAPTER 16

1 Letter to Toss Woollaston, 25 Nov 1980.
2 Letter to Jeffrey Harris, 24 Jan 1981.
3 Conversation with the author, 12 June 2012.
4 Letter to Neil McGrath, 23 July 1981. Unless otherwise noted, all quotations in this section are from this letter. Wystan Curnow, visiting a year later, found a similar reaction to PM: 'Mr Curnow, we are not interested in New Zealand art. End of conversation.' See 'New Zealand art – where in the world is it?', *New Zealand Listener*, 3 Apr 1982, p. 34.
5 The exhibition was organised and toured by the Los Angeles County Museum of Art.
6 They also went to New Haven to see the Yale University collection and the Yale Centre of British Art.
7 Letter to Richard Killeen, 27 Apr 1981. PM wrote to Colin McCahon on 16 Mar 1981, 'We had a fabulous time in New York. However, we both didn't feel overwhelmed by it. New Zealand is home and I've returned with a deeper sense of belonging to it.'
8 Another sculptor, Robert Jesson, had a solo exhibition in Mar–Apr 1982.
9 Hellyar and Dawson had only one solo exhibition each: Hellyar in Mar–Apr 1980 (ten works entitled *Folds and keeps*), and Dawson in July 1981 (seven works entitled *Escape*).
10 Neil Rowe, 'NAG event big', *EP*, 30 June 1979, p. 11.
11 Fraser first exhibited in Wellington in 1977 as part of the *Videostore* project on Lambton Quay organised by Nicholas Spill and Andrew Drummond, who were then on the National Art Gallery staff. She held her first dealer gallery show at the Bosshard Gallery in Dunedin in 1978.
12 Artist's statement, *NZ sculptors at Mildura*, 1978, p. 27.
13 Letter to Jacqueline Fraser, 8 Mar 1979.
14 Letter to Killeen, 23 July 1979.
15 PM included the quotation (from Emerson's *Nature*, chapter 1) on the exhibition catalogue.
16 Letter to Fraser, 29 Sept 1980.
17 Letter from Fraser to PM, 6 Oct 1980.
18 Letter to Fraser, 4 Dec 1980.

19 Letter to Fraser, 11 June 1981.
20 Letter to Ireland, 11 Sept 1981.
21 PM had, however, purchased works for the BNZ Art Collection in 1986 and 1988. In 1995, he sold a major installation, *The deification of Mihi Waka* (1995), to the Sarjeant Gallery.
22 Letter to Fraser, 8 Dec 1990.
23 Interview with the author, 10 Aug 2012. Unless otherwise noted, all quotations from Warren Viscoe in this section are from this interview.
24 Letter from Warren Viscoe to PM, 1 July 1980.
25 Letter to Viscoe, 4 July 1980. The next quotation is also from this letter.
26 *The quarryman's dream* (1985) was entitled *Rock salt aggregate, The quarryman's dream* in the exhibition catalogue. The National Art Gallery acquired a wall piece, *Puketi* (1984), in 1984, followed by a major installation, *Entries – an airmail letter from John Frumm; Exits – Captain Musick is missing* (1986), four years later.
27 Letter to Gordon Walters, 21 Nov 1975.
28 See Wystan Curnow, 'Report: The given as an art political statement: Nine works by Billy Apple 1979–1980', *Art New Zealand*, No. 15, Summer 1980, front piece, pp. 26–33, 60–61, 65.
29 Neil Rowe, 'Billy causes another stir with wild ideas', *EP*, 1 Dec 1979, p. 13. PM wrote to Apple's New York dealer, Leo Castelli, on 11 Dec 1979 with some documentation on the exhibition: 'We are a long way away from New York here; three islands on the edge of the world. Still, for that, we have an active scene. There are just a handful of dealer galleries in New Zealand. And we are supported by just a handful of people. I often think that my business survives on just 4 or 5 private collectors and a couple of institutions.'
30 Peter Ireland, who painted the gallery a number of times over the years, was entrusted with the task of painting out the 'red bits': 'The only difference was that Peter asked me to phone him the moment I finished eliminating the Apple work. Billy wanted to know.' Letter to the author, 17 Nov 2012.
31 Letter to Billy Apple, 20 Mar 1982.
32 Letter to Walters, 22 July 1982. In 1989, PM sold the suite of five works to the National Art Gallery.
33 Letter to Harris, 16 Aug 1982.
34 Letter to Apple, 20 Mar 1982.
35 Also important for New Zealand artists was *ANZART* (1981–87), which succeeded the *Mildura Sculpture Triennial*. Ian Hunter organised the first *ANZART* in Christchurch 1981 as a low-budget, artist-run project to encourage greater cross-fertilisation between New Zealand and Australian artists.
36 In 1979, the biennale director, Nick Waterlow, had initially planned to include six New Zealand artists. When the number was cut to two, local officials took drastic measures: as Wystan Curnow put it, 'An entire New Zealand art scene was air-lifted to Sydney.' See 'The Sydney Biennale', *Art New Zealand*, No. 13, 1979, p. 22. The contingent of 50, including Jacqueline Fraser, From Scratch, Peter Roche, Bruce Barber and Pauline Rhodes, staged an impromptu exhibition of installation and performance across Sydney.
37 The others were Ron Brownson, Boyd Webb and expatriate Annea Lockwood.
38 Letter to Colin [?], 19 May 1982.
39 Letter to Harris, 14 May 1982.
40 Letter to Milan Mrkusich, 13 May 1982.
41 Letter to Neil McGrath, 29 July 1983 [1982?].
42 Letter to Walters, 20 May 1982.

CHAPTER 17

1 Letter from Robin White to PM, n.d. [mid-Nov 1981]. The next quotation is also from this letter.
2 Letter to White, 20 Nov 1981. In an interview with the author (23 Aug 2012), White noted, 'I didn't want to be a missionary, that wasn't what it was about. But I kind of understood what he meant. To give yourself to something that was bigger than yourself. To take risks and to do things that are not just for yourself.'
3 Letter to White, 12 Dec 1981.
4 Interview with the author, 23 Aug 2012.
5 'Robin White: Painter', *Broadsheet*, No. 22, Sept 1974, p. 18.

6 Letter from White to PM, 29 Apr 1973.
7 Susanne Butler, 'Print will help convention fund', *EP*, 7 Sept 1978, p. 12.
8 Interview with the author, 23 Aug 2012.
9 *Sam Hunt at the Portobello* Pub (1978) is now in the DPAG. *Glenda at Tahakopa* (1978) came up for auction 10 years later, and PM bought it for the BNZ Art Collection.
10 Neil Rowe, 'Robin White's work continues to grow in stature', *EP*, 9 Sept 1978, p. 11.
11 *Robin White: New Zealand painter*, compiled by Alister Taylor and Deborah Coddington, 1981.
12 'Robin White talks to Abby Cunnane', www.youtube.com/watch?v=0APsHbMm0D8, accessed 16 Feb 2013.
13 Charmian Smith, 'Artists share friendship and working mother commitment', *Otago Daily Times*, 22 Oct 1992, p. 25.
14 Letter from White to PM, 16 June 1982.
15 Letter to White, 6 July 1982.
16 Letter to White, 6 Oct 1982.
17 Letter from White to PM, 16 June 1982.
18 Claudia Pond Eyley, 'Robin White in Kiribati', *Art New Zealand*, No. 31, 1984, p. 30.
19 Letter from White to PM, 28 Oct 1982.
20 *Ibid.*
21 The exhibition was entitled *Workbooks/Diaries*. The Women's Gallery in Wellington (Jan 1980–Feb 1984) provided a focus for the women's art movement in the early 1980s.
22 Letter from White to PM, 20 Nov 1983. All the quotations in this paragraph are from this letter.
23 Ian Wedde, 'Woodcut exhibition shows simple realism', *EP*, 23 Mar 1984, section 2, p. 15.
24 Letter from White to PM, 25 June 1984.
25 Letter from White to PM, 24 July 1984.
26 Letter to White, 3 Aug 1984. Ray Hughes (who established Gallery 1Eleven in Brisbane in 1969 and opened a second gallery in Sydney in 1985) represented White only briefly. In 1990, she began to show with Helen Maxwell, initially at aGOG (Australian Girls' Own Gallery) and from 2000 to 2010 at the Helen Maxwell Gallery.
27 Letter to White, 7 Sept 1984.
28 Letter from White to PM, 17 Sept 1984.
29 White's Tarawa work includes the following print portfolios: 'Beginners' guide to Gilbertese', 'Twenty-eight days in Kiribati', 'Naareau and the tree of creation', 'Saying goodbye to Florence', 'The fisherman loses his way', 'Sainimele goes fishing', 'Nei Tiein goes for a walk', 'Postcards from Pleasant Island', 'Te Rerenga Wairua' and 'Along the way of sorrows'.
30 Letter to Toss Woollaston, 7 Aug 1982.
31 Quoted in Gregory O'Brien, *We set out one morning: The BNZ Art Collection*, Bank of New Zealand, Wellington, 2006, p. 13. I'm grateful to O'Brien for his observations on PM's collecting for the BNZ.
32 Letter to JC Hiddleston, 22 June 1982.
33 Undated draft notes for BNZ collection policy [1982].
34 Others include Ralph Hotere, Robert McLeod, Gretchen Albrecht, Joanna Margaret Paul, Don Peebles, Stanley Palmer, Stephen Bambury, Melvin Day, John Drawbridge, Dick Frizzell, Peter Siddell, Hariata Ropata Tangahoe and others. Photography is well represented in the collection with work by Peryer, Aberhart, Bruce Foster, Peter Black, Mary Macpherson, Robin Morrison, Frank Hofmann, Ans Westra, Megan Jenkinson, Fiona Pardington and Margaret Dawson.
35 The bank's collection is especially rich in works by Stewart and Bensemann – artists who were underrated at the time.
36 Letter to Hiddleston, 9 Feb 1984. PM echoed these comments in an interview with Bryan Staff in *ChaCha*, June 1984, p. 11: 'I think that if New Zealand was to sink beneath the waters of the South Pacific tomorrow, perhaps the only thing we would be remembered for would be the great artworks that were created by the people who lived here before the Europeans came. I'm thinking of the masterpieces of Maori carving... And it is from this art that we can all learn so much... My personal love is the carving of the Maori, because that is the benchmark of the art that is produced in these islands.'
37 *Te Maori: Maori art from New Zealand collections* was subsequently shown in Saint Louis, San Francisco and Chicago before returning to New Zealand.

38 Memorandum from Hiddleston to general manager, 17 Feb 1984.
39 Draft press release, n.d. [Aug 1984].
40 Diary note, 10 Nov 1976.
41 Letter to Toss Woollaston, 14 Dec 1979.
42 Letter to Colin McCahon, 2 Mar 1978.
43 Letter to Jeffrey Harris, 19 July 1982.
44 Letter to Woollaston, 14 Dec 1978.
45 Letter to Harris, 21 May 1981. One of PM's first assistants was Janne Land, who later became an art dealer herself. 'He was very specific about how he wanted things done,' she recalled, 'but he was always very polite and he would show me what he wanted. I'd address envelopes for the openings, and I'd mind the gallery while he was away and see if I could sell something. We always got on very well and even after I stopped working for him we'd keep in touch.' Interview with the author, 12 Sept 2012. Other assistants included Anna Thurlin, Sandy Callister, Derek Cowie, Ivan Anthony, William Hedley, Victor Berezovsky, Daniel Mortimer and Daniel Unverricht. Their duties varied over the years, but included clerical work, packing and installing art, cleaning the gallery, and minding it while he was away.
46 Interview with the author, 19 Dec 2012.
47 Letter to Charles Tole, 10 Dec 1981.
48 Conversation with the author, 2 July 2012.
49 Letter to Laurence Aberhart, 10 Oct 1982.
50 Letter to Richard Killeen, 15 Apr 1983.
51 Letter to White, 10 Nov 1983.
52 Letter to Killeen, 2 Dec 1983.
53 Letter to Killeen, 21 Dec 1983.
54 PM in conversation with the author, 27 June 2012.
55 Interview with the author, 28 Nov 2012.
56 Letter to Peter Ireland, 19 Jan 1984. The next quotation is also from this letter.
57 Letter to Milan Mrkusich, 25 July 1984.
58 Letter to Ireland, 26 Mar 1984. PM's commission on sales nearly quadrupled from 1975 to 1985: by comparison, his rent more than doubled in the same period, his travelling expenses quadrupled and the cost of advertising increased sevenfold.
59 Letter to Pat Hanly, 28 July 1984.
60 Letter to Ireland, 26 June 1984.
61 Letter to Harris, 8 Oct 1984.
62 As early as 1 Mar 1979, PM had written to McCahon: 'I have found lately that my own religious background is surfacing and I seem to have a yearning to know God.'
63 Interview with the author, 25 Aug 2010.
64 Letter to Ireland, 27 Mar 1985.
65 Letter to Ireland, 3 Nov 1985.

CHAPTER 18

1 A top auction price in New York in the early 1980s was $3 million; by the end of the decade, works were selling for 10 to 20 times that amount.
2 Rosemary McLeod, 'The state of New Zealand art', *North & South*, Nov 1986, p. 46.
3 Rosemary McLeod, 'Towards 2000: Art', *North & South*, Apr 1987, p. 65.
4 Webb worked for the auction house George Walker in Auckland in the early 1960s, which occasionally sold works of art, and in 1963, in partnership with McCahon and others, established John Cordy Ltd. He left Cordy's to work as exhibitions officer at the Auckland City Art Gallery from 1970 to 1974, and in 1976 established the Peter Webb Gallery, which eventually became Webb's auction house, holding the first auction on 30 Nov 1978. Other art auction companies included Dunbar Sloane's in Wellington, and McCrostie's in Christchurch.
5 Letter to Peter Ireland, 27 July 1985.
6 It was only in the 1980s, however, that Walters earned a living from his art; prior to that he was partially supported by his wife, Margaret Orbell.
7 Diana Dekker, 'The art of buying art', *Dominion Post*, 10 Aug 2002, F3.

8 *Practical religion: the resurrection of Lazarus showing Mount Martha* (1969–70). Today's equivalent of $130,000 is $324,000.

9 Interview with the author, 16 Mar 2011.

10 Quoted in Peter Shaw, 'Auctions demonstrate market's erratic nature', *NZ Times*, 3 June 1984, p. 14.

11 Quoted in Garth Cartwright, 'Auction boom $ellout', *New Zealand Listener*, 28 Mar 1987, p. 35.

12 Twenty-two members signed up, contributing $500 at the outset and $250 every year to acquire works. They included businessmen James Wallace and John Fernyhough, and lawyers Julian Miles and Geoff Ricketts. The entire collection was sold at auction in March 1987.

13 Resales were an important part of PM's business from the late 1970s. Some of his clients preferred to sell works that had dramatically inflated in value to finance their ongoing acquisition of works by young artists.

14 Born and bred in Wellington, Jenny Gibbs was familiar with the PMG before the 1980s, and had begun to buy art from Barry Lett and Petar Vuletic in the previous decade.

15 Letter to Gordon Walters, 28 Aug 1985. Walters replied on 15 Sept: 'I agree too that the Auckland art scene is a destablising one, I feel the effects of this with just one show there, everything is hyped up and the emphasis on dollars & cents is bad.'

16 Artis was run by Trish Clark and Red Metro by Brad Smith, who had recently relocated the gallery from Dunedin. PM commented in a letter to Walters on 2 Apr 1985: 'I find Patricia Clark a very warm, charming person and I like her space. She should go well. I also found the Sue Crockford Gallery a beautiful space; probably the best in the country. She, too, is a very nice person and she should also go well. The more the better as it makes the whole thing tick over better and extends the market.'

17 Letter to Walters, 7 July 1985.

18 Galerie Legard was owned by Brooker & Friend, a firm of legal stationers, annotators and publishers. Land, who was PM's assistant in the mid-1970s, was appointed to run the Galerie Legard in 1977; when she left in 1981 to establish her own business, Kay Roberts took over. The gallery was renamed the Brooker Gallery in 1985.

19 They included Gregory Flint's Southern Cross Gallery (1986–90) and Lindsay Park's 33⅓ Gallery (1987–93). Catherine Scollay briefly took over Gregory Flint's space in 1990–91, and Gow Langsford ran a Wellington branch in 1991–92, which was managed by Hamish McKay (who opened his own eponymous gallery in 1993).

20 Notably, Artspace was established in Auckland in 1987 as a non-collecting, non-commercial venue to promote contemporary art. It was – and continues to be – supported by the arts council (now Creative New Zealand).

21 Wystan Curnow, 'New Zealand art – where in the world is it?', *New Zealand Listener*, 3 Apr 1982, p. 34.

22 Luit Bieringa in conversation with the author, 6 Oct 2012.

23 *ANZART-in-Edinburgh* presented the McCahon exhibition *I will need words* from the Sydney Biennale, as well as a New Zealand show, which included Trusttum, Killeen, Maria Olsen, From Scratch, Andrew Drummond and John Cousins. The project was coordinated by Wystan Curnow and Ian Hunter in association with the Richard Demarco Gallery, and supported by the Queen Elizabeth II Arts Council.

24 Bryan Staff, 'Peter McLeavey interviewed for ChaCha', *ChaCha*, June 1984, p. 11.

25 Interview with the author, 9 Aug 2012. Unless otherwise noted, the following quotations from Reynolds are from this interview.

26 Letter to John Reynolds, 13 Nov 1983.

27 The show comprised five large works, at $1000, and smaller oil and pastel sketches, priced from $180.

28 Ian Wedde, 'Way of life: Dealer punts on the new', *EP*, 29 Oct 1984, p. 39.

29 Letter to Julian Dashper, 29 Mar 1985. The next quotation is also from this letter.

30 Letter from Dashper to PM, 9 Nov 1985.

31 Letter to Reynolds, 8 July 1988.

32 Letter to Reynolds, 27 Jan 1986.

33 Rob Taylor, 'Dashper pursues pleasure', *Dominion*, 21 May 1986, p. 8.

34 Dashper later distanced himself from the apparently expressionist style of these early works: they were not about personal expression, he maintained; rather, they reflected on the nature of painting and the process of its production: 'I could have made them wearing three-piece suits.' Interview with Mark Kirby, *Luxus*, 1997; reprinted in *The twist*, Waikato Museum of Art and History, 1998, p. 3.

35 Letter from Killeen to PM, 20 Jan 1985.
36 Merrill Coke, 'Life is the next show', *New Zealand Listener*, 13 Dec 1986, p. 62. The next quotation is also from this article.
37 Letter from Dashper to PM, n.d. [*c.*Nov 1985]. Dashper had worked on a collaborative painting with Philip Clairmont, Adam Gifford and Maddox when he was still a student in 1978. Gifford recalled: 'Julian instigated the idea of a collaborative painting, and came round with a roll of the same jute canvas Phil was using at the time. It was tacked up on the wall of the sitting room and we tried to paint the road from Auckland to Wellington – because of course you didn't fly in those days as poor students/artists, you drove or in my case hitchhiked.' Email to the author, 23 May 2012.
38 As recalled by Peter Ireland in a letter to the author, 17 Nov 2012.
39 PM also purchased a work for the BNZ Art Collection: *Omaha Beach no. 3* (1986).
40 Ian Wedde, 'Beyond window shopping: Xmas art grottoes', *EP*, 17 Dec 1986, p. 30.
41 Letter from Dashper to PM, 23 June 1987.
42 Postcard from Dashper to PM, 20 Aug 1987.
43 Letter from Dashper to PM, 15 Nov 1987.
44 Letter from Dashper to PM, 15 May 1989.
45 Quoted in 'John Reynolds', *Kia Ora* (Air New Zealand magazine), Feb 2004, p. 71.
46 See, for example, Benjamin Buchloh, 'Figures of authority, cyphers of regression: Notes on the return of representation in European painting', in Brian Wallis (ed.), *Art after modernism*, New Museum of Contemporary Art, New York, 1984. This essay was first published in *October*, Vol. 16, Spring 1981.
47 In 1988, Jenny Harper curated an exhibition of Kruger's work for the National Art Gallery's Shed II, and Lita Barrie contributed an essay to the catalogue. See Jenny Harper, *Barbara Kruger*, National Art Gallery, Wellington, 1988.
48 Lita Barrie, 'McLeavey chimes for Julian Schnabel', *NBR*, 16 Oct 1987, p. 75.
49 For Reynolds, see 'Blurring the distinctions of modernism', *NBR*, 5 Feb 1988, p. 31; for Dashper, see 'Never mind the public: just take a look at all that "devajunk" piling up', *NBR*, 13 Oct 1989, p. W13, and 'McLeavey chimes for Julian Schnabel', *NBR*, 16 Oct 1987, p. 75. PM exhibited Schnabel's prints in 1987, see p. 333.
50 Letter from Dashper to PM, 14 Dec 1985.
51 Letter from Dashper to PM, n.d. [July–Aug 1986].
52 The National Art Gallery bought *P.M. in Brooklyn* (1988) from this show.
53 Letter from Dashper to PM, 4 May 1989.
54 Barrie, 'Never mind the public'.
55 The book was *Gordon Walters: Order and intuition*, a collection of essays edited by James Ross and Laurence Simmons for the artist's seventieth birthday (1989).
56 Letter to Dashper, 13 Oct 1989.
57 Letter from Dashper to PM, 17 Oct 1989.
58 Letter to Reynolds, 14 Oct 1989.

CHAPTER 19

1 Letter to Gordon Walters, 29 Mar 1985. The next quotation is also from this letter.
2 Letter to Peter Ireland, 4 July 1986.
3 Letter to Richard Killeen, 6 July 1985.
4 Letter to a client, 8 Oct 1985. The artist Tony Lane, who had five solo shows at the PMG from 1981 to 1985, recalled the dish as a combination of mince, cabbage and potato: 'It was rather awful. I remember having dinner there one day and there was an aluminium ladder in the room with five white shirts hanging off it, one for every day of the week. It was quite an eccentric household.' Conversation with the author, 3 Sept 2012.
5 Letter from Toss Woollaston to PM, 24 Aug 1985.
6 Interview with the author, 16 Oct 2012. The quotation in the next paragraph is also from this interview.
7 Letter to Woollaston, 12 July 1982.
8 Letter to Ireland, 4 July 1986.
9 Interview with the author, 28 Nov 2012.

10 This and the following quotations from Peter Black are from a conversation with the author, 4 June 2012. PM also commissioned a painting by Gavin Chilcott: *Peter at 50 with lares and saints* (1986–87); see Alexa Johnston et. al., *Dream collectors: One hundred years of art in New Zealand*, Te Papa Press, Wellington, 1998, pp. 136–37.

11 Ian Wedde, 'Mark Rossell's gothic biomorphs', *EP*, 22 July 1987, p. 38.

12 Letter to Ireland, 24 Sept 1986.

13 Letter to Ray Hughes, 1 Apr 1985.

14 Others to have solo shows included Janet Bayly (1985), Gail Wright (1990) and Helm Ruifrok (1989 and 1991).

15 Letter to Gordon Walters, 28 Aug 1985.

16 Interview with the author, 16 Mar 2011.

17 *Ibid.*

18 This and the following quotations from Don Binney are from an interview with the author, 31 Aug 2011.

19 Smither had 11 solo exhibitions at the gallery until 1980. Only Mrkusich had more, with 12.

20 Letter to Ireland, 10 June 1983.

21 Letter from Michael Smither to PM, 14 May 1984.

22 PM sold eight oils from the *Golden Age* show; the buyers included the National Art Gallery, the Ministry of Foreign Affairs and Victoria University.

23 Letter to Pat Hanly, 10 Dec 1987. The next quotation is also from this letter. See also PM's letter to Hanly of 20 Nov 1987.

24 Interview with the author, 31 Aug 2011.

25 Interview with the author, 2 Sept 2011.

26 They included *The illumination of festivals* (1954), *Six days in Nelson and Canterbury* (1950), *Easter morning* (1950), *North Otago landscape 4* (1967), all gifted to Auckland City Art Gallery between 1972 and 1979; *The Song of the Shining Cuckoo* (1974), gifted to the HL in 1977; *Hail Mary* (1948), gifted to the Govett-Brewster in 1978; and the *Parihaka triptych* (1972), gifted to the people of Parihaka and housed at the Govett-Brewster.

27 Letter from Colin McCahon to PM, 19 June 1980. The quotations in the next two sentences are also from this letter. On 11 July that year, McCahon wrote: 'My paintings do belong here & are painted for New Zealanders – whether they like them or not. In a way I'm trying to do something useful for New Zealand – this will become apparent in due time.' He told PM that working in the museum world had made him particularly aware of the 'lavish losses overseas', citing Ruatepupuke II, the nineteenth-century wharenui he had seen in the Field Museum in Chicago in 1958: 'it was so wrong there – a curio – here it would be splendid'.

28 Letter from McCahon to PM, [23?] June 1980.

29 Letter from McCahon to PM, 7 July 1980. In the following years, in consultation with his family and PM, McCahon gifted several more key works to public collections in New Zealand. They included *Caterpillar landscape* (1947), gifted to the Dowse Art Gallery in 1980; *Triple Takaka* (1948) and *The family* (1947), gifted to the Manawatu Art Gallery in 1983; *How is the hammer broken* (1961), *The Fourteen Stations of the Cross* (1966), *Will he save him?* (1959) and *The lark's song (A poem for Matire Kereama)* (1969), all gifted to Auckland City Art Gallery in 1981–82; *Storm warning* (1980–81), gifted to Victoria University in 1981; and *Crucifixion According to St Mark* (1947), gifted to the Robert McDougall Art Gallery on the death of Ron O'Reilly in 1982. *Storm warning* was sold by Victoria University in 1999, amid much controversy.

30 It was gifted, via PM, with the credit line, 'Gift of anonymous donors with assistance from the Willi Fels Memorial Trust'. Even director Luit Bieringa did not know the identity of the donor at the time.

31 Letter from McCahon to PM, 7 July 1980.

32 Letter to McCahon, 10 Oct 1982.

33 Letter from McCahon to PM, 9 Feb [1983].

34 *I will need words: Colin McCahon's word and number paintings* was held at the Power Gallery of Contemporary Art at the University of Sydney as a satellite exhibition of the fifth Sydney Biennale.

35 Terence Maloon, 'You've got to have faith to hear and see', *Sydney Morning Herald*, 21 Apr 1984, p. 30. See also Ian Wedde, 'McCahon excites Sydney critics', *EP*, 12 May 1984, p. 13.

36 The exhibition was part of *ANZART-in-Edinburgh*, coordinated by Wystan Curnow and Ian Hunter in association with Richard Demarco.

37 McCahon died in Auckland Hospital from bronchopneumonia complicated by dementia.
38 Deborah Hannan, 'Epitaph: Colin McCahon (1919–1987)', *EP*, 30 May 1987, p. 21.
39 Letter to Richard Killeen, 27 Jan 1986.
40 Letter from Michael Illingworth to PM, n.d. [early July 1988].
41 Letter to Ireland, 21 July 1988.
42 Letter to Dene Illingworth, 26 July 1988.
43 Letter to Ireland, 10 Mar 1986.
44 Letter to Julian Dashper, 30 Jan 1987.
45 Letter to Walters, 5 Feb 1987.
46 Letter to Milan Mrkusich, 30 Mar 1987.
47 PM had first seen Schnabel's work in the Whitney Biennial in 1981.
48 Letter to Barbara Tuck, 17 Sept 1987. After the exhibition, PM stored the Schnabel prints in his flat for some time. One night he cooked a meal for Peter Ireland: 'the usual dinner of fried chops, mashed potato and tinned Watties peas & coming out of the kitchen now & then in his pinny to make sure I still had something to drink. As he was leaving the room he paused and said reflectively, "I think this is the biggest collection of Schnabels in Brooklyn", but as he went through the door he popped his head back in and said very deadpan, "That's Brooklyn New Zealand"! It was consummate comic timing.' Letter from Ireland to the author, 17 Nov 2012.
49 Lita Barrie, 'McLeavey chimes for Julian Dashper', *NBR*, 16 Oct 1987, p. 75.
50 Ian Wedde, 'The Americans are coming', *EP*, 24 Sept 1987, p. 25.
51 Letter from James Mollison to PM, 16 Nov 1987. Encouraged by the response to his Schnabel show – although no prints were sold – PM also enquired about showing works by Anselm Kiefer.
52 Garth Cartwright, 'Auction boom $ellout', *New Zealand Listener*, 28 Mar 1987, p. 34.
53 Gilbert Wong, 'Galleries hanging in there', *NZH*, 16 June 1988, section 2, p. 1. The Gow Langsford Gallery had opened just weeks before the stockmarket crash.
54 *Ibid.*
55 Letter to Walters, 25 Nov 1988.
56 Conversation with the author, 16 July 2012.
57 'Art dealer positive about market', *Dominion*, 26 July 1991, p. 23. The next quotation is also from this article.
58 Interview with the author, 22 Sept 2012. Unless otherwise noted, all quotations from Bill Hammond in this section are from this interview.
59 Calvin Tomkins, 'Profile: A good eye and a good ear', *New Yorker*, 26 May 1980, p. 41.
60 Letter from Bill Hammond to PM, n.d. [mid- to late Sept 1990].
61 Letter to Peter Ireland, 30 Nov 1990.
62 Quoted in Gregory O'Brien, *Lands & deeds: Profiles of contemporary New Zealand painters*, Godwit, Auckland, 1996, p. 58. The next quotation is also from this page.
63 Letter to Hammond, 17 Sept 1991.
64 Letter to Hammond, 30 Dec 1991.
65 The first exhibition, 23 May–10 June 1995, was entitled *Bill Hammond: Unplugged*. PM felt these two shows had 'jump-started' Hammond's career; see his letter to Andrew McLeod, 20 Dec 2006.
66 On 28 July 2007, Celia Dunlop wrote to PM: 'I consider myself lucky to have enjoyed our happy association over 36 years now ... we have built a lot of my collection together.' Quoted in Jill Trevelyan, 'Introduction', *Thrill me every day: The Celia Dunlop collection*, Celia Dunlop Trust, Wellington, 2009, unpaged.
67 *Containers* (1998) was sold by Dunbar Sloane in Auckland in May 2002. The buyer was Sydney dealer Martin Browne, who purchased it for his gallery stock.
68 Letter to a client, 31 Oct 2002. The next quotation is also from this letter.
69 Letter to Hammond, 28 Sept 2002. The work was *Threshing dog, The golden bough* (2002), exhibited in *Self motivation* at the PMG, Sept–Oct 2002.

CHAPTER 20

1 Letter to Char Dales, 7 Oct 1988.
2 Letter to Kirstin Marks, 15 Apr 1990. The next quotation is also from this letter.

3 Letter to John Reynolds, 19 May 1989.
4 Letter from Derek Cowie to PM, 30 May 1989.
5 Email from Cowie to the author, 19 July 2012.
6 Email from Kathlene Fogarty to the author, 27 Aug 2012. PM commented in a conversation on 13 Dec 2012: 'It was actually corrugated brown paper: Colin had addressed it to me and signed it too.'
7 Interview with the author, 2 Sept 2011.
8 Email from Cowie to the author, 19 July 2012.
9 See PM's letter to McCahon, 4 July 1980.
10 Grant Smithies, 'Art and soul', *SST*, 29 May 2005, p.27.
11 Letter to Gordon Walters, 15 Aug 1978.
12 Interview with the author, 14 July 2011.
13 Letter to Cowie, 13 June 1989.
14 Letter from Cowie to PM, 3 July 1989.
15 Letter to Jacqueline Fraser, 16 Sept 1989.
16 Letter to Cowie, 3 Oct 1989.
17 Letter to Cowie, 3 Nov 1989. The next quotation is also from this letter.
18 Letter to Nevill Drury, 24 Sept 1991.
19 Interview with the author, 28 Nov 2012.
20 Letter to Murray Bail, 5 Nov 1993.
21 Interview with the author, 25 Aug 2011. The quotation in the next paragraph is also from this interview.
22 Mrkusich comments: 'It is worth noting that the two works in question and other similar works have been sold later at substantial prices without any issue arising.' Letter to the author, 12 Nov 2012.
23 The name has been changed to protect the clients' privacy.
24 Letter to Milan Mrkusich, 19 Mar 1991.
25 Letter to Billy Apple, 24 Dec 1990.
26 Letter to Apple, 5 May 1990.
27 On 24 July 1990, PM wrote to Apple, 'I do not wish this piece of furniture to be touched, at this stage. I need time to think.'
28 Letter to John Hurrell, 17 Mar 1992.
29 Letter to Reynolds, 31 Mar 2004.
30 Letter to Julian Dashper, 14 Feb 1991. The next two quotations are also from this letter.
31 Letter to Tim and Sherrah Francis, 8 Apr 1991.
32 Interview with the author, 16 July 2012.
33 The quotations in this paragraph are from an interview with the author, 25 Sept 2012.
34 Interview with the author, 25 Aug 2011.
35 Letter to Dashper, 22 May 1992.
36 Letter to Dashper, 3 Nov 1992.
37 Interview with the author, 28 Nov 2012.
38 Letter to Barry Brickell, 4 Dec 1991.
39 Artist's statement, 8 Dec 1992, exhibition file 290.
40 Letter to Merylyn Tweedie, 10 July 1991.
41 PM used these words in a note about the incident in the exhibition file.
42 Instead of an exhibition opening, PM arranged for Brian Sergent and The Flannelettes to perform a comedy piece.
43 Letter to Richard Killeen, 3 Apr 1993.
44 Interview with the author, 2 Sept 2011. Ivan Anthony was PM's assistant.
45 Conversation with the author, 16 July 2012.

CHAPTER 21

1 Letter to Murray Bail, 5 Nov 1993.
2 The exhibition was *Recognitions*, at the Robert McDougall Art Gallery Art Annex, curated by Lara Strongman; the other artists were Marianna Bullmore, Shane Cotton, Séraphine Pick, Kim Pieters and David Reid. PM made a note in the catalogue by Robinson's name: 'very impressed'.
3 Interview with the author, 10 Aug 2012. Unless otherwise noted, the following quotations from Robinson are from this interview.

4 Letter to Peter Robinson, 12 Aug 1992. *Shadow of style: Eight new artists* was curated by Greg Burke and Robert Leonard; other artists included Shane Cotton, Luise Fong, Ronnie van Hout and Giovanni Intra.
5 Letter to Robinson, 3 May 1993.
6 Artist's statement, artist's file, Te Aka Matua Research Library, TP.
7 Philip Matthews, 'A touch of tar', *Capital Times*, 18–24 Aug 1993, p. 15. The next quotation is also from this article.
8 Megan Tamati-Quennell, 'Peter Robinson: Pale by comparison', *Planet*, No. 14, 1994, p. 60.
9 Matthews, 'A touch of tar', p. 15.
10 The works were priced from $900 to $7000.
11 In 2012, Robinson commented, 'I'd be horrified if I heard of one of my students being treated like that. At least a part of me would be horrified. Now, we try to teach the students about installation, but it was different then – we didn't really have any training in it. You made the art and put it out there.' Interview with the author, 10 Aug 2012.
12 Paton was reviewing *New lines/Old stock*, an exhibition from the same series at the Brooke Gifford Gallery in Christchurch. See 'Market laughs last as fame comes courting', *Press*, 21 Sept 1994, p. 16.
13 Fax to Robinson, 23 Aug 1995.
14 Letter from Robinson to PM, 4 Dec 1995.
15 Peter Simpson, *Candles in a dark room: James K. Baxter and Colin McCahon*, Auckland Art Gallery Toi o Tāmaki, Auckland, 1996.
16 Letter to Robinson, 3 Aug 1996.
17 Fax from Robinson to PM, 5 Sept 1996. The Japanese artist was Yukinori Yanagi; Tane Norton captained the All Blacks and the New Zealand Maori team during the 1970s.
18 The show included 24 acrylic and oil stick paintings on paper, priced from $1800 to $2100.
19 See Leonard Bell, 'Pakeha have rights too: Peter Robinson's swastikas', *Pre/dictions: The role of art at the end of the millennium*, Department of Art History, Victoria University of Wellington, 2000, pp. 91–96.
20 Email from Robinson to PM, 26 May 1999.
21 Email to Robinson, 9 Apr 1999.
22 Letter to Karen Walker, 13 July 1999.
23 See, for example, 'Ngahuia Te Awekotuku in conversation with Elizabeth Eastmond and Priscilla Pitts', *Antic*, No. 1, June 1986, pp. 44–55. *Headlands: Thinking through New Zealand art* was shown at the Museum of Contemporary Art in Sydney. Walters himself saw his work as an homage: 'Traditional Maori art means a lot to me – it is the one distinctive art style that we have in this country. What I have done is a kind of tribute to this tradition.' See William McAloon, *Gordon Walters: Prints + design*, Adam Art Gallery Te Pātaka Toi, Wellington, 2004, p. 11.
24 Rangihiroa Panoho, 'Maori: At the centre, on the margins', in Mary Barr (ed.), *Headlands: Thinking through New Zealand art*, Museum of Contemporary Art, Sydney, 1992, pp. 122–34.
25 Letter to John Reynolds, 15 Apr 1992.
26 *Parallel lines: Gordon Walters in context* was on display from 22 Aug to 20 Oct 1994.
27 Letter to Gordon Walters, 8 Aug 1994.
28 Justin Paton, 'The ties that bind', *New Zealand Listener*, 8 Oct 1994, p. 44.
29 Letter to Walters, 25 Aug 1994.
30 Letter to Keith Stewart, 27 July 1994. The review was entitled 'Shapes that move people', *SST*, 24 July 1994, D5.
31 Letter to Walters, 1 Sept 1995.
32 Letter to Richard Killeen, 21 Sept 1995.
33 Letter to Knight Landesman, 11 Nov 1995.
34 Conversation with the author, 25 Oct 2012. The painting was *Untitled* (1993).
35 Letter from Laurence Aberhart to PM, 18 Dec 1995.
36 Letter from Reynolds to PM, 9 Nov 1995.
37 'This has been distressing to me,' he wrote to Julian Dashper in his last letter of 16 Mar 1994, 'and it's tainted my ability to handle your work. I now wish to be relieved from my position as one of your dealers.'
38 Letter to Reynolds, 7 Feb 1996.

39 Interview with the author, 9 Aug 2012.
40 Letter to Killeen, 26 Oct 1996.
41 Letter to Robin White, n.d. [late Aug 1996].
42 Letter from White to PM, n.d. [Sept 1996]. The next quotation is also from this letter.
43 Hugh Barlow, 'An artist's family comes to visit', *Wairarapa Times-Age*, 15 June 2002, p. 3.
44 Tom Fitzsimons, 'Visionary collaboration', *Dominion Post*, 27 May 2010, p. 14.
45 Justin Paton, 'The shock of the old', *New Zealand Listener*, 26 June 1999, p. 38.
46 Letter to Chris Heaphy, 26 May 1997.
47 David Eggleton, 'Mark Braunias', in Fiona Campbell (ed.), *Real art roadshow: The book*, The Real Art Charitable Trust, Waikanae, 2009, p. 18.
48 Letter to Diane Miller [PM's accountant], 29 Apr 2002.
49 Letter from Peter Ireland to PM, 26 July 1998.
50 Letter to Ian Brown, 23 Sept 1998.
51 Letter to Ireland, 13 Nov 1998.
52 Ian Wedde, 'McLeavey's pilot opera', *EP*, 25 June 1985, p. 37. Four years later, Miro Bilbrough reviewed a show with an unusual pairing: 'Peter McLeavey is up to his tricks with a show from stock where he mixes loud late 60s paintings by Ian Scott with recent and tranquil black and white photographs by Laurence Aberhart. It's a very cultivated looking mix of good and bad taste that provokes one to wonder: why these two together?' See 'Looking through a dark glass', *EP*, 25 May 1989, p. 19.
53 Damian Skinner, 'The dealer as curator', *Art New Zealand*, No. 88, Spring 1998, p. 41.
54 Letter to Robinson, 5 Aug 1998.
55 The work is *Glassman, Mexico City* (1994). *Blood brothers* also included work by Peter Robinson, Derek Cowie, Andrew McLeod, McCahon and Walters.
56 Interview with the author, 4 Aug 2012.
57 Conversation with the author, 13 Dec 2012.
58 Conversation with the author, 24 Nov 2012.
59 Letter to Helen Garner, 28 Feb 2005.
60 Exhibition catalogue, exhibition number 344.
61 The quotation is from Ireland's essay, 'Just looking thanks', in the exhibition catalogue.
62 The quotation, which introduces Ireland's catalogue essay, 'Poetic justice', is from Colette, *Journal à rebours* (1941).
63 Ireland was the only person PM ever entrusted to select work for the gallery, but he found it stimulating and rewarding to watch his exhibitions take shape; and, most importantly, he had complete confidence in his vision. 'I regard his taste,' he commented in 2001. See Lindsay Rabbitt, 'The dealer', *New Zealand Listener*, 17 Feb 2001, p. 50.
64 The quotations in this and the next paragraph are from an interview with the author, 25 Aug 2012.
65 'Dream song 352', in John Berryman, *His toy, his dream, his rest: 308 dream songs*, Faber & Faber, London, 1969, p. 284 (reproduced courtesy of Kate Donahue).
66 Letter to Mark Amery, 9 Apr 2007.

CHAPTER 22

1 This and the following quotations from Ivan Anthony are from an interview with the author, 9 Aug 2012.
2 'My mother thought I was crazy,' Anthony recalled. 'She screamed at me. She said, "I'm not going to bail you out when you get in trouble." She thought it was a complete folly.'
3 Interview, PM with Pip Oldham, 12 Sept 2007, Art Gallery Oral History Project, CD 1.
4 This and the following quotation from McLeod are from an interview with the author, 8 Aug 2012. McLeod left the PMG in 2012 for sole representation by the Ivan Anthony Gallery.
5 Letter to Andrew McLeod, 12 Nov 1998.
6 Letter to Darryn George, 21 July 2000.
7 Aaron Lister, 'Wellington', *Art New Zealand*, No. 93, Summer 1999–2000, p. 36.
8 Letter to McLeod, 11 Oct 1999.
9 Interview with the author, 10 Aug 2012.

10 Robert Leonard, 'Peter Robinson: The end of the 20th century', *Gallery News*, Mar–June 2004, p. 19.
11 In 2011, China moved ahead of both countries in money spent on art and antiques. See Clare McAndrew, 'The international art market in 2011: Observations on the art trade over 25 years', a report commissioned by TEFAF Maastricht, 2011.
12 On 30 Apr 1991, PM told the art council's John Leuthart that he could not entertain any possibility of exhibiting at ARCO in Spain: 'I am totally involved in the day to day business of "getting by" here.' Gow Langsford was one of the first New Zealand galleries to attend international art fairs; in more recent years, Starkwhite, Michael Lett, Jensen, Hamish McKay and others have led the way in participating.
13 The first Melbourne Art Fair was held in 1988; Gow Langsford was the first New Zealand gallery to exhibit in 1990.
14 This and the next quotation are from Jo McCarroll, 'A fair deal of exposure', *SST*, 5 Nov 2000, F4.
15 Letter to Knight Landesman, 24 Sept 2002.
16 Conversation with the author, 8 Nov 2012.
17 Letter to Peter Robinson, 25 June 2001.
18 Fraser left the PMG the year after the Venice Biennale to concentrate on exhibiting overseas.
19 Interview with the author, 23 Aug 2012.
20 Interview with the author, 25 Sept 2012.
21 Letter to Olivia McLeavey, 29 Oct 2002.
22 Ruffo Karl de Graine was an Aro Valley painter and muralist who spent much of his life on the street. See Geoff Cochrane's poem, 'Ruffo', *84-484*, Victoria University Press, Wellington, 2007, p. 75.
23 Interview with the author, 25 Sept 2012. The next quotation is also from this interview.
24 Letter to Knight Landesman, 30 Dec 2002.
25 Fax to Brent Hansen, 18 Mar 2003.
26 Interview with Ivan Anthony, 9 Aug 2012.
27 Interview with the author, 7 Aug 2012. Maw went on to have five solo shows at the PMG between 2004 and 2012, when Ivan Anthony became her exclusive dealer.
28 Conversation with the author, 15 Aug 2012.
29 This and the following quotations are from an interview with Yvonne Todd, 11 Aug 2012.
30 Letter to Sam Neill, 14 Aug 2002.
31 Email to the author, 24 Oct 2012. The following quotations are from an interview with Howard Greive, 2 Sept 2012.
32 This and the next quotation are from a letter to Richard Killeen, 31 Mar 2005. The Auckland Art Fair was first held in 2005, and has become a significant biennial event in the arts calendar. A precursor was Artex, initiated by dealer Warwick Henderson in 1986, a trade fair of historical and contemporary New Zealand art, although few of the major dealer galleries attended.
33 This and the next quotation are from Grant Smithies, 'Art and soul', *SST*, 29 May 2005, pp. 25–28.
34 Interview with the author, 23 Aug 2012. John Reynolds remarked in an interview with the author on 12 Aug 2012, 'I liked the fact that I could talk to Peter about what was happening in a gallery in Chelsea – or the latest Batman movie. He's not precious – he's interested in popular culture too, he constantly has that antennae up.'
35 Letter to Jane Campion, 27 Oct 2004.
36 Letter to Darren Knight, 10 May 2005.
37 Interview with the author, 23 Dec 2011. For more on Brown's collection, see Alisa Bunbury, *Making a mark: Prints and drawings gifted by Ian Brown*, National Gallery of Victoria: Melbourne, 2008.
38 Letter to John Reynolds, 30 Dec 2006.
39 Interview with John Reynolds, 9 Aug 2012. Unless otherwise noted, the following quotations from Reynolds are from this interview.
40 Nick Archer, 'Looking west, later afternoon, low water', *Salient*, 5 Oct 2012, also accessible at www.salient.org.nz/arts/visual-arts/looking-west-late-afternoon-low-water.
41 Interview with the author, 10 Aug 2012.
42 Letter from PM to an anonymous client, 16 Apr 2008.
43 These and the following quotations are from an interview with Robin White, 23 Aug 2012.
44 Letter from Robin White to PM, 8 Oct 2008.

45 Hamish Clayton, 'Art in the face of tragedy: A project by Robin White, Holly Jackson & Robyn McFarlane', *Art New Zealand*, No. 133, Autumn 2010, p. 29.
46 Interview with the author, 23 Aug 2012.
47 Letter to Gordon H Brown, 27 Dec 2007.
48 Interview with the author, 19 Dec 2012.
49 Interview with the author, 19 Dec 2012. All quotations in this and the next paragraph are from this interview.
50 Interview with the author, 19 Dec 2012. The next quotation is also from this interview.
51 Interview with the author, 30 Aug 2012.
52 www.nzonscreen.com/title/the-man-in-the-hat-2009, accessed 10 May 2013.

EPILOGUE

1 Letter, 19 June 2010.
2 All quotations from Olivia McLeavey in this section are from an interview with the author, 25 Sept 2012.
3 Interview with the author, 16 Oct 2012. The next quotation is also from this interview.
4 Interview with the author, 9 Aug 2012.
5 This and the following quotation are from a letter to Andrew Barber, 6 Nov 2010.

LIST OF EXHIBITIONS

1 Occasionally there is a slight discrepancy in dates between the exhibition file and the register, and in these cases I have consulted correspondence, diaries and exhibition reviews to determine the correct dates.
2 PM organised this exhibition in association with the Palmerston North Art Gallery.
3 This exhibition replaced a show of sculpture by Paul Beadle, cancelled by the artist.
4 PM showed Binney's prints to fill a gap when potter Adrian Cotter cancelled his November exhibition six days before the opening.
5 This exhibition was part of *Works on paper*, toured from the US by the director of the Govett-Brewster Art Gallery, Robert (Bob) Ballard.
6 This exhibition replaced *Bill Sutton: Paintings*, cancelled by the artist three weeks before the opening.
7 This exhibition was delayed several weeks at Smither's request; PM showed stock in the interim.
8 This exhibition replaced a show by Don Driver, rescheduled then cancelled by the artist.
9 This exhibition of freestanding sculpture overlapped with the previous show by two days.
10 The gap between this and the next show is due to Don Driver cancelling an exhibition scheduled for Oct 1973.
11 Killeen first exhibited in a stock show with Mrkusich, Smither and Woollaston in Jan 1972, but this is not listed in the exhibition register or exhibition files. See PM's letter to Killeen, 28 Jan 1972.
12 This show was toured by the Auckland City Art Gallery.
13 This show, initially scheduled for October, was delayed due to PM's post-operative convalescence.
14 The gap in the programme following this exhibition was due to PM's trip to Australia.
15 This show is not listed in the exhibition register.
16 This show is not listed in the exhibition register.
17 PM described this show as *Billy Apple: Sculpture* on the invitation; the preferred title is given in brackets.
18 This stock show replaced an exhibition postponed by Billy Apple.
19 Visitors to the opening on 18 Nov were met with a wall wrapped in brown paper, inscribed in red ink, 'The Billy Apple Show is in Transit'. Ian Wedde described the occasion in the *EP*: 'I'm told that unwitting offers were made for this display, although it was in fact the work of Peter McLeavey himself.' See 'McLeavey displays a little piece of Apple', *EP*, 26 Nov 1986, p. 132.
20 This title is from the envelope containing the exhibition file.
21 This show was exhibited at the Timurid Gallery, 134 Cuba Street.
22 PM gave number 233 – an 'unused' exhibition number – to Derek Cowie's exhibition in Mar 1989.
23 According to the exhibition chronology, this should have been number 243.
24 This is how PM described the works in the invitation.
25 Olivia Elizabeth McLeavey. PM had been rebuilding his relationship with his daughter, and this exhibition was a tribute to her.

26 Previously exhibited at PMG, Nov–Dec 1992.
27 The title is from a stencil by Louise Clifton which PM noticed in the gallery entranceway.
28 This was actually the fourth exhibition to use this title.
29 This exhibition, like numbers 405–407, was held at 151 Cuba Street.
30 PM also exhibited historical images in Melbourne: black and white photographs by Elizabeth Pulman, and chromolithographic prints by an anonymous photographer working for the New Zealand Tourist and Publicity Department.
31 The works in the exhibition catalogue were initially listed as *Great eagle*, and changed to *Giant eagle* during the show.
32 Hanly is listed in the invitation, but not in the exhibition catalogue.
33 The works by Meatyard, exhibited 'not-for-sale', were from PM's collection.
34 Olivia McLeavey comments: 'When Peter sent out his letter announcing that he had Parkinson's, he created an exhibition file. It was part of his record keeping, his way of marking the occasion, and in it he put all the correspondence he received and notes about who had popped in to the gallery – "Tina Barton called in with a pot of Floriditas' jam", that kind of thing. Peter said to me, "When the time comes for me to pass from this world to the next world, I want every piece of paper in that file pinned to the wall. And that will be my final exhibition."' Conversation with the author, 3 Mar 2013.
35 A note on the catalogue reads: '"For Oscar" marks the passing of a dear friend. He was much loved, patted, sung and whistled to. Admired by many of the gallery artists on whose laps he sat.'

BIBLIOGRAPHY

ARCHIVAL SOURCES

THE PETER MCLEAVEY GALLERY ARCHIVE

The Peter McLeavey Gallery archive contains exhibition files, correspondence files, diaries, sales books, newspaper clippings, exhibition catalogues, photographs and ephemera. It is especially rich in correspondence with Gordon Walters, Colin McCahon, Toss Woollaston, Richard Killeen, Robin White and Michael Illingworth. The archive is in the possession of Peter McLeavey. Some small changes have been made to the spelling and punctuation of Peter McLeavey's letters, in the interests of readability. All editorial insertions in the text are indicated by square brackets.

OTHER DEALER GALLERY ARCHIVES

Alexander Turnbull Library, Wellington
Peter Webb Galleries, MS-Papers-2362
Centre Gallery records, 89-152

Auckland Art Gallery Toi o Tāmaki
Ikon Gallery (The Gallery), RC 2001/23

Hocken Collections Uare Taoka o Hākena, University of Otago, Dunedin
Barry Lett Galleries/RKS Art, ARC-0190

Museum of New Zealand Te Papa Tongarewa, Wellington
Gallery of Helen Hitchings, CA000118-124, CA000600-601
Denis Cohn Gallery, CA000094-108
Janne Land Gallery, CA000380-384
New Vision Gallery, CA000001-CA000022
Louise Beale Gallery, CA000084-93
Elva Bett Gallery, CA000285

Macmillan Brown Library, University of Canterbury, Christchurch
Barbara Brooke papers (Gallery 91 and Brooke Gifford Gallery), MB-198

PUBLISHED WRITINGS BY PETER MCLEAVEY

'Wellington', in *New Zealand painting 1966*, Auckland City Art Gallery, Auckland, 1966, unpaged.
'Exhibition of influential French artist's works', *Dominion*, 17 June 1967, p. 7.
'What has Kelliher contest achieved?', *Dominion*, 24 June 1967, p. 9.
'Modest art show', *Dominion*, 22 July 1967, p. 8.
'Dominion controversy points up the need for city art gallery', *Dominion*, 29 July 1967, p. 9.
'Boost for visual arts in New Plymouth', *Dominion*, 5 August 1967, p. 6.
'Encouraging help for visual arts', *Dominion*, 19 August 1967, p. 9.

'Photographer's art over 100 years', *Dominion*, 26 August 1967, p. 7.
'Chance to study work of eminent cartoonist', *Dominion*, 2 September 1967, p. 9.
'Valuable sketches given to gallery', *Dominion*, 9 September 1967, p. 9.
'Auckland dealer has done much for visual arts', *Dominion*, 16 September 1967, p. 9.
'Contemporary art gets boost from Manawatu prize', *Dominion*, 23 September 1967, p. 9.
'Wyndham Lewis work bought for National Gallery', *Dominion*, 30 September 1967, p. 9.
'Revived interest in print-making', *Dominion*, 7 October 1967, p. 11.
'Unfortunate reaction greets sculptor's creation', *Dominion*, 14 October 1967, p. 11.
'"Ned Kelly" oils to be exhibited in Auckland', *Dominion*, 21 October 1967, p. 9.
'Poussin work for Christmas stamp', *Dominion*, 28 October 1967, p. 9.
'Academy out of step with creative art', *Dominion*, 4 November 1967, p. 9.
'Graham Sutherland a painter at top of profession', *Dominion*, 11 November 1967, p. 9.
'N.Z.-born artist has won renown in unusual idiom', *Dominion*, 18 November 1967, p. 8.
'Keen demand for NZ potter's art', *Dominion*, 25 November 1967, p. 8.
'Disturbing English painter and his striking work', *Dominion*, 2 December 1967, p. 8.
'Photographic collection hardly inspiring', *Dominion*, 9 December 1967, p. 11.
'Summer school for art students', *Dominion*, 16 December 1967, p. 8.
'Wellington artist wins Hodgkins fellowship', *Dominion*, 23 December 1967, p. 7.
'Loss of Tomory blow to NZ art', *Dominion*, 6 January 1968, p. 9.
'Artist shows value of Europe visit', *Dominion*, 13 January 1968, p. 9.
'Fine Gothic art group for New Zealand', *Dominion*, 20 January 1968, p. 9.
'Fuseli collection an exciting art find', *Dominion*, 27 January 1968, p. 7.
'Painter with devotion for NZ landscape', *Dominion*, 3 February 1968, p. 6.
'New Zealand artist with rare distinction', *Dominion*, 10 February 1968, p. 8.
'Keen interest in art biennales', *Dominion*, 17 February 1968, p. 6.
'Time ripe for a change at National Art Gallery', *Dominion*, 24 February 1968, p. 6.
'NZ art could be used on stamps', *Dominion*, 9 March 1968, p. 7.
'Centre Gallery in new home', *Dominion*, 16 March 1968, p. 7.
'Arts world indebted to Helen Hitchings', *Dominion*, 23 March 1968, p. 7.
'Good collection of NZ art in university', *Dominion*, 30 March 1968, p. 11.
'Painter who aims at clarity', *Dominion*, 6 April 1968, p. 9.
'Chance to study art of Petrus van der Velden', *Dominion*, 13 April 1968, p. 9.
'Exhibition to mark centenary of Frances Hodgkins', *Dominion*, 20 April 1968, p. 7.
'Van der Rohe: Master of the simple style', *Dominion*, 27 April 1968, p. 9.
'Rare masterpieces by Renaissance painters in private N.Z. collection', *Dominion*, 4 May 1968, p. 14.
'Record price paid for Nolan work', *Dominion*, 1 June 1968, p. 16.
'Exciting sculpture to grace building', *Dominion*, 8 June 1968, p. 12.
'Palmerston North gallery one of the liveliest', *Dominion*, 15 June 1968, p. 16.
'Leading US art critic to speak in capital', *Dominion*, 22 June 1968, p. 14.
'A clean, well-lighted place', *New Zealand Listener*, 6 December 1968, pp. 2–3.
'Gordon Walters: An interview', *Salient*, 7 May 1969, p. 8.
'When I first heard Colin McCahon's name', *Art New Zealand*, No. 8, November 1977–January 1978, pp. 40–41.
'The clothes we love', *Monica*, June–July 1996, p. 11.

INTERVIEWS AND PROFILES OF PETER MCLEAVEY

'Art dealer positive about market', *Dominion*, 26 July 1991, p. 23.
Blundell, Sally, 'I sell, therefore I am', *New Zealand Listener*, 28 November 2009, pp. 34–37.
Brett, Michael, 'Eyes opened in Sydney' (The Auckland Diary), *Auckland Star*, 11 July 1972, p. 8.
Butler, Susanne, 'Beauty through art', *Evening Post*, 30 August 1978, p. 4.
Cardy, Tom, 'The man under the hat', *Dominion Post*, 15 July 2009, p. 2.
Coke, Merill, 'Life is the next show', *New Zealand Listener*, 13 December 1986, pp. 62–63.
Corner, Katy, 'Living culture', *City Voice*, 16 April 1998, p. 16.
Dekker, Diana, 'The art of buying art', *Dominion Post*, 10 August 2002, F3.

———, 'Portrait of a salesman', *Dominion Post Weekend*, 31 May 2008, p. 5.
———, 'In her father's den', *Dominion Post,* Your Weekend, 5 March 2011, p. 6.
Rabbitt, Lindsay, 'The dealer', *New Zealand Listener*, 17 February 2001, pp. 50–51.
[Simmons, Beverley], 'Young man on way to the top', *New Zealand Herald*, 24 June 1967, magazine section, p. 2.
Smithies, Grant, 'Art and soul', *Sunday Star-Times*, 29 May 2005, *Sunday* supplement, pp. 24–28.
Staff, Bryan, 'Peter McLeavey interviewed for ChaCha', *ChaCha*, June 1984, p. 11.
Wedde, Ian, 'The Wellington art mafia dossier', *Wellington City Magazine*, June 1985, pp. 16–23.
Wilson, Simon, 'Gallery stakes', *New Zealand Listener*, 25 November 1991, pp. 42–43.

SELECTED BOOKS AND EXHIBITION CATALOGUES

Allen, Jim and Wystan Curnow, *New art: Some recent New Zealand sculpture and post-object art*, Heinemann, Auckland, 1976.
Barnett, Gerald, *Toss Woollaston: An illustrated biography*, Random Century, Auckland, in association with the National Art Gallery, Wellington, 1991 (exhibition catalogue).
Barr, Jim and Mary Barr, *Contemporary New Zealand painters*, Vol. 1, A–M, Alister Taylor, Martinborough, 1980.
———, *Michael Smither: An introduction*, Govett-Brewster Art Gallery, New Plymouth, 1984 (exhibition catalogue).
———, *When art hits the headlines*, National Art Gallery, Wellington, 1987 (exhibition catalogue).
———, *Hit parade: Contemporary art from the Paris family collection*, Wellington City Art Gallery, Wellington, 1994 (exhibition catalogue).
Barr, Mary (ed.), *Headlands: Thinking through New Zealand art*, Museum of Contemporary Art, Sydney, 1992 (exhibition catalogue).
Barton, Christina, *After McCahon: Some configurations in recent art*, Auckland City Art Gallery, Auckland, 1989 (exhibition catalogue).
Barton, Christina, (ed.), *Behind closed doors*, Adam Art Gallery Te Pātaka Toi, Wellington, 2011 (exhibition catalogue).
Beagehole, Tim, *A life of JC Beaglehole: New Zealand scholar*, Victoria University Press, Wellington, 2006.
Bieringa, Luit, *MT Woollaston, Works 1933–1973*, Manawatu Art Gallery, Palmerston North, 1973 (exhibition catalogue).
———, *McCahon: 'Religious' works, 1946–1952*, Manawatu Art Gallery, Palmerston North, 1975 (exhibition catalogue).
Bloem, Marja and Martin Browne, *Colin McCahon: A question of faith*, Stedelijk Museum Amsterdam; Craig Potton Publishing, Nelson, 2002 (exhibition catalogue).
Bloomfield, GT, *New Zealand: A handbook of historical statistics*, GK Hall, Boston, Massachusetts, 1984.
Brown, Gordon H, *New Zealand painting 1900–1920: Tradition and departures*, Queen Elizabeth II Arts Council of New Zealand, Wellington, 1972 (exhibition catalogue).
———, *New Zealand painting 1920–1940: Adaptation and nationalism,* Queen Elizabeth II Arts Council of New Zealand, Wellington, 1975 (exhibition catalogue).
———, *New Zealand painting 1940–1960: Conformity and dissension*, Queen Elizabeth II Arts Council of New Zealand, Wellington, 1981 (exhibition catalogue).
———, *Colin McCahon: Artist*, Reed, Wellington, 1993 (revised edition; first published 1984).
———, *Towards a promised land: On the life and art of Colin McCahon*, Auckland University Press, Auckland, 2010.
Brown, Gordon H and Hamish Keith, *10 years of New Zealand painting in Auckland*, Auckland City Art Gallery, Auckland, 1967 (exhibition catalogue).
———, *An introduction to New Zealand painting 1839–1967*, Collins, Auckland, 1969.
Brown, Warwick, *Ian Scott*, Marsden, Auckland, 1998.
Bunbury, Alisa, *Making a mark: Prints and drawings gifted by Ian Brown*, National Gallery of Victoria, Melbourne, 2008 (exhibition catalogue).
Burke, Gregory et al., *Bi-polar: Jacqueline Fraser and Peter Robinson*, Creative New Zealand Toi Aotearoa, Wellington, 2001 (exhibition catalogue).

Campbell, Fiona (ed.), *Real art roadshow: The book*, Real Art Charitable Trust, Waikanae, 2009.
Cann, Tyler and Wystan Curnow, *Len Lye*, Govett-Brewster Art Gallery; Len Lye Foundation, New Plymouth, 2009 (exhibition catalogue).
Caselberg, John, *A retrospective exhibition: MT Woollaston, Colin McCahon*, Auckland City Art Gallery, Auckland, 1963 (exhibition catalogue).
Cohen-Solal, Annie, *Leo and his circle: The life of Leo Castelli*, Alfred A Knopf, New York, 2010.
de Coppet, Laura and Alan Jones, *The art dealers*, Cooper Square Press, New York, 2002 (2nd edition; first published 1984).
Criticism in the arts, Australian UNESCO Seminar, University of Sydney, May 1968, Australian National Advisory Committee for Unesco, Canberra, 1970.
Curnow, Wystan, *McCahon's 'Necessary protection'*, Govett-Brewster Art Gallery, New Plymouth, 1977 (exhibition catalogue).
———, *I will need words: Colin McCahon's word and number paintings*, National Art Gallery, Wellington, 1984 (exhibition catalogue).
———, *As good as gold: Billy Apple, art transactions, 1981–1991*, Wellington City Art Gallery, Wellington, 1991 (exhibition catalogue).
Dashper, Julian, *This is not writing*, Clouds; Michael Lett, Auckland, 2010.
Dunn, Michael, *Gordon Walters*, Auckland City Art Gallery, Auckland, 1983 (exhibition catalogue).
Dunn, Michael and Petar L Vuletic, *Milan Mrkusich: Paintings 1946–1972*, Auckland City Art Gallery, Auckland, 1972 (exhibition catalogue).
Eggleton, David, *Into the light: A history of New Zealand photography*, Craig Potton Publishing, Nelson, 2006.
Five Auckland painters: Don Binney, Patrick Hanly, Ross Ritchie, Colin McCahon, Milan Mrkusich, Darlinghurst Galleries; Barry Lett Galleries; Wakefield Press, Auckland, 1966.
Garrity, Tim et al., *The Kennedy gift: Rodney Kennedy and his gift to the Hocken Library*, Hocken Library, University of Otago, Dunedin, 1990 (exhibition catalogue).
Green, Nicola, *By the waters of Babylon: The art of A Lois White*, Auckland City Art Gallery; David Bateman, Auckland, 1993 (exhibition catalogue).
Gribbon, Trish, *Michael Smither: Painter*, Ron Sang Publications, Auckland, 2004.
Hanfling, Edward, *Ian Scott: Lattices*, Ferner Galleries, Auckland, 2005 (exhibition catalogue).
Hanfling, Edward and Alan Wright, *Vuletic and his circle*, Gus Fisher Gallery, Auckland, 2003 (exhibition catalogue).
Hay, Jennifer (ed.), *Bill Hammond: Jingle jangle morning*, Christchurch Art Gallery, Christchurch, 2007 (exhibition catalogue).
Henderson, Warwick, *Behind the canvas: An insider's guide to the New Zealand art market*, New Holland Publishers, Auckland, 2012.
Horrocks, Roger, *Len Lye: A biography*, Auckland University Press, Auckland, 2001.
Ireland, Peter, *Views/Exposures: 10 contemporary New Zealand photographers*, National Art Gallery, Wellington, 1982 (exhibition catalogue).
———, *Looking back*, Peter McLeavey Gallery, Wellington, 2001 (exhibition catalogue).
———, *Victory over death: About photography*, Peter McLeavey Gallery, Wellington, 2003 (exhibition catalogue).
Johnston, Alexa M, Gordon H Brown, Wystan Curnow and Tony Green, *Colin McCahon: Gates and journeys*, Auckland City Art Gallery, Auckland, 1988 (exhibition catalogue).
Johnston, Alexa M et al., *The 1950s show, New Zealand Home & Building*, souvenir edition Auckland City Art Gallery, Auckland, 1992 (exhibition catalogue).
Johnston, Alexa M and Ian Wedde, *Dream collectors: One hundred years of art in New Zealand*, Te Papa Press, Wellington, 1998 (exhibition catalogue).
Kay, Robin and Tony Eden, *Portrait of a century: The history of the NZ Academy of Fine Arts, 1882–1982*, Millwood, Wellington, 1983.
Keith, Hamish, *Eight New Zealand artists*, Auckland City Art Gallery, Auckland; Wakefield Press, South Australia, 1965 (exhibition catalogue).
———, *Native wit*, Random House, Auckland, 2008.
Kerr, Donald (ed.), *Enduring legacy: Charles Brasch, patron, poet and collector*, University of Otago Press, in association with the University of Otago Library, Dunedin, 2003.

Kirby, Mark, *The twist*, Waikato Museum of Art and History, Waikato, 1998.
Klein, Ulrike, *The business of art unveiled: New York art dealers speak up*, Peter Lang, Frankfurt, 1994.
Leonard, Robert (ed.), *Dead Starlets Assoc. by Yvonne Todd*, IMA, Brisbane, 2007 (exhibition catalogue).
Lilburn, Douglas, *A search for tradition & a search for a language*, Lilburn Residence Trust, in association with Victoria University Press, Wellington, 2011.
McAloon, William, *Gordon Walters: Prints + design*, Adam Art Gallery Te Pātaka Toi, Wellington, 2004 (exhibition catalogue).
McAloon, William (ed.), *Victoria's art: A university collection*, Adam Art Gallery Te Pātaka Toi, Wellington, 2005.
———, *Art at Te Papa*, Te Papa Press, Wellington, 2009.
McAndrew, Clare, *The international art market in 2011: Observations on the art trade over 25 years*, a report commissioned by TEFAF, Maastricht, 2011.
McCahon, Colin, *Colin McCahon: A survey exhibition*, Auckland City Art Gallery, Auckland, 1972 (exhibition catalogue).
McIvor, Lois R, *Memoir of the sixties*, Remuera Gallery, Auckland, 2008.
Milbank, Bill and D'Arcy Dalzell, *Friends of the family: From the Bieringa family collection*, Sarjeant Gallery Te Whare o Rehua, Wanganui, 2001 (exhibition catalogue).
NZ sculptors at Mildura, Queen Elizabeth II Arts Council, Wellington, 1978 (exhibition catalogue).
O'Brien, Gregory, *Lands and deeds: Profiles of contemporary New Zealand painters*, Godwit, Auckland, 1996.
———, *We set out one morning: Works from the BNZ Art Collection*, Bank of New Zealand, Wellington, 2006.
O'Brien, Gregory (ed.), *Hanly*, Ron Sang Publications, Auckland, 2012.
Paton, Justin, *Warren Viscoe: Life and limb*, Sarjeant Gallery Te Whare o Rehua, Wanganui, 2000 (exhibition catalogue).
———, *Jeffrey Harris*, Victoria University Press, Wellington; Dunedin Public Art Gallery, Dunedin, 2005 (exhibition catalogue).
———, *Aberhart*, Victoria University Press, Wellington, 2007.
———, *Reboot: The Jim Barr and Mary Barr collection*, Dunedin Public Art Gallery, Dunedin, 2007 (exhibition catalogue).
Pound, Francis, *Stories we tell ourselves: The paintings of Richard Killeen*, Auckland City Art Gallery, in association with David Bateman, Auckland, 1999 (exhibition catalogue).
———, *The invention of New Zealand: Art and national identity, 1930–1970*, Auckland University Press, Auckland, 2009.
Ross, James (ed.), *New Zealand modernism – in context: Paintings from the Gibbs collection*, J & A Gibbs, Auckland, 1995.
———, *New Zealand modernism: Figuration and expressionism: Paintings from the Gibbs collection*, J & A Gibbs, Auckland, 1996.
Ross, James and Laurence Simmons, *Gordon Walters: Order and intuition – a festschrift of essays presented to Gordon Walters on the occasion of his seventieth birthday*, Walters Publication, Auckland, 1989.
Salinger, Lesleigh (ed.), *The Todd corporation art collection*, Wellington, 2010.
Simmons, Laurence (ed.), *Certain words drawn: John Reynolds continued*, Godwit, in association with Dead Letter Office, Auckland, 2008.
Simpson, Peter, *Candles in a dark room: James K Baxter and Colin McCahon*, Auckland Art Gallery Toi o Tāmaki, Auckland, 1995 (exhibition catalogue).
———, *Answering hark: McCahon/Caselberg, painter/poet*, Craig Potton Publishing, Nelson, 2001.
———, *Colin McCahon: The Titirangi years*, Lopdell House Gallery, Auckland, 2006.
Simpson, Peter and Peter Peryer, *Peter Peryer: Photographer*, Auckland University Press, Auckland, 2008.
Skinner, Damian, *Don Binney: Nga manu/nga motu – birds/islands*, Auckland University Press, Auckland, 2003 (exhibition catalogue).
———, *Luncheon under the ash tree: The Ian & Elespie Prior collection*, Aratoi Wairarapa Museum of Art and History and the Willi Fels Memorial Trust, Masterton, 2005 (exhibition catalogue).
Skinner, Damian, Aaron Lister and Kevin Ireland, *A tourist in paradise lost: The art of Michael Illingworth*, City Gallery Wellington, Wellington, 2001 (exhibition catalogue).

Taylor, Alister and Deborah Coddington (comps), *Robin White: Painter*, Alister Taylor, Martinborough, 1981.
Tomory, PA (ed.), *New Zealand art: Painting 1890–1950*, AH & AW Reed, Wellington, 1968.
Trevelyan, Jill (ed.), *Toss Woollaston: A life in letters*, Te Papa Press, Wellington, 2004.
Vial, Jane, *The gallery of Helen Hitchings: From fretful sleeper to art world giant*, Museum of Wellington City & Sea/Te Waka Huia o nga Taonga Tuku Iho, Wellington, 2008 (exhibition catalogue).
Wallis, Brian (ed.), *Art after modernism*, New Museum of Contemporary Art, New York, 1984.
Watson, Peter, *From Manet to Manhattan*, Random House, New York, 1992.
Wedde, Ian, *How to be nowhere: Essays and texts, 1971–1994*, Victoria University Press, Wellington, 1995.
———, *Making ends meet: Essays and talks, 1992–2004*, Victoria University Press, Wellington, 2005.
White, Pat, *How the land lies: Of longing and belonging*, Victoria University Press, Wellington, 2010.
Wilson, Rodney and Peter Leech, *Milan Mrkusich: A decade further on, 1974–1983*, Auckland City Art Gallery, Auckland, 1985 (exhibition catalogue).
Woollaston, MT, *Far-away hills: A meditation on New Zealand landscape*, Auckland Gallery Associates, Auckland, 1962.
Wright, Alan and Edward Hanfling, *Mrkusich: The art of transformation*, Auckland University Press, Auckland, 2009.
Young, Mark, *New Zealand art: Painting 1950–1967*, AH & AW Reed, Wellington, 1968.

ARTICLES, ESSAYS, THESES

'$900 painting bamboozles passers-by', *Dominion*, 3 May 1971, p. 3.
'$1000 painting on move in city', *Dominion*, 24 September 1971, p. 1.
AB, 'Happenings', *Thursday: The magazine for modern women*, 29 October 1970, p. 40.
'Art appreciation as part of life', *Evening Post*, 14 December 1965, p. 16.
'Art blossoms where art is nourished', *Evening Post*, 3 July 1968, p. 10.
'Art notes: Wellington: French Maid Coffee House art shows', *Art in New Zealand*, Vol. 14, No. 3, March 1942, pp. 148–49.
'Art's place in the capital', *Evening Post*, 12 February 1966, p. 20.
Barlow, Hugh, 'An artist's family comes to visit', *Wairarapa Times-Age*, 15 June 2002, p. 3.
Barr, Jim, 'The Les and Milly Paris family collection', *Art New Zealand*, No. 4, February–March 1977, pp. 18–23.
Barrie, Lita, 'McLeavey chimes for Julian Schnabel', *National Business Review*, 16 October 1987, p. 75.
———, 'Blurring the distinctions of modernism', *National Business Review*, 5 February 1988, p. 31.
———, 'Never mind the public: Just take a look at all that "devajunk" piling up', *National Business Review*, 13 October 1989, W13.
Bayly, Janet, 'Laurence Aberhart – Peter McLeavey Gallery', *PhotoForum* newsletter, No. 16, March 1984, pp. 8–10.
Bell, Dr Gerda E, 'The arts in Wellington', *Home & Building*, 1 November 1969, p. 59.
Bell, Leonard, 'Pakeha have rights too: Peter Robinson's swastikas', *Pre/dictions: The role of art at the end of the millennium*, Department of Art History, Victoria University of Wellington, 2000, pp. 91–96.
Bellette, Tony, 'Galerie Legard', *Art New Zealand*, No. 38, 1986, p. 62.
Benjamin, Walter, 'Unpacking my library: A talk about book collecting', in Hannah Arendt (ed.), *Illuminations*, Harcourt, Brace & World, New York, 1955, p. 60.
Bilbrough, Miro, 'Looking through a dark glass', *Evening Post*, 25 May 1989, p. 19.
Blackley, Roger, 'The 4th Biennale of Sydney: New Zealanders in Australia', *Art New Zealand*, No. 24, 1982, pp. 26–31.
Blackman, Gary, 'The photographic experience: A report from Dunedin', *PhotoForum Supplement*, No. 3, Spring 1979, p. 5.
Brasch, Charles, 'Art gallery policy', *Landfall*, Vol. 3, No. 2, June 1949, pp. 176–82.
———, introduction, *A private collection of New Zealand paintings: Thirty-seven New Zealand paintings from the collection of Charles Brasch and Rodney Kennedy*, Auckland City Art Gallery, Auckland, 1958.
'Breathtaking canvas – so is the price', *Evening Post*, 29 July 1971, p. 8.

Brown, Gordon H, editorial, *Auckland City Art Gallery Quarterly*, No. 44, 1969, p. 2.
Brunton, Alan, 'Art people: Dealing court cards in Cuba Street', *Art New Zealand*, No. 4, 1977, pp. 14–15.
Butler, Susanne, 'Print will help convention fund', *Evening Post*, 7 September 1978, p. 12.
Calhoun, Ann, 'Two Wellington entrepreneurs of the thirties: The Murray Fullers: Part I, Edwin Murray Fuller', *Art New Zealand*, No. 23, Autumn 1982, pp. 20–23.
———, 'Two Wellington entrepreneurs of the thirties: Part II, Mary Murray Fuller', *Art New Zealand*, No. 24, Winter 1982, pp. 22–25.
Cape, Peter, 'Art gallery round-up', *National Business Review*, 23 September 1971, p. 11.
———, 'The arts in Wellington', *Arts & Community*, Vol. 10, No. 5, 1973, p. 13.
Cartwright, Garth, 'Auction boom $ellout', *New Zealand Listener*, 28 March 1987, pp. 34–35.
Clayton, Hamish, 'Art in the face of tragedy: A project by Robin White, Holly Jackson & Robyn McFarlane', *Art New Zealand*, No. 133, Autumn 2010, pp. 28–31.
'Contrasting art in two displays', *Evening Post*, 18 April 1970, p. 3.
Curnow, Allen and Ngaio Marsh, 'A dialogue by way of introduction', *First year book of the arts in New Zealand*, No. 1, 1945, pp. 1–8.
Curnow, Heather, 'Developing art form', *New Zealand Listener*, 22 September 1979, p. 24.
Curnow, Wystan, 'High culture in a small province', in Wystan Curnow (ed.), *Essays on New Zealand literature*, Heinemann, Auckland, 1973, pp. 155–71.
———, 'The Sydney Biennale', *Art New Zealand*, No. 13, 1979, pp. 22–23.
———, 'Report: The given as an art political statement: Nine works by Billy Apple 1979–1980', *Art New Zealand*, No. 15, Summer 1980, front piece, pp. 26–33, 60–61, 65.
———, 'New Zealand art – where in the world is it?', *New Zealand Listener*, 3 April 1982, pp. 34–35.
Dart, William, 'Rodney Kirk Smith: 25 years with art', *Art New Zealand*, No. 55, Winter 1990, pp. 49–50, 90.
'Dim view of other cities: Aucklanders "see the light" on modern art', *Evening Post*, 5 June 1958, p. 20.
Docking, Gil, 'The Arts Council and the visual arts', *Arts & Community*, Vol. 5, No. 9, 1969, pp. 1–2.
Dunn, Michael, 'Ian Scott talks about his Lattice series', *Art New Zealand*, No. 13, 1979, pp. 32–35.
Eastmond, Elizabeth and Priscilla Pitts, 'Ngahuia Te Awekotuku in conversation with Elizabeth Eastmond and Priscilla Pitts', *Antic*, No. 1, June 1986, pp. 44–55.
Emsley, Bill, untitled article, *Dominion*, 18 April 1969, p. 18.
———, 'Where was the gallery?', *Dominion*, 22 August 1969, p. 22.
'Exhibition sales have soared rapidly', *New Zealand Herald*, 20 May 1966, section 1, p. 5.
Fairburn, ARD, 'Some reflections on New Zealand painting', *Landfall*, Vol. 1, No. 1, March 1947, pp. 49–56.
———, 'The Wertheim collection', *Year book of the arts in New Zealand*, No. 5, 1949, pp. 2–9.
Fitzsimons, Tom, 'Visionary collaboration', *Dominion Post*, 27 May 2010, p. 14.
Foster, Hugh, 'The rationale of a private collector', *Art New Zealand*, No. 9, 1978, pp. 28–31.
Fraser, Ross, 'An independent gallery', *Home & Building*, Vol. 20, No. 7, 1 December 1957, pp. 44–45.
———, 'Peter Peryer: The photograph as a portrait of the self', *Art New Zealand*, No. 8, 1978–79, pp. 25, 65, 67.
———, 'Looking back: Memories of painting in Auckland through the 1950s', *Art New Zealand*, No. 66, Autumn 1993, pp. 56–57.
'Gallery decision unanimous: Two grounds stated for refusing show', *Evening Post*, June 1958, p. 7.
Gibblin, Ross, 'Beyond the crash', *Evening Post*, 23 September 1989, p. 29.
Green, Anthony (Tony), 'Peter Webb's gallery', *Bulletin of New Zealand Art History*, Vol. 1, 1972, pp. 12–24.
———, 'Colin McCahon's paintings and drawings at the Ikon Gallery', *Bulletin of New Zealand Art History*, Vol. 2, 1974, pp. 28–43.
———, 'More about Peter Webb's gallery and some unpublished lithographs', *Bulletin of New Zealand Art History*, Vol. 2, 1974, pp. 44–48.
Green, Stephen, 'Karl Sidow [*sic*] – sculptor', *Arts & Community*, Vol. 6, No. 6, June 1970, p. 7.
———, 'Wellington – Don Binney', *Arts & Community*, Vol. 6, No. 9, September 1970, p. 11.
Guiney, JS, 'Swinging London has enlivened our art gallery', *Evening Post*, 18 February 1969, p. 35.
Hall, David, 'Venus rising', *New Zealand Listener*, 2 May 2009, pp. 40–41.
Hall, Ken, 'A progressive champion: RN O'Reilly, Colin McCahon and the Canterbury Public Library art loan collection', *Journal of New Zealand Art History*, Vol. 31, 2010, pp. 52–72.

Hannan, Deborah, 'Epitaph: Colin McCahon (1919–1987)', *Evening Post*, 30 May 1987, p. 21.
Hayward, Dai, 'Muldoon confesses: Art gift a stunt', *The Australian*, 17 March 1978, p. 1.
Hewson, Paul, 'Snaps Gallery and the exhibiting of photographs', *Art New Zealand*, No. 12, 1978, p. 14.
'Highest price for NZ painting?', *Evening Post*, 19 September 1972, p. 7.
Illingworth, Michael, 'Adam and Eve', letter to the editor, *New Zealand Listener*, 10 April 1976, p. 6.
Ireland, Kevin, 'Hung, drawn and courted: Your guide to the art galleries of Auckland', *New Zealand Listener*, 15 October 1990, pp. 104–05.
Ireland, Peter, 'The recent small paintings of Jeffrey Harris', *Art New Zealand*, No. 6, 1977, pp. 12–13.
———, 'Laurence Aberhart: Nineteen photographs 1974–1978', *PhotoForum*, No. 43, March 1979, pp. 43–46.
James, Judith, 'Smither: So stones make a mountain', *Dominion*, 4 December 1971, p. 18.
'John Reynolds', *Kia Ora* (Air New Zealand magazine), February 2004, p. 71.
Keith, Hamish, 'Painting in New Zealand', *Salient*, 5 October 1964, p. 3.
———, 'Auckland is so "big-headed!"', *Auckland Star*, 16 December 1964, p. 24.
———, 'A living can now be made', *Auckland Star*, 5 November 1965, p. 10.
———, 'Colin McCahon', *Art & Australia*, Vol. 6, No. 1, June 1968, pp. 61–69.
———, 'The art scene', *Vogue New Zealand*, Summer 1968, pp. 86–89.
———, 'Painting in the sixties', *New Zealand Listener*, 11 July 1969, p. 10.
———, 'Capital neglects the NZ scene – why?', *Auckland Star*, 20 June 1970, p. 16.
———, 'Dealer galleries tin anniversary', *Arts & Community*, No. 7, July 1970, p. 11.
———, 'A happy return to old style', *Auckland Star*, 1 April 1972, p. 11.
———, 'Illingworth: Tales of the outlaw artist', *Sunday Star-Times*, 10 February 2002, F3.
Kember, Olivia, 'State of the art', *New Zealand Listener*, 15 May 2004, pp. 16–21.
Lee-Johnson, Eric, 'Eric Lee-Johnson', *Year book of the arts*, No. 3, 1947, p. 74.
Leonard, Robert, 'Peter Robinson: The end of the 20th century', *Gallery News*, March–June 2004, p. 19.
Leonard, Robert and Stuart McKenzie, 'Surf: Recent works by Julian Dashper', *Sport*, No. 4, 1990, pp. 107–11.
Lister, Aaron, 'Wellington', *Art New Zealand*, No. 93, Summer 1999–2000, p. 36.
'Lower Hutt councillor elaborates on his urges', *Evening Post*, 28 February 1978, p. 1.
Lynn, Elwyn, 'Colin McCahon: The view from across the Tasman', *Art New Zealand*, No. 31, Winter 1984, pp. 24–26.
'McCahon panels go to gallery for $25,000', *Evening Post*, 11 May 1978, p. 4.
'McCahon works on show', *New Zealand Herald*, 25 July 1969, section 1, p. 6.
McCarroll, Jo, 'A fair deal of exposure', *Sunday Star-Times*, 5 November 2000, F4.
McCredie, Athol, 'Peter Black: 2 Brooklyn Terrace', *Art New Zealand*, No. 46, Autumn 1988, pp. 82–83.
———, 'Going public: New Zealand art museums in the 1970s', MA thesis, Massey University, Wellington, 1999.
McDonald, John, 'A star in our backyard', *Sydney Morning Herald*, 29 January 1994, p. 121.
McLeod, Rosemary, 'The state of New Zealand art', *North & South*, November 1986, pp. 46–57.
———, 'Towards 2000: Art', *North & South*, April 1987, p. 65.
McNamara, TJ, 'Avant-garde in their time', *New Zealand Herald*, 29 May 2003, B5.
Maloon, Terence, 'You've got to have faith to hear and see', *Sydney Morning Herald*, 21 April 1984, p. 30.
Matthews, Philip, 'A touch of tar', *Capital Times*, 18–24 August 1993, p. 15.
Melville, Robert, 'A stranger in N.Z.', *Architectural Review*, December 1968, pp. 443–45.
'Michael Illingworth: Alienation and search for innocence', *Craccum Art Supplement*, 2 September 1968, p. 10.
Miles, Anna, 'Stranded in paradise', *Pavement*, April–May 2000, pp. 130–33.
Millar, David, letter to the editor, *AGMANZ News*, Vol. 3, No. 1, May 1972, p. 12.
Moir, Christine, 'His art is strictly from the intellect', *New Zealand Woman's Weekly*, 10 March 1969, p. 16.
'Nearly sold out', *New Zealand Herald*, 28 September 1968, magazine section, p. 5.
'New Zealand's gift "Muldoon's revenge?"', *Sydney Morning Herald*, 17 March 1978, p. 11.
'Notable art not expected from NZ', *Press*, 1 July 1968, p. 10.
Orbell, Margaret, 'Landscapes on show', *Dominion*, 9 September 1968, p. 23.
———, 'McCahon's panels', *Dominion*, 28 October 1968, p. 4.

'Painting is superb says expert', *Auckland Star*, 17 March 1978, p. 1.
'Paintings fetch $17,500', *Press*, 24 May 1980, p. 6.
Panoho, Rangihiroa, 'Maori: At the centre, on the margins', in Mary Barr (ed.), *Headlands: Thinking through New Zealand art*, Museum of Contemporary Art, Sydney, 1992, pp. 122–34.
Paton, Justin, 'Market laughs last as fame comes courting', *Press*, 21 September 1994, p. 16.
———,'The ties that bind', *New Zealand Listener*, 8 October 1994, pp. 44–45.
———, 'The shock of the old', *New Zealand Listener*, 26 June 1999, pp. 38–39.
Pond Eyley, Claudia, 'Robin White in Kiribati', *Art New Zealand*, No. 31, 1984, pp. 30–33.
Pound, Francis, 'Petar Vuletic: Art dealer, critic, heretic', *Metro*, August 1981, pp. 44–48.
Ralston, Bill, 'Art for art's sake', *New Zealand Listener*, 19 May 2007, pp. 28–29.
Ray, Pauline, 'The good offices of art', *New Zealand Listener*, 2 December 1991, pp. 48–49.
'Rejection of art display defended', *Taranaki Herald*, 18 November 1954, p. 1.
'Robin White: Painter', *Broadsheet*, No. 22, September 1974, p. 18.
Roberts, John, 'Theirs sincerely', *New Zealand Listener*, 10 September 1977, p. 29.
Rowe, Neil, 'Don Binney at the Peter McLeavey Gallery', *Salient*, 22 March 1976, p. 16.
———, 'Killeen's impeccable art: Enigmatic and witty', *The Week*, 6 August 1976, p. 15.
———, 'A whole lot of grids', *Evening Post*, 18 June 1977, p. 10.
———, 'Late recognition for major painter', *Evening Post*, 29 October 1977, p. 12.
———, 'Michael Illingworth: Looking for a subject', *Evening Post*, 8 April 1978, p. 14.
———, 'Where is the retrospective?', *Evening Post*, 5 August 1978, p. 11.
———, 'Robin White's work continues to grow in stature', *Evening Post*, 9 September 1978, p. 11.
———, 'A mature artist with a formidable talent', *Evening Post*, 30 September 1978, p. 11.
———, 'Smither takes a new direction', *Evening Post*, 18 November 1978, p. 19.
———, 'NAG event big', *Evening Post*, 30 June 1979, p. 11.
———, 'McLeavey show important', *Evening Post*, 7 July 1979, p. 13.
———, 'Everyone is going "click"', *Evening Post*, 18 August 1979, p. 13.
———, 'Billy causes another stir with wild ideas', *Evening Post*, 1 December 1979, p. 13.
———, 'Illingworth comes back', *Evening Post*, 12 June 1980, p. 11.
Seear, Annette, 'Artist paints about death', *Evening Star Saturday Magazine*, 12 February 1977, p. 9.
Shaw, Peter, 'Auctions demonstrate market's erratic nature', *New Zealand Times*, 3 June 1984, p. 14.
'"Shut" call to gallery', *Dominion*, 30 October 1965, p. 6.
'Simple art for homely walls', *Evening Post*, 18 December 1965, editorial, p. 20.
Skinner, Damian, 'The dealer as curator', *Art New Zealand*, No. 88, Spring 1998, pp. 40–41.
Smith, Charmian, 'Artists share friendship and working mother commitment', *Otago Daily Times*, 22 October 1992, p. 25.
Spens, Michael, 'Meaning, excellence & purpose: ANZART in Edinburgh', *Art New Zealand*, No. 33, 1984, pp. 28–31.
Stewart, Keith, 'Shapes that move people', *Sunday Star-Times*, 24 July 1994, D5.
Stratford, Stephen, 'Would you buy a used painting from this man?', *Metro*, October 1987, pp. 142–54.
Tamati-Quennell, Megan, 'Peter Robinson: Pale by comparison', *Planet*, No. 14, 1994, p. 60.
Taylor, Rob, 'Dashper pursues pleasure', *Dominion*, 21 May 1986, p. 8.
'The Gallery: 64 Symonds St, Auckland', *Home & Building*, Vol. 23, No. 2, 1 July 1960, pp. 56–57.
Tomkins, Calvin, 'Profile: A good eye and a good ear', *New Yorker*, 26 May 1980, pp. 40–73.
Tomory, PA (Peter), 'Unifying art – in New Zealand', *The Connoisseur*, March 1959, pp. 91–93.
———, 'What's different about NZ art?', *New Zealand Listener*, 30 October 1964, pp. 3, 22.
———, 'It started in the thirties', *New Zealand Listener*, 6 November 1964, pp. 5, 21.
———, 'Art can't be taught', *New Zealand Listener*, 20 November 1964, p. 3.
———, 'New Zealand sculpture', *Art & Australia*, Vol. 3, No. 2, September 1965, pp. 108–13.
Trevelyan, Jill, introduction, *Thrill me every day: The Celia Dunlop collection*, Celia Dunlop Trust, Wellington, 2009, unpaged.
'US collector pays well for NZ work', *Evening Post*, 24 March 1972, p. 2.
Veysey, Alex, 'Artist finds life has no rosy hue', *Dominion*, 1 September 1972, p. 1.
von Meier, Kurt, 'Contemporary painting in New Zealand', *Art & Australia*, Vol. 2, No. 3, December 1964, pp. 190–202.

'"Way out" gallery exhibits attacked', *Evening Post*, 28 February 1978, p. 17.

Wedde, Ian, 'Woollaston', *Spleen*, No. 4, July 1976, unpaged.

———, 'Woodcut exhibition shows simple realism', *Evening Post*, 23 March 1984, section 2, p. 15.

———, 'McCahon excites Sydney critics', *Evening Post*, 12 May 1984, p. 13.

———, 'Way of life: Dealer punts on the new', *Evening Post*, 29 October 1984, p. 39.

———, 'McLeavey's pilot opera', *Evening Post*, 25 June 1985, p. 37.

———, 'Beyond window shopping: Xmas art grottoes', *Evening Post*, 17 December 1986, p. 30.

———, 'Mark Rossell's gothic biomorphs', *Evening Post*, 22 July 1987, p. 38.

———, 'The Americans are coming', *Evening Post*, 24 September 1987, p. 25.

Wilkinson, Tanya, 'A survey of the primary players in the establishment of New Zealand dealer galleries', School of Art & Design, UNITEC Institute of Technology, 1996.

Wong, Gilbert, 'Galleries hanging in there', *New Zealand Herald*, 16 June 1988, section 2, p. 1.

Young, Christine, 'Another opening, another show: Inside Auckland's art world', *Metro*, May 1984, pp. 71–80.

Zeplin, Pamela, 'The "neglected middle distance": Australian and New Zealand visual art exchanges, 1970–1985', DPhil thesis, School of Art History and Theory, University of New South Wales, 2005.

IMAGE CREDITS

Except for the sources credited below, all images are from the Peter McLeavey Gallery archive or McLeavey family collection, and were photographed by Michael Hall, Te Papa. All digital imaging by Jeremy Glyde, Te Papa.

Alexander Turnbull Library, Wellington, Dominion Post Collection 115, 126, 200, 217, 302, 342, 394–95
Amelia Handscomb 494–95
Aratoi Wairarapa Museum of Art and History 203 (photographed by John Casey)
Art New Zealand 289
Art+Object 137
Auckland Art Fair 380
Auckland Art Gallery Toi o Tāmaki 146, 206, 211, 233, 253, 316; EH McCormick Research Library 106 (photographed by S Pilkington), Marti Friedlander archive 170, 175, 236, 241
Bank of New Zealand Art Collection 282–83
Billy Apple archive 279 (photographed by Geoffrey Palmer)
Bridgeman Art Library, London 375
Christchurch Art Gallery Te Puna o Waiwhetu 164, 340
Dunedin Public Art Gallery 214, 234, 287
Getty images, Central Press 34
Govett-Brewster Art Gallery, New Plymouth 94, 104 (photographed by Mark Ashkanasy)
Hocken Collections Uare Taoka o Hākena, University of Otago 156
Ivan Bootham 41, 61
The James Wallace Arts Trust 181, 188
Jim and Mary Barr 263
Luit Bieringa 357
Matthew O'Reilly and Rachel Watson 47 (photographed by John Ashton)
Museo di Capodimonte, Naples 30
Museum of New Zealand Te Papa Tongarewa 3, 50, 70, 80–81, 125, 132–33, 140, 155, 158, 171, 178, 192, 194, 198, 205, 226, 243, 246, 248, 254, 260, 264, 268, 273, 284, 290, 295, 310, 311, 322–23, 329, 361, 369, 377, 378, 390; Woollaston archive 53 (photographed by Inksters Ltd)
National Gallery of Australia, Canberra 220–21
Peter Fleischl collection 54
Queensland Art Gallery 28, ©Pablo Picasso/Succession Picasso, licensed by Viscopy, 2013
Richard Brimer 402
Richard Killeen ii, 186, 197, 230, 368
Robyn McFarlane 397
Sarjeant Gallery Te Whare o Rehua, Whanganui 276
Te Manawa Art Society Inc., Te Manawa Museums Trust 64, 250
Victoria University of Wellington Art Collection 38, 93, 182

All Colin McCahon works are reproduced courtesy of the Colin McCahon Research and Publication Trust.

INDEX

A

B

C

D

E

F

G

H

I

J

K

L

M

N

O

P

Q

R

S

T

V

W

Y

Z